The New England Town
in Fact and Fiction

Other books by PERRY D. WESTBROOK

Author:
  Acres of Flint: Writers of Rural New England, 1870–1900
  Biography of an Island
  The Greatness of Man: An Essay on Dostoyevsky and Whitman
  Trail Horses and Trail Riding (with Anne Westbrook)
  Mary Ellen Chase
  Mary Wilkins Freeman
  John Burroughs
  William Bradford
  Free Will and Determinism in American Literature

Editor:
  Pembroke
  Seacoast and Upland: A New England Anthology

The New England Town
in Fact and Fiction

Perry D. Westbrook

Rutherford • Madison • Teaneck
Fairleigh Dickinson University Press
London and Toronto: Associated University Presses

©1982 by Associated University Presses, Inc.

Associated University Presses, Inc.
4 Cornwall Drive
East Brunswick, N.J. 08816

Associated University Presses Ltd
27 Chancery Lane
London WC2A 1NF, England

Associated University Presses
Toronto, Ontario, Canada M5E 1A7

Library of Congress Cataloging in Publication Data

Westbrook, Perry D.
  The New England town in fact and fiction.

  Bibliography: p.
  Includes index.
  1. American literature—New England—History and
criticism. 2. Cities and towns in literature. 3. New
England in literature. 4. City and town life—New
England—History. 5. New England—Historiography.
1. Title.
PS243.W43   810'.9'3274   80-67077
ISBN 0-8386-3011-1   AACR2

Contents

Preface

This book is a study of the development and the influence of an institution and a myth. The institution is the New England town in all its aspects; the myth is the assumption, shared by many, that the New England town is the high point in mankind's social and political evolution. Hence the title *The New England Town in Fact and Fiction*. The fiction-making, or myth-making, was not, nevertheless, solely the activity of writers of short stories and novels; political theorists and historians from Thomas Jefferson and George Bancroft onward also engaged, when discussing New England towns, in idealization sufficiently romantic to border on fiction. And, conversely, some of the authors of tales and poems attained a level of realism that placed their works closer to fact than to fiction. Thus the division between the supposedly factual and the imaginative should not be rigidly insisted on. Like most human institutions, the New England town in certain times and places came close to living up to the expectations of its most enthusiastic apologists, while in other times and places it fell spectacularly short of the perfection it was supposed to have attained. The truth for average towns lies somewhere between the extremes.

But my concern is not to establish the ultimate objective truth as to the worth of the New England town as a societal unit. My interest, rather, is in examining the town as it impinged upon, and molded, the American imagination during two centuries of nationhood. The impact, which has undoubtedly been great, has often been useful and constructive—for example, in providing models for the orderly organization of new communities in the Middle West. But in other instances the influence has occasioned sentimental, even spurious, imitations of town institutions, as for instance in the meaningless use of the term *town meeting* ("Town Meeting of the Air" or the "town meeting" that a former president of the United States held during a visit to West Berlin). Such looseness of usage attests to the persistence of a myth—that the New England town meeting is a cure for all social and political ills—but it is scarcely accurate historically.

Perhaps in a preface it is permissible to express one's personal views. I have lived in towns in five of the New England states, and I have lived elsewhere in towns that may or may not have been influenced by the New England system. The differences between the New England and the other

[9]

towns, from the point of view of efficient government, neighborliness, civic pride, and the like, seem slight. Corruption, pettiness, downright meanness are present in all towns, small and large, no matter where they are located. All of this is entirely predictable and not of primary importance or concern in this study. What I am attempting to do is to present widely held views— sometimes delusions—and to indicate how they have contributed to the formation of an American mystique of democracy, or, less frequently, in their negative aspects have generated misgivings concerning our national political and social norms.

My materials are drawn mainly from writers of fiction and nonfiction, belletrists and historians, who have been, or are, New Englanders by birth and upbringing or, though native elsewhere, have acquired a deep interest in the region. The majority of the authors whom I discuss and from whose works I draw are at least moderately well known to the educated public— authors like Timothy Dwight, Ralph Waldo Emerson, Sarah Orne Jewett, James Gould Cozzens. But I have also given attention to the writings of less famous persons or of ones scarcely known at all today. Various periodicals—for example, the *New England Magazine,* the *Atlantic Monthly,* and *Harper's*—have supplied much of this more or less fugitive material, which has value in indicating trends in public interests and views.

I have not attempted to survey all literature dealing with my subject; the mere mass of relevant writing would doom such an effort to failure. Thus I have had to be selective; and I have also had to be impartial, for my purpose has not been to demonstrate one thesis or another about New England towns—to ascertain conclusively, for example, whether life in them is stunting or stimulating to the growth of the human mind and spirit. Yet I take into account those who set about demonstrating various theses. I repeat: my intention has been to examine ideas *about* the towns—not the towns themselves—and in doing so, to trace the growth and the persistent life (along with occasional temporary declines) of a social and political preconception that is embedded with the tenacity of a myth in the national imagination.

Many have undertaken to debunk this preconception; many more have labored to idealize and perpetuate it; and a sizable number of able writers have produced objective and carefully researched studies of towns as (supposedly) they actually are. The works of all these authors have aided me in my own effort, and indeed they constitute much of the subject matter of my study. I am particularly grateful, however, to certain scholars whose books and essays have served as guides through some of the windings of the labyrinth into which my own researches have led me. There are many such writings, and some that have been extremely helpful to me are Irma Honaker Herron's *The Small Town in American Literature* (1939), John

Fairfield Sly's *Town Government in Massachusetts* (1930), and Ernest Lee Tuveson's *Redeemer Nation* (1966). As indicated in my notes, my debt to other books is also great, but always my main reliance has been upon primary materials: poems, fiction, drama, reminiscences, autobiographies, reportage, and local histories.

The New England Town
in Fact and Fiction

[1]
"God Has Never Forsaken That Country"

We shall finde that the God of Israell is among vs, when . . . he shall make us a prayse and glory, that men shall say of succeeding plantacions: "the lord make it like that of New England."
John Winthrop, "A Modell of Christian Charity" (1630)[1]

A gentleman of great respectability in the State of New York, and of Dutch extraction too, being asked in a late critical period by a circle of his friends what measures he would advise them to take, replied, "Go with the people of New England. So far as I can find, God has never forsaken that country."
Timothy Dwight, *Travels in New England and New York* (1821)[2]

During the years from 1783 to 1795 the Reverend Timothy Dwight looked out on New England and America from the vantage point of his parsonage in Greenfield Hill, a rural parish in the town of Fairfield in southwestern Connecticut, and he was pleased with what he saw. He was so impressed, indeed, that he was inspired to write a poem praising the goodness of New England village life and avowing his belief that this goodness would radiate outward and encompass first the nation and finally the world. He was conscious that he was dealing with a great subject, no less a one than a divinely decreed historical movement with millennial implications. Convinced that he was present at the time and place of this critical point in the affairs of men, he dutifully and gladly took upon himself the role of its bard and prophet.

A Lovely Village and a Mediocre Poem

Situated on a ridge commanding a view across several miles of countryside to Long Island Sound and the Island itself, Greenfield Hill was, and still is, a gem among Connecticut villages. As pastor, Dwight in traditional Puritan fashion was the cultural as well as the spiritual leader of the community. For the times he was well compensated, receiving a salary of five hundred dollars a year and an additional one hundred dollars to help him get "settled." A handsome parsonage and six acres of land for his own use were provided, along with a promise of twenty cords of firewood a year.[3] A grandson of Jonathan Edwards, he was a moderate "New Divinity" Calvinist, thus rejecting doctrines such as that of the Half-Way Covenant, which he deemed inconsistent with orthodoxy.[4] He had been called to Greenfield Hill from his native Northampton, Massachusetts, where, after having returned from a year's service as a chaplain in the Continental Army, he had been occupying himself with preaching, studying, and working on his father's farm. Before his war service he had been a tutor at Yale College, from which he had graduated in 1769 at the age of seventeen. From 1795 until his death in 1817 he was president of Yale, as well as one of the most influential religious leaders in New England. In the literary history of the United States he takes his place as the outstanding member of that early group of authors known as the Connecticut Wits.

At Greenfield Hill, Dwight became convinced that New England villages represented the highest, most Christian civilization ever to have existed; and he found that a comparison between conditions in these communities and those of Europe was to the disadvantage of the latter. To express his conviction of New England's superiority he published in 1794 the didactic and tendentious poem *Greenfield Hill*. He had already won some renown as the author of a turgid patriotic "epic," *The Conquest of Canaan* (1784).

Greenfield Hill reveals its author's literary learning as well as his religious and cultural enthusiasms. Of the poem's seven sections, two are in blank verse, two in heroic couplets, one in Spenserian stanzas, and two in tetrameter couplets. Yet for all its variety of meter and form, the verse is consistently undistinguished. Imitative as it is of the standard British poets of the previous two centuries—John Dyer, Spenser, Goldsmith, Pope, Wharton, Milton—it seldom rises stylistically above the level of mediocrity. Pomposity, affectation, and triteness are the rule. Long Island is renamed Longa; the Connecticut river, Connecta; and Greenfield Hill, Verna. The birds invariably *carol*, the winter *glooms*, the herds *low*. Rhyme, when employed, is mechanical, unimaginative, and repetitious, as for example in countless pairings of *rise* and *skies*. Dwight was a bookish man who in his youth had ruined his eyes by incessant reading, and he was an ardent—too ardent—admirer of the poets he imitated. Like many a better writer of the times, he saw no need for innovation. The old literary paths trodden by so many of the great were good enough for him, as was his grandfather's religion. But unfortunately his poetry fell far short of his models.

Yet *Greenfield Hill* is an important early statement[5] of certain American ideals and attitudes that were emerging in the decades immediately following the Revolutionary War and that have persisted to the present time in various guises. Quite clearly, Dwight, a Calvinist minister in religiously conservative Conneticut, subscribed to that perennial Puritan belief that New England, in Governor Winthrop's words, was destined to be "as a citty on a hill," a New Jerusalem for all nations to admire and emulate. Reformed religion and a harmonious civil order were to be the foundations of a redeemed society where there would flourish the traditional Puritan virtues of fear of God, love of one's fellows, honesty, hard work, and plain living. Symbolic of the successful establishment of such a society—after the first years the settlers spent in clearing the forests—were the fertility and loveliness of the countryside and the compact self-sufficiency of the towns with their churches, their schools, and their town-meeting governments.

In Dwight's view New England, which in his time and earlier was expanding westward and northward, was already leading the country in the continuing effort to build the New Jerusalem. The strengths that qualified New England for this leadership were to be found mainly in the rural communities of self-governing farmers and artisans with their strong commitment to church and school. Situated on its "eminence"[6] above the Sound, Greenfield Hill was the New Jerusalem in miniature.

But Greenfield Hill had other than geographical qualifications. According to ancient Puritan doctrine, based on Puritan surmises as to the nature of the primitive Christian church and reaffirmed in the Connecticut churches' Saybrook Platform of 1708, the members of an individual congregation should not be excessively numerous and should live near one another. Each church should constitute a closely knit, largely autonomous unit. Greenfield Hill exactly answered to these specifications.

The intent of Dwight's poem is to present Greenfield Hill as typical. Dwight supplies much lengthier accounts of numerous other New England villages in his *Travels in New England and New York* (1821–22), which will be the subject of the next chapter. But even in the case of his poem, he adds a prose commentary in the form of extensive notes offering factual data about the village and the state of Connecticut and New England at large. Both the prose and the verse, despite their limitations as literary art, convey an idyllic picture—the first that strives to present the New England town as a culmination in the history of civilization.

From its lovely "eminence"—Dwight uses the word in its spiritual as well as in its geographical sense—Greenfield Hill looks out upon the world, rather smugly aware of its own superior merits and of its mission as a light for all mankind. Here, Dwight assures us, the inhabitants taste

> every good
> Of competence, of independence, peace
> And liberty unmingled; every house
> On its own ground, and every happy swain
> Beholding no superior, but the laws,

> And such as virtue, knowledge, useful life
> And zeal exerted for the public good,
> Have raised above the throng.[7]

This representative New England community, moreover, enjoys "The noblest institutions, man has seen"[8]—the Congregational Church, town-meeting government, education for all, and the ownership of family farms in fee simple,

> to every child
> In equal shares descending; no entail
> The first-born lifting into bloated pomp,
> Tainting with lust, and sloth, and pride and rage,
> The world around him.[9]

New England Land Tenure

In Greenfield Hill and elsewhere in his writing Dwight makes very clear his conviction that the ownership of land in small farms and the absence of entail are fundamental to the economic, political, and even spiritual health of New England. In this conviction he was echoing sentiments that can be traced back to the first colonists, for many of whom a major inducement to emigration was the opportunity of possessing land free of feudal or manorial encumbrances. The strength of this motive was demonstrated in Plymouth, where in the first years of its settlement, the land was cultivated in common. But when it became apparent that this arrangement did not make for abundant crops, parcels of land—at first small but soom more extensive—were assigned to individual inhabitants to own outright, and the result was a greatly improved yield. In early New England towns much land continued to be held in common—especially pastures and woodland—but each settler owned at least his home-plot and some acreage in meadows and arable fields, scattered perhaps in various parts of the township. The hunger for one's own land was always keen, and within a century most New England farmers had consolidated their holdings and common land of all types had become almost nonexistent.[10] Such had been the case in the town of Fairfield, founded in 1639, where Greenfield Hill was situated. Towns settled after the first half century or so of colonization contained little or no common land at any time. The rule in New England was separate and individual ownership whenever and wherever feasible. From common ownership in the early years of a settlement, the townspeople may have learned valuable lessons in cooperation, so essential to the functioning of a community; but they had no wish to perpetuate a system that, after all, resembled too closely what they had left behind in Europe.

Dwight was not the first to comment glowingly on the New England land system as compared to that in the Old World and in other colonies in North America. Another Connecticut parson, Jared Eliot of Killingsworth, had anticipated Dwight's enthusiasm by a generation. Eliot, also a Yale graduate, was not only a minister but a physician as well—as were many of the clergy in his day—and a skillful one, who made calls throughout Connecticut and occasionally in neighboring colonies. Thus, like Dwight, he was well traveled; and also like Dwight, he had a keen interest in farming. The result was that between 1748 and 1759 he published six papers on agriculture, which appeared as a book in 1760 under the title *Essays upon Field-Husbandry in New England, as it is or May be Ordered.* This interesting little volume has been called "one of the earliest attempts ever made in this country to reënforce by science the empiricism of agriculture."[11] On its pages practical advice and information are mingled with comments on New England's past and present, and throughout are copious biblical quotations and allusions emphasizing the godly nature of the farmer's calling.

But most significant, Eliot in his sixth essay, first printed in New Haven in 1759, stated in brief what was later to be the main thesis of Dwight's *Greenfield Hill* and of much of his *Travels in New England and New York.* Eliot had read in a British magazine "a Dissertation" arguing "that the extensive, uninhabited, Parts of *North-America* ought to be so planned, and settled, that every Planter should have several Thousand Acres of Land, to enable him to become useful; and that this is the sure Way to render those Countries eminently beneficial, to our Mother Country." As Eliot rather unsyntactically reported him, the British writer "observes, that *New-England,* as to their Manner of Settlement, Course of Business, Way of living together in Towns, being similar to that of *England;* therefore he concludes, that we can be but of little service to *Great-Britain.*"[12]

Eliot took "Leave to differ from that polite Writer, and retain a good Opinion of our Tenure of Land, and Manner of Settlement, as being divided into small Freeholds; as it is an arduous Work, to clear Land, overgrown with Wood, and drain Land, immerged [*sic*] in Water, and bring it into a State of Fertility; and as nothing will inspire Men with Resolution, to undertake, and Patience, to persevere, like the Pleasure, and Advantage, of having a Right to call it their *own.*"[13] Freehold tenure, Eliot went on to say, encourages early marriages and large families, and the consequent rapid increase in population hastens further colonization, which in turn results in increased trade with the mother country. But above all, Eliot believed, the "Collection of People, in Towns, gives Opportunity for the

Exercise of Social Virtues,"[14] offers education for children, encourages the pursuit of arts and sciences, stimulates trade, and, most important, provides "The Benefit of social Worship."[15] It is to promote and perpetuate this wholesome community life that Eliot sought to increase the productivity of New England's agriculture, which he admitted had to contend with difficult conditions of soil and climate. The small freehold family farm, providing what Dwight called "a competence" rather than wealth, was best suited, Eliot thought, for coping with these conditions. Dwight in *Greenfield Hill* went a step further than Eliot by celebrating in full physical and spiritual detail a village made up of such freeholders.

Community Life in Greenfield Hill

But communities like Greenfield Hill, Dwight was at pains to inform the reader, did not come into existence and continue to flourish without great suffering and effort. Section 3 of his poem describes the siege and burning of nearby Fairfield by the British in 1779;[16] and section 4 goes back to the Pequot War of 1637 to tell of a decisive victory gained by the colonists close to the spot where Fairfield was to be settled two years later. Only after such ordeals could New England pursue in security her mission as a light to all America and the world.

Having put on record these successfully encountered trials, Dwight returned to his presentation of the Edenic charms "of a happy village in New England"[17] and introduced the reader to the local pastor, who is nearing the end of a long and saintly life. Venerated and loved by all, this man of wisdom and benevolence favors his flock with a final exhortation to continue in their happy Christian ways that it had been his life's purpose to lead them in; for, he assures them, such ways alone can bring them joy in this world and in the next. Bible reading, keeping the Sabbath, daily family prayers, education of the young, and "the duties of charity" demand the attention of every villager, and any one who ignores these obligations does so at the risk of eternal damnation.

But the old minister does not have the last word in the poem. That is reserved for a wise and highly esteemed farmer, who discourses to his neighbors on thrift and industry, shares with them the secrets of successful farming, and emphasizes the importance of education and the strict disciplining of children. He ends with remarks on neighborliness and good citizenship. Aware apparently of the readiness of New Englanders of that time to go to law against one another, he urges friendly, out-of-court settlements of disputes.

Each cause let mutual friends decide,
With common-sense alone to guide.[18]

For unless Greenfield Hill and its sister villages of New England were havens of brotherly love and civic harmony, they could not qualify as the nearly perfect Christian communities that Dwight demanded that they be.

Prophecy

Greenfield Hill closes with a "Vision" in which "the Genius of . . . [Long Island] Sound appears, and declares the future Glory of America."[19] The New England towns, we are assured, will provide the model and stimulus for this future, and their influence will spread outward across the continent and the world. The mission of New England was to be truly messianic, millennial—no less than the establishment of the Kingdom of Christ on earth, an event which Dwight elsewhere predicted would occur "not far from the year 2000."[20] Places like Greenfield Hill would be the foci on which God's millennial grace first would shine, soon to radiate outward[21] to redeem the human race. Then the angels would rejoice,

As, from the tomb, when great MESSIAH rose,
Heaven bloomed with joy, and Earth forgot her woes.[22]

Greenfield Hill is the first—and certainly one of the most enthusiastic—poetic celebrations of the New England town as a way of life; and as such it was important in launching the myth, or image, of the New England town as a second Eden or a new Zion[23]—a myth that had been taking shape over many years and was discernible in germ even in William Bradford's *Of Plimmoth Plantation*. Not that Dwight was consciously establishing a myth. He was being entirely literal, as he made very clear in 1817 in *An Address to the Emigrants from Connecticut, and from New England Generally, in the New Settlements in the United States*,[24] written by him as a member of a committee formed by the General Association of the Congregational Church of Connecticut. The *Address*, which speaks of course for the committee in general, loses no time in getting to the point: "Our fathers were your fathers. They were the pious pilgrims, who first came to New England, and laid the foundation of all our invaluable civil, literary, moral and religious institutions."[25] Another member of the committee was Lyman Beecher, one of the great Calvinist preachers of the day, who later moved to Cincinnati, where he was president of a theological seminary. To the Connecticut churchmen it was the sacred trust of those Yankees emigrating to settle new territories, whether in northern New England, in New York, or in the West, to carry with them their native institutions and establish them as extensions of the parent culture. If the emigrants tarried long in founding schools, churches, and civil governments resembling as closely as possible those of the New England towns, the committee feared that they would sink into a condition not far from barbarism. New England ways were the best. They should spread as the dominant civilizing force with the west-ward-moving frontier. To a limited extent this is exactly what happened, so that in his *Travels in New England and New York* (1821 and 1822) Dwight referred to the western sections of New York as "a colony from New En-gland."[26]

Yet Dwight was a realist, well aware that Eden could not be created in a day. He made clear, in his *Travels,* that in any newly settled territory an interval of lapsed civilization must be expected—hence the urgency of his warnings. The first settlers, or "foresters" as he called them,[27] lacked the time—if not the desire—to concern themselves with the niceties of religion and education and cared little for well-ordered civil government. They at first would lead a rough, hard, semisavage life, but in the normal course of events this advance guard soon was transformed to, or gave way to, a more permanent population of earnest, socially and religiously responsible citi-zens. The state of Vermont furnished Dwight with striking examples of this process. Though mainly New Englanders, the first settlers were from among those who had "met with difficulties at home."[28] Following close after would be families in search of large farms at low cost, and among them would be a certain number of "the discontented, the enterprising, the ambitious, and the covetous."[29] But eventually schools and churches would be instituted and a more stable social order developed under the influence of teachers, clergymen, and the civic leaders who would naturally emerge from a group of New Englanders.

Dwight saw Vermont, in the early 1800s, as being in the first stages of this sort of evolution. Ethan Allen, whom Dwight despised as an infidel despite his exploits at Ticonderoga and elsewhere, typified the earliest pioneer stage of settlement. But Allen had long since been dead when Dwight traveled in Vermont, and many of the rougher elements had left for other frontiers. Though Dwight still found the Vermont constitution to be defec-tive because of its one-house legislature and its provisions for selecting judges by popular vote, he saw many signs of continuing improvement. Log cabins (to Dwight a sign of an imperfect society) were being replaced by frame houses; ministers in growing numbers were being settled throughout the state; the manners of the people were undergoing refinement.

Typical of the gradual change toward more civilized conditions in Vermont was the case of the little Champlain Valley town of Benson, situated in a "rough and unsightly"[30] terrain. For a number of years the inhabitants, "influenced by the turbulence of the times and by the vice that necessarily grows out of that turbulence," had persecuted their pastor with "derision and insult. . . . The young people in particular became grossly hostile to him, merely because he was a minister of the Gospel and a virtuous man." But just as the despairing clergyman was on the point of leaving, a revival of religion occurred. "The people dropped their animosity against their minister; vice and licentiousness fled; peace, order, and good will took their place. . . . The church was enlarged by the accession of multitudes; and all the blessings of Christian neighborhood sprang up in the place of tumult and confusion."[31] The New England way had worked. The presence of a church and a pious minister had had the inevitable effect. Benson and the state of Vermont, indeed all territories settled by New Englanders, could look forward to "the more extensive improvement rationally promised by the influence of . . . New England institutions," which would transform them into localities "where a great mass of happiness and virtue [might] be fairly expected in future ages."[32]

The Church as Redeemer of Society

In assigning an all-important civilizing influence to the church, Dwight was drawing from his knowledge of New England history, to which he devoted much space in his *Travels*. He was aware that the Congregational churches had originally been—and, he hoped, would continue to be—the intellectual, spiritual, even geographical centers of the life of the towns. Built into the Congregational system was the idea of the covenant— between God and His people, between the people and their pastors, and among the people themselves. As William Bradford and others have recorded, the very first churches, some of which originated in England, were gatherings that covenanted together and with their ministers to live and worship as a group in the ways directed by the Bible. One such covenant— that of Salem in 1630—was worded as follows:

We, whose names are here underwritten, being by [God's] most wise and good providence brought together into this part of America, in the Bay of Massachusetts; and desirous to unite into one congregation or church, under the Lord Jesus Christ, our head, in such sort as becometh all those whom he hath redeemed, and sanctified to himself, do hereby solemnly and religiously, as in his most holy presence, promise and bind ourselves to walk in all our ways according to the rule of the Gospel, and in all sincere conformity to his holy ordinances, and in mutual love and respect to each other, so near as God shall give us grace.[33]

Other covenants might be worded differently, but that of the Salem congregation is typical of those entered into throughout New England down to Dwight's time, and no Congregational church could exist without one. Although the salvation of each individual rested entirely on the divine will in granting grace, the church was considered an indispensable "means" by which God brought about the predestined conversion and sanctification of His elect. But the church also—perhaps because of its immensely important function in the works of salvation—was the strongest unifying force in a community. At least men like Dwight regarded the church as serving this end, and other commentators saw the origin of town government itself in church polity. Of course, in addition to being a channel for the flow of grace from God to the elect, the church had always taken on itself the closely related role of preparing the world for the establishment of Christ's kingdom on earth—the millennium that would supposedly precede the second bodily advent of Christ.

This dual purpose—the salvation of souls and the preparation of the world for the millennium—did doubtless have a direct and decisive bearing on the organization and planning of a community, though it was far from the sole influence. It must be remembered that the Puritans and Separatists who settled in New England believed that their churches were modeled upon those of the primitive Christians; and this belief, as has been mentioned earlier, is basic to the Saybrook Platform of the Connecticut churches. Accordingly, each congregation would be a more or less self-governing group of individuals bound together in close fellowship. But for the fellowship to exist among all members of a church, the congregation must not be excessively large—several hundred was considered the ideal number for a church in New England—and the members must reside within reasonable distances of one another. The planning of a New England town was thus normally based, in part at least, on these considerations. The location of a meetinghouse, which would determine the location of a village, was always a matter of grave concern and sometimes of bitter contention, as Charles Francis Adams has recorded in his history of Braintree and Quincy, Massachusetts.[34] Often the church building would be used for town meetings. In Massachusetts and Connecticut the appointment of the Congregational pastor was a matter in which all voting inhabitants, not just church members, had a voice, since the pastor's salary would be paid from town taxes. This "standing order," as it was called, was slowly eroded and early in the nineteenth century discarded altogether, as other denominations won converts and formed congregations in the various towns. But for almost two hundred years the Congregational church—in the true sense an established church—was a focal point of New England town organization. Though in theory the church and the civil affairs of a town were separate and distinct, most community leaders would be members and perhaps officers in the church. The values, ideals, and social and spiritual goals promoted by the church would perforce be those of the community at large.

Reports on the Promised Land: Dwight's *Travels in New England and New York,* and Other Commentators

A succession of New England villages, composed of neat houses, surrounding neat schoolhouses and churches, adorned with gardens, meadows, and orchards, and exhibiting the universally easy circumstances of the inhabitants, is, at least in my own opinion, one of the most delightful prospects which this world can afford.
Timothy Dwight, *Travels in New York and New England*[1]

While living on Greenfield Hill, Dwight had the impulse to be the bard and prophet of the New England village and of its importance in God's plan for this world. In later years he dropped the bardic and prophetic roles and assumed those of historian and reporter.[2] The result was the four-volume *Travels in New England and New York,* which is his work of chief interest to the modern reader and was held in high esteem by such writers as Emerson, Thoreau, and Hawthorne. Finished before Dwight's death in 1817, *Travels* was published by his family, in accordance with his dying wish, in 1821 and 1822. In these volumes he described his frequent and lengthy journeys in the two areas during the period from 1795 to 1815. Traveling by horse and, occasionally, on foot, he covered, by his own calculation, an aggregate distance equal to two-thirds of the circumference of the world.[3] The format that he chose for his account was that of letters supposedly "addressed to an English gentleman,"[4] and he had as one of his purposes the correction of errors contained in the published narratives of foreign travelers in the newly founded republic. He did, in fact, give considerable attention to such corrections, but he insisted that he was writing primarily for Americans and that what he had to report was of most concern to them.

Inklings of the Millennium

The northern states, as Dwight designated New England and New York, were in his opinion "that part of the American republic in which its strength is principally found,"[5] and he discerned in this region a common culture dominated by that of New England. To begin with, he considered "the scene . . . a novelty in the history of man."[6] The conversion of a wilderness into what he described as the site of a mild-mannered, benignly governed social order where education, the arts and, above all, the Christian religion flourished, and where poverty was almost unknown, was an achievement of enormous significance to Dwight and must, he thought, be valued as such by the American people. Dwight proposed to report not only on the end product of this civilizing process in the older parts of the area but, more important, on its continuing operation in northern New England and large sections of New York.

Dwight emphasized the uniqueness of the colonizing to which he was to devote so much descriptive effort and commentary and which to him, as a clergyman, ranked as a crucial phase of God's working out of His plan for the world. Dwight, it will be remembered, was a grandson of Jonathan Edwards and much of his life a close follower of his grandfather's theology. One of Edwards's major subjects of speculation was the form and manner in which the millennium would arrive. Like many other Protestant theologians in his century he could not accept the traditional and widely held belief that the millennium would be ushered in by the return of Christ in body with accompanying cataclysms and catastrophes; that Satan at such a time would be totally crushed; and that Christ would then reign during one thousand years of peace and joy, at the end of which Satan would revive, briefly throw the world into turmoil, but soon would be destroyed in a final great battle—Armageddon. Ever since the formulation in 1658 of the Savoy Confession of Faith of the English Congregational Church, there had been a tendency to reject this dramatic scenario and substitute for it a more allegorical view of the millennium; and this tendency was evident in the Saybrook Platform of 1708, which subscribed to the Savoy Confession in all matters of doctrine and which Edwards, as a Yale graduate, highly esteemed. The question of course was argued, and the allegorical approach was elaborated by a number of theologians. Edwards ranked first among them for the forcefulness of his reasoning and, as concerned America at least, for certain elements of originality in his conclusions.

Simply stated, the concept of the millennium that was emerging in Edwards's time and that he aided in establishing was this: In accord with evidence provided in the Revelation of Saint John, the church in the eighteenth century was in the sixth of seven stages through which it must pass before the end of history. Each stage thus far had been marked by hardships for the church, though progress had been made in alleviating these hardships. The seventh stage, to begin in the not-too-distant future, would be the millennium. But contrary to the earlier and more spectacular concept, this last period would not involve Christ's coming in person. It would be a time in which the spirit, not the person, of Christ would reign worldwide through His church and in which the Devil would be suppressed but not destroyed. It would be a time of peace, of happiness, of material prosperity, of the easing of labor by means of technological inventions. In short, many of the effects of the fall of Adam—such as hard labor—would be either alleviated or eliminated, and humanity would be reinstated in a new, though perhaps slightly imperfect, Eden. The spirit of Edward Hicks's "Peaceable Kingdom" paintings—themselves allegorical representations of the millennium—would prevail. The people of this age would no longer be wanderers in exile, would no longer toil so hard for their bread, nor would they destroy themseves in bloody wars. They would now have time and energy to pursue their loftiest mission on earth—the loving worship of God, their creator, and the furthering of His kingdom. After many years of this blissful dispensation, however, Satan would rise up for one last stand, as predicted in older millennial theories. Christ would now indeed descend in person to rout the forces of evil and preside at the final judgment and the end of history.

The salient feature of this concept of the millennium is that, unlike the rather simplistic earlier ones, it envisioned the redemption of society (not only of individuals) here on earth without the preliminary return of Christ to overthrow the Devil and anti-Christ. Also it differed from the pessimistic view of John Calvin, who anticipated no literal earthly millennium but interpreted the idea of it symbolically. On this sinful earth, Calvin thought, the church of Christ, which was the whole body of the elect and the regenerate, would never be dominant but would endure as a suffering minority sustained and protected, until the Last Judgment, by the grace of the Holy Spirit, whose presence among the elect would constitute a millennium of sorts.

Thus Edwards's earthly millennium was markedly different from that accepted by Calvin, whose doctrine in most other matters Edwards so highly venerated and did so much to restore in the New England churches. Edwards, in fact, thought he had already seen signs of the imminent coming of this sort of millennium, and saw signs pointing to the English North American colonies, especially to New England, as being the first areas to feel its effects. Recent victories over the French—to Edwards the minions of the pope, whom he considered to be the anti-Christ—notably at Cape Breton, and the restoration to New England of many captives taken by the

French seemed to him to bear out this view. A further indication was "a very great awakening, in the county of Hampshire, in the province of Massachusetts Bay . . . and also in many parts of Connecticut."[7] This awakening, Edwards carefully noted, *preceded* similar awakenings "of many thousands in England, Wales, and Scotland, and almost all the British Provinces in North America."[8] Edwards mentioned revivals in Germany and in the United Netherlands, but clearly God was favoring Britain and her colonies, and New England most of all, in His outpouring of grace. The tokens were impressive; God was using New England as a chief, though perhaps not the only, instrument of His will. The duty of New England was clear and her responsibility was awesome.

It was true that the upsurge of piety known as the Great Awakening, which swept the whole English-speaking world in the first half of the eighteenth century, had been particularly intense in Edwards's own Northampton. Edwards was even accused of claiming that the millennium had actually begun in his parish,[9] but he denied this, stating that the events at Northampton might be regarded as harbingers but not the actual commencement of the millennium. Nevertheless, in this small Connecticut River town occurred stirrings that gave promise of much greater glories to come. And it was this typical New England town—not Boston, which was a spawning ground of Arminianism—that had, under Edwards's ministry, been the central point whence emanated a newly revived Calvinist orthodoxy. Despite his disclaimers, Edwards had described Northampton as "a city set on a hill, to which God has in so great a degree entrusted the honor of religion."[10] Dwight, a native of Northampton and grandson of Edwards, would have been impressed by all that had taken place in the town. In the first volume of his *Travels* he devoted two chapters[11] to a description and historical account of Northampton, which he presented as a community outstanding for its freedom from litigation, its piety, the high caliber of its ministers, its fair treatment of the Indians, its material prosperity, the large size of its families, and the longevity of its citizens—all signs of divine approval and all millennial characteristics.

Whether or not Edwards actually believed that the Great Awakening in New England was a prologue to the millennium, he did definitely hold, as we have seen, that the English colonies in America would be the first eventually to experience it—a view that was a logical extension of the conviction that sustained the Pilgrims and the Puritans in their migrations to the New World. These first New Englanders compared their journeying to that of Moses and Joshua seeking and conquering the Promised Land. They thought of themselves as modern Israelites, divinely directed to found a New Jerusalem, a western Zion, far from the centers of corruption in the Old World. In the next century the idea that North America was to be the site of a new religious dispensation was broadened to include the concept of the *translatio imperii,* which held that high civilization follows a course from east to west and was now about to cross the Atlantic from its present location in Europe. Bishop Berkeley's famous lines written in 1752 are an expression of the idea:

> Westward the course of empire takes its way;
> The four first acts already past,
> A fifth shall close the drama with the day:
> Times noblest offspring is the last.

Later still, in the nineteenth century, the idea of the New Jerusalem merged with the notion that the United States was also a New Eden, a spot where humanity would have an entirely new beginning in "the garden of the world,"[12] to use Whitman's phrase. Thus, in New England at least, there had always been a sense of messianic mission, the New World as the redeemer of mankind, an idea that Englishmen during the Reformation held in regard to England's predestined role in history.[13] Later these beliefs coalesced in the United States in the concept of manifest destiny and in Britain in the concept of the white man's burden; and both nations, convinced of their roles as redeemers, sent out armies of missionaries, preceded by armies of soldiers, "from greenland's icy mountains to Afric's coral strands."[14] But missionary activity within the United States reached its peak long after Edwards's day, in the nineteenth century, with Dwight incidentally one of its most fervid sponsors.

Dwight and the Millennium

As a theologian and pastor, Dwight admired his grandfather Edwards and those clergymen who most closely followed his teachings, Samuel Hopkins and Joseph Bellamy, for example, both of whom entertained New Light evangelical, strictly Calvinistic views and shared Edwards's ideas about the millennium. The New Light segment of the Congregational Church held that divine grace, evidenced by the experience of conversion, was the sole means of achieving a sanctified life in this world and salvation in the next. Since in normal times grace could be expected to descend upon only a small portion of mankind—the elect—in accord with God's eternal decrees, a sudden increase in the number of conversions, as during the Great Awakening in the Connecticut Valley, would indicate something was afoot, since it was the belief of the New Light divines that during the millennium most of the human race, instead of the usual tiny part of it, would be regenerate and thus saved—for how else could the millennium deserve to be called the kingdom of Christ on earth?[15] Here again was a compelling reason for sending out missionaries. Unless the heathen masses were instructed in the truths of Protestant Christianity, they would hardly become fit vessels to receive the outpouring of grace in the glorious era to come.

Referring to his grandfather's theology in general, Dwight wrote in his *Travels:* "The scheme of Mr. Edwards is true. Of its truth I have not a question...,"[16] and surely he made no exception of Edwards's views on the millennium. In respect to the doctrine of election, however, he did deviate from Edwards's and the New Lights' opinions, in that, unlike such men as Hopkins and Bellamy, he assigned to an individual's own efforts a major, if not decisive, role in achieving salvation.[17] Indeed he seemed to believe that salvation was within the grasp of all who really strove for it, though he did not deny God's ultimate sovereignty in granting grace. By thus modifying the predestinarian theory of regeneration, Dwight accomplished two things. First, he held out the hope of full church membership to greater numbers of persons by making conversion—which was a prerequisite for membership—appear more attainable than under the doctrine of strict election. Second, as a consequence of this view of conversion he enhanced among the nonmembers an interest in the church, which resulted in increased attendance at services, for he insisted that only through the church as a "means" of salvation could one hope to be saved. The results of this modified Edwardsian doctrine would correspond to much that was envisioned as millennial—a greater number of saved souls, fuller pews at church, and greater prestige and influence for the ministers.

Writings during the eighteenth century and later in regard to the millennium were numerous and complex, and their nature and variety have only been touched on here. Many of the niceties of biblical interpretation—especially of Daniel and Revelation—are of slight interest today. But the general concept of a millennium occurring in this world as a reign of Christ through His church, beginning quite possibly in New England, is of the greatest significance in a consideration of the almost mythical qualities that have come to be associated with the New England town. There is no more remarkable demonstration of this significance than Dwight's *Travels,* which might be termed—only half facetiously—a record of its author's tours of inspection of the progress being made in anticipation of the millennium in outlying areas of the northeastern United States.

Before accompanying Dwight on his rounds, let us review and summarize briefly the millennial characteristics, many of them already mentioned, that he, along with others in the Edwardsian tradition, was seeking and sometimes, he thought, actually finding—as, for example, in his beloved and archetypal Greenfield Hill. The church, of course, would preside over the new era, for the Edwardsian millennium was in its broadest definition simply the reign, benign but complete, of Calvinistically oriented Protestantism—the Church of Rome, considered the anti-Christ, having been overthrown. This would be true not only in America but eventually in Europe and the rest of the world, the conversion of which required the immediate deploying of armies of missionaries. Hand in hand with the spread of true religion would be the spread of education; for ignorance, in the Calvinist view a bulwark of Romanism, had no place in the millennial scheme. The importance of knowledge and education as prerequisites of the millennium could not be overemphasized, and had been specifically mentioned by those two highly influential New England divines in the tradition of Edwards—Samuel Hopkins in *A Treatise on the Millennium* (1793)[18] and Joseph Bellamy in *The Millennium, Or the Thousand Years of Prosperity* (1758).[19] Schools, academies, and colleges must therefore be as numerous as meetinghouses, and learning of all sorts must flourish. In addition, advances must occur in technology, in agriculture, and in communication and transportation. Yankee mechanical ingenuity would thus be one of God's means in His millennial providence. Finally, every one must be materially prosperous and poverty must cease to exist.

The overall result of all this would be manifold. There would be increased time for the cultivation of religion. Living conditions and the health of the people would improve and life spans would lengthen. Though death would not yet be banished—that awaited the final coming of Christ—death would no longer be feared. With the improvements in transportation, the world would become one vast, brotherly neighborhood—a universal New England town—and wars would be no more. Love and respect would be the rule among nations as among persons, and the law courts would for the most part be unused. Crime would have vanished from the earth; litigation would be an outdated bad habit.

Progress of the Millennium in New England and New York: Religion

What indications, then, of millennial conditions did Dwight find on his tours of inspection through New England and New York? We have seen that in his own Greenfield Hill, where previous to his systematic travels he had served as pastor and schoolmaster—two functions indispensable in a perfected society—conditions were already close to millennial. The four volumes of the *Travels* assess the situation in literally hundreds of other communities. Dwight omits few details. For each town or district that he visits or merely passes through he gives information on such matters as geographical location, climate, the health and morals of the inhabitants, history, population statistics over a period of several decades, economic conditions, industries and manufactures, the architecture of the dwellings and public buildings, and, above all, the state of education and religion. In addition he includes lengthy general discourses on the political, religious, and educational practices of the northeastern region as a whole and of the individual states, and he has other sections on the general social and personal characteristics of the people of the region. The result is an amazing body of fact and opinion, sometimes entertaining, sometimes tedious, but always informative, even when most colored by its author's prejudices. The *Travels*, indeed, serves as a sort of encyclopedia, written with a Calvinist bias, of New England and New York in the late eighteenth and early nineteenth centuries. Like *Domesday Book*, though compiled with a very different purpose, it is an invaluable source of information about its time and place. But today, and for this study, the chief interest of the *Travels* is the idealized conception it gives of the New England town; for it supplements the poeticized description of Greenfield Hill with a factual report, the main purpose of which is to establish the poet's vision as a present, or imminent, reality for the extensive and populous region that Dwight considers will play the leading role in the future of the nation.

In the series of "Letters" that constitute the chapters in *Travels* that deal with "Religion of New England," Dwight states in the strongest terms his conviction that religion is the very basis of an orderly, civilized society. Morality and justice depend on it. "Oaths of office and of testimony alike, without the sanctions of religion, are merely solemn farces,"[20] he declares. Thus, as was the case in Connecticut in Dwight's time, the legislature has the duty and right "to establish the worship of God"[21] in towns within its jurisdiction. Nor does he find it undesirable that in towns where there is only one church society, or organization, the selectmen, who are the chief civil officers, also "perform the duty of a [church] society's committee"[22]—a flaunting of the principle of separation of church and state that would shock many today. Dwight, of course, was well pleased with the existence of an established church—the Congregational—supported by town taxes in every New England state except Rhode Island, and he vigorously opposed efforts to effect disestablishment in his own state of Connecticut. Yet he was pleased to report that in recently settled New York towns, where religion was not supported by public moneys, New England emigrants rapidly organized churches and appointed ministers. Wherever New Englanders went, he found, they took their benign customs and institutions with them. To encourage them in this laudable practice, the missionary societies and church associations in the home states stood ready with advice and exhortation, as can be seen in *An Address to the Emigrants from Connecticut . . .*, written, it will be recalled, by a committee chaired by Dwight. Also these organizations aided the struggling communities financially and assisted them in finding pastors, and the Connecticut General Association of the Congregational Church even got its state legislature to appropriate money for these purposes.[23] But the concern was not only with religion. The Connecticut Association, in the same *Address* in which in 1793 it urged emigrants "to gather and organize churches,"[24] also drew attention to the need of "good schools for the instruction of [their] children."[25]

Though in some recently settled towns, such as Benson, Vermont, the pastors at first had difficulty gaining the confidence of the people, these problems usually had favorable outcomes as the New Englanders' traditional respect for religion asserted itself. To Dwight, of course, the pastor was the most important person in a community, since the purpose of his presence was no less than "the salvation of his flock."[26] The minister's "office is, and is acknowledged to be, sacred, instituted by God himself, eminently useful to the present and immensely important to the future well-being of mankind."[27] Dwight outlines the specific duties of the pastor, such as delivering two lengthy sermons each Sabbath in addition to giving lectures on other days, officiating at funerals, making and receiving parochial visits, and attending ordinations and ministers' meetings within his district. In the older sections of New England, Dwight in his travels most invariably found the religious life to be thriving. In most newly settled areas, it was either thriving or gave promise of so doing in the near future. Even if one community had to share its minister with others or if members of different denominations (as long as they were Protestant) agreed to unite in appointing a minister, Dwight was happy, for such expedients showed concern with what to him was of first importance.

Progress of the Millennium: Education

"Attachment to education in New England is universal,"[28] Dwight proudly stated, and of his own Connecticut he wrote: "There is a schoolhouse sufficiently near to every man's door . . . to allow his children to go conveniently to school most of the year."[29] Altogether in the state, he calculated there were between 1,400 and 2,600 schools, with an average of thirty pupils in each. In 1790 in the parish of Greenfield Hill alone there were eight schools and one academy (of which Dwight was the master). Elsewhere, even in areas where "the inhabitants were still living in log huts," he reported, "they had not only erected schoolhouses for their children, but had built them in a neat style"[30] The situation was the same throughout most of New England, where, since earliest colonial times,

towns had been legally obliged to provide education for the young. Ignorance, especially illiteracy, could not be tolerated under a religious dispensation that emphasized for all persons the reading and study of the Bible,
and the learning of the catechism, which latter was taught in the schools,
being included in the famous *New England Primer*. Also, as we have seen, in
Dwight's day as well as earlier, it was believed that the confidently expected
millennial future would be marked by the spread and improvement of
learning among all peoples.

In the regions of New York settled by New Englanders, Dwight was
happy to report that schools were "established with a celerity delightful to
the eye of benevolence, which cannot fail to foresee in this propitious
institution the elevation, not of a few privileged individuals, but of the
whole rising generation; the children of the poor as well as of the rich, to
intelligence and worth; the exaltation of man, and not of those merely by
whom man is usually controlled."[31]

Dwight made clear that he favored the kind of education prevalent in
rural areas—schooling leading to useful and enriched lives. He wrote
scornfully of the fashionable education to which many of the children of
the well-to-do in the cities were subjected and which had as its chief end the
teaching of "accomplishments" considered desirable in high society. This
sort of education, he complained, produced "not a man, nor a woman, but
a well-dressed bundle of accomplishments. Not a blessing, nor an heir of
immortality, but a fribble or a doll."[32] The New England that commanded
Dwight's attention and respect was the New England of farms and villages.
Here he expected that the ideal Christian society, already taking shape,
would in the not-too-distant future be realized.

Dwight dilated at length on the happy results, as he saw them, of universal education in New England and New York. The beneficial effects on the
religious life of the people were, of course, obvious and of first importance.
Another result was that universal education prevented the formation of a
peasant class. "Our common people," he asserted, "are far better educated
than [those of England and Europe], both in the school and in the church.
. . . All of them can read; and write, and keep accounts. Almost all of them
do read; and many of them, much."[33] Indicative of the intellectual level of
the people was the excellence of their English as compared to that of the
masses in Britain. Dwight pointed out several reasons for this linguistic
superiority. The schools themselves were taught in many cases by college
graduates. The ministers in the churches, which most people habitually
attended, were scholars who wrote and spoke the language according to
the highest standards. In a relatively classless society, people of all educational levels conversed with one another and thus the speech of the highly

educated was regularly heard and was available for imitation by the less well educated. Also the popularity of reading among the people provided exposure to standard literary English.

A final effect of the system of compulsory education on the people of New England stemmed from the fact that they themselves directly controlled their schools and thus developed a sense of civic responsibility and an interest in, and knowledgeability about, matters outside their private and family affairs. Maintaining a school system was only one of the responsibilities of the citizens of a New England town, but it was an important one, for its efficient discharge made possible the meeting of other responsibilities connected with the government of the community. Education and its administration were phases of a larger corporate life.

Finally, educational opportunities were not confined to those offered by the local schools. Dwight drew attention to the academies and colleges scattered throughout the region, and glowingly described their role in training ministers and teachers and in generally raising the intellectual level of the populace. Every town would have a number of young men— and as time went on, young women—educated beyond the common-school level.

Progress of the Millennium: Civil Government

Dwight regarded universal elementary education as a necessity for the efficient functioning of town governments. As is well known, these governments were participatory democracies, in which by Dwight's time almost every male inhabitant, with only minimal property qualifications, had a voice. Meeting at least once a year, usually in March, and at other times if the need or demand arose, the men of a town would vote on taxes, on projects such as bridges and road improvements, on appropriations for the care of the poor, and on any matters of public concern that might come up. In the March meeting also, the voters would elect the three or more selectmen who would be in charge of town affairs during the ensuing year, and would choose other officers, including a town clerk, fence-viewers, haywards, chimney-viewers, listers of rates (taxes), and sealers of weights and measures. Indeed, the New England town in Dwight's time was an almost autonomous unit.

At town meeting any one could speak his mind on any matter under consideration. Also, during the course of his lifetime any male inhabitant would probably be elected to at least one office, even if a very minor one; and in the early days if he refused to serve, he would be subject to a fine. It is true that the most important offices—those of selectmen, town clerk, and moderator—were usually held by the wealthier, more prominent citizens and would tend to remain in families, and thus a sort of aristocracy existed.[34] But this situation was always remediable by the election process, and a dissatisfied citizenry could have terminated it at will. Any one in office, however, would have the tacit backing of the church, which taught that all magistrates or government officials, once chosen by the people, must be respected and obeyed. The church and town, though strictly separate in theory and to some extent in fact, were opposite sides of a coin. The same persons were often involved in the governance of each; many a deacon had served as a selectman or town clerk. In addition, if a male citizen were a church member, he would participate in church meetings and be eligible to hold office in the church society, for each parish of the Congregational Church, the most numerous denomination in New England, was also virtually autonomous.[35] Thus there existed a sense of community—enhanced by the spirit of covenant so vital in New England history—in which almost every townsperson shared, unless he were a thorough recluse or curmudgeon—and such did exist.[36]

Obviously, a number of conditions were prerequisite to the successful functioning of a New England town. First, the town must be limited in population and geographical area if all inhabitants were to participate in its spiritual and civil life. Thirty-six square miles of territory occupied by perhaps one thousand or at most two thousand persons was average and ideal. Second, as we have seen, a usable level of education was highly desirable, if not a necessity, for effective town-meeting government; for useful participation in town affairs—which in itself constituted a sort of continuing education—drew upon one's knowledge and intellectual skills. Finally, the fact that most families in a town owned their land contributed an important economic incentive to maintaining a stable and harmonious community. "You are to understand," Dwight informed his fictional English correspondent in *Travels,* "that every man in this country [New England], almost without exception, lives on his own ground. The lands are held in fee simple and descend by law to all the children in equal shares. . . . Every farmer in Connecticut and throughout New England is, therefore, dependent for his enjoyments on none but himself, his government, and his God; and is the little monarch of a dominion sufficiently large to furnish all the supplies of competence."[37] With so much at stake, the landowner would be vitally involved in local government—which to him would be of more immediate importance than state or national government. That Dwight's assessment was overly favorable we shall see in later chapters. Indifference to local government was not uncommon. Many a townsman struggled hard not to have to serve in some official capacity.

A happy result of the general prosperity, the piety, and the harmonious community life of the people of New England was, Dwight points out, the almost total absence of crime in the region. Proudly he affirmed: "There have been fewer capital crimes committed in New England since its settlement than in any other country on the globe, Scotland [a sound Calvinist country] perhaps excepted, in proportion to the number of its inhabitants. Half, or two thirds, of these inhabitants sleep, at the present time, without barring or locking their doors. Not more than five duels have been fought here since the landing of the Plymouth colony. . . . During the last fourteen years, I have traveled not far from twelve thousand miles in New England and New York, and in this extensive progress have never seen two men employed in fighting."[38] Elsewhere he asserted that in New Haven (population six thousand), during the sixteen years that he lived there, not one house was broken into.[39] The Devil himself had apparently been put to rout in New England—the final step before the onset of the millennium. Biblical prophecy was being fulfilled; theology was being vindicated.

Scenery and Architecture

In volume 4 of his *Travels* Dwight quotes extensively from the British author John Lambert, who had published in London in 1810 a book titled *Travels in Lower Canada and North America.* Dwight found many inaccuracies in Lambert's account, but he was entirely in agreement with and quotes the following passage:

Throughout the states of Connecticut, Massachusetts, and New York, a remarkably neat, and indeed elegant style of architecture and decoration seems to pervade all the buildings in the towns and villages; and I understand is more or less prevalent in the northern and middle states. The houses in the small towns and villages are mostly built of wood, generally one or two stories above the ground floor; the sides are neatly clapboarded and painted white; the sloping roofs are covered with shingles and painted of a slate color; and with sash windows, green venetian shades outside, neat white railings, and steps have a pretty effect. Sometimes the entrance is ornamented with a portico. The churches, or as they are oftener termed meetings, are constructed of similar materials, painted white, and frequently decorated like the houses with sash windows and green venetian shades. The building is also surmounted by a handsome spire or steeple with one or two bells. A small town composed of these neat and ornamental edifices, and situated in the neighborhood of well-cultivated farms, large fields, orchards, and gardens, produces a most agreeable effect, and gives the traveler a high opinion of the prosperity of the country, and of the wealth and happiness of its inhabitants. Indeed those parts of the northern and middle states through which I traveled have the appearance of old well-settled countries. The towns and villages are populous; provisions are cheap and abundant; the farms appear in excellent order; and the inhabitants, sober, industrious, religious, and happy.[40]

Lovely villages, Dwight thought, could be found everywhere in New England, but in the Connecticut River Valley he was convinced that they had reached something near perfection architecturally as well as spiritually and culturally, and on these river towns he lavished many pages of description. Dwight's enthusiasm may have been heightened by the fact that he was a native of the valley, having been born at Northampton, Massachusetts. Furthermore, he subscribed to the orthodox religion of which, since the days of his grandfather Jonathan Edwards, the valley had been a stronghold as contrasted to the slackening zeal in eastern Massachusetts. At any rate, Dwight found the valley altogether to his liking. In the first place, he considered it to be, in its geographical aspects, a veritable Eden—a proper setting for a millennial society. "Beauty of landscape," he wrote, "is an eminent characteristic of this valley. From Hereford Mountain [on the Canadian border] to Saybrook, it is almost a continued succession of delightful scenery. No other tract within my knowledge, and from the extensive information which I have received, I am persuaded that no other tract within the United States of the same extent, can be compared to it with respect to those objects which arrest the eye of the painter and the poet. . . . The first object, however, in the whole landscape is undoubtedly the Connecticut itself. This stream may perhaps, with as much propriety as any in the world, be named the beautiful river. From Stewart [in northern New Hampshire] to the Sound it uniformally sustains this character."[41] Dwight fills a long paragraph with a list of the beauties of the river, and one wonders if he is attributing to it a religious significance suggestive of that of the River Jordan. Here, he seems to say, is a Promised Land where true Christians flourish and whence radiates a spiritual light destined to redeem the nation and all mankind.

Dwight was always keenly aware of the physical aspects of the regions through which he traveled. His eye for impressive scenery, indeed, places him in the vanguard of that large group of artists and writers—including Thomas Cole, Asher Durand, William Cullen Bryant, James Fenimore Cooper, Washington Irving, and Nathaniel P. Willis—who specialized in celebrating the American landscape. Yet for all his love of the beauties of nature, Dwight's overriding interest was in the condition of the farmlands and the appearances of the farmhouses and the villages. As a onetime farmer himself, he was concerned with agriculture and could tell at a glance how expertly the farms of an area were tilled, and from the condition and architecture of the dwellings and other buildings he could gauge a town's prosperity. As a matter of course he would comment on meetinghouses and schoolhouses and was always pleased when these were substantial and attractive to the eye—for what better evidence could one have of thriving religion and education and hence of a thriving community? Log huts pained him, though he recognized that in newly settled territory they were temporary necessities. But he hoped they would soon be demolished and be replaced by the neat, clapboarded houses that he so much admired in the older towns.

Thus the crowning ornaments of the valley were "its numerous towns, villages, and hamlets almost everywhere exhibiting marks of prosperity and improvement . . . , the numerous churches lifting their spires in frequent succession, the neat schoolhouses everywhere occupied, and the mills busied on . . . a multitude of streams."[42] The towns, moreover, were "not like those on the Hudson, mere collections of houses and stores clustered round a landing, where nothing but mercantile and mechanical business is done."[43] New England villages, Dwight pointed out, are carefully planned, especially those of the Connecticut Valley. A healthy, sightly spot was first selected. The site, Dwight explains, was then divided among the settlers into lots of two to ten acres, on which a house and a barn were erected. This home lot was usually used for a meadow, a garden, an orchard; and the owner, if a farmer, would in the early days of settlement have other holdings outside the village. The aspect of the village would be one of spaciousness, with the houses and other structures situated at considerable distances from one another. Of the grounds and outbuildings of each dwelling, Dwight remarked that "it is hardly necessary to observe that these appendages spread a singular cheerfulness and beauty over a New England village, or that they contribute largely to render the house a delightful residence."[44] Of course, Dwight would realize that there would be isolated farms in the township, established usually well after the original settlement, but the farms would be within manageable distance of the central village or of a parish church and district school, and would share in the social, political, and religious activities of the town. Here, the idealist would believe, mild manners, love of learning, respect for government, love of liberty, and many other virtues would flourish.[45] The valley was quintessential New England, according to Dwight; it was the best that the New or the Old World had to offer—a foretaste of the Kingdom of God on earth.

Thus in Dwight's *Travels* as in *Greenfield Hill* is found a systematic idealization, amounting to mythologizing, of the New England town. Others from Governor Bradford onwards had idealized their communities as they had existed in the past before debilitating forces had set in. But Dwight made no such comparisons between the past and the present. In the New England town as he knew it he found qualities in no way inferior to those of the past and perhaps superior. The world, to him, was moving toward universal betterment—the millennium—and New England was leading the way by the example of her towns, which, Dwight repeatedly affirmed, represented the highest form of civilization yet seen on this earth.

Other Early Commentators on the New England Town

Dwight was not alone in the early nineteenth century in his admiration of the moral, spiritual, and physical aspects of New England towns. In fact, the admirers were a multitude, and they were both domestic and foreign. One of them—perhaps the best known today—was James Fenimore Cooper, a man not noted for his love of New Englanders. Cooper had grown up in Cooperstown, New York, which had been founded by his father, a New Jerseyman, but which was populated primarily by settlers from what Cooper in his novel *The Pioneers* (1823) rather disparagingly called "the moral states of Connecticut and Massachusetts." But in this same novel he recorded less disparagingly that these settlers soon directed their "attention to the introduction of those customs and observances which had been the principal care of their forefathers." Education and religion—with much discussion "of grace and free-will"[46]—were, of course, foremost among the matters to receive attention, and Judge Temple, modeled on Cooper's father, is most cooperative in introducing these civilizing forces. However, Cooper depicted many of the Yankees in the settlement as opinionated, wasteful, or downright foolish.

In a later work, *Notions of the Americans*, Cooper treated New England and Yankees with a much less grudging approval. This two-volume work, published in 1828 only a few years after Dwight's *Travels*, was, like Dwight's book, composed of letters—in this case supposedly written by an Englishman visiting the United States—explaining American ways. And as regards New Englanders this fictitious correspondent's enthusiasm equals Dwight's. "New-England may justly glory in its villages!" he exclaims. "In space, freshness, and air of neatness and of comfort, they far exceed anything I have ever seen, even in the mother country."[47] The writer proceeds to describe the white buildings and the tranquillity and idyllic beauty of the surrounding countryside. He applauds the New Englanders' commitment to education, and he praises their "frugality, order, and intelligence," as well as their "self-respect, decency . . . , and individuality."[48] The New Englanders, he asserts, have "a better right to claim an elevated state of being than any other people I have ever visited";[49] and he finds that the influence of New England is felt far beyond its borders, for there is "scarcely a State in the whole confederation which has not imbibed more or less of the impetus of its inexhaustible activity."[50] New England, he avows, is the source of the "moving principles" and "peculiar tone" of "American character."[51] Such encomium from the pen of such a popular and respected author as Cooper was in the 1820s could go far in establishing New England's reputation, whether warranted or not, as an especially favored region.

Insofar as Cooper's and Dwight's purposes were to correct erroneous foreign accounts of the United States, they were not engaged in an entirely uphill struggle. Many foreigners, including travelers from England, wrote glowingly about early-nineteenth-century America, and New England received its share of praise. Even as early as 1794 and 1795 the Englishman William Strickland, whose chief interest was agriculture, toured New England, and had only good things to say about Dwight's beloved Connecticut River towns, the neatness and prosperity of which reminded him of England. A generation later in 1821, Frances Wright, a Scotswoman recounting her travels in North America, wrote enthusiastically of Burlington, Vermont, which with its white houses and orderly appearance she presented as a typical village of the region. New Englanders, she thought, were "the Scotch of North America."[52] Like so many other observers, she commented on the Yankee emphasis on education and the cleanliness of the children.

The most eloquent British travel writer was the author Harriet Martineau, who sojourned in the United States from 1834 to 1836, spending much of her time in New England. Out of her American experience came two books: *Society in America* (1837) and *Retrospect of Western Travel* (1838). A description of Northampton, Massachusetts, where she was visiting the historian George Bancroft, would have gladdened the heart of Dwight. "The villages of New-England are all more or less beautiful," she wrote, "and the most beautiful . . . is Northampton."[53] Her enumeration of the attractions of a New England village is the standard one; it includes the white churches, the elms, the respect for education, and the tolerance of the people in matters of taste and occupation, though not so much in religion. In her belief, "most enlightened and virtuous residents in the villages of New-England are eager to acknowledge that the lines have fallen to them in pleasant places."[54] Her most intimate contacts with New England village life were made, however, not in Northampton but in Catharine Sedgwick's Stockbridge, where she spent a summer—an experience that she described at length in *Society in America*.

Thus the fame—perhaps the myth—of the New England village was crossing the ocean, repeating and supporting what Dwight, Cooper, and many others were saying in America. The most impressive and authoritative endorsement from abroad appeared in 1838 (in English) in Alexis de

Tocqueville's *Democracy in America*—the year of publication of Martineau's *Retrospect of Western Travel*. With Tocqueville, whose views will be discussed in a later chapter, the New England town was becoming the subject of worldwide interest and acclaim.

[3]
Emerson and Thoreau and the Town of Concord

It is the consequence of this institution [the town meeting] that not a school-house, a public pew, a bridge, a pound, a mill-dam, hath been set up, or pulled down, or altered, or bought, or sold, without the whole population of this town having a voice in the affair. A general contentment is the result. And the people truly feel that they are lords of the soil. In every winding road, in every stone fence,in the smokes of the poor-house chimney, in the clock on the church, they read their own power, and consider, at leisure, the wisdom and error of their judgments.

Ralph Waldo Emerson, "A Historical Discourse"[1]

Emerson as a Citizen of Concord

In 1834 Ralph Waldo Emerson left Boston to make his permanent home in the country town of Concord, some twenty miles northwest of the city. Two years before, he had resigned as pastor of the Unitarian Second Church in Boston, because his theology had become too liberal for his congregation. Now, recently returned from an extended trip to Europe, he was ready to enter a new life of lecturing and writing; and like so many intellectuals since his day, he sought a congenial rural environment. In his case the move was no mistake. He flourished in Concord, and soon his name made the town famous; it became the most widely known small town in America.

"Hail to the quiet fields of my fathers!"[2] he wrote in his journal shortly after his arrival in Concord. He had, in fact, returned to the home of his ancestors, for he was the direct descendant of Concord's first two parsons—Peter and Edward Bulkeley—and of two later ones. During his childhood he had frequently visited the Old Manse, where his grandfather William Emerson and his great-grandfather Daniel Bliss had resided when they were the village pastors and which was now occupied by his grandmother and his step-grandfather, the Reverend Ezra Ripley. It was in the Old Manse that Emerson lived during the first months following his move to

Concord in 1834. The next year he bought a house on the opposite side of the village, and there he remained till his death forty-seven years later.

His ancestral roots were an asset to Emerson in establishing himself in the town. Though a Bostonian by birth and a Harvard graduate, he could not be taken as a complete outsider by the townspeople, who like country people everywhere might hold a newcomer from the city at arm's length. Emerson had Concord forebears—and he also had the sponsorship of the venerated Ezra Ripley. Thus he was accepted. Having married his second wife in 1835—the year in which he moved into his own house—he was promptly elected at the next town meeting to the post of hogreeve, an honor reserved according to New England rural custom for widowers newly remarried. One assumes that Emerson took the gesture for the semiofficial practical joke that it was and considered it an oblique Yankee way of saying, "You are one of us." It is doubtful that he tracked down and impounded many stray hogs. In that same year he was elected, more appropriately, to the school committee, of which he was soon made chairman. But he found the drain on his time too costly and soon resigned from the committee altogether. Once again, many years later, he was elected to the same committee as its chairman and again quickly resigned. He persisted, however, in another post, that of a director of the Concord Atheneum.

Further evidence of his acceptance by the townspeople was his election in 1839 to the Social Circle, of which he wrote later: "Much of the best society I have ever known is a club in Concord called the Social Circle, consisting always of twenty-five of our citizens, doctor, lawyer, farmer, trader, miller, mechanic, etc., solidest of men, who yield the solidest of gossip. Harvard University is a wafer compared to the solid land which my friends represent. I do not like to be absent from home on Tuesday evenings in winter."[3] He was a member of the group for the rest of his life.

Thus Emerson entered as fully as his calling of scholar and lecturer permitted into the community life of his ancestral town. He attended town meetings regularly and was impressed by the eloquence and good sense of the townsmen, though he seldom spoke himself. He also entered into the everyday activities appropriate to a countryman—keeping a garden and an orchard and becoming something of an authority on horticulture—and he became a landowner of some consequence. Among his holdings was the property on Walden Pond where Thoreau had his permission to build his famous hut. Most important to him, probably, in Concord was the opportunity for the woodland walks and the solitary contemplation that the countryside offered. Emerson was very much a "man thinking," to use his phrase from "The American Scholar"; he often said his important work was done in his ramblings in the woods and fields and his indoor study was simply a place where he wrote down his ideas. But always a good citizen, a good neighbor, Emerson shared his thoughts with his fellow townspeople, often lecturing in the Concord Lyceum and occasionally preaching in the Concord Church.

Emerson as the Historian of Concord

Emerson's enthusiasm for Concord and New England town life in general was demonstrated in an address he was invited to make in 1835 in celebration of the two-hundredth anniversary of Concord's founding. That he was asked to do this so soon after his move is additional evidence of the respect in which he was held. He took the assignment very seriously, studying the town records, interviewing old inhabitants, and reading whatever he could find that was related to the town's history. His numerous footnotes in the printed address—under the title "A Historical Discourse, Delivered before the Citizens of Concord, 12th September 1835"—attest to the pains he went to.

Sixty-four pages in length—including several appendixes—the speech required an hour and forty-five minutes for delivery. In it Emerson reviewed Concord's history from its founding to the ratification of the federal Constitution in 1788. But the "Discourse" is much more than a chronology of events. Its value and interest lie in its author's comments on the political and social organization that made possible two hundred years of prosperous town life. Emerson vies with Dwight in his enthusiastic admiration for New England towns. He does not, however, see in these communities hints of fulfillment of a biblical prophecy of a millennium, as Dwight did. Emerson had rejected formal theology, and from Dwight's standpoint would have been a hopeless heretic. To Emerson the potential of millennial bliss and peace existed in the here and now—was always immanent in the human spirit, which was an outlet of the world spirit or oversoul. He thought that each individual or group of individuals who lived by their highest spiritual capabilities would already have attained a state of perfection. "Five minutes of to-day," he wrote, "are worth as much to me as five minutes in the next millennium."[4] In Concord during at least part of its existence, this potential, Emerson thought, had in large measure been realized; and the result, rather than the cause, of this realization was the social and political institutions of the community.

All systems of government, religion, and economic organization and the like are to Transcendentalists like Emerson manifestations of the human spirit and hence reflections, albeit sometimes quite dim, of divinity. In some cases such manifestations may seem to bear very little relation to their divine source, but that is the result of a temporary imbalance in human affairs. In his essay "Politics" Emerson traces all political activities and systems to various material and spiritual needs of mankind. And if some form of government ceases to serve the most basic needs of the governed, it will quickly be eliminated, as, for example, the monarchy was discarded in the American Revolution.

The same was true in theology, Emerson thought. Though he rejected Puritanism as far as the present was concerned, he wrote favorably of it in his "Discourse" and elsewhere. Indeed, on reading some letters written by his aunt Mary Moody Emerson, a staunch Calvinist, he acknowledged "the debt of myself & my brothers to that old religion which in those years [of his youth] still dwelt like a Sabbath peace in the country population of New England, which taught privation, self denial & sorrow. A man was born not for prosperity, but to suffer for the benefit of others, like the noble rock-maple which all around the villages bleeds for the service of man. Not praise, not man's acceptance of our doing, but the Spirit's holy errand through us, absorbed the thought. How dignified is this! how all that is called talents & worth in Paris & in Washington dwindles before it!"[5] To the Transcendentalist, the Holy Spirit works through human beings in many theological guises in different times and places. Puritanism, though on the wane, was no exception. Concord, Emerson was aware, owed to the old religion some of its finest qualities.

It has frequently been observed that Transcendentalism provides the ultimate justification for democracy. If each individual in a society contains a particle of the divine—of the oversoul—within him, then the collective voice of that society, if each member of it is true to the best within himself, must be grounded on divine authority. *Vox populi* then is indeed *vox Dei.* In the early colonies of seventeenth-century New England the Old World obstacles to clear and unobstructed manifestations of the oversoul in the political and social realm were conspicuously absent. Outworn customs and deeply entrenched institutions had been left thirty-five hundred miles across the ocean and the human spirit was alone in a new environment and faced with new needs. Considering the divine foundation of the spirit, a Transcendentalist like Emerson would assume that the emergence of a social order perfectly suited to the spiritual requirements of the people and the physical conditions of their new home would have been inevitable.

Emerson's theory of the origin of New England town organization and government was a simple one: they grew out of the needs of the people and the demands of the place and times. In 1635 the land now occupied by Concord and several adjacent towns was settled by a group of newly arrived English under the spiritual guidance of Peter Bulkeley. Twenty miles from Boston, the area was accessible only by the most primitive forest paths. Boston was under the corporative government specified by the Massachusetts Bay charter, but new and outlying towns could not be governed directly from Boston, nor could they conveniently or effectively exist merely as parts of Boston. The towns, because of their isolation and special problems, must be nearly self-governing, at least in matters involving their daily life and their defense. Necessity demanded strong, harmonious local governments in which *all* inhabitants would participate for the benefit of all. The result, which emerged with the blessing of the colony administration, was town-meeting government, with its roster of elected officers from selectmen to hogreeves.

In the colony government there were restrictions as to who could qualify as a freeman and hence as a voter or office-holder. But in the towns, where each depended on all, virtually all male inhabitants, from very early times, could vote in town meetings and were eligible to hold office. Conditions demanded no less. The whole populace was committed to establishing and maintaining a community in the wilderness. The whole populace must be involved equally, and—in accordance with the Transcendentalists' view of human nature as divinely grounded—the whole populace rose to the occasion, completely refuting most of the political theory of the period, which held democracy in abhorrence. The very name Concord, Emerson explained, was chosen by the Puritans "to keep the remembrance of their unity with one another."[6] The unity, of course, was expressed in their church covenant, and its extension to civil government would be no surprise to Emerson, who could describe Puritanism as "a Sabbath peace in the country population of New England." New England town government and the covenanted church would be manifestations of the divine in man.

In Concord records, Emerson came upon a town-meeting vote in 1654 assigning three pounds to the north quarter of town to defray the costs of maintaining roads there. "Fellow citizens," he explained in his address, "this first recorded political act of our fathers, this tax assessed upon its inhabitants by a town, is the most important event in their civil history, implying as it does, the exercise of a sovereign power, and connected with all the immunities and powers of a corporate town in Massachusetts."[7] Referring to the relations of town with colony, Emerson continued: "For the first time, the ideal social compact was real. The bonds of love and reverence held fast the little state, whilst they untied the great cords of authority to examine their soundness and learn on what wheels they ran. They were to settle the internal constitution of the town, and, at the same time, their power in the commonwealth."[8] Thus the towns were to a great extent independent, "enjoying, at the same time, a strict and loving fellowship with Boston."[9] When the "ideal" becomes "real," as Emerson said of "the social compact" in Concord, the oversoul is indeed in evidence; for the oversoul and the ideal are one and the same in the thinking of a Transcendentalist.

Thus growth of local government in Massachusetts was, according to Emerson, spontaneous—an emergence of the spiritual resources of the human race. In his essay "Politics" Emerson later wrote: "The power of love, as the basis of a State, has never been tried."[10] Perhaps this was true of a state. But in his "Discourse" Emerson seems to say it *had* been tried in a town and had worked. One must read the whole of the "Discourse" to appreciate Emerson's joy in what he sincerely thought he had discovered in the Concord town records. Yet, though excerpts do not convey the intensity of his enthusiasm, they do convey the flavor of his thought, as in the following:

> In a town-meeting the great secret of political science was uncovered, and the problem solved, how to give every individual his fair weight in the government, without any disorder from numbers. In a town-meeting the roots of society were reached. Here the rich gave counsel, but the poor also; and moreover, the just and the unjust. He is ill informed who expects, on running down the Town Records for two hundred years, to find a church of saints, a metropolis of patriots, enacting wholesome and creditable laws. The constitution of the towns forbid *[sic]* it. In this open democracy, every opinion had utterance; every objection, every fact, every acre of land, every bushel of rye, its entire weight.[11]

The continuous working of these principles over the years of Concord's history before 1788 is the subject of most of the "Discourse." Particularly impressive to Emerson is the account of the Concord town meeting's practical and moral support of the American Revolution. Acting as usual as an almost autonomous political unit, it nevertheless joined in concert with other similarly self-governing New England towns and with the Continental Congress in the struggle for national independence.

The "Discourse," one of Emerson's earliest writings, deserves more attention than it has received. The obviously meticulous research that the author did into the history of the town must have had its influence on his later thought. His optimistic Transcendental views on human nature, already pretty well formed, could only have been strengthened by his delving into the town's past, just as his interpretation of that past was colored by the degree of Transcendentalism he had already arrived at. Most interesting is his admission that all that occurred in a town meeting did not bespeak the divinity of man. The good and the bad, the admirable and contemptible, rose to the surface at these gatherings, and usually the admirable prevailed. But not always. Though the earliest relations of the town with the Indians were amicable and harmonious—again justifying the name Concord—later relations with them, including several wars, were hostile and discordant. Emerson does not gloss over these blemishes on the town's and New England's history—these lapses from the rule of love that he recommended as "the basis of a state."

But the broader picture was good, and it boded well for the future, as Emerson wrote:

> I believe this town to have been the dwelling place, in all times since its planting, of pious and excellent persons, who walked meekly through the paths of common life, who served God, and loved man, and never let go the hope of immortality. The benediction of their prayers and of their principles lingers around us. The acknowledgment of the Supreme Being exalts the history of this people. It brought the fathers hither. In a war of principle, it delivered their sons. And so long as a spark of this faith survives among the children's children so long shall the name of Concord be honest and venerable.[12]

Sentiments like these, phrased in conventional rather than Transcendental terms, could easily be ascribed to Dwight, whom Emerson included among "the sterling chroniclers"[13] of New england. For like Dwight, Emerson not only regarded the New England town in its religious and political aspects as preeminent among American institutions but strongly hinted that it would serve as a model in the inevitable evolution of the nation and the world toward perfection. Referring to a recent gift from the British government of copies of *Domesday Book* and "other ancient public records of England,"[14] to certain American libraries, Emerson suggested:

> I cannot but think that it would be a suitable acknowledgement of this national munificence, if the records of one of our own towns,—of this town for example,—should be printed, and presented to the governments of Europe; to the English nation, as a thank-offering, and as a certificate of the progress of the Saxon race; to the Continental nations as a lesson of humanity and love. Tell them, the Union has twenty-four States, and Massachusetts is one. Tell them, Massachusetts has three hundred towns, and Concord is one; that in Concord are five hundred ratable polls, and every one has an equal vote.[15]

Again like Dwight, Emerson was convinced that in the vanguard of human progress would be "the Saxon race," that is, England and the United States. Foremost of all would be New England and her towns.

Thus Emerson and Dwight—the Transcendentalist and the Calvinist— warmed to their subject with equal fervor. To Dwight the New England town, dominated by the Protestant Church (preferably Congregational or Presbyterian), offered the most effective armament for attacking Satan and his legions, who, faced by such formidable forces, would retire for a thousand years. To Emerson, who as a Transcendentalist did not literally believe in the existence of Satan, the towns offered unprecedented conditions for the growth and flourishing of the divine seed planted in each human individual, and to him the town itself was a result as much as a cause of the flourishing. But for both Dwight and Emerson the end was the same: the reign on earth of the Kingdom of God, whether God was named Jehovah or the Oversoul.

Emerson and Brook Farm

Indeed the Transcendentalists were perhaps the most convinced millennialists of their times, though they would avoid using the term. Utopia was for them not a condition for some future era, dependent on God's not always predictable providence. It was, rather, a certainty attainable in the present, and they hastened to establish various Utopian communities. Bronson Alcott, Emerson's neighbor in Concord founded his short-lived Fruitlands in the nearby town of Harvard. More enduring and better known was Brook Farm, established by George Ripley, in West Roxbury in 1841. There is significance in these idealistic New Englanders' faith that the perfection of civilization could best be accomplished by isolated communities that would lead the way into a bright and blissful future. This had been one of the impulses behind the planting of the first New England communities. Winthrop, addressing the passengers of the *Arbella* on their voyage to New England in 1630, admonished: "For wee must Consider that wee shall be as a Citty upon a hill, the eies of all people a vppon vs."[16] And the Transcendentalist Ripley, in a letter urging Emerson to join the Brook Farm experiment, said of the venture: "If wisely executed, it will be a light over this country and this age. If not the sunrise, it will be the morning star."[17]

The Puritan and the Transcendentalist impulses or purposes were thus analogous, and Nathaniel Hawthorne, who shared neither point of view, was quick to see the likeness. In *The Blithedale Romance* (1852), based on his own experience as a Brook Farmer, Hawthorne's persona, Miles Coverdale, compares the founding of the community to the Pilgrims' founding of Plymouth,[18] at the same time ironically alluding to the community as a step toward "the millennium of love."[19] Referring to the lighted windows of the farmhouse on a blizzardy night, he remarks: "These ruddy window-panes cannot fail to cheer the hearts of all that look at them. Are they not warm and bright with the beacon-fire which we have kindled for humanity?"[20] It is interesting, too, that Brook Farm, like the first New England colonies, was organized as a stock company, though in this respect it borrowed from blueprints that Charles Fourier had devised for community living.

Ripley had urged Emerson to join Brook Farm, but Emerson in a now famous letter applauded the idea of the community, but regretfully, even penitently, declined the invitation. Among the reasons he gave was his lifelong conviction, not shared by all Transcendentalists, that reform must begin with individuals, who, when in sufficient numbers, would automatically constitute a Utopian society—an idea suggestive of the belief of Edwards, Dwight, and others that during the millennium almost all persons would be numbered among the elect, that is, filled with God's grace. Emerson would say that his perfected individuals were in tune with the oversoul rather than filled with grace, but the result would be the same. His point as regards Brook Farm, however, was that a rigidly, self-consciously organized community life would probably be no more conducive to human improvement than the more genial environment of Concord or other New England towns. In his answer to Ripley he wrote, "it would not be worth my while to make the difficult exchange of my property in Concord for a share in the new household. I am in many respects suitably placed, in an agreeable neighborhood, in a town which I have many reasons to love, & which has respected my freedom so far that I may presume it will indulge me farther if I need it."[21]

What Concord offered was the opportunity to live in a well-structured societal unit, in whose political, social, religious, and educational activities each resident was guaranteed a part if he wished it, but in which he would be reasonably free to pursue his own purposes and whims without interference other than normal village gossip. In such a setting, as Emerson knew, one belonged to the community and belonged to oneself at the same time without serious inner or outer conflict.

Thoreau as Citizen of Concord

Thoreau, too, was well aware of the advantages to himself of living in Concord, though he sometimes spoke acerbically about its citizens and its institutions. In all events, he much preferred it to Brook Farm, to which he was referring when he wrote in his *Journal:* "As for these communities, I think I had rather keep bachelor's hall in hell than go to board in heaven."[22] A native of Concord, Thoreau lived there all his adult life. In his Harvard class book he wrote: "I shall ever pride myself on the place of my birth," and, in unexpectedly Puritan fashion implying an analogy between Concord and Jerusalem, added a verse slightly altered from Psalm 137: "If I forget thee, O Concord, let my right hand forget her cunning."[23]

Later he stated that he had "been born into the most estimable place in all the world, and in the very nick of time, too."[24] Thus Thoreau was well content to live out his life in Concord; and with the exception of a short sojourn on Staten Island and a number of excursions to such nearby localities as the Maine Woods and Cape Cod and occasionally a bit farther, he remained at home. He preferred to journey vicariously by means of travel books; and, among the great number of these that he read, Dwight's *Travels* was a favorite, if one may judge by the frequency with which he quoted it.[25] From Dwight—as doubtless from other sources—obviously he learned much about New England and its social, religious, and political institutions, concerning which, as we shall see, his feelings were mixed. Yet Dwight at the very least must have sharpened his sense of Concord's participation in the larger historical culture of New England and the nation.

When asked why he did not wish to see more of the world, he protested that he had traveled far in Concord and still had more to see and learn there. Even his residence of a year and two months at Walden Pond can not in any sense be considered an absence from the town, for he was still within its boundaries and only a mile and a half from its business and civic center. The remainder of his life he lived in the village itself. He did not, however, belong to the church or take part, as did Emerson, in town affairs. There is no record of his ever having proposed a motion in town meetings or that he even attended them; nor did he ever hold a town, church, or school office—which in New England must have taken some determined no-saying.[26] He did, however, serve for a short term as secretary of the Concord Lyceum. He also worked for the town as a surveyor and a boundary perambulator, and he received public money in payment. In addition he was employed in various capacities by private citizens, such as Emerson, and for a brief time he kept, with his brother, a private school in Concord.

His views regarding town government were tinged with none of the enthusiasm noted in Emerson, though he was not completely condemnatory. During his "perambulation" (the word tickled Thoreau) in 1851 of the Concord town lines, he met the selectmen of the adjacent towns and remarked on the experience in his *Journal:* "I trust that towns will remember that they are supposed to be fairly represented by their *select* men. From the specimens which Acton sent, I should judge that the inhabitants of that town were made up of a mixture of quiet, respectable, and even gentlemanly farmer people, well to do in the world, with a rather boisterous, coarse, and a little self-willed class; that the inhabitants of Sudbury are farmers almost exclusively, exceedingly rough and countrified and more illiterate than usual, very tenacious of their rights and dignities and difficult to deal with."[27] There is a tone of sarcasm in these remarks; yet in his essay (first a speech) "Slavery in Massachusetts" he could remark quite glowingly on town government: "When, in some obscure country town [e.g., Acton or Sudbury], the farmers come together to a special town meeting, to express their opinion on some subject which is vexing the land, that, I think, is the true Congress, and the most respectable one that is ever assembled in the United States."[28] The opinion of such a group on a moral question, like that of slavery, would be worth more to Thoreau than the collective opinions of New York or Boston.

Thoreau in his writings makes numerous derogatory remarks about his fellow Concordians. According to him, their values are false, they lack a sense of right and wrong, they are blind to the beauties and meanings of nature—in short, they are in need of an awakening. The fact that Thoreau exerted considerable effort in his writing and public lectures to arouse his fellow townsmen and other Americans from their torpor would indicate that he did not consider them hopeless. Indeed, to the end he made use of the most characteristic personal right accorded citizens of New England towns—the right to voice their opinions in public meeting. Though he did not exercise this privilege in regular town meetings, he spoke frequently at the Concord Lyceum and elsewhere and sometimes on topics of national political importance. Thus after his experience in jail for refusal to pay his poll tax, he delivered a lecture on "the relation of the individual to the State,"[29] later printed and known today under the title "Civil Disobedience." It is interesting and suggestive of at least some of the townspeople's open-mindedness that this lecture was given by their request. His audience was attentive; and to satisfy those who had not been present he repeated the lecture three weeks later.

The question of slavery aroused in Thoreau a latent social consciousness. The passage of the Fugitive Slave Law and the oppressive actions it prompted on the part of the government were the occasion of his great speech "Slavery in Massachusetts," delivered not at Concord but at nearby Framingham. At Concord in 1859, after the raid on Harpers Ferry, he made his famous "Plea for John Brown." The decision to do so was sudden. As a citizen, Thoreau had the right to use the Concord town hall, but the selectmen, opposed to his speaking on so controversial a subject, refused to ring the bell as was customary before a meeting. Thoreau, who had previously made known his intention to speak, rang the bell himself and spoke before a full house. He repeated this speech, too, in Worcester and Boston. Later he called another meeting in Concord Town Hall to make plans for a memorial service on the day Brown was to be hanged. He also asked permission to toll the bell at the time set for the hanging, but again the selectmen refused his request. Since by this time a large number of Concord people had turned against Brown, and a counterdemonstration, with the burning of Brown's effigy, was being arranged, the memorial service was conducted in a lower key than planned.

Judging by events like these, one realizes that Thoreau did concern himself with current affairs of the nation and state, and that he fully availed himself of traditional channels and customs in a New England town in making known and promoting his beliefs. In this respect his record is much more impressive than Emerson's, who despite his participation in civic affairs, was only with reluctance brought into the abolition controversy. Thoreau's efforts to involve his fellow citizens in a major national crisis were directly in the tradition established among the towns in earlier crises, such as the Indian Wars and the Revolution. As for Concord when the Civil War finally came—when the time for debating was over—the town meeting functioned much as Emerson reported it had during the Revolution, encouraging recruitment among the local young men and doing whatever it could in aid of the Union cause.

Intellectuals like Emerson, Thoreau, Alcott, and other Transcendentalists constituted a minority in the predominantly agricultural community of Concord. The fact that they were not simply tolerated but were respected and even loved is a tribute to the citizenry and to the spirit of the town. Thoreau at times became quite sentimental about the Concord farmers, as in this entry in his *Journal:* "How I love the simple, reserved countrymen, my neighbors, who mind their own business and let me alone, who never waylaid nor shot at me, to my knowledge, when I crossed their fields, though each one has a gun in his house! For nearly twoscore years I have known, at a distance, these long-suffering men, whom I never spoke to, who never spoke to me, and now feel a certain tenderness for them, as if this long probation were but the prelude to an eternal friendship."[30]

Thoreau was considered odd, for how else could the townspeople regard a man who went to jail rather than pay his poll tax, who went off to a forest hut to live like a hermit—or so he liked to think—for more than two years, who worked only a small part of each year and spent the rest of his time walking in the woods and fields, and, to cap it all, once carelessly set fire to the very woods he so much admired. Thoreau thought Concord "a desperate odd-fellow society."[31] Surely he realized that he was himself one of oddest.

Bronson Alcott, too, was considered strange, and yet he was given the responsible position of superintendent of schools. Oddity was not grounds in New England towns in the nineteenth century for ostracism or condemnation. In fact, most of the towns had odd persons in their midst and these "characters" were frequently a cause of pride—objects to be pointed out or described to visitors as contributors to the local color. As one commentator remarked: "Eccentricity was not only tolerated by the community, it was often actually encouraged because it made people more interesting. It was a luxury a person certain of his social status could afford to indulge. Besides, a man's peculiar habits and tastes were his own business. No check to the development of individuality was needed or applied so long as it did not become anti-social, or interfere with the community ideal."[32] In many cases such persons were more or less harmless cranks or eccentrics of the sort described in great numbers in the fiction of Mary Wilkins Freeman and Sarah Orne Jewett. But occasionally, as with Thoreau, Alcott, and Emily Dickinson of Amherst, they were persons of talent or genius who made their villages famous in later generations.

To persons like Emerson, who was not an eccentric, and Thoreau, who was, or was considered so, the advantage of living in a place like Concord was that they could be themselves and follow their callings or whims without being objects of antagonism or vicious derision, and yet be a part of an old and traditionally organized community. They could belong to Concord without being owned by it. This is at least the impression of their feelings as conveyed by their writings; and thus they may be counted among the encomiasts of New England town life.

Village Fiction before 1850

The importance of the fact I state—the progress and improvement of the country towns—is plain, when we consider that here, and not in the great cities—New York, or Boston, or Philadelphia—are the hope, strength, and glory of our nation. Here, in the smaller towns and villages, are indeed the majority of the people, and here there is a weight of sober thought, just judgment, and virtuous feeling, that will serve as a rudder and ballast to our country, whatever weather may betide.

Samuel Griswold Goodrich, *Recollections of a Lifetime* (1856)[1]

Catharine Maria Sedgwick: *A New-England Tale*

In 1822, the same year in which Dwight's *Travels in New England and New York* was completed, a western Massachusetts author, Catharine Maria Sedgwick, published *A New-England Tale; or, Sketches of New England Character and Manners.* Having its setting in a Berkshire town, obviously modeled on Sedgwick's native Stockbridge, this novel was the first noteworthy attempt in prose fiction to depict life in rural and village New England. Countless stories and novels by other writers with a similar intention were soon to follow, and they continue to appear to the present day. Sedgwick's book is a landmark in American regional literature, especially that of New England. It was also inevitable that such a book should be published and such a trend begun in the decade of the 1820s. American readers were ready for fiction and verse dealing with American scenes and subjects, as is amply attested by the interest Washington Irving had already aroused with his *Knickerbocker History of New York* (1809) and, more strikingly, with his *Sketch Book* (1819–20). The time was ripe for *A New-England Tale,* and the novel made its author famous.

Catharine Sedgwick was the daughter of a prominent lawyer, Theodore Sedgwick, of Stockbridge, whose career included terms in the Continental Congress, in the Senate, in the United States House of Representatives (he was Speaker from 1799 to 1801), and, in later years, on the bench of the Supreme Court of Massachusetts. A staunch Federalist, a suppressor of

Shays's Rebellion, during which his house was looted, Squire Sedgwick was no egalitarian and despised the views of Thomas Jefferson. His daughter Catharine said of him: "He was born too soon to relish the freedoms of democracy, and I have seen his brow lower when a free-and-easy mechanic came to the *front* door."[2] Yet he was fair-minded and actually served as lawyer for several Shaysites who had been sentenced to death. His presence in Stockbridge brought there visitors of national eminence who would otherwise probably never have heard of the town. Furthermore, Stockbridge was on the stagecoach route between Albany and Boston—coaches each way regularly stopping there—and thus was easily accessible. The town was far from being the crude, backwoods community that its mountain location would lead one to suspect it to have been.

Naturally, the daughter of a man of Theodore Sedgwick's wealth and influence would lack no opportunity to develop whatever talents and intelligence she had, and Catharine Sedgwick had plenty of both. The stream of visitors and the cultured atmosphere of her Stockbridge home supplied ample stimulus, which was supplemented by lengthy visits to New York and other cities. Eventually, indeed, she resided half of each year in New York and the other half in the Berkshires, not in Stockbridge but in Lenox, a few miles to the north. The Berkshires were her home, and she never thought otherwise.

Yet her first book, *A New-England Tale*, was far from uncritical of village life. Her chief objection was to the rigid Calvinism still lingering in the backcountry of New England. She herself had become a Unitarian, and her original intention had been to write a Unitarian tract, but her storytelling impulse got the better of her and she wrote a novel instead. Berkshire County had been, and remained until well on in the nineteenth century, a stronghold of religious orthodoxy. In fact, it was in Stockbridge that Edwards, serving as missionary to the Housatonic Indians after his dismissal from his pulpit at Northampton, had composed his treatise on freedom of the will, by many still considered the most carefully and cogently reasoned philosophical and theological work ever to be produced in America. But whatever its merits, Edwards's treatise served as a major bulwark of high Calvinism. The ministers following Edwards at Stockbridge carried on the tradition, and one of his most faithful disciples, the Reverend Samuel Hopkins, was pastor at nearby Great Barrington. Edwards and Hopkins met frequently for theological discussions. "Old Benevolence," as Hopkins was called, though basically an Edwardsian, preached a brand of Calvinism that came to be labeled Hopkinsianism, best known to the popular mind for the question its proponents were fond of asking to test the sincerity of one's faith: "Are you willing to be damned for the glory of God?"[3]

This "Berkshire Divinity" was characterized by revivalism, full acceptance of the doctrine of election, recognition only of faith and divine grace as means of salvation, and, as a corollary, complete denial of the redemptive value of good works. It was the religion, though in a different locale, that Harriet Beecher Stowe later described—and deplored—in *Oldtown Folks*, (1869) particularly as set forth in the chapter "My Grandmother's Blue Book," the Blue Book being a compendium of doctrine put together by the Reverend Joseph Bellamy, another Edwardsian whose church was in the northwestern Connecticut town of Bethlehem, in the foothills of the Berkshires. It was also the religion of the grim Reverend Dr. Stern in *Oldtown Folks*. Indeed Mrs. Stowe's own father, the Reverend Lyman Beecher, held views only slightly less uncompromising, and, as we shall see, she rejected them not only in her novels but in her life as well.

Catharine Sedgwick, as she was growing up, was exposed to high Calvinism by the two wholly orthodox clergyman who succeeded Edwards in Stockbridge—the Reverend Stephen West, who served there for fifty-seven years (from 1759 to 1816), and the Reverend Dudley Field, who followed West—and she found, after reaching adulthood, that she could not accept the doctrines these men preached. Thus, though one of the earliest recorders in fiction of New England village life, she was also one of its first critics. She loved Stockbridge and the Berkshires. The very subtitle of her first book, *Sketches of New England Character and Manners*, testifies to her attachment. Yet she realized that her own towns, Stockbridge and Lenox, were church-dominated—we must remember that the Congregational Church in Massachusetts was supported by public moneys until 1833—and the dogma of this established church did violence to both her feelings and her intellect. Equally abhorrent to her was the pharisaism of the orthodox believers, who thought that a single experience of conversion released one from any obligation to engage in "good works"—that is, to behave like decent human beings—and her characterization of such persons is devastatingly condemnatory. She does not directly attack the village clergy, but she does not spare the church members whom she deems to be hypocrites. Part of her method is to compare the Edwardsian Congregationalists to the Methodists, who were also present in the town, and to the Quakers, both of which groups placed great store in "good works."

Sedgwick had plenty of company in rural New England in her revolt against Calvinist orthodoxy. Unitarianism, which she adopted, was beginning to become a force in areas more and more distant from Boston, where it had got its start; but for many rural people it would have been too intellectually cold. The Methodist, and to a lesser extent the Episcopal, Church constituted the greatest threat to the established church. Methodist preachers, who frequently were more emotional than educated, exerted a strong appeal in the countryside. One of their major points of attack was against the Calvinist doctrine of the perseverance of saints—which taught that once converted a person could not backslide, however questionable at times his conduct might be. In contradiction, the Methodists preached the concept that a convert might *fall from grace* and again be as subject to damnation as before his conversion experience. Since in every town a critical observer could point to at least one or two church members, or "saints," whose redemption was supposedly irrevocably assured but whose actions gave no evidence of their ever having received saving grace, the Methodist clergymen could graphically and convincingly demonstrate that it was possible to fall from grace.[4] In more and more communities as the century progressed, Methodist congregations were formed. In *A New-England Tale*, of the two more importnt "good people," other than the angelic and saccharine heroine,one is a Methodist and the other a Quaker recently arrived from Pennsylvania.

Yet despite the dominance of Calvinism, the heroine and the Quaker and the Methodist, along with several other admirable characters, find their Berkshire village to be a place in which above all others they wish to dwell. Here they can flourish; here they can realize their full capacity for happiness. The fact is that skepticism and tolerance were on the increase. Even Catharine Sedgwick's father confessed just before his death that he was not an orthodox believer. Like his daughter he seems to have veered toward Unitarianism. Times were changing, as were prevalent modes of thought and belief. Yet the New England village, even in Calvinist Berkshire County, could weather the change and perhaps be the better for it. Not even the religion of the Puritans was indestructible. Other things—the community itself and the landscape—were more permanent. The Quaker in Sedgwick's novel remained and married the heroine, herself at odds with the Calvinism she had been brought up in. The town held them; the beauty of the countryside exerted its pull. The community was capable of absorbing change and diversity and above all was becoming a place where persons of varying beliefs and backgrounds could find peace and spiritual well-being. Despite her ambivalence about the town as it was, Sedgwick's confidence in it and love of it infuse her book and make it a strong and unequivocal tribute to New England village culture. Indeed this ambivalence is prototypal, because it is discernible in most of the fiction about New England village life during the century and a half that followed.

The blight on the town in Sedgwick's opinion was Edwardsian Calvinism, and it was a severe blight indeed, as is illustrated in the lives of the children of one of the main characters, the widow Mrs. Wilson, who is the personification of orthodoxy combined with hypocrisy. Entirely self-serving, Mrs. Wilson is convinced she is one of the elect and hence need not trouble herself about being a considerate or kindly person. She browbeats her orphaned niece, the heroine of the tale, but spoils her own children, a son and a daughter, who hold her and her beliefs in contempt. Sedgwick's point is that old-time Calvinism does not inculcate virtue because in Calvinism virtuous action is not deemed a means of acquiring saving grace. Nor are ministers' threats of hellfire of any effect other than inducing fear and melancholy in the unredeemed or those not sure of their regeneration. The elect, according to the doctrine of irresistible grace, will eventually be converted and saved no matter what they do. Virtue in this system has to be its own reward or it will go unrewarded altogether. Seeing no advantage in good behavior or in obedience to their mother, Mrs. Wilson's children act accordingly. One of her daughters elopes with a French confidence man who poses as a dancing master. The son, while a student at Williams College, seduces a girl and leaves her and her baby to die. He next steals five hundred dollars from his mother, holds up a mail coach, is imprisoned, but eventually escapes to the West Indies. Perhaps in reporting these sorry results of the young man's so-called religious upbringing, Sedgwick had in mind Aaron Burr, grandson of Jonathan Edwards and thus well known, by his unsavory reputation at least, in Stockbridge. Years later Harriet Beecher Stowe in *The Minister's Wooing* (1859) also presented Burr as unscrupulous and immoral, and attributed these flaws of character to the effects of his grandfather's theology.

But under the sway of milder doctrines like those of Methodism, quakerism,or Unitarianism, Sedgwick believed that New England villages would be places where virtue and happiness could be universal and unalloyed. Dwight had regarded the ancestral religion as the main generator of the millennial qualities in New England village life; Sedgwick saw the old religion as a major hindrance to the full flowering of village life.

Sedgwick's feelings about her characters deserve attention. She herself was as aristocratic as a New England countrywoman could be, and she was well acquainted with the fashionable life of the larger cities. Nor did she ever entirely cease to live and act as an aristocrat—following her father's example—but she did cease to think like one, especially in her attitudes toward the common people. Politically, at least, she rejected her father's rigid Federalism and became sympathetic with Jeffersonian and, later, Jacksonian concepts of democracy. Thus in *A New-England Tale* she introduced a number of the humblest townspeople—servants and mountain dwellers—and depicted them as morally superior to many of the wealthy in the village. More notable was the sympathetic discussion of Shays's Rebellion that she appended as a note of several pages at the end of the book. There was no artistic reason for this note; Shays had been mentioned only once, in passing, in the body of the novel. But the Rebellion must have been a frequent topic of conversation in the Sedgwick family. The Federalist

Theodore Sedgwick, though he had aided some of the rebels legally after the Rebellion, would, of course, have considered Shays and his men to be a rabble menacing the foundations of the state and nation; this was the generally held view among most Massachusetts historians and intellectuals until Edward Bellamy, as we shall see later, presented the rebels' side of the affair in *The Duke of Stockbridge* (1879). Thus Catharine Sedgwick's note, unnecessary as it was in the structure of her book, was a gratuitous statement of views not in harmony with those of her family or of her class. The Rebellion, she writes, was a blemish on the otherwise fair pages of the history of Massachusetts. But the blemish was not solely the insurgency itself. The causes behind the revolt were equal, perhaps greater, blemishes. These causes she presents in some detail: economic depression, seizure of property and imprisonment for debts unpayable in the depreciated currency of the times, the arrogance and high-handedness of the courts. The farmers of Massachusetts, she seems to be saying, had reason to rebel; and after all, she adds, they were not guilty of severe excesses.

Catharine Maria Sedgwick: *Redwood*

This rather restrained championing of the poor people of New England became more marked in Sedgwick's next novel, *Redwood* (1824). In it the novelist has attempted to present a large variety of characters representative of American society—among them a Virginian gentleman, a Southern belle, several Philadelphia persons of fashion, Shakers, a drunken Indian, and a number of Yankee farm folk. Her process of bringing together this motley assortment is perhaps better left unexamined, for her art was not wholly equal to the task. The interesting point is that the farm people, especially the Lenox family in Vermont, are shown to be simply better human beings—morally, spiritually, even intellectually than the aristocrats, both Northern and Southern, with whom they have dealings. The values of the rural folk, Sedgwick obviously thinks, are the right ones—the ones that last and form a sound basis for a healthy society. The aristocrats dawdle away their time unproductively in coquetry, in directionless intellectual speculation, and in pursuit of the fashionable life; the country people work long hours in the fields or in the kitchen, but still find time to walk a mile to the village to hear a lecture, or attend church, and they see to it that their children get an adequate education. The farm family's life is more cohesive; sons and daughters respect their parents; and all work together for their common livelihood. The aristocrats and people of fashion are at loose ends, children pitted against parents, a sense of common purpose completely lacking. The aristocrats travel from one city or watering place to another; the farmers are rooted in one locality—in a delightful landscape,

Miss Sedgwick carefully points out—and travel only when necessary and then not far.

The outstanding character in *Redwood* is Deborah Lenox, who combines most of the Yankee female strengths and has come to be considered prototypal, so often have similar women—for example, Sarah Orne Jewett's Almira Todd in *The Country of the Pointed Firs*—been depicted in New England fiction. Deborah is plain in looks, unstylish in dress, blunt in speech, physically strong, dependable, utterly self-reliant, but unselfish, warm-hearted, and hard-working. She contrasts sharply with the Southern belle, Caroline Redwood, who is pretty, fancily dressed, physically weak, unreliable, dependent, selfish, unfeeling, and idle. Deborah is the product of the New England rural town and its values; Caroline is the result of faulty education and the indulgent upbringing typical of city-bred daughters of wealthy families. Dwight would have recognized in her a deplorable example of the product of fashionable city education: "a well-dressed bundle of accomplishments . . . a fribble or a doll."[5]

In *Redwood*, although Sedgwick did not describe the social structure of the town in which the farmers live, the town is there in the background, imparting its values and ways to its inhabitants. It is a real and decisive influence, for it is the totality of the culture of which these people are representative. Indeed, Sedgwick is very conscious of community and the part played by it in the lives of its members. Her own life of alternate periods of residence in the cities and in the Berkshires made her fully aware of the contrasts between urban and village life—and her preference, at least emotionally, was for the village and for a closely knit rural family, like that of the Lenoxes, which seemed to thrive in country towns.

But Sedgwick again emphasizes that community life must not be subjected to, and overshadowed by, religious fanaticism. In *Redwood* she does not rail against Calvinism, whose presence is scarcely intimated. Instead she presents us with the example of another set of zealots, the Shakers. Several of the Lenox kin have been induced to join that sect and reside at its community in Hancock, Massachusetts, a few miles from Stockbridge and thus well known to Sedgwick. This and other Shaker communities had aroused the interest of many American authors of the nineteenth century, notably Herman Melville, Nathaniel Hawthorne, and William Dean Howells; and Timothy Dwight in his *Travels* had devoted two of his "Letters" to a discussion of the Shakers. He admired their industry and skill as workmen but condemned vehemently their religious practices; and of course he totally rejected their theology and their polity, which placed despotic power in the hands of the elders.[6] In fact, the Shaker communities were successful as agricultural and industrial enterprises, and the idea of community was as strong with them as it had always been with all New Englanders.

The Shakers, indeed, despite their wholly unorthodox beliefs, had had much the same motivation in founding their communities as did the early Puritans in founding theirs. Shakerism, among other things, was entirely millennial, and the Shakers thought they were preparing the way for the Second Coming, much as the early Puritans thought of themselves as establishing a new Zion and their later descendents fancied that they were leading the way to the millennium.

The Shakers also shared the Protestant work ethic with the rest of New England and practiced it with vigor, so that the resulting economic success of their communities added to the prosperity of the towns in which they were located. Indeed their prosperity could not be ignored. After all, the orthodox Calvinists believed that God favored in this life those whom He chose for the eternal life hereafter. Like Dwight, Sedgwick did not shut her eyes to the admirable qualities of the Shakers. There in nearby Hancock was a community, one of several, exhibiting much that she and other New Englanders valued—simplicity, industry, community spirit. Yet beneath these assets was a dogmatism of the most uncompromising sort—a dehumanization, as Hawthorne might have called it[7]—which Sedgwick could not accept. She could accept the values but not the fanaticism. Like Hawthorne, she felt that an environment free of oppression was necessary for the full development of the potential of human nature.

In her day Sedgwick was ranked with William Cullen Bryant, James Fenimore Cooper, and Washington Irving as one of the American writers who were demonstrating that the republic was not without literary talent. The validity of this ranking need not be argued here. Popular in the United States and abroad, she enjoyed a reputation not far behind Cooper's. Without question her prose style was superior to Cooper's, and her plots, in general, were no sillier than his. In the creation of believable characters, especially of women, she was far his superior. But quite aside from any comparison with Cooper, she succeeded in conveying the notion that New England rural and village culture offered a most favorable milieu for the nurture of human happiness and virtue, providing the blight of fanaticism could be removed.

Catharine Sedgwick: *Home*

Sedgwick's conviction that the perfectibility of the human race, both socially and individually, was attainable under the conditions prevalent in a New England town ideally conceived is most explicitly expressed in her didactic tale *Home* (1835), which presumably draws heavily on her memories of her own childhood.[8] Greenbrook, the town in which the story is laid, is thus Stockbridge, though the author assures the reader that it might be located anywhere in New England, in which region she finds the people and conditions of life to be remarkably uniform. The story deals with a countryman, William Barclay, whose trade as a printer requires him and his family to move to the city. Though the printer and his wife would much prefer to live in Greenbrook, they set about successfully to provide their children with the kind of life they would have in a New England town. Besides inculcating the usual Christian virtues, they give them the sound moral and intellectual education so important to New Englanders. Above all, the father wishes to convince his children of the dignity of all labor and teach them not to consider the working man intrinsically inferior to the physician or lawyer. Sedgwick, through the example of this printer, thus upholds the equality of all who work honestly and live virtuously. She thinks that when all persons in a city, a state, or a nation learn this lesson that is so indispensable to a democracy, they will treat one another considerately and courteously, for Sedgwick believes good manners are essential to harmonious community life. In rural New England towns this sense of equality and an innate courtesy among the people already exists, she finds; and, curiously echoing the Puritans' concept of their newly founded villages, the printer's family regard their native Greenbrook as their "Jerusalem, to which the heart made all its pilgrimages."[9]

Barclay the printer's urban household is thus an urban outpost of New England rural culture, retaining faithfully all the best that that culture had to offer. Similar outposts, some of them consisting of whole towns, would be established elsewhere in America, most notably in the western lands to which in Sedgwick's day so many New Englanders were emigrating. Echoing, probably unknowingly, Timothy Dwight's views on the spread of the Yankee way of life across the continent, Sedgwick points out that each emigrant carried with him or her a New Englander's love of education and religion and the respect for "the intrinsic claims of each individual"[10] that is so basic to the political and social life of New England towns. Like Dwight, Sedgwick tended to think of all of the northern United States as a cultural colony of New England; and for the New Englander, whether exiled in the city or the West, the memory of home and its values remained alive. "His heart lingers in the homestead,"[11] Sedgwick wrote, and eventually he might return to it for a visit.

Sylvester Judd: *Margaret*

Another novel laid in a western Massachusetts town, on the edge, if not quite in, the Berkshire Hills was Sylvester Judd's *Margaret: A Tale of the Real and the Ideal, Blight and Bloom* (1845). In it, as in Sedgwick's *A New-England*

Tale, Calvinism is deplored and a substitute is suggested. Judd was born in 1813 in Westhampton, Massachusetts, lived for part of his boyhood in adjacent Northampton, attended Yale College and Harvard Divinity School, and spent the last thirteen years of his short life (he died in 1853) as pastor of a Unitarian church in Augusta, Maine. While at Harvard he was converted from Calvinism to Unitarianism, in which sect he remained, though he became so idealistic and liberal that he is commonly numbered among the Transcendentalists, and *Margaret* has been described as the only truly Transcendental novel that we have. Perhaps we may be thankful that other Transcendentalists eschewed the genre if Judd's effort represents what they might have produced, for *Margaret* is notable for long-windedness, a grinding tedium produced in the reader, and incredibly awkward prose. Yet at the time it was published it received some highly favorable notices, along with unfavorable ones, and no less accomplished a critic than Margaret Fuller singled it out for special praise, perhaps because the achievements of the heroine Margaret in redeeming a community appealed to Fuller's feminism. Indeed, Fuller found the book to be "a harbinger of the new era."[12] More recently Van Wyck Brooks claimed to have discovered rare talents in Judd, asserting that in *Margaret* "his best scenes were almost as good as Hawthorne's."[13]

Few would share Brooks's opinion today. Yet the novel has some worth as social history combined with the presentation of its Transcendentalist point of view. The setting is a small, rather primitive town located on or near the west bank of the Connecticut River. Before writing the novel Judd had returned to Westhampton to gather material concerning life in the area during the two or three decades immediately following the Revolutionary War, the time in which his plot is laid. And his research, which was painstakingly thorough, deserves praise. His description of various aspects of village life in late-eighteenth-century New England are admirable. The daily existence of villagers and country people, the militia trainings, a revival meeting, even a public execution provide a convincing background for what action *Margaret* contains. Most striking is the picture, in direct contrast to Emerson's depiction of Concord, that Judd provides of rural degeneracy rampant in the town even at this early date. Slovenliness, idleness, poverty, habitual drunkenness, violence are the rule among large numbers of the population—conditions hinted at in Sedgwick's fiction as existing in the 1820s and presented in highly advanced stages a hundred years later in Edith Wharton's Berkshire novel *Summer* (1917). Religion in Livingston, Judd's fictitious town, is the doctrinaire Calvinism found in other Berkshire novels. Preached by a narrow, unimaginative, unsympathetic drudge of a parson, it has no effect in raising the abysmally low moral and spiritual tone of the community.

Livingston is located, we are told, a day's journey north of Hartford. This is exactly the region—in the same post-Revolutionary decades—described by Dwight in his *Travels* and praised by him as being the culmination of the civilization of New England and hence of the world. But Judd did not rely on Dwight for the sociological facts. His own researches resulted in sharply different conclusions, and indeed he relied on another traveler, the ornithologist Alexander Wilson, to corroborate his own rather shocking findings. He quotes parts of the following excerpt from a letter written by Wilson in 1808 just after a protracted tour of New England: "My journey through almost the whole of New England has rather lowered the Yankees in my esteem. Except a few neat academies, I found their school-houses equally ruinous and deserted with ours [Scotland's]; fields covered with stone; stone fences; scrubby oaks, and pine trees; wretched orchards; scarcely one grain field in twenty miles; the taverns along the roads, dirty and filled with loungers, brawling about lawsuits and politics; the people snappish and extortioners, lazy, and two hundred years behind the Pennsylvanians in agricultural improvements. I traversed the country bordering the river Connecticut for nearly two hundred miles [most of its length]. . . . The plains are fertile, but half cultivated."[14]

In another letter describing the same journey Wilson again wrote that, despite the fact that the region had been settled for 150 years, little grain was raised and there had been no advances in agriculture: "In short, the *steady habits* of a great portion of the inhabitants of those parts of New England through which I passed, seem to be laziness, low bickerings, and [whoring?]."[15] The one exception to these unflattering descriptions was the region around Middletown, Connecticut, which Wilson found beautiful and where the rich soil was productively cultivated.

The contrasts between Wilson's and Dwight's accounts are dramatic. Judd was in agreement with Wilson, though he may not have read Dwight. But Judd was a Unitarian and a Transcendentalist and hence no chamion of the Calvinism to which Dwight ascribed the superiorities of New England. Indeed, Judd, like Sedgwick, considered Calvinism an obstacle to the spiritual, intellectual, and social development of New England.

Judd did, however, share with Dwight, and even with Edwards, a belief in the millennium—a reign of christ, or of the Christian spirit, introduced not by devastating war and natural catastrophes but taking hold gradually in the hearts of men and women and spreading outward into larger and larger units of society. But the process, as Judd envisioned it, would be brought about by very different means from those foreseen by the orthodox Dwight. Judd shared the ideas of the Transcendentalists—themselves millenialists of a sort, for the idea would not be expunged from the New England imagination. The impulses that established Brook Farm and sent Thoreau to Walden Pond were in the last analysis millennial ones, stemming from a conviction that the supposed divinity in every human being—the spark of the oversoul—could prevail over the negative influences of a corrupt society and would eventually fashion a social order commensurate with the race's divine potential. As Sacvan Bercovitch has pointed out, New Englanders, indeed most Americans, were still enthralled by the dream of establishing a cisatlantic New Jerusalem, though perhaps a more secular one than that projected by the Puritans.

Judd's first biographer, Arethusa Hall, states that he "yearned for a generally improved state of society, for a millennium; such, in its spirit, as has been long expected by the great mass of Christians."[16] With more assurance than Edwards and as confidently as Dwight, Judd, in the words of his heroine's future husband, states the idea that New Englanders "might lead the august procession of the race to Human Perfection; that here [in New England] might be revealed the Coming of the Day of the Lord, wherein the old Heavens of sin and error should be dissolved, and a New Heaven and New Earth be established wherein dwelleth righteousness."[17] The beginning of this Day of the Lord occurs in Livingston, which, under the benign influence of Margaret herself, a prodigy of intellect and virtue, and her almost equally saintly and learned husband, abandons its drunken, shiftless, bigoted ways in favor of joy, love, tolerance, and beauty. Indeed, a forest fire that sweeps through the town parallels the catastrophes that are traditionally supposed to announce the millennium. Significantly, among the buildings destroyed is the old church; in its place, after considerable discussion in town meetings, a new, Grecian-style temple of worship is erected; and, to convene in it, a new church society, called simply Christ Church, is founded. Christ Church, we shall see, closely resembled the religion with which Longfellow's Kavanagh, in the novel of that name, hoped to replace old-time Calvinism. As Margaret says, the Livingston religion represents the triumph of Christ over "Isms";[18] spirit supplants dogma.

Livingston as a community is in fact regenerated. Margaret in a letter assures a friend that a "New Earth" is "in the process of creation."[19] Locally the signs are impressive. Temperance (one of Judd's favorite reforms) has largely replaced drunkenness; training days with their accompanying brawling have been abolished; life has become so attractive "that the mania for removing to the West, which prevails all over New England, has here subsided."[20] Women seem to be rising from their lowly status. The town has a neat, pleasing physical appearance, suggestive of Dwight's white-clapboarded villages. Roads are good. Real estate values have risen. Schools are thriving. The number of paupers has shrunk. Various festivals and innocent recreations, anathema to the Calvinists, have been instituted. The fame of this redeemed town draws visitors from all over the world and of all religions—Mohammedans, Jews, Hindus. Presidents John Adams and Thomas Jefferson come to view "Livingstonian re-Christianization"[21] (to use Margaret's husband's phrase), and both presidents are properly impressed. Prophecy has been fulfilled; New England is indeed the site of millennial beginnings. By the end of the book Livingston's influence is being felt nationally and worldwide and three of their festivals "have . . . become national, or at least New England."[22]

Yet Livingston remains in its physical aspects very much the New England town it was before its rebirth. It is "eight miles long by six broad, it contains two hundred farms, three stores, two taverns [relics of the unregenerate times, apparently], one Church, six School-houses,"[23] and an assortment of joiners' shops, fulling mills, grist mills, and the like. Along with their spiritual, intellectual, and aesthetic interests, the townspeople have, as a common, unifying interest, the practical political and economic functioning of their community. In the last section of *Margaret,* Judd is describing a Utopia, but it is a Utopia erected on the familiar and solid foundations of a traditional New England town.

Longfellow: *Kavanagh*

During Sedgwick's lifetime many writers, artists, and intellectuals were drawn to Berkshire County partly because of her residence there. They came for short visits or lengthy sojourns—and still do—making the region a center of American cultural achievement. By the 1840s and 1850s the list of such persons included Hawthorne, Melville, Longfellow, and Oliver Wendell Holmes. Of these, all but Hawthorne wrote novels with settings strongly suggestive of Berkshire County, and Hawthorne did place on the slopes of Mount Greylock the action of one of his greatest stories, "Ethan Brand."

Among the novels, Melville's contribution was perhaps the least germane to the present study. The first part of *Pierre* was obviously laid in a town modeled after Pittsfield; and many features of the surrounding countryside—Mount Greylock and the Balanced Rock, for example—figure importantly in the book. But the village life, where it is touched on at all, is in no way distinctive of New England or any other region; the social system, indeed, is virtually feudal, and may well have been drawn in part from Melville's knowledge of the Hudson Valley patroonships, with the history of which his mother's family, the Gansevoorts, were closely connected. Some of Melville's shorter pieces, like "The Piazza," "The Lightning-Rod Man," and the second part of "A Paradise of Bachelors and a Tartarus of

Maids," have distinctively New England settings, as do the first pages of *Israel Potter,* where Melville does a fine job of catching the atmosphere of the townships strung along the higher ridges of the Berkshires.

Longfellow, however, in his short novel *Kavanagh* (1849) focuses on a village, Fairmeadow, that has many resemblances to both Lenox and Pittsfield.[24] But the resemblances are not decisive. The location of Fairmeadow is in Massachusetts in the mountains and on the banks of a river, which in the Berkshires would have to be the Housatonic, scarcely more than a large brook in that region. Yet, strangely, a coasting schooner belongs to Fairmeadow and there is mention that the town might someday be a seaport. Obviously there is no community in Massachusetts whose location combines a navigable river, closeness to the sea, and proximity to mountains. The situation is further confused by mention that Fairmeadow contains one of the oldest houses in New England, which could not possibly be true of any town in Berkshire, which was not settled until well into the eighteenth century. Yet Berkshire is an unmistakable presence in *Kavanagh,* on which Longfellow was working in the summer of 1848 during the second of his two extended visits to Pittsfield (the first had been during his wedding trip in 1843). Though he did not complete *Kavanagh* until after his return to Cambridge, he makes use in it of material garnered during his summer vacation.

The question of what actually geographical setting Longfellow had in mind, if any, is not of first importance. What is significant is that culturally Fairmeadow is very much a New England town in transition and that it in many ways resembles a Berkshire town. Large parts of Berkshire County before the mid-nineteenth century, despite its growing popularity as a summer resort, were still backcountry, along with most of Vermont, much of New Hampshire and Maine, and perhaps the northwest corner of Connecticut. Berkshire, like these other areas, had been settled by one of the first outpourings of immigrants westward and northward from the older towns on or near the coast and in the larger river valleys. In other words, it resulted from the first wave of expansion that Dwight and others felt would people the continent with a God-fearing, orderly educated populace worthy of being the vanguard of the millennial bliss and prosperity he thought was soon to follow. Of course, the participants in this early eruption into the outer reaches of New England were mostly orthodox Congregationalists—a fact that gladdened the heart of Dwight. Berkshire, being thus populated and being guided by such preachers as Edwards, Hopkins, West, and Field, became a bulwark of Calvinism—one of the strongest and one of the last in New England—and this, as we have seen, distressed Catharine Sedgwick, who believed that New England should lead the nation culturally and spiritually but was herself a Unitarian and would have spiritual leadership based on something less rigid than the *Institutes* of Calvin.

Longfellow, too, was a Unitarian, and he was from eastern Massachusetts, where for many years Calvinism had been on the defensive in a losing battle. In Berkshire he found an amazing and apparently perdurable survival of the old order, and to him it seemed, as it had to native-born Sedgwick, to be an archronistic blemish on the culture of the region. *Kavanagh* is not a great novel: though better written, it is in other ways weaker than Sedgwick's *A New-England Tale* and *Redwood*. In plot it represents the opposite extreme from Sedgwick's melodrama, for *Kavanagh* contains virtually no action at all. It evokes an atmosphere that in many respects is unreal, and it belabors a rather feeble love triangle involving the romantic and ecumenical clergyman Kavanagh and two seemingly homoerotic girls who communicate with each other by carrier pigeon. One of these nymphs dies of consumption and the survivor, of course, marries the minister. Another character, who occupies much space in the novel but has no discernible function in the plot, is a Mr. Churchill, the local schoolmaster, who dreams of writing a romance but never gets the first sentence on paper. As a schoolmaster, too, he is ineffective. Education at Fairmeadow reflects an imperfect reality rather than the bright ideal that many authors, including Sedgwick, had seen as the standard for New England.

But if education leaves something to be desired, religion at Fairmeadow is entirely deplorable as described in the opening pages of the novel. The village pastor, the Reverend Mr. Pendexter, is a stodgy representative of the old school, whose views are symbolized by his aged and plodding white horse and antiquated chaise, which seems to anticipate by a decade Oliver Wendell Holmes's "One Hoss Shay." Because of a quarrel with his congregation—for one thing, over pasture rights for his horse—Pendexter is ousted from his church, to be regretted by "only a few old and middle-aged people. . . . They missed the accounts of the Hebrew massacres, and the wonderful tales of the Zumsummims [*sic*]; they missed the venerable gray hair, and the voice that had spoken to them in childhood, and forever preserved the memory of it in their hearts."[25]

But the younger generation did not miss the old parson. They were ready for something new, and therein lies the point that Longfellow wished to make about Fairmeadow and similar villages in New England. While writing the novel, he felt that it lacked something—a misgiving that does credit to his powers of self-criticism. It was becoming, he thought, a sentimental romance, with many pretty atmospheric effects but little more. It needed, he at last concluded a spiritual dimension. While finishing it in Cambridge in March 1849, he wrote in his diary: "My mind is perplexed about *Kavanagh*. . . . One more long, spiritual chapter must be written for it. The thought struck me last night. It must go into the book as the keystone into the arch."[26]

On a previous brief visit to Pittsfield in 1846, Longfellow had been appalled by a sermon preached by the local pastor, the Reverend John Todd, who among other things made the following comment about reprobates: "'Nay, they may go up Calvary so far that they can hear the blood dropping from the Saviour's side upon the stones below, and yet they will not be moved.' The parish consider it a great sermon."[27] To a Cambridge Unitarian this sort of preaching would come as a surprise and a shock; yet such was the religious climate of Berkshire in the 1840s. The spiritual dimension that Longfellow thought his book needed would be supplied by offering a substitute for the ugly, outdated Calvinism still lingering among the lovely hills. New England, he thought, must be healed of this sort of spiritual deformity.

Dogmatic Calvinism was not the only ugliness that Longfellow found in the life of the region. In *Redwood* Sedgwick had castigated the Shakers for their fanaticism. In *Kavanagh* Longfellow introduces the Millerites, to whose "camp-meetings, held in the woods near the village . . . many went for consolation and found despair."[28] The Millerites were millennialists of the most extreme sort, since they set dates—in the very near future—for the Second Coming and the consequent end of the world, and whole congregations of them, dressed in ascension robes, waited upon hilltops at the times set for the final cataclysm. The hymns of these zealots, sung in their "white tents and leafy chapels"[29] filled the balmy evening air, to the horror of the schoolmaster and Arthur Kavanagh, the new pastor, who had finally been chosen to replace the plodding Pendexter.

In the young Reverend Arthur Kavanagh, Longfellow presents not only a welcome successor to Parson Pendexter but also a wholly new theology to supplant the town's traditional doctrines. Interestingly, Kavanagh had been born and educated a Roman Catholic in Maine, where in early times a family of that name and religion had figured importantly.[30] Thus Longfellow was hinting that New England had long contained the seed of a religion that was different from and in some ways, he obviously thought, more humanistic than Puritanism and that one day might make its influence felt in beneficial, if indirect, ways.

In his young manhood Kavanagh had become converted to Protestantism, but not to that brand of it which had dominated New England's spiritual life for over two hundred years. For example, he embraced the doctrine of good works—rather than election—as a means of salvation. "Out of his old faith he brought with him all he had found in it that was holy and pure and of good report. Not its bigotry, and fanaticism, and intolerance; but its zeal, its self-devotion, its heavenly aspirations, its human sympathies, its endless deeds of charity."[31] Kavanagh "preached holiness, self-denial, love."[32] In selecting texts for his sermons he drew "as much as possible from the words of Christ."[33] He infrequently drew from Paul—from whom the doctrine of election had been derived—or from the Old Testament, which the orthodox Calvinists relied on for their depictions of a God of wrath and vengeance. "He did not so much denounce vice, as inculcate virture; he did not deny, but affirm; he did not lacerate the hearts of his hearers with doubt and disbelief, but consoled and comforted, and healed them with faith."[34]

Abhorring narrow sectarianism, Kavanagh dreamed of "the union of all sects into one church universal"[35]—a vision no less millennial, though in a far different way from that of Edwards, Bellamy, and Hopkins, and curiously parallel to Dwight's, insofar as a New England village was chosen as an appropriate scene in which the beginning of the dream might be realized. How closely Kavanagh's vision of a universal church reflects Longfellow's own hopes for humanity is not easy to gauge. It is significant that, like Longfellow, Kavanagh went on far journeys, in his case to Italy and the East, in preparation for his great mission of drawing all churches "into one universal Church of Christ."[36] Thus Kavanagh gives evidence of being possessed of the New England missionary spirit so prominent in men like Dwight, but the mission is not to establish the dominance of one sect. Longfellow's possible sympathy with the idea of universality as opposed to sectarianism is suggested by the frequently quoted section of *Kavanagh* in which the schoolmaster Churchill rejects the notion that the United States is under some sort of obligation to prove its nationhood by developing its own unique literature. Churchill argues—and these *are* Longfellow's views—that literature by its very nature must contain much that is universal; a great American literature would be one that shares in, and contributes to, the greatness of literature the world over. What is true of literature, Longfellow might argue, is even truer of religion. Fairmeadow in New England is doubtless a likely seedbed for the growth of a religion with a potential of universality, but first Fairmeadow must purge itself of the bigotry, the smug self-satisfaction of Orthodox Congregationalism. Parochialism is the enemy, both in literature and in religion.

One may wonder whether Longfellow, in choosing a liberal and ecumenical clergyman as the instrument of Fairmeadow's redemption, was taking a cue from Sylvester Judd, the transformation of whose fictional town in *Margaret* from a morass of vice and bigotry was effected by a liberal minister working in alliance with the saintly heroine. In both cases the clergyman was of a Unitarian coloration, though not definitely described as Unitarian, and in both cases the new and redeeming religion was defined simply as one of Christ, notably lacking the doctrinal and dogmatic encrustations of the orthodox sects. Longfellow, we know, read Judd's second novel, *Richard Edney and the Governor's Family* (1850), which he found completely devoid of artistic merit. Though there seems to be no proof that he was aquainted with *Margaret,* that novel appeared in 1845, four years before the publication of *Kavanagh,* and might well have lingered as an influence in Longfellow's conscious or unconscious memory.

Oliver Wendell Holmes: *Elsie Venner*

Sedgwick, Longfellow, and Judd saw in the New England town the potential for an ideal society, which indeed was already partly realized and would be fully so once the shadow of Calvinist orthodoxy could be dispelled from the land. Another author associated with Berkshire County— the focal point of so much writing about New England in the nineteenth century— was Oliver Wendell Holmes, who spent seven summers, from 1849 to 1856, in Pittsfield in a house named Holmesdale, which he had built at Canoe Meadows close to Melville's home. Holmes, a product of Boston and Cambridge, took a somewhat condescending attitude toward New England country people, but he entered wholeheartedly into Pittsfield village life, writing verse for various occasions, including an ode in honor of the Berkshire Fair, at which in 1849 he officiated as a judge of the ploughing contest. More to his taste was the society of the region, including the Sedgwicks, Fanny Kemble, Melville, and other people of intellect and culture living in the Lenox and Pittsfield area.

In 1860 Holmes published serially in the *Atlantic Monthly* his first novel, titled *The Professor's Story,* which drew heavily, especially for its setting, from his observations during his Pittsfield summers. Though this novel, which in book form was named *Elsie Venner: A Romance of Destiny* (1861), is neglected today, it ranks high in American fiction for its depiction of village characters, its authentic atmosphere, the grace of its tyle, its wit, and above all its treatment of New England religious and intellectual life. *Elsie Venner,* along with Sedgwick's *A New-England Tale,* Judd's *Margaret,* and Longfellow's *Kavanagh,* belongs in what one critic termed "the main liberal theological stream of Berkshire fiction,"[37] and it is a much better book than any of the others.

The son of an orthodox minister, Holmes had rejected his father's theology and had long been a Unitarian; and, living in Cambridge, he might easily have concluded that Calvinism had ceased to be a major force in New England. But his experience of Berkshire would have disillusioned him and would have aroused his antipathies. The setting of *Elsie Venner* is a country village, Rockland, overshadowed by a rattlesnake-infested mountain that was probably suggested by Mount Greylock, though Greylock is in no way so grim and foreboding. The fact is that in the novel the Mountain, as it is simply called, is a symbol of the frightening presence of the traditional theology that overhangs the lives of the inhabitants of Rockland and darkens their days. The snakes on the Mountain are, of course, associated with Satan, the instigator of original sin, because of which, according to Christian orthodoxy, Eden was blasted and the human race morally tainted ever afterward. A God who, like that of the Calvinists, would consign countless individuals to eternal damnation as a result of a transgression committed by their remote ancestors is, Holmes points out, a monstrous despot unworthy of respect or worship. The ingenious fable by which the novel makes this point is based on the folk belief in prenatal influences—a belief that we may assume Holmes did not share. A girl living in Rockland is afflicted with ophidian traits stemming from her mother's having been bitten by a rattlesnake while the child was still in the womb. Is the girl responsible for the unfortunate effects this incident has had on her personality? If the answer is negative, as of course it is, the conclusion must also follow that it is untenable to hold human beings responsible for the choices and actions of Adam and Eve.

In Holmes's view all New England in the past and in its outlying regions at the time he was writing had been overshadowed by a vision of a pitiless Deity, as Rockland had been overshadowed by its snake-infested Mountain. The vision must be banished if Rockland and New England were to be wholesome places for the life of the spirit. Holmes concedes that God created snakes, that evil exists, that certain warped wills perpetrate crimes. These are the facts of the univese that we must accept without attributing to the Creator the character of a vengeful tyrant more deserving of our hatred than our love. Indeed, Holmes kept a caged rattlesnake in his Berkshire home—as an interesting specimen of God's handiwork, not as an evidence of the blight the Fall of Man had brought upon the once paradisal world. The shadow of the Mountain need not eclipse all sunlight from the New England village of Rockland, which provided wide scope as a place for human beings to live in happily and prosperously.

Julia Caroline Ripley Dorr and Donald Grant Mitchell

Among nineteenth-century novelists who deplored lingering Calvinism in rural New England, two others, Julia Caroline Ripley Dorr (1825–1913) and Donald Grant Mitchell (1822–1908), warrant more than passing attention, though their writings are seldom read at the present time. Dorr was born in Charleston, South Carolina, where her father, a Vermonter, was in business as a merchant. Her mother, of French extraction, died when the child was very young, and soon after, the father and daughter moved back north, eventually settling in Rutland, Vermont. After her marriage in 1847, Dorr lived for ten years in Ghent, New York, near the Connecticut border. The remainder of her life she resided in Rutland, where her husband, Seneca Dorr, joined her father in his marble business. Her books, written under the pseudonym Caroline Thomas, were much admired by Emerson and by her good friend Oliver Wendell Holmes.

Two of Dorr's novels, *Farmingdale* (1854) and *Lanmere* (1856), are highly critical of certain aspects of New England religious life. The former is an attack on the Protestant work ethic—so sacred in agricultural New England—which takes precedence over the famed Yankee respect for education. As Dorr makes amply clear, the obsession with work among Vermont farmers literally left their children no time to attend school. *Farmingdale* is in essence a polemic, and a forceful one, against child labor. The novel *Lanmere* somewhat resembles Sedgwick's *A New-England Tale* in that it exhibits the harm a woman can do to her family in the name of religion—in this case a woman whose zeal leads her to spoil one daughter, mentally torture another, and mercilessly beat her son until he runs away from home. Two clergymen, both basically kindly, figure in the story: one old-fashioned in his beliefs and quite ineffective; the other and younger one, less rigid and very effective. The younger minister marries the maltreated daughter, and the novel ends with a general reconciliation of all concerned.

Equally critical of the harshness and bigotry seemingly generated by Calvinist orthodoxy is the novel *Dr. Johns: Being a Narrative of Certain Events in the Life of an Orthodox Minister of Connecticut* (1866), by Donald Grant Mitchell, himself a native of Connecticut and a graduate of Yale, who wrote under the pseudonym Ik Marvel. Like Henry Ward Beecher's *Norwood*, Mitchell's novel depicts village life in detail and for the most part admiringly; and, again like *Norwood*, it presents the reader with a gallery of portraits of interesting village characters. As local color the book is charming, somewhat nostalgic over the vanishing pre-railroad simplicity of country ways, yet not unduly sentimental. But in his title character, the clergyman Dr. Johns, Mitchell portrays a man whom he clearly considers to be an almost grotesque, if not obnoxious, relic of the early days of Puritanism. The Reverend Dr. Johns, educated at Andover Theological Seminary in the sternest Calvinist dogma, sees beauty and justice in the doctrine of election, is convinced that his rather irreligious father has been damned to eternal hellfire, and inspires in his own son a spirit of rejection that results in the youth's inability to experience saving conversion. Dr. Johns appears in an even worse light in his dealing with a young Catholic girl with whose upbringing he has been entrusted. The child is the offspring of an illegitimate union between Johns's best friend and a Frenchwoman and has been brought up in the Roman church. Indeed, horror of horrors, she wears a crucifix about her neck. In the minister and in his even more intolerant sister, not to mention the ultra-Protestant villagers in general, the presence of a Catholic, even though a child, arouses a three-centuries-old antagonism. The girl, however, is converted to Calvinism; and, after a rather complex plot involving her French mother and aunt has worked itself out, she marries a local youth and thus becomes fully absorbed into the community.

Mitchell in this novel was dealing with a widespread and, to him, deplorable New England prejudice. To his credit he has dealt with it firmly but genially. Like Beecher, Stowe, Longfellow, and Holmes, he is pointing to what he considers a blemish—that of a fanatic orthodoxy—in an otherwise estimable social order. Like them he refrains from rejecting the whole fabric because of one stain.

"A Delightful Village on a Fruitful Hill": Lyman and Henry Ward Beecher and the New England Town

> A delightful village, on a fruitful hill, richly endowed with schools both professional and scientific, with its venerable governors and judges, with its learned lawyers, and senators and representatives both in the national and state departments, and with a population enlightened and respectable, Litchfield was now in its glory.
> Quoted by Lyman Beecher, *Autobiography*[1]

The output of fiction with New England village settings continued unabated during the second half of the nineteenth century. Prominent among the later writers were Henry Ward Beecher, whose one novel, *Norwood; or, Village Life in New England* (1867) was a resounding popular success, and his sister Harriet Beecher Stowe, whose New England fiction, though overshadowed by *Uncle Tom's Cabin* (1851 and 1852), is a major literary achievement. Before considering the work of these two, we should glance briefly at their early background and at the career of their famous and influential father, the Reverend Lyman Beecher, one of Timothy Dwight's most faithful protégés, whose forceful personality is reflected in much of their work and in their outlook on life.

The Reverend Lyman Beecher: Progenitor of a Famous Family

Born in New Haven in 1775 of parents of limited means but of ancient and honored Puritan stock, Lyman Beecher, whose mother died when he was two years old, was brought up by an aunt and uncle on a farm in North Guilford, a district of Guilford, one of the oldest towns in Connecticut and completely under the sway of Calvinist orthodoxy. Thus his childhood and youth were spent in exactly the kind of environment that Dwight believed nurtured the purest religion and hence bred persons of exemplary Christian character. Beecher had the normal upbringing of a New England farm boy. Hard work, respect for parental and other authority, devotion to religion, and a sense of duty and responsibility were the values of rural New England, and Beecher's character was molded by them. Deciding that he wanted to go to college, Beecher prepared himself accordingly and entered Yale in 1793, with the half-formed purpose of studying for the ministry. In his junior and senior years he attended classes taught by Dwight, who had become president of the college in 1795. Beecher is recorded as saying in his old age: "Dwight had the greatest agency in developing my mind. . . . I loved Dwight as my own soul and he loved me as a son."[2]

Under this influence, Beecher experienced in his junior year a religious awakening,[3] which sealed his determination to become a preacher. On graduating he entered Divinity School at Yale, and continued his studies under Dwight, whose admiration for Jonathan Edwards he came to share. But he also concurred with the modifications that Dwight had made in Edwardsian doctrine, especially in regard to predestination, so as to make Calvinism more palatable than formerly to the unredemmed. This New Haven or New School Divinity, as it was variously called, was later described by Henry Ward Beecher as "alleviated Calvinism."[4] It was a necessary compromise with High Calvinism and was followed by Lyman the rest of his life. He also adopted Dwight's millennialism: "I had studied the prophecies," he recalled in his *Autobiography* (1865), "and knew that the punishment of the Anti-Christian powers was just at hand. I read also the signs of the times. I felt as if the conversion of the world to Christ was near."[5]

Beecher, after finishing his "divinity year,"[6] quickly got a call to serve as minister at East Hampton, Long Island, essentially a New England community in that part of the Island which had once been under the jurisdiction of Connecticut. There he remained for eleven years before being called to Litchfield, Connecticut, where he was Congregational minister from 1810 to 1826. It is his years there that are directly relevant to the present study, but the remainder of his life deserves brief attention. After his Litchfield ministry, he served as pastor of the Hanover Street Church in Boston, where it was hoped he would be a counterforce to the Unitarians, who were becoming a major threat to orthodoxy in eastern Massachusetts. Like Dwight, he was a strong advocate of revivals, in conducting which he was active in Boston. In 1832 he went west to Cincinnati to become head of the Lane Theological Seminary.

Again following Dwight's lead, Beecher was a firm believer in the duty of the New England Congregational church to carry its pure form of Christianity to the new settlements of the West and elsewhere in the world. Thus

he was an active member of the General Association of Congregational
Churches in Connecticut, which, under the chairmanship of Dwight, published in 1817 an *Address to the Emigrants from Connecticut and from New
England Generally in the New Settllements in the United States.* Later during his
stay in Ohio he became convinced that the scene of the future greatness of
the country and of the onset of the millennium would be in the American
West, "where the religious and political destiny of our nation is to be
decided,"[7] as he wrote in a book titled *A Plea for the West* (1835). He considered that the East was obligated to plant the seeds that would fructify so
gloriously. "The corn and the acorn of the East are not more sure to
vegetate at the West than the institutions which have blessed the East are to
bless the West."[8] To him the great danger was that the Roman Catholics,
whom he denounced with all the fury of a seventeenth-century Puritan,
would shoulder out the Protestants. He viewed with xenophobic horror the
influx of Catholic immigrants from Europe and was enraged at the activity
of priests among them. The most surely redemptive religion, he thought,
was that based on the doctrines of Calvin. Anglo-Saxon greatness owed its
being to Calvinism, which was also responsible for the civil liberties in the
United States and the United Kingdom. Beecher's thinking was not un-
touched by racism as well as religious bigotry; both were common among
Protestant Anglo-Americans in his day.

Beecher involved himself in other causes. He was a founder of the
American Bible Society; he worked vigorously for temperance; he
preached against dueling. He was primarily a man of action rather than
thought. During the final decade of his life, his health broken, he lived in
Brooklyn with his son, Henry Ward Beecher, who as pastor of Plymouth
Church in that city had become one of the most influential clergymen in
America. During these years his *Autobiography* was written, not by him in his
weakened health, but by three of his children—Harriet (Stowe), Charles,
and Catharine—who drew from their own recollections and prodded their
father's memory with questions, the answers to which they wrote down in
his own words. Charles, in addition, gathered and organized the papers,
such as letters and sermons, that were to be included. In this way Harriet
received vivid impressions of places, people, customs, and events that she
later put to good use in her novels and tales dealing with New England life
during the first fifty or sixty years of American independence. The father's
memory of his boyhood and youth in North Guilford were detailed and
sharp, and were conveyed not only with a strong flavor of his former
country dialect but also with the lively humor that Harriet Beecher Stowe
always claimed was one of the traits of the New England clergy as a class.
The resulting *Autobiography* was a success not only as the narrative of a

man's life but as a record of the places and times in which he lived and worked.

Of major interest are Lyman Beecher's reminiscences of Litchfield, which village provided models for fiction written by two of his children, Harriet and Henry. Though not so old as towns nearer the sea or on the Connecticut River, Litchfield, beautifully situated on a ridge among the hills of northwestern Connecticut and containing superb specimens of late-colonial architecture, set a standard against which other New England towns may be compared. Lyman Beecher's *Autobiography* gives a full description of the town, beginning with details about its geographical location and assets, its fauna and flora, and its early history. We learn that at the time of the Revolution, Litchfield, though small in population, contributed much to the colonists' cause. It was "visited by Washington, Lafayette, Rochambeau, and by most of the principal officers of the army," and was "the residence of a remarkable number of educated and distinguished men. Of these, three were members of the State Council; four, members of Congress; seven, captains in the army; four rose to the rank of general officers; two became chief justices; and two governors of the state."[9] Among the famous men born there was Ethan Allen, though Lyman Beecher would hardly have considered this a mark of distinction for the town, in view of Allen's hostility to orthodox religion. In addition to its illustrious citizens, or perhaps because of them, Litchfield contained a nationally famous "female academy" and the first law school in the United States, founded by Judge Reed, who had married a granddaughter of Jonathan Edwards. (She was the sister of Aaron Burr, who for a number of years also resided in Litchfield.)

At this time Litchfield had two churches, the smaller one Episcopal and the dominant one Congregational. The *Autobiography* quotes at length a description of the Congregational meeting house and the services held within it—a description that had formerly appeared in an essay by Harriet Beecher Stowe published long before the writing of the *Autobiography* was undertaken. In its detailed fidelity to the structure of a New England meetinghouse and the worship that took place within it, this essay, "The Old Meeting House—Sketches from the Notebook of an Old Gentleman," deserves the attention of students of New England daily life. But more significant is the spirit in which it was composed. Harriet Beecher Stowe in this, as indeed in all her writing about New England, was clearly enthralled by her subject. She herself had been born in Litchfield and lived there fifteen years, and, as her sister Catharine remarked, Lyman Beecher himself enjoyed there the happiest years of his life. He was in his prime, his family was growing, the location was beautiful, his ministry flourished.

Henry Ward Beecher as a Writer of Village Fiction

For the whole Beecher family the Litchfield days seem to have been idyllic. "Surely, Old Litchfield was a blessed place for one's birth and one's childhood,"[10] Henry Ward Beecher wrote in 1864. In a later work, the novel *Norwood* (1868), he drew heavily from his Litchfield memories. The book, though mediocre as literature, is a detailed and popular treatment of the strengths, and of a few of the weaknesses, of New England village life, and as such deserves attention. But it is important, too, as an assessment—and an encomium—of the social and spiritual values it depicts as flourishing in a New England town. Henry Ward Beecher's novel is very much in the tradition that began with Dwight's *Greenfield Hill*.

The importance of Beecher's views may seem questionable to some. In our century he has been derided as "the Barnum of religion," and he is generally believed to have been an adulterer, even though the jury in his notorious trial for adultery could not reach a verdict and a council of the Congregational Church exonerated him. And, as a final put down, he has been compared by Sinclair Lewis to Elmer Gantry.[11] Although there may be some basis for Beecher's current unenviable reputation, the fact remains that he was one of the most respected preachers of his generation, as his father had been in the preceding generation. For forty years, beginning in 1847, Henry Ward Beecher presided over the large, prosperous, and fashionable congregation of Plymouth Church in Brooklyn, New York, from which vantage point he held the ear of the nation and achieved a popularity as a religious leader that may be compared to that of Harry Emerson Fosdick, Norman Vincent Peale, or Father Coughlin in our century. Not confining himself to preaching sermons, he delivered innumerable lectures throughout the nation and in England, edited for a time a prestigious religious periodical, the *Independent,* wrote a weekly column for the New York *Ledger,* and published many books.

Any one so much in the public eye would be bound to become controversial and the object of attack, whether deserved or not. Also, if he was a religious figure, connected by ancestry with Puritanism, such a person would inevitably become a target for the sarcasm of early twentieth-century writers like Sinclair Lewis and H. L. Mencken, both of whom could find nothing bad enough to say about anyone or anything even faintly associated with Puritanism—that is, with virtually the entire culture of the northeastern United States. But Henry Ward Beecher's memory cannot be erased from the American consciousness; he is still a subject for scholarly and not-so-scholarly discussion. Not too long ago a major article in the *New Yorker* rehashed his trial, finding the defendant guilty;[12] and on a more serious level William G. McLoughlin, in a study entitled *The Meaning of*

Henry Ward Beecher: An Essay on the Shifting Values of Mid-Victorian America (1970), attempted to assess Beecher's impact, both in his preaching and in his writing, on American thought and religion. McLoughlin found the impact to be great, and he credited Beecher with formulating and introducing into the United States a liberal Protestantism with a strong romantic and Transcendantal emphasis on nature as a revelation of God. Without making any claims for Beecher as an original thinker, McLoughlin does not regard him as a hypocrite or a mountebank but as an interpreter of, and contributor to, middle-class American thought and attitudes in the nineteenth century. In this role Beecher *was* a major influence. For example, without being a member of the Transcendantalist group, he had in one way or another absorbed enough of its ideas to write in 1857 in one of his *Ledger* columns this entirely Transcendentalist sentiment: "The roots of Nature are in the human mind. The life and meaning of the outward world is not in itself, but in us"[13]—which amounts to saying that the Bible is not the only source of divine revelation. Nature, as it exists in our minds, is also a source, and a very important one. This was one of the directions Protestant theology was taking, and Beecher early recognized, followed, and encouraged the tendency.

Not that Beecher ever formally renounced religious orthodoxy, but he could sense, and adapt to, the spirit of the times. He served as a guide, an intermediary between the Calvinism, already somewhat modified, of his father, Lyman Beecher, and the liberal Protestantism of the East Coast, with its burgeoning Emersonian emphasis on nature as a manifestation, if not an embodiment, of the divine.

McLoughlin finds that Henry Ward Beecher has given in his novel, *Norwood,* a full and forthright expression to these tendencies in his own religious orientation. The two preoccupations of the novel—religious meanings in nature and the celebration of village life—are, moreover, intimately connected; for the New England village is essentially rural, and its inhabitants are in close contact with the changes in the weather and the seasons, are situated in the midst of the fields and forests and hills, and are acquainted with the agricultural activities of the surrounding countryside. At home in nature as well as in the social, political, and religious life of the little community, the Norwood villager becomes a living proof of the spiritual and physical wholesomeness of his environment. The situation is idealized, but the novelist had no reason to be other than sincere and doubtless did not think he was straying a bit from reality.

Norwood has been ignored almost entirely by literary scholars; and if it is to be judged by literary standards alone, it deserves to be ignored. As a specimen of the art of the novel it merits no attention whatsoever. Henry Ward Beecher himself was fully aware of this, as a widely circulated anecdote makes evident. In 1882 at a garden party given in honor of his sister Harriet, he remarked: "For a long time after the publication of Uncle Tom's Cabin there were a great many very wise people who said they knew that she never wrote it herself, but that I did. The matter at last became so scandalous that I determined to put an end to it, and therefore I wrote Norwood. That killed the thing dead."[14] The reviewers agreed that *Norwood* was not the work of a professional novelist, seeing its chief worth in its character sketches and vignettes of New England village life and its major defect in its incessant sermonizing that brought an already sluggist plot to a standstill. But sermonizing was what Henry Ward Beecher could do best and what his readers apparently expected from him and wanted.

As already mentioned, he had been writing weekly columns for the New York *Ledger*. The subjects of his contributions were by no means exclusively religious; he touched on a variety of topics, many of them having to do with nature and country life. In 1865 Robert Bonner, editor of the *Ledger,* asked Beecher to write a novel for the newspaper, and Beecher consented. He found the going difficult at first in this unfamiliar genre, but soon he gained momentum and the weekly installments flowed steadily from his pen. An incentive to persistence could have been the $30,000 compensation for his efforts.

In a letter to Bonner outlining his intention, Beecher wrote: "I propose to delineate a high and noble man, trained to New England theology, but brought to excessive distress by speculations [of the mental sort] and new views. . . . The heroine is to be large of soul, a child of nature, and, although a Christian, yet in childlike sympathy with the truths of God in the natural world, instead of books. These two, the man of philosophy and theology and the woman of nature and simple truth, are to act upon each other and she is to triumph."[15] There is, in fact, a plot of sorts, a sentimental one involving lovers eventually caught up in the turmoil of the Civil War, but all that need concern us here is the depiction of the New England village of Norwood and Beecher's views in the 1860s regarding its cultural and spiritual importance to the present and future of America. What he said on this and other matters reached a large audience, for the *Ledger* boasted a circulation upwards of 300,000,[16] and the first edition of *Norwood* as a book, running to over 500 closely printed pages, was "a better seller" in 1868, trailing *Little Women* and *The Moonstone,* but still doing very well.[17] It went through a number of editions, one of them illustrated (1886), the last appearing in 1895. Thus *Norwood* was read widely over a period of many years. It made an impression totally out of proportion to its literary worth. Indeed, one commentator credited it with initiating the Lincoln legend in America.[18]

The Location of Norwood

Norwood is intended to be typical of the older and more prosperous New England communities. There is much that resembles Litchfield in it. Its population of five thousand, the impressive intellectual attainment of some of its citizens, and its generally thriving condition are all suggestive of Litchfield at the time when Henry Ward Beecher was growing up there. But also the Berkshire town of Lenox, where Beecher spent many summers, may have contributed to his depiction of Norwood. Lenox, too, is beautifully situated among the hills and had many highly intellectual and prominent persons among its population.

Norwood has characteristics of both these towns. But founded "not far from thirty years after the Pilgrims' landing,"[19] it is close to a hundred years older than either. Furthermore, Norwood is situated in the Connecticut River Valley, across the river and "not a score of miles"[20] from Amherst, and not in the hills of western Connecticut or in the Berkshires. Two possible reasons may be given for Beecher's thus locating his fictional village. First, he had resided in Amherst for a number of years, attending Mount Pleasant Classical Institution there and later Amherst College. He would have known the surrounding countryside well and would have learned much about its history and traditions. Actually, the village of Deerfield, across the river and about twenty miles from Amherst, almost exactly tallies with Norwood in location, age, and physical attractiveness. It seems more than likely that, along with Litchfield and Lenox, Beecher in his descriptions of Norwood had Deerfield in mind—a village that is still one of the showplaces of New England.

A second and more subtle reason for placing Norwood in the Connecticut Valley can be found in Beecher's knowledge of that region's tradition of zealous and orthodox piety. Timothy Dwight, as has been seen, regarded the valley, his native region, as the most favored area physically and spiritually in New England and hence in the nation. Its religion was the purest, its fields were the most fertile, its villages and dwellings and meeting houses the most beautiful. Here had occurred the triumphs of Jonathan Edwards, the champion of unvitiated Calvinism; and the valley remained a stronghold against the rising heresy of Unitarianism, which indeed Amherst College had been founded to combat.

In Henry Ward Beecher's day the valley was still religiously conservative, and the minister of Norwood's Congregational Church, the Reverend Mr. Buell, was a stodgy and dull upholder of the most conventional Calvinism. There could be no more appropriate setting in which to introduce and test the innovative doctrines that Beecher was espousing. The town and its inhabitants not only were steeped in orthodoxy but they were thoroughly earnest, in no way tainted with hypocrisy, in their spiritual convictions. They would not lightly relinquish the old faith, but once they adopted a new one, they would cling to it with equal tenacity. All of Norwood, of course, was not won over to the new ways, which were represented by the highly educated village physician, Dr. Wentworth, but a few were; and among them was the novel's hero, Barton Cathcart, who attended Amherst College and was in love with the doctor's daughter Rose. What Beecher was saying was that Norwood, a typical New England village, was not doomed perpetually to be an ice-house of frozen and antiquated doctrines but was, potentially at least, the scene of a vital and varying spiritual life, just as Northampton in the days of Edwards and his grandfather Solomon Stoddard before him had been the scene of religious change and revival in forms suitable to the needs of their generations.

Beecher started his novel with a comment on "the thousands of curious travellers" who "every summer have thronged New England,"[21] and deplored the fact that they had not become better acquainted with the region's more out-of-the-way places. "The remote neighborhoods and hill-towns yet retain the manners, morals, institutions, customs and religion of the fathers. The interior villages of New England are her brood-combs."[22] Norwood was a fine specimen of what New England had to offer; and having introduced the reader to this particular village, Beecher sang the praises of New England as a whole with an enthusiasm that equaled Dwight's: "Single spots, finer than any in New England, there may be in other lands; but such a series of villages over such a breadth of country, amidst so much beauty of scenery, enriched, though with charming and inexpensive simplicity, with so much beauty of garden and yard and dwelling cannot elsewhere be found upon the globe. No man has seen America, who has not become familiar with the villages of New England and the farms of the Northwestern States."[23] Beecher ended this first chapter with eloquent praise of the elm trees of New England, the trunks of which he suggested are symbolic of "Puritan inflexibility" while "their overarching tops, facile, wind-borne and elastic, hint the endless plasticity and adaptableness of this people."[24]

Whether intentionally or not, Beecher in this novel was appealing to the constantly increasing interest in New England which resulted from its recent greater accessibility by railroad. Tourists and summer vacationers were coming in large numbers, and resorts in the White Mountains, the Berkshire Hills, and the Green Mountains were booming at the time he wrote, and he himself, in addition to keeping a summer home in Lenox, made lengthy sojourns in northern New Hampshire.

New England Ways and Values in Norwood

But Norwood offers more than scenic beauty and pastoral peace. The reader is invited to this fictional town not primarily for aesthetic pleasure and restoration of city-jaded nerves—for tranquility beneath the elms, as it were. Rather, he is invited mainly to observe the inner workings of the hive, the "brood-comb" not only of New England's but of all America's religious and political life, the breeding place, as Beecher saw it, of the ideas and spiritual forces upon which the nation depended for its present existence and future progress. If the claim seems excessive, Beecher did his best to substantiate it, as in later chapters he came to grips with the Civil War, in dealing with which his regional chauvinism, augmented perhaps by the emotions aroused by that conflict, reached its greatest intensity.

One of Beecher's points in the novel was that New England institutions as they existed in the mid-nineteenth century were expressions of New England character. So also were its architecture and the layout of its towns. Institutions and character, he implied, cannot be neatly separated in a cause-and-effect or any other relationship. Thus Dr. Wentworth, a free-thinking physician in *Norwood,* points out that "New England character and history are the result of a wide-spread system of influences of which the Sabbath Day is the type—not only so, but the grand motive power. Almost every cause which has worked benignly among us received its inspiration and impulse largely from One Solitary Day of the week."[25] The doctor goes on to say that as the sun is the cause of all vegetable growth, so is the sun's day "a generic and multiplex force"[26] in the formation of the New England personality.

The doctor was speaking in regard to efforts, of which he approved, to retain the traditional Sabbath, and those efforts, of course, were expressions of the very character that the Sabbath had helped to create. This sort of conservatism, in which institutions are self-perpetuating because the people whose character traits they have formed perceive and cherish their value, at least as symbols, was to Beecher a sign of a healthy society. Religion, of which the Sabbath was obviously a symbol, thus lay at the basis of New England character, but the religion itself did not need to be static. Indeed, Beecher believed it should not be. Rigid Calvinism, for example, could and should be modified to become a religion of nature and love as well as of doctrine. But the religious impulse should be nurtured and retained with all the earnestness with which older generations cherished their sterner faith. The old-time Sabbath consequently should remain, with only slight relaxation, for it was the expression, as it was formerly the cause, of the religious and intellectual strengths of New England life. Emerson must have had something of this sort in mind when he referred to "that old religion which [in his youth] still dwelt like a Sabbath peace in the country population of New England."[27]

The old-time Sunday, described by so many writers on New England, was a day intended for deep and demanding thought as well as for worship. During two lengthy sermons the churchgoer would listen to his minister expound the intricacies of such doctrines as election, predestination, irresistible grace, or perseverance of saints, or dilate on some knotty passage of Scripture. These expositions would be the starting point, and provide the material for dinner-table or hearthside discussions during the week. Beecher writes: "Now and then, and in New England often, are to be found plain and uncultured persons, whose unconscious thoughts deal habitually with the profoundest questions which man can ponder. The very intensity of religious conviction . . . tends, at length, to breed among the common people an aptitude for deep moral problems."[28] Thus the whole community "is seasoned with religious thought."[29] If this were true of the "common people," how much more given to ethical and religious discussion would be the educated townspeople, who Beecher says constituted "the nearest approach . . . to an aristocratic class in New England."[30] The lengthy dialogues in *Norwood* carried on by Dr. Wentworth, Parson Buell, and Judge Bacon, the local man of law, are ample evidence of the penchant among the educated for pondering abstract subjects.

The New England Mind and Conscience in Norwood

The propensity of the New England mind for analyzing problems in their spiritual, ethical, as well as practical aspects is most impressive in those who, like the two lovers, Rose Wentworth and Barton Cathcart, are intelligent but not yet highly educated or deeply read. An example is a conversation between Barton and his mother about his desire to go to college—something new among Cathcarts, who had always been content with their calling as farmers. Having announced his desire, Barton says that he will give it up if his mother wishes him to stay on the farm. She does wish him to stay, but her answer is shaped more by her theological beliefs than by personal preference, which as a true Puritan she suppresses. She replies: "When God stirs in us deep thoughts for things that are right, they are prophecies, and we must heed them. Should I keep you back and hide you from God's decrees, could I prevail? If we follow duty willingly, we are treated kindly; but if we resist, Duty hunts us down and drags us to answer to our conscience."[31] Thus does she state the ancient Puritan doctrine of following one's calling, which comes from God.

The mother continues: "Oh, my son, I know not why God has shaded life to my eyes. His will be done! Life seems so deep, so awful in meaning, and infinite—infinite in its results. It is like an ocean, with great storms travelling over it always, and many enemies. Yet every one must venture. If I were sure that you had made your peace with God—."[32]

Barton has not made his peace with God—yet. That will come later but not in the form of a conventional conversion, with its overwhelming sense of sin, its repentance, its abject surrender to omnipotence. His conversion will be of the Transcendental sort—an ecstatic consciousness of divinity in nature and of the goodness of God and His creation. Barton is to exhibit a new religious awareness, not less intense than the traditional one but more in harmony with the times. But now, in his conversation with his mother, he sidesteps the question as to whether he has made his peace with God (i.e., experienced conversion), and replies to a second question of hers as to whether he will be able to succeed in college. His words are a striking statement of the work ethic to which his family and culture are dedicated: "Did you ever know me to give up any thing that I had undertaken? Did not father say that he didn't believe any body else would have got down that wood, on the mountain-lot, in the deep snow, that I did? But he never knew half that I went through. Didn't I finish that piece of wall that father said nobody could do in two days? But you didn't know, nor he either, that I went out after you were abed, and worked all night, by the moon. It was four o'clock in the morning when I quit. There's something in me that won't let go when I take hold in earnest. I can't help it!"[33] Barton does go to college, but only after he has obtained his father's permission, which hinges upon Barton's proving his intellectual ability by learning how to survey, and then drafting a map of the family farm. In Puritan fashion, the father did not believe in making anything too easy either for himself or for others.

Like Dwight, Beecher placed education second only to religion—mind second only to conscience—at the base of New England village culture. "Intelligence and morality are the household ideals of New England,"[34] he wrote. Norwood itself had an academy; within twenty miles was Amherst College, founded as a bastion of orthodoxy so that the Connecticut Valley youth would not have to attend Unitarian Harvard. But in addition to the college's religious emphasis—its early presidents were clergymen and revivals were yearly events on the campus—it offered a sound education in the arts and sciences. The Norwood Academy was under the direction of a Mr. Edwards, who during forty years of undivided service had gained for it a sound reputation. As much a pillar of the community and as indispensable to it as the minister or the doctor, he was always ready to help boys like Barton realize their educational ambitions, for he knew that a college education in New England constituted a claim to social as well as intellectual superiority. "If a man has been to college," Beecher wrote, "he has a title,"[35] and the seriousness with which New Englanders observed commencement exercises bears out this statement. Moreover, Beecher believed "that a majority of the graduates of New England colleges [he must have meant rural ones like Amherst] were farmers' and mechanics' sons."[36]

Insofar as social stratification existed in New England towns, college education provided the best means of upward mobility, and upon graduation Barton soon succeeded the retiring Mr. Edwards as headmaster of Norwood Academy. But college also provided stimuli to religious growth beyond the accepted orthodoxies—or at least this was the case with Barton and Dr. Wentworth, the two most highly educated persons in Norwood. The process of growth was not easy with Barton, and Beecher in a rare instance of negativism about Norwood makes clear his aversion to the morbidity that often characterizes the New England religious conscience and nowhere more frequently than in the Connecticut Valley. Barton, having trained his reason, employs it in examining "the great truths of the Bible,"[37] and he finds that he can no longer accept the Bible as the sole and ultimate authority. He is thus going counter to what he had been taught by his parents and minister since earliest childhood. The result is a cruel inner conflict, which he keeps to himself so as not to distress his family and friends.

Doubts and guilt combine to make Barton wretched. Only under the influence of Dr. Wentworth can Barton bring himself to accept nature as well as Scripture as a revelation of religious truth and thus attain spiritual well-being and be able to accept the basics of his "childhood faith."[38] His conversion experience, which leads to his "making his peace with God," resembles Wordsworth's theophany above Tintern Abbey or that of Emerson on a bare common at twilight.[39] It occurs spontaneously in a lovely, tranquil natural setting, and not as a result of the traditional Puritan "means of grace," such as interminable praying, exposure to two-hour-long sermons, or attendance at revivals. Yet Barton's is a real and impressive conversion, and it bespeaks the full health of his and New England's changing religious life.

Norwood in the Civil War

Beecher desired to establish that the Norwood way of life had more than local or regional significance. Like Dwight and his father, Lyman Beecher, he recognized the far-flung influence of New England emigrants who implanted their institutions, especially education and religion, from coast to coast. As he puts it elsewhere, "the New England farmers came across the continent driving their lowing herds and schools and churches, their courts and lyceums before them."[40] But Beecher was able to find for New England an even more dramatic role than that of provider of the nation's culture. This role was no less than that of preserver of the Union, under the benign leadership of Abraham Lincoln, himself a descendant of New England Puritans.

Norwood was serialized and published as a book directly following the Civil War, and, perhaps with an eye to public appeal, Henry Ward Beecher has that conflict figure prominently in his plot and in the development of his theme. Some of the actual fighting, including that at Gettysburg, is described in some detail; but more important, a love triangle involving Barton Cathcart, Rose Wentworth, and a young Virginian, Tom Heywood, is introduced into the novel, much to its detriment as literature but very conveniently for its author's didactic purposes. From Beecher's point of view, Heywood is an exemplary Southerner. A scion of a First Family of Virginia, he is cultivated, courteous, altogether charming. Far from being rabidly pro-slavery, he regards "the institution as a misfortune" and he apologizes "for it, as a thing entailed upon the South, and for which no present remedy could be found."[41] He is also a staunch Unionist, who is later horrified at the irrevocable act of secession, which he himself witnesses in Charleston in the seizure of Fort Sumter. Furthermore, while on extended visits with his aunt, who lives in Norwood, he learns to admire New England and the New England character, especially as exemplified in Rose Wentworth, with whom he falls in love. Yet when the war finally comes, he joins the Confederate forces as an officer and is killed at Gettysburg, where Rose Wentworth and Barton's sister, Alice, who is secretly in love with Heywood, have gone as nurses. The situation oozes with sentimentality, which does much to cloud Beecher's message that the North, especially New England, possessed spiritual resources superior to those of the South and hence was destined to win the war.

In contrasting North and South, Beecher puts many of his ideas in letters that Heywood writes to his brothers in Virginia. For example, Heywood finds in the North a greater respect for, and reliance on, the law. In a situation in which two Southerners would resort to personal combat to settle their grievances, Northerners would go to court. Heywood is perhaps most impressed by the "liberty" of thought that he finds in the North, along with an intellectual curiosity, a love of reading, and a respect for ideas. He is, in fact, an admirer of almost all that he finds in New England, and as a result he shocks his family and friends, who regard Yankees as stingy, mean-minded, and cravenly unwilling to fight for the Union or for any other cause.[42]

As the inevitable conflict approaches, Heywood warns that the North will fight and that the South will be bitterly surprised at the determination with which secession will be resisted. His prediction was, of course, right, and the reason he was able to make it was that he had lived for lengthy periods in a New England town and had perceived the caliber of the people in closely knit communities like Norwood. According to Beecher, the determination, the morale of the Northern country people and villagers, especially those of New England, made possible the Union victory. Barton, Dr. Wentworth, Rose, are all at the front or assisting just behind it. Beecher's contention is obviously that the North won the war, despite its inferior generalship, because of the character of the Northern people and their awareness of the justice of their cause. Certainly they were no braver, Beecher says, nor were they better than their adversaries. "Two battles were waged in one," Beecher writes in regard to Gettysburg. "Principles were contending in the air, while men were fighting on the ground. And when on the night of the fourth of July, the army of the South, sullenly and in the dark, drew back from the farms of Pennsylvania and retreated southward, it was not alone the defeat of the army, but far more of the political economy, the genius of the government, and the evil spirit of a perverted religion, that had inspired the conflict and given moral significance to the rebellion."[43] To Beecher, it seems, Gettysburg suggested Armageddon.

But if the rightness of the Northern cause—which Beecher tends, perhaps unwittingly, to make almost exclusively the cause of New England—is demonstrated by military victory, the superiority of Northern character (i.e., New England character) is dramatized—sentimentally and clumsily, to be sure—by the fact that the Northerner Barton Cathcart eventually marries Rose Wentworth, with thom the Virginian Tom Heywood had also been in love. Heywood's convenient death at Gettysburg, where he was fighting somewhat reluctantly against the Union he respected and would have liked to have perpetuated, does not alter the symbolic significance of Barton's marriage to Rose. Rose represents the finest human product of New England culture. Brought up in the benign village atmosphere of Norwood, she has the added advantage of having a father who is a highly educated professional man acquainted with the more sophisticated culture of urban New England. Barton, on the other hand, is the son of a farmer; his background and upbringing are in every way admirable but are entirely lacking in the leaven of sophistication that characterizes Rose's upbringing. But Barton, availing himself of the academy and nearby college, both of which are typical of the New England countryside, readily attains equal educational and cultural status with Rose. The inevitable result, marriage, validates the whole mystique of the New England village.

Thus the significance of the novel *Norwood* as a cultural phenomenon is great; but its aesthetic merit is negligible—an evaluation that would not have distressed Henry Ward Beecher, to whom art had worth mainly insofar as it encouraged religion and morality. The primary message that *Norwood* carried to the American people in 1867 and 1868 may be summarized as this: We have just gone through a terrible war fought so that the Union might survive. The northern cause triumphed because it was the just cause, which inspired the people of the North to exert themselves far beyond the expectations of the enemy. The people of the North aligned themselves with justice and were victorious because their religion, their inquiring habits of mine, their sense of individual human worth as embodied in their political institutions, particularly on the town level, were sources of strength largely absent in the South.

But in addition, New England and the North had another advantage, and this was the strength of the work ethic among the people. A second part of Beecher's message to Americans is the lesson to be learned from the New Englanders' devotion to and respect for work. "All hail, Work!" Beecher exclaims in *Norwood*. "Man lost Paradise by temptations that beset indolence. He will gain it again by those wholesome qualities which are the fruit of intelligent work!"[44] A society like the South, where work is associated with slavery, Beecher tells us, is basically rotten at its foundation.

The slain Heywood in one of his prewar letters to his brothers had commented almost with awe on the place of work in the New England way of life: "Working people, in a community where work is a badge of servitude, cannot represent the value and personal excellence of working men in a different state of society where nothing is more honorable than labor [again the Judaic and Protestant work ethic]; where all, more or less, perform it; where men are taught from childhood that manliness and honor require one to be personally as much as possible independent of others' help, and to perform with one's person a large part of the offices which, with us, servants are expected to render."[45]

Beecher embodies the strengths of the North and weaknesses of the South in Barton and Heywood respectively, employing the two almost as allegorical figures. The contrast is very explicit. Heywood, for all his basic decency, "had been reared in affluence, and had never learned to work, nor to have sympathy with those that did. Barton Cathcart had been inured from childhood to toil, and was drawn by vital sympathy to all who labored. The Virginian was born to command [hence the fine generalship of the confederate army]. . . . The New Englander had been reared in a true democracy, in which classes represent the relative forces of the actors, into which and out of which men passed at their pleasure, and in which there were few leaders and no aristocracy—except that which was conferred by consent of all."[46] Beecher proceeds to point out the contrasts in the religious training and beliefs of the two. As an Episcopalian, Heywood accepted the doctrines and rituals of his church without questioning. Never did he subject even one of the Thirty-nine Articles to intellectual analysis. On the other hand, Barton Cathcart, in the true tradition of New England, subjected his beliefs "to the utmost scrutiny of Reason. Cathcart, from an early 'period, felt himself drawn into deep thought. He could not rest with traditional knowledge and hereditary faith."[47] This "free spirit of inquiry and discussion"[48] repelled Heywood. The fact that the two men were good friends in no way weakens the impact of the contrast Beecher was trying to make. For him the differences were all in Barton's favor.

Beecher's Neglect of Town Government in Norwood

It is noteworthy that in *Norwood* almost no mention is made of town government. The emphasis is on religion and character. Character, as Beecher sees it, is closely related to religion, which even though in the process of liberalization exerts the same powerful influence that it had exerted during the past two centuries. But, as Dwight had perceived and explained at length, the system of town government in New England, in which every male over twenty-one years of age might participate as a voter and, if he had the slightest inclination, as a functionary, carried an influence comparable to that of religion and education. Emerson, going farther than Dwight, emphasized the virtues and influences of town government and took only rather perfunctory notice of the church.Beecher's lack of attention to this important phase of village life was unfortunate from the point of view of his own desire to illustrate the superiority of new England culture. Among the traits of New England rural character that he most admired were its intellectual vigor and independence and its devotion to principles that have been thoroughly examined and tested. But the free and intense discussion that such examination and testing involve were not limited to religious or philosophic topics. From the earliest colonial times, as writers like Charles Francis Adams have demonstrated from surviving town records, New England townspeople discussed, argued, and analyzed all manner of matters that affected their daily lives. Many of these matters were of a completely practical nature, such as the management of common pastures, the building of bridges, and the upkeep of fences. But others involved general policies: for exasmple, the desirability of admitting new inhabitants to the town and the status of such, if admitted, as shareholders in the undivided or common land; or the question of precisely what powers should be delegated to the selectmen; or the pros and cons of instituting a new church society in an expanding town. Matters such as these, as well as setting tax rates and establishing schools, all were subjects for town-meeting debate in which every voter was entitled to join, and yet Beecher ignored this basic element in the life of the village he presented in such a shining light. The New England villager is a political as well as religious person. By failing to recognize one of the two major forces in the formation of character in a town like Norwood, Beecher did himself and his book a disservice. The full picture would have been much more impressive than the incomplete one that he provided.

Yet Beecher's readers apparently either did not notice or did not resent his omissions. Nor did they complain of similar omissions in other writers of fiction depicting life in village and rural New England. All during the century, authors of far greater skill than Beecher were as neglectful as he of the political dimension of the communities in which they laid their stories and novels, or about which they wrote poems. Among these writers were Beecher's sister, Harriet Beecher Stowe, Sarah Orne Jewett, Emily Dickinson, Mary E. Wilkins Freeman, Rose Terry Cooke, and Catharine Maria Sedgwick. One could argue—perhaps convincingly—that since these writers were women they would have had no voting privileges in town affairs (except sometimes in matters connected with the schools) and hence would not be experienced in town politics or concerned about them. But these authors made up for their omissions with literary skills, acute character analyses, and psychological insights for the most part beyond Beecher's abilities. Their successes lay in catching the atmosphere of the scenes they described and in revealing the emotions and motives of the people about whom they wrote. Though they gave some attention to religion and its influences, they left the town meeting and its origins and significance to the historical societies and the numerous band of scholars, who kept the presses busy with a steady stream of publications on the subject. These scholars, and the writers of fiction and poetry, will be treated in later chapters. They must be mentioned at this point as evidence of what was fast becoming a fad, perhaps a cult, centered on New England village and rural life.

[6]
Harriet Beecher Stowe: Interpreter of New England Life

> My object is to interpret to the world the New England life and character in that particular time of its history which may be called the seminal period. I would endeavor to show you New England and its *seed-bed*, before the hot suns of modern progress had developed its sprouting germs into the great trees of today.
>
> Harriet Beecher Stowe, *Oldtown Folks*[1]

Henry Ward Beecher was only incidentally a writer of fiction, and not a very able one at that. His sister, Harriet Beecher Stowe, on the other hand, won herself a world-wide reputation as a novelist of skill and influence. Throughout her literary career she wrote about New England places and persons, drawing from her childhood memories, her father's and husband's reminiscences, and her experiences when, after her marriage, she lived in Maine and Massachusetts. Her second published story, titled "A New England Sketch" (later retitled "Uncle Lot"), was a character study of Lyman Beecher's eccentric but kindly foster-father, Lot Benton of North Guilford, Connecticut, about whom she had heard many anecdotes. Printed in 1834 in the *Western Monthly Magazine*, this story, which incidentally won a fifty-dollar prize, is an early example of that kind of New England writing which specializes in presenting the oddities and quirks of Yankee character. Uncle Lot's stubbornness and quaint contrariness were indeed qualities that later appeared in many another character in Stowe's own fiction and in that of authors like Mary E. Wilkins Freeman and Rose Terry Cooke. Again establishing a convention for later New England regional fiction, Stowe set "A New England Sketch" against a carefully lined background of village life, emphasizing, in this case, its serenity and stressing the centrality of the church and the prestige of its pastors.

Stowe's first book of consequence, *The Mayflower; or, Sketches of Scenes and Characters among the Descendants of the Pilgrims* (1843), contains "Uncle Lot" and a fine description of the Litchfield church (which Lyman Beecher quoted at length in his *Autobiography),* and a piece named "Old Father

Morris: A Sketch from Nature," one of the best of Stowe's sympathetic studies of New England clergymen.[2] In this volume Stowe had found her subject. During the next thirty-five years she continued to add to her list of books dealing with New England, among them another volume of short stories and sketches, *Sam Lawson's Oldtown Fireside Stories* (1872), with a Massachusetts setting, and four novels: *The Minister's Wooing* (1859), *The Pearl of Orr's Island* (1862), *Oldtown Folks* (1869), *Poganuc People* (1878). Of the novels, *Poganuc People*, which relies heavily on Stowe's memories of Litchfield, is the most impressive as a depiction of New England village ways, but the other three novels are well worth more than perfunctory attention.

The Minister's Wooing

The first of these novels, *The Minister's Wooing*, has its setting in Newport, Rhode Island, soon after the Revolutionary War. Newport, though not a large city, was sophisticated and cosmopolitan to a degree that was not typical of the New England communities—including even Litchfield—with which Stowe was most familiar. Also, tainted as it had been in Colonial times, by a thriving slave trade, it hardly provided an example of the democratic strength and moral virtues so valued by idealizers of New England life. The characters of the novel, among them Aaron Burr, are less provincial in their style of living and in their attitudes than are the inhabitants of the smaller New England towns that are the locales of most of Stowe's regional fiction. The important aspect of the book, however, is its presentation of a strain of stern Calvinism widespread in New England and particularly in rural areas. The minister to whom the title refers was an actual clergyman, Dr. Samuel Hopkins, one of the most uncompromising exponents of Jonathan Edwards's theology, even surpassing his master in the rigidity of his opinions on election.

Hopkins in real life served as minister in Newport, having gone there after being dismissed from the church at Great Barrington, Massachusetts, because of the harshness of his views. Stowe's discussion of his teachings and of their origins and influence is of major importance in understanding her own feelings about her ancestral religion. Though she alludes to Hopkins's ideas throughout the book, she devotes chapter 22, headed "Views of Divine Government," in its entirety to them and their effect on the mind of one of the main characters, Mrs. Marvyn. This conscientious and intelligent woman has received word that her son, who is still in an unregenerate state, has been drowned at sea. The situation suggests the circumstances of the death by drowning of the fiancé of Stowe's sister, Catharine Beecher.

Knowing that the man was unconverted, and learning later that he was a complete skeptic, Catharine, as a Calvinist, could only believe that her intended husband was doomed to eternal damnation, a conclusion that her father, Lyman Beecher, could not deny. Though this event occurred many years before Stowe wrote the *Minister's Wooing,* the memory of it haunts this chapter that so relentlessly demonstrates the havoc wrought on human actions and emotions by Calvinist dogma. Even more contributory to the emotional power of Stowe's presentation of Mrs. Marvyn's agony is the fact that Stowe herself had experienced similar distress when her own son, Henry, a student at Dartmouth College, was drowned before having experienced conversion.

"It is impossible," Stowe asserts, "to write a story of New England life and manners for superficial thought or shallow feeling. They who would fully understand the springs which moved the characters with whom we now associate must go down with us to the depths."[3] She then presents the reader with a summary of Calvinist doctrine as held by Jonathan Edwards and, with alterations in the direction of even greater severity, by Samuel Hopkins. Her exposition of these puzzling and appalling views has the clarity of which only one who understood them all too well could be capable. Methodically, step by step, she lays bare the essentials of the theology inherited by her father and passed on by him to his family, though perhaps in slightly "alleviated" form.

This, in paraphrase, is how she describes the Beecher theology: Mankind, because of the sin of Adam, lives under the curse of an outraged God. Nothing that one can do will be pleasing to God until and unless one undergoes the inflowing of grace known as conversion or regeneration. But man in his utter depravity and helplessness is incapable of achieving regeneration unless elected for this benefit by God's eternal decrees as made before the Creation. If one's name is in the book of the elect, one's conversion will be irresistible and inevitable. If not so listed, one is a reprobate and inevitably will burn in hell through all eternity. But in spite of the inevitability of the fulfillment of God's decrees, each person *is free* to choose whether or not to become converted. This is Stowe's summary of a crucial part of high Calvinist dogma. The problems, agonizings, and rebellions that this set of doctrines occasioned are dealt with in her novel, either directly or implicitly.

The obvious contradictions in the Calvinist teaching on election and conversion gave rise to endless debate and explanations, none of them convincing enough to save high Calvinism, in New England, beyond the nineteenth century. In general the explanations were to the effect that the nonelect innately desired evil and were free to choose evil, and hence were exercising freedom of will. Similarly, after conversion, the elect were able to desire good and were free to act upon their desire. In brief, what one desires is controlled by forces beyond human capacity to direct, but one is always free to act upon these desires. Will is free but desires are not—a quibble not very convincing to Harriet Beecher Stowe.

A major problem was to identify a true conversion. The criteria were so exacting that no one, not even the most pious preachers, could be perfectly sure of being among the elect and regenerate, who indeed would at best comprise but a small fraction of the human race. Yet one fairly sure "evidence" of a genuine influx of saving grace would be the recipient's total acceptance, after conversion, of the ways of God as taught by Calvin, even to the extent of rejoicing in his own possible damnation as part of God's scheme for His universe. To question for a moment any divine decree, even of one's own assignment to everlasting hellfire, would be damaging evidence of one's own unregeneracy.

Harriet Stowe and Catharine Beecher, and Mrs. Marvyn in *The Minister's Wooing*, all rebelled against the doctrine of election when they were faced with applying it to persons they had loved and knew to be decent and good. Catharine rejected the doctrine of Original Sin also, and became an exponent of a more thoroughgoing freedom of the will than that posited by Calvin and his adherents. Harriet, after the death of her son, joined the Episcopal church, which by that time had discarded, or was ignoring, much of its original Calvinism. And Mrs. Marvyn, in a state of near insanity, is saved from going over the edge only by her Negro servant, Candace, who assures her mistress that we should rely on Jesus' love rather than on Samuel Hopkins's dogma. Interestingly, Henry Ward Beecher in his Plymouth Church in Brooklyn was also preaching a religion of love quite different from the orthodox preaching of his father and of his own earlier ministry in Indiana. New England theology was undergoing radical change.

Yet Stowe did not look upon her father's religion with hatred or scorn, despite the pain that it had caused her in her personal life. In all her writing on New England she expresses deep reverence for the clergy, no matter how stern their orthodoxy. In *The Minister's Wooing* she writes: "The rigid theological discipline of New England is fitted to produce rather strength and purity than enjoyment. It was not fitted to make a sensitive and thoughtful nature happy, however it might ennoble and exalt. . . . It is not in our line to imply the truth or falsehood of those systems of philosophic theology which seem for many years to have been the principal outlet for the proclivities of the New England mind, but as psychological developments they have an intense interest. He who does not see a grand side to these strivings of the soul cannot understand one of the noblest capabilities of humanity."[4]

Stowe believed that the Calvinist minister who would welcome his own damnation, if it is willed by God for the betterment of the universe, is comparable to the artist or philosopher who gladly rises "to the height of utter self-abnegation for the glory of the invisible. . . . These hard old New England divines were the poets of metaphysical philosophy, who built systems in an artistic fervor, and felt self exhale from beneath them as they rose into the higher regions of thought."[5] The poetry of New England life, then, was Calvinist theology as taught by the ministers, and it was a tragic poetry, with all the terror and grandeur of true tragedy, as Stowe was perceptive enough to see. Just as one would not reject Greek tragedy because it is based on polytheistic and fatalistic concepts of nature no longer held, so Stowe, though her own temperament compelled her to reject much of Calvinism, still recognized its tragic beauty. Thus in *Oldtown Folks* she points out that for New England students of Greek literature "the Calvinism of the old Greek tragedian mingling with the Calvinism of the pulpit and of modern New England life, formed a curious admixture in our thoughts."[6] Perhaps also she saw that the Aristotelian concept of the tragic flaw, which inevitably destroys the protagonist of tragedy, whether in the work of a Greek or a later playwright, is not so different from the doctrine of election. She isolates perfectly the essence of tragedy when she states in *The Minister's Wooing* that according to the Calvinist doctrine "the individual entered eternity alone, as if he had no interceding relation in the universe."[7] For a more poetic statement of the tragic and Calvinist concept of humanity's relation to God and the universe one should turn to Emily Dickinson's great poem:

> This Consciousness that is aware
> Of Neighbors and the Sun
> Will be the one aware of Death
> And that itself alone
>
> Is traversing the interval
> Experience between
> And most profound experiment
> Appointed unto Men—
>
> How adequate unto itself
> It's properties shall be
> Itself unto itself and none
> Shall make discovery.
>
> Adventure most unto itself
> The Soul condemned to be—
> Attended by a single Hound
> Its own identity.[8]

Thus Stowe could admire, even stand in awe of her father's Puritan religion—and appreciate its profound meanings—and yet, under stress, she found herself unable to sustain its teachings. Her objections, indeed, were largely emotional. Intellectually, as far as the old-time ministers were concerned, all she could bring herself to say in mild denigration of them was that they transferred to the Deity the concept of total sovereignty that the British kings took for themselves. She goes on to say that only a generation after the Revolution this mode of thought began to lose its hold on the clergy. As a result the ministers lost some of their prestige, especially when religion ceased to be supported by public taxes, though able ministers by their own merits and some softening of their doctrines continued to exert an extremely strong influence.

On the other hand, and paradoxically, Stowe realized that Calvinism ultimately favored and promoted democracy. According to men like Edwards and Hopkins—and Stowe concurred—each individual soul is important enough to engage God's attention in making a decision whether to save it or damn it. In the Greek tragedies, as well as in Shakespeare's and those of other Renaissance authors, the protagonists were kings or counselors, but in New England's Calvinist views, all persons from the lowest to the highest rated some notice from God. Thus the tragic potential was extended from the limited class of aristocrats and the wealthy to entire populaces. The meanest and the highest could rank as heroes, or victims, of tragedy. Here was the basis for the democracy of the New England town.

A further contribution to New England life and thought with which Stowe credits the early divines was that they provided "the strong mental discipline needed by a people who were an absolute democracy. The Sabbath teaching in New England has been a regular intellectual drill as well as a devotional exercise."[9] The difficulties in reconciling seemingly contradictory concepts like the doctrines of free agency and election called for vigorous exercise of the mental powers of the pastor in his pulpit and of his parishioners in fireside discussion. In their town meetings—where democracy could be "absolute" if the voters rose to the occasion—conclusions also had to be reached, and conflicting views reconciled, and the practice in dealing with knotty theological problems could only have an advantageous effect.

The Pearl of Orr's Island

Stowe is more concerned with theology in *The Minister's Wooing* than in her other novels, though in all of them it receives ample attention. The second of her New England novels, *The Pearl of Orr's Island* (1862), is a classic among innumerable works of fiction with Maine Coast settings and characters. Written from firsthand knowledge that she gained while living at Brunswick, Maine, where her husband taught at Bowdoin College, this work, despite much sentimentality, is still a fine evocation of coastal scenes, occupations, and people. Sarah Orne Jewett, today considered the most perceptive writer about Maine, found in Stowe's book the inspiration that led to her own writing. The tone and theme of *The Pearl of Orr's Island* is strikingly conveyed in the words of one of its characters, the Reverend Mr. Sewell. Addressing Moses Pennel, a Spanish boy saved from a wrecked vessel and adopted by the sea captain Zephaniah Pennell and his wife, the minister says: "You have the greatest reason to bless the kind Providence which cast your lot in such a family, in such a community. I have had some means in my youth of comparing other parts of the country with our New England, and it is my opinion that a young man could not ask a better introduction into life than the wholesome nurture of a Christian family in our favored land."[10]

The Old Testament names that abound in *The Pearl of Orr's Island* are typical of New England during the times about which Stowe was writing. But she particularly relishes them in this book because they harmonize with her conviction, repeatedly stated in her works, that New England during its first two centuries or longer was essentially a Hebraic society. "Zephaniah Pennel," she writes, "was what might be called a Hebrew of the Hebrews. New England, in her earlier days, founding her institutions on the Hebrew Scriptures, bred better Jews than Moses could, because she read Moses with the amendments of Christ."[11] In Stowe's sketch "Old Father Morris" in *The Mayflower and Miscellaneous Writings* (1855), she had the aged preacher delivering in New England dialect sermons in which he describes the landscape, villages, and people of the Holy Land precisely as if they resembled New England in every detail, so that, for example, the road to Emmaus becomes a New England turnpike with tollgates.[12]

"The state of society in some districts of Maine," Stowe goes on to say in *The Pearl of Orr's Island*, "in these days, much resembled in its spirit that which Moses labored to produce in ruder ages. It was entirely democratic, simple, grave, hearty, and sincere,—solemn and religious in its daily tone and yet, as to all material good, full of wholesome thrift and prosperity. . . . Its better specimens had a simple Doric grandeur unsurpassed in any age."[13] Many students of New England have commented upon the Hebraic flavor of its life and worship, but the grafting of Doric qualities upon the Hebrew seems to be original with Stowe, whether justifiable or not. At any rate, as a community, she thought that Orr's Island shared the best of each of the two ancient cultures. In *The Country of the Pointed Firs* (1896) Sarah

Orne Jewett, very likely taking a cue from Stowe, was to emphasize the Greek qualities she found among the dwellers along the Maine Coast.

Oldtown Folks

The third of Harriet Beecher Stowe's New England novels, *Oldtown Folks* (1869) is by many considered her best. It is the longest and surely contains the greatest wealth of details about New England life in the post-Revolutionary decades in which it is laid. Oldtown is modeled upon Natick, Massachusetts, the native town of Harriet's husband, Calvin Stowe, whose reminiscences were the source of much of the material in the book. Natick had been the scene of a large part of the Reverend John Eliot's missionary work among the Indians in the seventeenth century, and at the time of the novel's action a number of Indians, in a sad condition of demoralization, remained there. Otherwise the town was typical of New England, though its proximity to Boston—three hours by coach—gave it closer contact with urban life than most towns had. Stowe unquestionably wished to present Oldtown as representative. Of *Oldtown Folks* she wrote to her publisher, James Fields: "It is more to me than a story; it is my résumé of the whole spirit and body of New England, a country that is now exerting such an influence on the civilized world that to know it truly becomes an object."[14]

Stowe in her remarks to Fields had more in mind than the increasing and spreading recognition of New England literature, education, and learning. She was also doubtless thinking of the westward movement of New England people and their way of life, a movement with which her father and Timothy Dwight had been so deeply concerned and in which the Beecher family had taken an important part during their years in Cincinnati. In her Preface to *Oldtown Folks,* she writes, again employing a Greek analogy: "New England has been to these United States what the Dorian hive was to Greece. It has always been a capital country to emigrate from, and North, South, East, and West have been populated largely from New England, so that the seed-bed of New England was the seed-bed of the great American Republic, and of all that is likely to come of it. New England people cannot be thus interpreted without calling into view many grave considerations and necessitating some serious thinking."[15]

Serious thinking abounds in *Oldtown Folks,* and it is doubtful if Stowe, a daughter of the Puritans, could with a clear conscience write a novel without a serious purpose and serious thoughts. Indeed, in the Lyman Beecher household novels had not been considered appropriate reading. Thus Stowe points out in her preface that in *Oldtown Folks* "Calvinist, Arminian, High-Church Episcopalian, sceptic, and simple believer all speak in their

turn";[16] and though she claims to be an impartial "observer and reporter,"[17] she quite clearly betrays her preferences for a milder theology
than orthodox Calvinism. Imbedded in the novel is a religious tract plus a
summary of various denominational beliefs in her times. She did most
assuredly approach her subject—the delineation of the temporal and spiritual life of a New England town—with seriousness of intent and thought.

The strictest Calvinist in *Oldtown Folks* is the grandmother of Horace
Holyoke, the first-person narrator. In a chapter headed "My Grandmother's Blue Book" are described precisely the beliefs the grandmother
adheres to. They are those presented in Dr. Joseph Bellamy's *True Religion
Delineated and·Distinguished from All Others* (1750), which is the Blue Book. A
disciple of Jonathan Edwards, Dr. Bellamy advanced a set of doctrines
differing somewhat in detail but not in the least in grimness from those of
Dr. Samuel Hopkins as described in *The Minister's Wooing*. They need not
be outlined here. Stowe finds them typical of New England at the time of
her novel's action, and she comments on their effect in terms even more
somber than any she used in *The Minister's Wooing:* "The underlying foundation of life, therefore, in New England was one of profound, unutter-
able, and therefore unuttered, melancholy, which regarded human
existence itself as a ghastly risk, and, in the case of the vast majority of
human beings, an inconceivable misfortune."[18]

The tragic sense of life that sets the tone in *The Minister's Wooing* is
supplanted in *Oldtown Folks* by a tone bordering on despair. Yet Stowe
refrains from condemning, here as elsewhere, the clergy who preached
these depressing doctrines. In *Oldtown Folks* she presents in rather admiring terms just such a minister, the Reverend Moses Stern. Interestingly,
Moses Stern is modeled upon the Reverend Nathaniel Emmons, for sev-
enty-one years pastor at Franklin, Massachusetts, where Catharine
Beecher's fiancé had lived and attended the Reverend Emmons's church.
Stern's views yield not an inch in bleakness to those of Hopkins or Bellamy.

Yet, however admirable the old-time Calvinist ministers may have been
in their devotion to duty and in uprightness in their personal lives, Stowe,
as a result of her own and her sister's sufferings concluded that it was time
for a change, and the direction this change should take is indicated toward
the end of *Oldtown Folks,* when the scene for a number of chapters shifts
from eastern Massachusetts to a mountain town called Cloudland, a two-
day journey distant. The symbolic meaning of this shift is patent. As Governor Winthrop had stated in 1630, New England's mission was to be a city
upon a hill—a New Jerusalem—for all the world to gaze on as an inspiration to holiness. Oldtown is in the lowlands; Cloudland is on a hill, a
fresher, newer community than Oldtown, and though there is much that is
admirable in Oldtown, and the winds of change are stirring there also,

Cloudland with its invigorating mountain air and inspiring scenery offers something better, something more promising for the future than does Oldtown with its patina of two hundred years of history. In Cloudland, at least, three adolescents, sent there from Oldtown, flourish and mature as they attend the academy and share in the local social and religious life.

Insufficient notice has hitherto been taken of Stowe's moving the action of her novel up into the hills. Nothing in the plot, itself a flimsy structure, compels her to do so. Her young persons could just as well have got their education in Oldtown or nearby. But the fact is that Oldtown, for all its attractions, has become stagnant. It has lost the vigor, the drive that in earlier Puritan times characterized the old New England that it represents. Its minister is secretly a skeptic concerning the Calvinist dogma of his church. An Arminian at heart, he preaches a cold, passionless religion suggestive of the Unitarianism that was gaining a foothold in the area, and Stowe was never sympathetic with Unitarianism. Nor do the beliefs of other Oldtown people offer alternatives that she would consider seriously. Grandmother Badger, with her Blue-Book Calvinism, and her husband, who is an outspoken Arminian, are entertaining, even instructive, but create a confusion of ideas unconducive to a vital choice as to one's spiritual life. Even Anglicanism, which Stowe herself adopted in the 1850s and which has some representation in the novel, is presented as unpromising as a spiritual force. Significantly, the most memorable and likable character— and the most successfully drawn among all the characters in Stowe's fiction—is Sam Lawson, the town loafer and raconteur of gossip and tall stories. Piety and work—esteemed in New England as indispensable to salvation—play no part in Sam's existence. He is kind, he is humorous, and he immensely enjoys his daily living. More one cannot say for him. Stowe obviously likes him and has fun reproducing his dialect and recording his Yankee witticisms and mannerisms, but his uncommitted way could not be hers.

Cloudland, unfortunately, enjoys no such colorful inhabitant as Sam Lawson, but it has much that Oldtown lacks. Most important, it has an excellent academy and a flourishing church presided over by a sincere, enthusiastic, and popular minister. Timothy Dwight, at a first glance, would have been delighted. Cloudland, he would have thought, had the best of what made New England great, and he would have placed the town in the forefront of the march toward the millennium.

"The academy in Cloudland," Stowe wrote, "was one of those pure wells from which the hidden strength of New England is drawn, as her broad rivers are made from hidden mountain brooks."[19] After taking notice of the custom in every New England community "to establish a school-house"[20] along with a church, she laments the passing of that phase of New

England history which made it "the vigorous, germinating seed-bed of all that has since been developed of politics, laws, letters, and theology, through New England to America, and through America to the world."[21] The seedbed no longer existed at the time she was writing—for *Oldtown Folks* was laid in a time sixty years earlier—and the events recorded in it could not have occurred in the later atmosphere of "the hurry of railroads, and the rush and roar of business."[22] But the seeds once planted and germinated resulted in wholesome growth—first in the older towns and, when they became unfavorable places for spiritual growth, as seemed to be the case with Oldtown, in newer, more remote places like Cloudland. "It was necessary," Stowe concludes, "that there should be a period like the one we describe, when villages were each a separate little democracy, shut off by rough roads and forests from the rest of the world, organized round the church and school as a common centre, and formed by the minister and the schoolmaster."[23]

Cloudland thus supplants Oldtown in social and spiritual significance. Aside from the reasons already given, there may be another impulse behind Stowe's favorable treatment of this hill town. The fact is that Cloudland in many particulars resembles her native Litchfield, her memories of which were always remarkably happy and which would at any rate remain in her mind as an archetypal image of what a New England, or any other, village should ideally be. Litchfield, though not in the high mountains, is situated like Cloudland on a hill. In both the real and the fictional town, the socially prestigious families dwelt in the village center, while the poorer people, the farmers, dwelt in the surrounding countryside—a situation that jars a bit with the symbolism of the hill as a New Jerusalem. Also as in Cloudland, education flourished in Litchfield.

But a more striking parallel between the real and the fictitious town was the fact that the Cloudland minister, the Reverend Mr. Avery, closely resembled Stowe's father, Lyman Beecher, the Congregationalist minister at Litchfield. The likeness will be immediately apparent to any one who reads Lyman Beecher's *Autobiography*. Henry Ward Beecher, it will be recalled, described his father's theology as an "alleviated Calvinism," in which conversion was to some extent, though not entirely, a matter of one's own choice and effort and hence more accessible to the unregenerate. Thus in the revivals, which he conducted frequently, Beecher was able to offer a real hope to the participants; the high Calvinist stand that conversion was God's work alone and that nothing one could do would influence God's choice would not be very effective in a revival sermon.

The schoolmaster in Cloudland writes to his sister in Oldtown concerning Parson Avery:

My good friend preaches what they call New Divinity, by which I understand the Calvinism which our fathers left us, in the commencing process
of disintegration. He is thoroughly and enthusiastically in earnest about
it, and believes that the system, as far as Edwards and Hopkins have got
it, is *almost* [emphasis added] absolute truth; but, for all that, is cheerfully
busy in making some little emendations and corrections, upon which he
values himself and which he thinks of the greatest consequence. . . . Now
my friend the parson is an outgrowth of the New England theocracy,
about the simplest, purest, and least questionable state of society that the
world ever saw. He has a good digestion, a healthy mind in a healthy
body; he lives in a village where there is no pauperism, and hardly any
crime,—where all the embarrassing, dreadful social problems and mys-
teries of life scarcely exist. . . . His preaching suits the state of advance-
ment to which New England has come; and the process which he and
ministers of his sort institute, of having every point in theology fully
discussed by the common people, is not only capital drill for their minds,
but it will have its effect in the end on their theologies, and out of them
all the truth of the future will arise.[24]

The New Divinity was the theology preached by Timothy Dwight at Yale
while Beecher was a student there. The "emendations and corrections" that
Dwight and Beecher, along with Parson Avery of Cloudland, made in the
doctrines of Edwards were designed to demonstrate "the free agency of
man,"[25] which the old Calvinists had upheld in theory but virtually
nullified with their simultaneous insistence on the inviolability of divine
decrees regarding election. But now Parson Avery, following the New Divinity (sometimes called the New Haven Divinity) preached to his congregations the unequivocal message: "You are free, and you are able."[26] This
shift in New England preaching from a crushing emphasis on God's absolute sovereignty to a liberating affirmation of man's free agency was to Mrs.
Stowe a natural development corresponding, as we have seen, to the political shift from monarchy to democracy. A people free to govern themselves, as were the New England villagers, must be able to consider
themselves free agents endowed with the power to make their own choices
and to act upon them.[27] God's sovereignty still remained, but—somewhat
mysteriously—it did not deprive the human will of its freedom.

Furthermore, Parson Avery, like Dwight and Beecher and a multitude of
other preachers of the time, believed that the millennium was coming in
the very near future. Since the millennium would be a period in which
Christ would rule the world unopposed by Satan, it was also supposed that
it would be a time when most of the population of the world would be
regenerate. Toward the realization of this condition Parson Avery, like his
real-life counterparts throughout New England and elsewhere, conducted
revivals and rejoiced when the harvest of souls was plentiful. In keeping

with the trends of the times, he preached a God of love, eager to save His creatures if they were willing and deserving, though he still relied on logic in his preaching and he did not go so far as to deny the existence of hell. The converted Christian, of course, would love God, but Avery did not teach that love of God in itself was necessarily an evidence of conversion. Thus he does not represent Stowe's thinking in all its aspects. At the time of writing *Oldtown Folks* she agreed with her brother, Henry Ward Beecher, that love, not just of God but of humanity, was not only an evidence of conversion but in itself constituted salvation. Neither Lyman Beecher nor Parson Avery, nor their congregations, were ready for quite so radical an "emendment or correction" of the forefathers' belief. Conversion to them was more than the glow of love, though love could and should be a part of it. Stowe was sympathetic with Parson Avery's and her father's efforts to modify Calvinism, but their teachings remained too strong for her after middle life. She could commend and approve, but not fully accept, the conclusions of these milder Calvinists.

Poganuc People

Ten years after *Oldtown Folks,* Harriet Beecher Stowe published her last novel, *Poganuc People,* in which the setting and many of the characters derive from her childhood memories of Litchfield much more directly than in any of her other novels. In her personal copy of the book she indicated by marginal notes the material she had taken from her own early years in Litchfield as well as from her father's reminiscences of North Guilford. Thus in *Poganuc People* we find that the heroine, Dolly, resembles Harriet herself in character and childhood experiences. Dolly's father, pastor of Poganuc, is clearly Lyman Beecher. The aristocratic Colonel Davenport, formerly a major in Washington's army, is drawn from a Colonel Tallmadge of Litchfield. This was preeminently a Beecher book, even in the circumstance of its first publication, serially, in the *Christian Union,* of which Harriet's brother, Henry, was editor. Moreover, *Poganuc People* is more compact in structure and readable in style and narrative flow than the three novels by Stowe already discussed. But, most important, in it Stowe shares with the reader her final views on and assessment of New England village life, and both are very positive. Actually, *Poganuc People* continues in tone and theme the Cloudland portion of *Oldtown Folks;* the spiritual and social assets of Litchfield were those of both Cloudland and Poganuc.

Some of the characteristics of Litchfield as Lyman Beecher saw them have already been discussed. Another witness, Timothy Dwight, a connoisseur of New England towns and a self-appointed expert in gauging their relative merits as examples of New England civilization, devoted to Litchfield and its inhabitants a number of pages in volume 2 of his *Travels*. Approaching from the south, he reported that South Farms, one of the parishes of the town, consisted of a cluster "of good farmers' dwellings, of which a little village is formed around the church. The inhabitants are industrious and thrifty, and distinguished for good morals, good order, and decency of deportment."[28] Since South Farms also had a good academy for boys and girls, it met all of Dwight's requirements for an exemplary New England village. Indeed, this parish may have recalled to Dwight his own Greenfield Hill, a parish in the town of Fairfield, consisting of farms, a church, and an academy, of which he was headmaster.

The village of Litchfield itself, according to Dwight, was "a handsome town,"[29] with fine houses and the architecturally most pleasing court house in the state. He remarks that the village proper is called "the Hill," that the town contains "a respectable female academy" and a famous law school, and that many of the citizens are notable for their intelligence or their achievements in public office.[30] To Dwight, Litchfield ranked not far behind the white-clapboarded towns of the Connecticut River Valley, which he considered the repositories of New England civic and religious virtues in their purest and most concentrated form.

Stowe's description of Poganuc could be applied to Litchfield with changes only in proper names. "A pretty mountain town in Connecticut,"[31] Poganuc is a county seat, contains a jail, a court house, a Congregational meetinghouse, and an Episcopal church. In the village reside a number of persons corresponding in importance and occupation to actual residents of Litchfield while Lyman Beecher was minister there. Surrounding the village are the farmfolk—all of them churchgoers and town-meeting attenders. Dr. Cushing, the minister, is firm but kindly and keeps up a civilized debate with the Episcopal priest, who has lured away some of Dr. Cushing's congregation and regards him as improperly ordained. Dr. Cushing is a New Divinity man, like Parson Avery in Cloudland, and is a strong believer in revivals, which he conducts with gratifying success.

The time of the major action of the novel is in the second decade of the nineteenth century—about a generation later than the time of *Oldtown Folks* and *The Minister's Wooing*—when the Standing Order (ie., state support of the Congregational Church) was subjected to attacks from political groups under the influence of Jeffersonian concepts of democracy just beginning to be felt in New England. A strength and interest in *Poganuc People*— lacking in Stowe's other New England novels—is that it takes into account this political trend. The older New England towns like Litchfield or the fictional Oldtown did contain small numbers of families of some wealth and political and social status who enjoyed considerable prestige and influence in the community, despite the fact that the local governments were thoroughly democratic in theory if not in practice. Such families would quite naturally be Federalist politically, along with the merchant classes of the cities and larger seaports. The ministers, for a number of obvious reasons, would tend to ally themselves with these interests, and would vote Federalist because that party supported the idea of an established church. Timothy Dwight was a Federalist and a firm establishmentarian, and one reason why he was so enthusiastic about the Connecticut River towns may have been that they were generally Federalist, in addition to being pious and architecturally handsome.[32]

Poganuc in Stowe's novel was undergoing a process of democratization, to which Dr. Cushing was opposed. In an election the farmers and common people voted for candidates of the anti-Federalist Democratic-Republican party—usually referred to simply as the Democratic party—which upheld Jeffersonian concepts. Dr. Cushing was crushed by the resulting defeat of the Federalists and the disestablishment of his church. But years later, he "could say with another distinguished Connecticut clergyman 'I suffered more than tongue can tell for the best thing that ever happened to old Connecticut.'"[33] The other clergyman was Lyman Beecher, whose remark his daughter transferred word for word to the novel. The people, whether Jeffersonian or not, had been right in rejecting the Standing Order.

Democracy in Poganuc was indeed advancing. Stowe recognized that there were two classes of citizens in the town. But the simpler people—the farmers, the artisans, the tavern-keepers—were asserting themselves and refusing to take second place to any one, and Stowe approved. She reports a considerable amount of demagoguery in Poganuc, led by the weekly newspaper, which specialized "in coarse and scurrilous attacks upon ministers in general, and Dr. Cushing in particular" and "ridiculed . . . every custom, preference, and prejudice which it had been the work of years to establish in New England."[34]

But beyond setting the tone of conversation among some of the tavern-haunters, this sort of journalism had little effect. The people still attended church, respected their ministers, and clung to old ways. And despite the defeat of Federalism, Poganuc still remained a town where doors did not need to be locked at night and "an almshouse was almost a superfluous institution."[35] Jeffersonianism, if we believe Stowe, did little beyond making the people more keenly aware than hitherto of the fact that their nation, their state, and, above all, their town were democracies, and that it was their privilege and duty to exercise their suffrage along with the wealthiest and grandest citizens.

Thus on election days the good citizens go to the polls in large numbers and vote the Federalists out of office. At town meetings they appear in force, and again have their way over the Federalists, whom, in the words of one of the farmers, "it takes a yoke of oxen to get ; . . out."[36] Not that the town meetings always deal with matters of vital importance. For example, a proposal to install a heating stove in the church—presumably before disestablishment when the town controlled such matters—carried only after a lengthy wrangle.[37] A more prolonged and acrimonious debate takes place over the question of moving a district school to a more convenient location. After several unproductive and time-wasting meetings, the issue is decided by the willful and opinionated Zephaniah Higgins, who, without further consulting the town, hitches two yoke of oxen to the building and drags it to the spot where he wants it. This episode, incidentally, was suggested by a similar one remembered by Lyman Beecher from his boyhood in North Guildford and related by him in his autobiography.[38]

Zeph Higgins, the most colorful figure in the book, is indeed endowed with a strong will that serves him well in farming his rocky acres, but it is an overdeveloped will that, as a fellow townsman puts it, makes him hate "to do the very thing he wants to, if any one else wants him to do it."[39] The subject of the will—its "freedom" or its bondage to divine decree—had been a matter of serious debate among Calvinists for centuries, and it had been of particular concern among New England clergymen and theologians at least since Jonathan Edwards wrote his famous treatise. The conceding of some freedom to the will—the promotion of a doctrine of "free agency"—we have seen to be a major innovation of the New Divinity. Zeph Higgins, whose stubborn will was not untypical of New England farmers, though somewhat exaggerated, thus assumes an importance in the novel other than merely being an amusing local eccentric. In later chapters Dr. Cushing conducts one of his revivals among the rural people of Poganuc. The prospect of a golden harvest of souls is heartening, but Zeph, who is already a church member and has been attending the revivals, is determined, as only he can be, not to be among the saved. At one of the meetings, after Dr. Cushing has preached, Zeph rises and denounces himself:

> "I hain't never ben a Christian—that's jest the truth on't. I never had oughter 'a' ben in the church. I've been all wrong—*wrong*—WRONG! I knew I was wrong, but I wouldn't give up. It's ben jest my awful WILL! I've set up my will agin God Almighty. I've set it agin my neighbors— agin the minister and agin the church. And now the Lord's come out agin me; he's struck me down. [Zeph's meek and saintly wife has recently died.] I know he's got a right—he can do what he pleases—but I ain't resigned—not a grain. I submit 'cause I can't help myself; but my heart's hard and wicked. I expect my day of grace is over. I ain't a Christian, and I can't be, and I shall go to hell at last, and sarve me right!"[40]

Zeph's case is interesting theologically. As a "free agent," which Beecher and Cushing would insist he was, he had willed himself into a conversion that would entitle him to church membership. But he had not really been converted, as he now realizes and thus even his terrific will proves insufficient to achieve regeneration. High Calvinists like Hopkins and Bellamy might see in Zeph's discomfiture an instance of the truth of their doctrines. Only God can supply the influx of grace necessary for conversion; the human will alone is inadequate. But when Zeph understands his situation, he sets his will with equal obduracy against regeneration. The high Calvinists might again shake their heads knowingly and say: "See, this man is hardened. He now appears in his true colors as a reprobate. He is now capable only of willing his own destruction. Furthermore, he refuses to realize that his damnation will be for the greater glory of God. Yet," the high Calvinists would continue, "Zeph is wrong to be so certain of his damnation, for grace can come to anyone, even the seemingly most depraved, and when it comes it is irresistible, even by Zeph's vaunted will."

And indeed grace does come to Zeph in the form of a child's irresistible pleading with him to believe in Christ's love for him. The solution is sentimental and the scene presenting it is mawkish; yet it is valid in terms of Stowe's own theology, which was closer to that of her brother, Henry Ward Beecher, than to her father's. Zeph conceived of God as a wrathful despot—somewhat as pictured by Edwards—with whom one must wage a battle of wills in order to become converted; and indeed orthodox Calvinists did believe that to be converted one must exercise one's will to that end, though the very act of sincere volition required the support of God's free grace. Thus Zeph, endowed with unyielding willpower that he had acquired during his lifetime of moving rocks from his sterile Connecticut fields, decided he would be converted, was converted, later found it was not a genuine conversion, became hostile to God, and finally actually wills his own damnation.

Stowe realizes that Zeph's will is not free; it is bound by the flaw of stubborn pride in his own character—a diagnosis that would please the High Calvinists because they believed that character faults were the result of original sin, the effects of which we can not overcome without Divine assistance. But Stowe believed that such flaws may be removed and that as a result the direction of one's will may change, and to this extent she believed in a "free agency" that seems a lot freer than that postulated by the New Divinity men. Once Zeph, under the influence of the minister's little daughter, relinquishes the idea that God is an enemy against whom he has to pit his own will and thinks of God, in the person of Christ, as loving and compassionate, his will succumbs and he submits to an inflow of grace.

Zeph's regeneration is thus only partly the result of Dr. Cushing's revival.

Much more important as an instrument of grace is Dr. Cushing's daughter Dolly, who we recall was modeled on Stowe herself as a little girl. Yet Dr. Cushing, with his New Divinity and his doctrine of "free agency," has advanced a considerable distance along the road to a religion in which the individual has some control over his choices. Dolly in her childish simplicity makes a further advance from Calvinistic dogma to a faith based on assurances of God's love of His creatures.

Poganuc, experiencing its upsurge of democracy and its revivals of religion, is expansively alive and healthy in spirit. Stowe presents the town and its people with an optimistic zest, justifiable or not, that echoes Dwight's enthusiasm for New England and its towns and that coincides with her brother Henry Ward Beecher's high opinion of Norwood. New England to all three is still "the vine which God's right hand had planted,"[41] as it had been with the Pilgrims and with the Puritans of Massachusetts Bay. For to Dr. Cushing, as to so many New England ministers, the millennium was a reality soon to be experienced, and his face "was set eastward, towards the dawn of that day"[42] when Christ would begin to reign supreme without the opposition of Satan. The clergy and presumably parishioners "were children of the morning."[43] At a Fourth of July celebration Dr. Cushing spoke feelingly about the country's future because he assumed that the future would be millennial. And faith in the coming of the millennium inspired his revival prayers and preaching. Souls in increasing numbers must be won for that day when most would be regenerate. The new political climate in which all the people exercised their rights could be a sign of the times, for a total and vigorous democracy could flourish only among a population where most of the individuals were imbued with grace. God's preparations were going on apace.

These were thoughts that Lyman Beecher, Dr. Cushing's real-life counterpart, also entertained and preached. But Lyman Beecher's optimism was not so unalloyed. In a jeremiad called "A Reformation of Morals Practicable and Indispensable," delivered at New Haven on October 27, 1813, he announced the near approach of the millennium but at the same time warned that New England was backsliding from its great heritage and might lose its place in the forefront in the march toward the day when Christ would reign supreme.[44]

Harriet Beecher Stowe as Representative of Her Times

Stowe doubtless shared her father's views and his hopes regarding New England's role in bringing on the millennium, even though she had ceased to be a Calvinist herself. In fact, millennialism was by no means a monopoly of the Calvinists. Millennial hopes—or at least hopes for the perfection of life on earth—were rife throughout the nineteenth century, and nowhere were they so apparent as among those arch-anti-Calvinists, the Transcendentalists, who in the generation after Lyman Beecher, were in the foremost ranks of "the children of the morning." Thoreau's *Walden* is a prolonged prose hymn to the dawn in which individuals, and at last perhaps society as a whole, would awaken to a new spiritual life, and Thoreau preached to this end as lustily as any revivalist. Brook Farm, an offshoot of Transcendentalism, was instituted to be a guiding beacon for its own and future generations. The Transcendentalists' view that all persons had a spark of the divine actually amounted to assuming that all persons were in a state of grace, if only they knew it and acted accordingly, and thus were at least potentially regenerate. As one nineteenth-century commentator put it, "Transcendentalism simply claimed for all men what Protestant Christianity claimed for its own elect."[45]

The great reform movements of the day were also symptomatic of millennial expectations, whether consciously held or not. Lyman Beecher himself, as we have seen, was a pioneer in temperance agitation and preached against dueling. Among the educated, feminism was gaining momentum. Henry Ward Beecher and Harriet Beecher Stowe were ardent and influential abolitionists. Stowe, it should be recalled, claimed that God, not she, actually was responsible for the composition of *Uncle Tom's Cabin.* God's leaven was at work in the minds of His elect, and most of the workers for various reforms felt that they were under some sort of divine influence— were God's instruments in leading the nation and the world forward to a regenerate society, whether one used the word *millennium* or not. This was frighteningly true of John Brown, whom Thoreau honored by calling him a Transcendentalist and comparing him to that other self-designated doer of God's work, Oliver Cromwell.[46] Both Thoreau and Emerson, as the Civil War approached, hailed the resurgence of the Puritan spirit in the nation—a spirit that, despite Puritan theology, they highly admired. And Julia Ward Howe's "Battle Hymn of the Republic," borrowing imagery from Revelation, may be taken—and by many very likely was—as celebrating the onset of the millennium, which would be preceded by mighty conflicts.

It is a matter of historical fact that the reforms in America during the first half of the nineteenth century had either their rise or very strong support in New England. To people like Dwight and the Beechers such places as Oldtown, Norwood, Poganuc, and the Connecticut River towns represented the essential New England from which redemptive influences streamed out into the regional and national life. Hence a knowledge of such towns is important for one who would understand our national character and history. The persons who wrote about New England in the last century, whether clergy or laymen, focused upon towns, congregations, communities, when describing the region and its culture. From Governor Bradford of Plymouth onward the importance of the towns as nuclei of New England culture was invariably emphasized by apologists for New England, for it was in these compact communities that man's most pressing purposes on earth—the salvation of his soul and the perfection of society—must take place. Groups of Christians, small enough and living close enough together to allow for fellowship in their worship and temporal pursuits, had the best chance of achieving these ends, or so the Puritans and their descendants, basing their views on biblical descriptions of the early church, were convinced. Everything that affected the life of these communities was thus of crucial concern—the form of their government, the success of their agriculture and industry, the size and layout of their towns. But above all the theology and discipline of their churches concerned the townspeople. On doctrine and religious practice all else hinged, and thus these were the preoccupation of writers like Dwight and Stowe and Henry Ward Beecher. Later writers had other preoccupations.

Essays, Sketches, Humor

> The more the ancient rural life receded into the background of
> men's lives, the more it roused their feelings of romance. The
> farm, the village ways, harsh enough in actuality, seemed, to the
> barefoot boys who had gone to New York or were making their
> fortunes in State Street, merry and jolly or softly sweet as
> Goldsmith's scenes of Auburn.
> Van Wyck Brooks, *The Flowering of New England*[1]

In the years 1819 and 1820 the New Yorker Washington Irving published
The Sketch Book, which, as was noted earlier, was profoundly to influence
American literature for the next half century. The essays, sketches, and
tales in Irving's book touched on a great variety of subjects. They included
idyllic pictures of English country life, treatment of such unrelated topics
as "English Writers on America" and "Traits of Indian Character," and the
two famous stories "Rip Van Winkle" and "The Legend of Sleepy Hollow,"
both laid in the Hudson Valley and strong in descriptions of scenery and
the way of life of the Dutch inhabitants of the region. These two tales are
still American classics and are still good reading.

The Sketch Book immediately started a vogue. In addition to the two famous tales, the vignettes of rural England are themselves charming, as are
the essays on other English subjects like "The Stage Coach" and "West-
minster Abbey." Indeed, Irving devoted to England much more space and
attention than he did to the United States. But no one seemed to object,
and the British even began to wonder if Sir Walter Scott had written *The
Sketch Book,* so much did they admire its prose style and its contents. In
America, Irving had many imitators. Henceforth a collection of localized
sketches, mainly with rural settings, spiced with a few stories either purely
fictional or based on legends, could be relied on to make a salable book.
New England writers did not ignore the trend. From Irving they learned
that American materials could be fictionalized or romanticized to suit the
literary tastes of the times.

Nathaniel Hawthorne

Catharine Sedgwick's New England novels belong in the trend popularized by Irving. So also does much of Nathaniel Hawthorne's work. His *Twice-Told Tales* (1837) is clearly patterned on *The Sketch Book*, in that it consists of a number of stories, some legendary and historical and others purely fictional, mixed with sketches, vignettes, and essays—a potpourri with something for every reader's taste. The chief difference between Hawthorne's and Irving's two books is that Hawthorne's material and settings were almost entirely related to one region, New England—"Wakefield" and "The Wedding Knell" are exceptions—while Irving shifted back and forth across the Atlantic Ocean for his subjects and scenes.

Yet Hawthorne, in spite of his concentration on the limited area of New England, was not in *Twice-Told Tales,* or in any of his writing, primarily a depictor of community life, any more than was Irving in *The Sketch Book.* Hawthorne's first concern was with individuals, some of them isolates. In many of his stories the community is there in the background—for example, in "The Gentle Boy," "Young Goodman Brown," and "The Minister's Black Veil." But it often exists as a threatening rather than a supportive force, though many of Hawthorne's characters long for some sort of community identity. Thus in *The Scarlet Letter* (1850) and in *The Blithedale Romance* (1852) Hawthorne placed his major characters, Hester Prynne and Miles Coverdale, in tightly structured social settings and presented them as being oppressed rather than sustained by it. Yet in *The Scarlet Letter* seventeenth-century Boston, though oppressive, provided an environment in which the sinner Hester could work out her own bitter redemption. Hawthorne frequently in his writing made reference to the "great warm heart" of humanity, which is ready to forgive if not forget. It is true that most of his characters, except perhaps Hester, were never really irradiated with this warmth so essential to their peace of mind and soul. What Hawthorne is saying is that an individual's peace is to be found at last only within a community, in association with one's fellow human beings, no matter how harsh the demands of the community are. That so many of his characters, like Roger Chillingworth and Ethan Brand, fail utterly to find peace anywhere is their tragedy, which Hawthorne fully realizes and exploits for his literary purposes. One feels, in reading his works, that Hawthorne himself thirsted for the feeling of belonging, which he conceived of as being provided only by living as a member of a well-defined community like a New England town. And one knows that he was never able to achieve this—not in Salem, in his day a small city; not at Brook Farm; nor in Concord, though he seemed more at ease there then anywhere else. Paradoxically, Thoreau, who prided himself on being a loner, was actually very much a part of Concord life, while Hawthorne remained aloof. The result is that in his writings village life plays a secondary part. When he does describe the life of a community—as in sketches like "Main Street" and "The Town Pump"—he does so in the role of an onlooker standing apart from a scene that fascinates him, perhaps, but in which he is not, or cannot be, an actor.

Nathaniel Shatswell Dodge of Massachusetts

Though influenced by Irving's example, Hawthorne was too talented an author to mimic any one. Another, and lesser, New England author, one who provides an instructive example of such mimicry and therefore is a useful example of a trend, was Nathaniel Shatswell Dodge (1810–74). Under the pseudonym John Carver (Dodge claimed to be descended from the *Mayflower* Pilgrims) a volume titled *Sketches of New England, or Memories of the Country* and published in 1842 displayed a strong Irving influence. Five of these sketches, the preface informs us, were previously published in the *Knickerbocker Monthly Magazine*—an indication that interest in New England was by no means confined to those residing within its borders.

Nathaniel Dodge, to refer again to his preface, was born in New England "on the banks of one of her beautiful rivers, and was nurtured among her mountains."[2] The river was the Merrimack, for his birthplace was Haverill, Massachusetts, and the mountains, judging from evidence in his book, were those in the vicinity of Ossipee, New Hampshire. He had studied at Andover-Newton theological Seminary—a Calvinist stronghold—and had served as principal of Maplewood Institute, a school in Pittsfield, Massachusetts. He also was an author and a journalist.

Sketches of New England is dedicated "to Yankee absentees, than whom none better know that 'home is home though never so homely'"—an appeal to nostalgia that was to sound more and more insistently as the century progressed, eventually finding expression in the semicommercialized institution of Old Home Week. Dodge in his *Sketches* touched on a broad variety of topics, some of them already standard in writings about New England, and others soon to become so. There are two pieces on the surefire subject of the New England Sabbath—"Saturday Evening" and "Sunday in the Country"—recording residual Puritan practices. There are descriptions of Mount Washington and Crawford Notch (both later to become hackneyed subjects) and Ossipee Falls, all in New Hampshire. In line with Irving's *The Sketch Book*, Dodge included several stories that differ from Irving's work in being overly sentimental in tone and completely lacking in humor. There is a lengthy string of pieces with titles beginning with the word *country*—"Country Girls," "Country Weddings," "Country

Burial Places" (again a perennial favorite)—all clearly in imitation of Irving's vignettes of English rural scenes and activities.

But most significant and interesting is Dodge's piece "The Village," which is obviously a description of Pittsfield. Like all others in the collection, this essay is idyllic in tone, utterly affirmative and laudatory. Here, too, much of what Dodge writes is standard for the subject, dating back at least to Dwight's "Greenfield Hill" and repeated frequently in the four volumes of *Travels*. For example hardly a writer on New England omits mention of the elm trees that overarch the village streets. Thus Dodge devotes a paragraph to the famous Pittsfield Elm—later celebrated by Melville and now long since cut down, but once supreme among its species. Like Dwight he comments on architecture—the "neat white buildings . . . with tasteful and productive gardens running off in the rear."[3] Asserting that the village he is describing is typical of "the thousands spread all over the plains and hillsides of New England," he characterizes the inhabitants as "intelligent, thriving, and happy."[4] Tolerance, good feeling, attachment to old traditions are the norm. He sketches the local eccentrics with sympathy, regarding them as assets to the community, to which their presence contributes a certain distinctiveness. Important figures in the town's history are introduced with pride, one of them Parson A—(actually Thomas Allen), "the stanch defender of his country's rights,"[5] who had shouldered a musket at the Battle of Bennington. Elsewhere in the essay the village pastimes are described, such as angling, sleighriding, and hunting matches. The completed picture is one of almost heavenly bliss—an idealization surpassing Dwight's efforts in his most enthusiastic moments.

In literary skill Dodge fell far short of his model, Washington Irving, whose romanticism he adopted without his humor and gentle irony. Yet Dodge is not wholly contemptible in his role of a magazine journalist. He gave his readers what they wanted, and he was sincere in the feelings and impressions he conveyed. If he was sentimental to a fault by present standards, so were most other popular writers of the time. What he felt and thought about New England was what his reading public also felt and thought. Likewise, from every point of view he stands in totally unfavorable contrast with Hawthorne, who had preceded him as a writer of tales and sketches drawn from New England life and history. But the fact that Dodge had an appeal on his marginal literary level suggests the breadth of popular interest in New England subjects.

Seba Smith of Maine

Another author of rather meager reputation at present but widely read in his day was Seba Smith (1792–1868). A native of Maine and a graduate of Bowdoin College, he founded a newspaper, the *Courier*, in Portland in 1826, in which he began to publish a series of letters supposedly submitted by Jack Downing, a fictitious small-town Maine Yankee who commented in dialect and bad spelling on current political and other issues. More will be said later about Downing, who soon attracted national notice, and about other fictitious home-grown New England rustic philosophers, for they are an interesting outgrowth of the public's concept of the New England town. But now attention should be given to Seba Smith's volume of sketches and tales *'Way Down East; or, Portraitures of Yankee Life* (1854). The fare offered by this book, as by Dodge's, is local color of an anecdotal, descriptive sort. But unlike Dodge, Smith follows Irving's lead in presenting material drawn from the remote past as well as the present. The word *Portraitures* in the volume's subtitle is the equivalent of *Sketches* as used by Dodge, by Irving, and even by Catharine Sedgwick, whose *New England Tale* was subtitled *Sketches of New England Character and Life*. Seba Smith was writing in a prolific and popular tradition.

In choosing selections for *'Way Down East* Smith permitted himself considerable geographic latitude, because four of the stories are set in New York State, including one in New York City, and another is laid in Illinois. Perhaps Smith thought that he covered himself in this seeming discrepancy by his reference to "Yankee Life" in his subtitle, which to all but a New England chauvinist could be applied to other areas than that of the six states. At any rate, his characters are for the most part country people and the settings rural—with the exception of the tale "Peter Punctual," which deals with New Englanders in New York City. "A Dutch Wedding," which occurs in the Mohawk River Valley, and "The Pumpkin Freshet," which has its setting on the Susquehanna River among emigrants from Connecticut, could both have taken place in New England, as far as the traits of the characters and the incidents are concerned. Another piece, "Seating the Parish," which describes the ticklish process of assigning church pews to the members of a congregation according to their status in the community, is laid in the Long Island town of Brookhaven, which Smith carefully points out was settled by New Englanders and was formerly a part of Connecticut. The meeting at which the seating arrangements are determined resembles in every way a New England town meeting.

By broadening his geographic base Smith offended no one and doubtless pleased many. His style is easy, his tone light, and most of the material amusing. Though *'Way Down East* does not rank even as a minor classic, it still has the force of a book that aims to please an acceptable public taste while at the same time forming that taste. It reflected and added to the general reader's concept of the lighter side of life in New England and in several other rural areas.

In general *'Way Down East* does not focus on community life so much as on individuals and episodes. This, though true of Hawthorne's work also, is somewhat exceptional among writers dealing with rural and village New England. Most are concerned with individuals, but within the context of community environment and mores, and this emphasis is frequently indicated by the titles and subtitles of their books, whether of fiction, essays, or sketches, or a combination of all three: Harriet Beecher Stowe's *Oldtown Folks*, Sarah Orne Jewett's *Deephaven*, Henry Ward Beecher's *Norwood*, Mary Wilkins Freeman's *Pembroke*, Rowland Robinson's *Danvis Folks*. The list, which could be extended to great length, constitutes a simple indication of where the authors' and readers' interests lay.

George Lunt, Chronicler of Newburyport

George Lunt (1803–85), a native of Newburyport, Massachusetts, and an author of considerable reputation in his day, exemplifies this intense interest in community life. A graceful stylist, a close observer, and an enthusiast about all things connected with New England, Lunt deserves not to be entirely forgotten. His *Eastford, or Household Sketches* (1855), though in the form of a loosely constructed novel, is a compendium of folkways, local customs, and anecdotes, all gleaned from the author's memory and from his experiences in the town of his birth. A later book of his, *Old New England Traits* (1873), drops the pretense of being fiction and simply addresses itself to its subject—that is, to the recording of manners of the past. Drawing again from his own life in Newburyport, he touches on a great variety of topics, among them the former prestige of Hopkinsian theology, the carrying of New England ways into the West by emigrants, the absence of crime in the old days, the existence in colonial times of social rank (which he admits had not entirely disappeared), the distinctive New England pronunciation of English, the lingering of witchcraft in remote parts of the region, and the difficulties of the selectmen in determining the political preferences of the townspeople. The preoccupations of Lunt thus correspond closely to those of Dwight in his *Travels*. Though not so concerned with religion, Lunt finds the same strengths of character in New England as does Dwight, neither one admitting to the existence of any serious shortcomings. The chief difference is that Lunt recorded the blessings of a past to which the present compares unfavorably, while Dwight considered the civilization of New England in his day to be at its highest point, and hence he placed in it his confident hopes for the country's future.

But since Dwight's day, the fictional and nonfictional recorders of life in New England had come more and more to dwell nostalgically on bygone, or almost vanished, times. In the multitudinous writings on the subject there was an abundance of chapters and individual pieces with titles like "An Old-Time Thanksgiving," "An Old-Time Sabbath," "A Husking [or any other] Bee," "A Barn Raising," all dealing with customs and activities no longer widely practiced. Interest in country cemeteries and in gravestone inscriptions was keen, and people began to trace their genealogies and the histories of their towns. The discovery of some custom lingering from the distant past was cause for rejoicing. Nathaniel Hawthorne's writing perfectly illustrates these interests, as do many of the stories by Sarah Orne Jewett, who in addition to fiction wrote a meticulously researched pamphlet on the history of her native South Berwick, Maine, and frankly announced in the preface to *Deephaven* (1877), a depiction of York, Maine, that her purpose was to seek out and record the old ways that still lingered among the elderly citizens of that ancient seaport. But the authors were far from alone in their researches into the past. Large numbers of New Englanders and persons descended from New Englanders had similar concerns. In 1847 a periodical designed to appeal to such readers was founded. This was the *New England Historical and Genealogical Register*, still being published, which is a vast storehouse of all sorts of information relating to New England throughout its history.

Thus writers like Nathaniel Dodge, Seba Smith, and George Lunt were part of a trend in public interests that they very likely in turn did much to sustain. The number of authors of miscellanies containing stories, sketches, and essays was large, and all of them need not, and cannot, be discussed here. But among them three others—Thomas Wentworth Higginson, James Parton, and Rowland Robinson may serve as representative and somewhat meritorious in their own right.

Thomas Wentworth Higginson, Chronicler of Newport

In 1873 Thomas Wentworth Higginson (1823–1911) published a book with the title *Oldport Days,* Oldport very obviously being Newport, Rhode Island. Higginson was not a native of Newport, but he had lived there for a number of years, knew the town well, and was obviously fascinated by it. His intention was to transmit a sense of the atmosphere of the place as he had felt it. The subject was attractive, though demanding. Newport not only had fine coastal scenery and close contact with the ocean, but it also had a rich history and a complex social structure. Once among the most thriving seaports in the nation, it was in 1873 the victim of prolonged commercial decline. But as shipping fell off, the fortunes of the town as a resort rose. By the time Higginson was writing, it had long since been attracting, from all over the eastern and southern United States, persons of fashion and wealth, who built palatial "summer cottages" of twenty to fifty rooms and anchored their luxurious yachts in the excellent harbor.

Nor were the rich the only newcomers. Newport also drew its share of intellectuals and artists, among them Henry James, Sr., and his family. The contrast between the atmosphere of Newport in the summer months and that of the rest of the year, when the ancient town was left to its permanent residents, was enormous, and one of Higginson's tasks was to make this contrast as vivid as possible for his readers, many of whom knew the town only in its summer mood. His descriptions of the natural setting—the ocean, the famous cliffs, the bay, and the hills beyond—in its seasonal guises are designed to point up the contrast, though he emphasizes the winter and autumnal moods above those of the warm months. So also does he devote much attention to the old houses and wharves of the once-prosperous seaport and makes little mention of the showy villas of the summer visitors. Higginson is interested in highlighting the old New England town that still remained in his time and that carried on its own slow-paced but self-sufficient life during the ten months when the glitter and bustle of wealth and fashion were gone and even the memory of these was shut away much as the mansions were boarded up during the long off-season.

But basic community remained—perhaps as a similar heritage remains in much of our nation—drawing vitality from its old roots and from the beauty of its island setting. Permanence, then, is the theme of Higginson's book, and it is a theme that would be appropriate to the literary treatment of many New England towns that had become summer resorts but that each year, after the withdrawal of the urban vacationers, were left to their ancestral culture and values. *Oldport Days* is not a profound book; it was not intended to be such, though it does seem to say that beneath the superficial flashiness of modern American life there is a substratum of standards that have withstood the years and may continue to do so. The book's style is light; its contents are the usual Irving-like medley of descriptive essays, short tales, sketches. But in its day—and perhaps in our own—it would provide the outsider, or the visitor, with a deeper understanding of the town and the culture that produced it than he could get elsewhere. Newport in Higginson's time was an exclusive summer resort, but it was something else besides—a New England town with traditions, though not all of them admirable—and its sense of identity as part of a larger culture was quite alien to the New York bankers and Philadelphia industrialists who came there in their yachts in July and August. Noteworthy, rather than ironical, is the fact that Higginson, an arch-abolitionist and the leader of a black regiment in the Civil War, chose the New England town most closely

connected with the evil of slavery to demonstrate the enduring qualities of
New England civilization.

James Parton, A British-born New Yorker Writing on New England

James Parton (1822-91) was born in England but in early childhood was
brought to New York. Here he later made for himself a substantial literary
reputation, as the author of popular biographies of Horace Greeley, Aaron
Burr, Andrew Jackson, and other famous Americans. He also worked on
the weekly magazine *Home Journal*, edited by the fashionable author
Nathaniel Parker Willis, a New Englander by birth, whose sister Sara Willis
(a sentimental essayist better known as Fanny Fern) Parton married. In
1869 Parton published in the *Atlantic Monthly* a piece ironically titled "The
Mean Yankees at Home," later included in his volume *Topics of the Times*
(1871). The Yankees whom Parton described were in fact the very opposite
of "mean." Drawing from observations he had made in the Berkshires, in
or near Stockbridge, he was moved to nothing but praise.

He began his essay with a famous anecdote concerning Cyrus Field, who
as a way of celebrating the success of his Atlantic cable wished to treat the
paupers of his native Stockbridge to a banquet, but was informed by the
selectmen that they could find no paupers. Thus launched into his subject,
Parton presented a lengthy list of assets characteristic of New England
towns. An illiterate, he affirmed, was a rarity. Black people enjoyed equal
political and educational privileges with whites, though they lived in separate sections of the towns. As Parton saw them, they seemed to illustrate
various ancient stereotypes of their race: carefree happiness, a slight propensity toward thievery, robust animal health. Most striking about the Yankees, Parton thought, was their possession of "qualities requisite for
holding a public meeting in a higher degree than any other people,"[6] and
he commented on the irony that a people believing in the doctrine of total
depravity could devise a town-meeting system dependent on the wills of the
people in general.

Parton described the Berkshire region as being economically prosperous, with a healthy diversity of industries and thriving farms (others have
found that agriculture was in serious trouble in the area at that time).
Though he conceded that some of the factory towns were ugly, he spoke
with admiration of the villages, especially the older ones, the beauty of
which was preserved and enhanced by improvement societies modeled
after one founded in Stockbridge in 1853. He was impressed also by the
libraries and literary societies present in almost every community. As for
religion, he noted approvingly that the old-time Puritan intolerance had

softened, so that even Roman Catholicism was experiencing a moderate measure of acceptance. On the other hand, he alluded with some disdain to the growing numbers of "foreigners" (not only in the factory towns), who he believed were not being rapidly enough assimilated.

Parton also had considerable to say about the composition of village and rural populations. Along with other commentators he noted the preponderance of women. The men had left in large numbers either for the West or the large cities, with the result that some communities might have twenty marriageable girls "and not one marriageable young man."[7] For example, five of the six sons of the prominent Field family of Stockbridge had left Stockbridge. Like many another observer, Parton remarked on the great number of eccentrics in New England communities, but did not consider them as liabilities. Lastly he commented on the contribution of summer residents in the variety of rural life for several months each year.

Few writers have outdone—or equaled—Parton in his admiration for New England towns in all their aspects. These communities he regarded as future models of the whole world living in harmony. Thus, without Dwight's religious fervor, he curiously echoed, probably unknowingly, Dwight's millennial expectations for the region.

Rowland Robinson of Vermont

Vermont Quaker Rowland Robinson (1833-1900) is the last of the nineteenth-century writers of New England sketches, essays, and tales, as distinguished from those authors who wrote fiction almost exclusively. The fact is that much of Robinson's writing defies classification as either fiction or nonfiction. The characters who keep reappearing in his books and shorter pieces are, technically, not actual people, but they are so closely based on rural and village types that they cannot be called fictitious. He is not a writer of short stories and novels, as Sarah Orne Jewett or Mary Wilkins Freeman are, for his characters, plots and situations are scarcely the products of his imagination, as theirs were. In reading his works one seldom feels that one is reading anything other than factual reporting.

Robinson's locale was the Champlain Valley near Ferrisburg, Vermont, about eighteen miles south of Burlington, and areas in the nearby foothills of the Green Mountains to the eastward—more specifically, the towns of Starksboro and Lincoln, which in his writing he combines into the composite quasi-fictional town of Danvis. Like William Faulkner, though in no way comparable to him in artistic genius or psychological insight, Robinson staked out a literary territory corresponding to an actual geographical area in its cultural and physical features. Robinson concerned himself with many aspects of this rather limited region that could easily be included in a square of fifteen miles on each side, but that he found more than adequate for the needs of a lifetime of writing, much as Thoreau had found Concord. The history of Lake Champlain which figured importantly in the French and Indian Wars, in the Revolution, in the dispute with New York State, and in the War of 1812, carries him somewhat farther afield, but even these events are for the most part narrated in the words of people living in Danvis or thereabouts. He did, however, write a history of the state, *Vermont: A Study of Independence* (1892), which is today perhaps the best known of his books. In his childhood some of the older inhabitants could tell him of the struggles with the British and the Yorkers, for the deeds of Ethan Allen, Remember Baker, and John Stark were on everyone's lips. The naval battles on Lake Champlain in the War of 1812 were virtually contemporary local history. Within his own lifetime Robinson witnessed the activities of the Underground Railroad, on which his Quaker father made his house a stopping place, providing a secret chamber for the fugitives. Robinson wrote several pieces about these abolitionist activities.

But most of Robinson's writing did not have to do with military or other momentous historical events. Like so many authors concerned with the New England countryside, the past of the area interested him more than the present, and his main fascination was with the way of life of the preceding generation or two. Thus in his introductory note to *Danvis Folks* (1894)—highly typical of his output—he states that he had written "with less purpose of telling any story than of recording the manners, customs, and speech in vogue fifty or sixty years ago in certain parts of New England. Manners have changed, many customs have become obsolete, and though the dialect is yet spoken . . . it is passing away."[8] But elsewhere he states that beneath the superficial changes "the Vermonter of to-day [1892], when brought to the test, proves to be of the same tough fibre as were his ancestors."[9] Nor had surface things changed as much as Robinson feared. Even today, eighty years after he wrote *Danvis Folks*, the rural New England he described is still recognizable in parts of the three northern states.

The town of Danvis is prototypal and timeless. It is representative of the multitude of up-country towns that Dwight had described in his *Travels* with such optimism as to their influence in perpetuating New England ways and values, particularly Christianity as interpreted by the Congregationalists. Yet Robinson is not so laudatory as Dwight, though he seldom condemns. A Quaker, and hence a member of a tiny minority, he has little to say about religious practices in Danvis. Nor does he dwell much on education, and, in fact, many of his characters are only meagerly educated. In Danvis education takes second place to more serious occupations, such as hunting and fishing. In one sketch Robinson describes a school meeting that, having degenerated into a chaotic wrangle, ends only when the partipants rush off to chase some raccoons that have been sighted nearby.

Robinson is not blind to some real shortcomings in the social structure of rural Vermont and in the conditions of village life. In a realistic story, "The Fourth of July at Highfield Poorhouse,"[10] the reader is introduced to the dismal New England way of caring for the indigent and is made vividly aware that all was not well, economically at least, with the region. The Highfield poorhouse is run by a mean-minded and penny-pinching woman who forbids the inmates, including two charming orphan children, to engage in any form of pleasure, even on the Fourth of July, that most sacred of local holidays. When the orphans celebrate defiantly by blowing up some elm logs with gunpowder, a selectman intervenes and takes them to the local festivities. Later the selectman's wife adopts the children.

In another story, "The Purification of Cornbury,"[11] the selectmen perform less creditably. A local woman, who is a member of the "Moral Reform Society," nags her husband, "Square" (Squire) Dana, the head selectman, into going with the other selectmen to turn out of doors a woman "living in sin" with her employee and his daughter. The brow-beaten officials reluctantly comply, and after some difficulty evict the woman and move her furniture into the yard. Despite a happy ending, which need not concern us here, the selectmen are made to appear spineless and unworthy of their public trust. Robinson looked upon New England town institutions somewhat more critically than did Dwight or most of the historians of the time, though Robinson was by no means a debunker.

In a piece titled "An Old-Time March Meeting," published posthumously in the *Atlantic Monthly* in 1902, Robinson presents with humor and realism the workings of town democracy. He begins by quoting verbatim a Ferrisburg warning of town meeting as posted sometime in the 1840s. Thus, though Robinson may have been too young to attend this particular meeting, it resembled many in which he later took part. He then proceeds to describe the "town house" of Danvis, "an unpainted, weather-beaten, clapboarded building of one story, with one rough, plastered room,"[12] which also served on alternate Sabbaths as a meetinghouse for the Congregationalists and the Methodists—a combination of religious and civic use as old as New England. On the appointed day the freemen, or voters, converge on this unpretentious building to elect officers and attend to town business, including the levying of taxes and the support of the poor. First the townspeople choose a moderator, then a clerk, the selectmen, and so on, till it is time to elect the hogreeves, or, as they were apparently called in Vermont, the haywards, or hog-howards. At this point the mood of the meeting shifts from seriousness to humor. Let Robinson tell of it in his own words:

> It was a common custom in Vermont, in the first half of this century, to permit all kinds of stock to run at large in the highways, which made it necessary to appoint several poundkeepers and as many haywards, or hog-howards, as they were commonly called, whose duty was to keep road-ranging swine within the limits of the highways. Six poundkeepers were now elected, and their barnyards constituted pounds. There was a merry custom, of ancient usage, of electing the most recently married widower to the office of hayward, and it then chanced that Parson Nehemiah Doty, the worthy pastor of the Congregationalists, had been but a fortnight married to his second wife. So an irreverent member of his own flock nominated him for hayward. The nomination was warmly seconded, and he was almost unanimously elected, even the deacons responding very faintly when the negative vote was called; for the parson was a man of caustic humor, and each of its many victims realized that this was a rare opportunity for retaliation. Laughter and applause subsided to decorous silence when the venerable man arose to acknowledge the doubtful honor which had been conferred upon him; and he spoke in the solemn and measured tones that marked the delivery of his sermons, but the clerical austerity of his face was lightened a little by a twinkle of his cold gray eyes:—
> "Mr. Moderator and fellow townsmen, in the more than a score of years that I have labored among you, I have endeavored faithfully to perform, so far as in me lay, the duties of a shepherd: to keep within the fold the sheep which were committed to my care, to watch vigilantly that none strayed from it, and to be the humble means of leading some into its shelter. Thus while you were my sheep I have acted as your shepherd, but since you are no longer sheep I will endeavor to perform as faithfully the office of your hayward."[13]

One recalls that Emerson, newly arrived in Concord and newly remarried, was elected hogreeve at his first town meeting. The joke was standard, and in these two instances, at least, the victims were clergymen—though this is probably coincidence. Those who attend New England town meetings in our time will notice that this sort of spicing of serious business with levity still persists, has indeed become part of the institution. Some of the ancient and obsolete offices like that of hogreeve are still filled solely for fun. Other opportunities for a touch of lightness present themselves. For example, in a certain town one of the citizens had the habit of falling asleep and snoring loudly toward the end of each meeting. When all business had been completed, the moderator would announce that a motion for adjournment had been made by the sleeping member. Would anyone second the motion? Amid an outburst of hilarity there would be a dozen seconds and the meeting would terminate—and as likely as not the sleeper had been feigning all along simply to perpetuate a merry custom.

An institution that can function with an infusion of humor, even of irreverence, is probably on a rather sound foundation. The March meeting at Danvis, as Robinson describes it, had its lighter moments, but much of it was conducted on a very serious level; and it became a bit appalling when the question arose as to how to provide for the local paupers. In New England until quite recently the towns were responsible for aiding the poor—hence the phrase *on the town* to denote a state of indigence. And the poor usually did not fare so well. The town either maintained a poorhouse—the lesser of two evils—or it "let out" the care of the poor to the lowest bidders—an arrangement that would ensure lean times for the unfortunate paupers. The evils of the latter system are demonstrated in Sarah Orne Jewett's story "The Town Poor."[14] In Robinson's "An Old-Time March Meeting," this procedure is followed also. Robinson describes not only the despair of the recipients of such aid but also the indignation of the more sensitive voters at the auctioning off of human misery, and his own disapproval is evident. Robinson, as a Quaker, was just sufficiently outside the generality of the townspeople without being alienated from them, to see with the critical eye. On the whole the March meeting he records is a success, a credit to the town, but it is not without major blemishes; it is an eminently human, and hence imperfect, occurrence—which within a few hours can be the occasion of a glow of approval, a burst of good, honest laughter, and a surge of indignation.

Robinson's Quakerism is more evident in his description of another New England institution—now long since extinct—the June Training Day. Singled out by John Adams as one of the cornerstones of American freedom, the training of troops of militia in New England towns for many years had contributed to the survival of frontier communities and to the successful waging of colonial wars and the winning of the struggle for independence. But after the eighteenth century the training became an anachronism and was taken less and less seriously and finally was abandoned altogether. Robinson looked upon this custom even less favorably than most, and in *Danvis Folks*, in the sketch "June Training," he bluntly brands the exercises as farcical, and his description of them is one of his more humorous efforts. Yet, though well-merited disparagement is heaped upon an outworn institution, the sense of community that still perpetuates it is honored.

A sense of community, indeed, is the pervasive impression conveyed in Robinson's writing. The fictional town of Danvis, which is most frequently the setting of his stories, is on the whole friendly and self-sufficient; but according to Robinson it has lost some of its neighborliness. Like many rural New England writers during the years after the Civil War, he was in the grip of a nostalgia for the past. Particularly, he regretted the dispersion of Vermonters and other New Englanders to the West—to the 'Hio, as they called it, and elsewhere. And in his book *Vermont: A Study of Independence* he deplores the large-scale influx of French-Canadians and other aliens— poor substitutes, he thought, for the vanished Yankees. Twenty or more residents of Danvis have emigrated, taking advantage of the comparative ease of travel via the newly opened Champlain and Erie Canals and the steamers on the Great Lakes.

Only the elderly were reluctant to depart, held by an attachment to the native soil that Robinson dramatizes in a short tale "The Goodwin Spring."[15] A couple, grown too old to continue farming their hilly acres, think of selling, but they know of no buyers except French-Canadians, against whom they entertain the prejudice common to their time and place. On their land is a spring of water of uncommon purity. In the midst of their quandary the husband fetches a pail of the water, from which they drink reverently. The spring, unbeknown to them, has become a symbol of the integrity of their lives on their rocky farm. As in Robert Frost's "Directive," the water exists to be drunk and to make the drinkers whole. On a less spiritual level, to Robinson it may represent the "purity" of the old Vermont stock now threatened by newcomers from foreign lands.

Humor: Seba Smith's Major Jack Downing

Robinson's humorous treatment of the Danvis town meeting and the fact of the essay's publication in the *Atlantic Monthly* are marks of a continuing tradition of Yankee humor that had had its inception some sixty-five years earlier in Seba Smith's creation of the Down-East farmer's son, Jack Downing. We have already glanced at Smith's book of Yankee portraitures, *'Way Down East,* but Downing is the character for whom he is best known today. In 1830 Smith began to write and publish in his own newspaper, the Portland *Courier,* a series of letters signed with the name Jack Downing. Smith himself was from rural Maine, and Jack Downing of Downingville "'way down-east in the State of Maine," as he gave his address, was of identical background. During his many-sided career he became commissioned a major of the Downingville militia, which saw inaction in the bloodless "Madawaska War" (a dispute with Great Britain over the Maine-New Brunswick boundary, ending with the Webster-Ashburton Treaty). His father was a perennial "squire" (justice of the peace) and moderator of the town meetings. Others of Jack's relatives were intensely interested in local politics, as indeed he was himself. He was thoroughly steeped in the ways of New England town government.

While still a youth Jack set off for Portland to peddle a load of "ax-handles and a few notions."[16] Not being lucky in selling his wares, he remained in the city some time, observed the workings of the Maine legislature meeting there, and wrote home his impressions—the letter being printed in the *Courier*. As letter followed letter, they were reprinted in newspapers elsewhere and Jack Downing soon became nationally known. He ran for governor of Maine; he ran for president of the United States; he became acquainted with Andrew Jackson and commented in his sly, ironical way on the policies of the Jackson administration. Smith himself did not remain in Portland; he wandered about in the literary and journalistic scene and eventually acclimated himself to New York, where he served in various editorial and authorial capacities. In his last years he was a resident of Patchogue, Long Island.

Major Jack Downing is in many ways authentic. His dialect is the best reproduction, in this author's opinion, of Down-East speech yet to appear: a speech that can still be heard on the offshore islands and in the remote inland regions of the state. Like Sarah Orne Jewett, the only close competitor, Smith caught the rhythms as well as the dialectal words and the pronunciations; and the essence of New England rural speech is in its rhythms. But Smith caught another more important quality of the New England villager—a combination of innocence that is at least half feigned and an astuteness based on common sense that is not in the least feigned. Smith gently satirizes Downing's seeming naiveté, but generally approves of his native wit. For example, in the second letter from Portland, Jack writes about a certain legislator, a Mr. Roberts, who, because his election was in dispute, was denied a seat in the assembly. Downing writes: "I can't see why they need to make such a fuss about it. As they've got seats enough, why don't they let him have one, and not keep him standing up for three weeks in the lobby and round the fire. It's a plaguey sight worse than being on a standing committee, for they say the standing committees have a chance to set most every day."[17]

One's first impression on reading such remarks may be that Downing is simply an ignorant rube. But then one reconsiders. Downing is not so innocent or so ignorant as he seems; he must realize that the phrase *seating a delegate* is metaphorical and that the word *standing* in reference to a committee does not allude to physical posture. Thus the reader recognizes that Jack Downing is acting a part—is playing with the reader's credulity— for no one could be that stupid or "numb," as they say in Maine. Jack is impersonating the rube. His role is self-conscious, just as, according to Constance Rourke and J. R. Lowell, the country Yankee's dialect is self-conscious.[18] Secure in his awareness of the practicality and, as he sees it, integrity of town-meeting government—in which the voice of the people speaks directly and without possible misinterpretation by representatives— he can look upon the parliamentary shenanigans of a legislature from a standpoint of uncorrupted innocence. The rube is thus also the sage, and his quaint dialect, the more "authentic" the better, contributes to his identity as both. What has worked in Downingville, under generations of Downing leadership, may seem primitive when compared to state and national governmental procedures. But the Downingville way has been successful, and the state and national systems have been known frequently to falter. The message is: good old Yankee common sense cannot be beaten—and the avid readers of Jack Downing accepted the message gladly. The countryman from Down East is presented as a hick, but also he is presented as possessing a fund of native good sense and basic morality that the higher levels of government sadly lack. To these readers the towns still were the source of values, still represented the desirable norm—which the state and national governments would do well to abide by.

Jack Downing is essentially Seba Smith himself. The ironical content of Downing's comments may seem to be the work of a professional writer rather than of a simple villager; yet Downing and Smith had much the same origins, though the latter went on to get an education at Bowdoin College. At any rate, the possibility of a relatively uneducated Down-Easter engaging in effective irony, along with a pose of calculated naiveté, cannot be discounted. One need not have gone to Bowdoin to achieve the following put-down of Manifest Destiny, though one would need a certain amount of political sophistication: "I dreamt t'other night that we had got through annexin' all North and South America; and then I thought our whole country was turned into a monstrous great ship of war, and Cape Horn was the bowsprit and Mr. [President] Polk the captain. And the captain was walking the deck with his mouth shet, and everybody was looking at him and wondering what he was goin' to do next. At last he sung out, 'Put her about; we'll sail across now and take Europe, and Asha, and Africa in tow—don't stop for bird's-egging among the West India Islands; we can pick them up as we come back along—crowd all sail now and let her have it.'"[19] The last sentence is pure Maine dialect and typical Downing irony of overstatement, as the following, spoken on the same subject of annexation, is of understatement: "Uncle Joshua always says, in nine cases out of ten it costs more to rob an orchard than it would to buy the apples."[20] Earlier, Downing had calculated that it would take twenty-five years of warfare to annex all of Mexico. The seeming bumpkin, as well as being a cracker-barrel philosopher, is a cracker-barrel diplomat of the type that in the weeks before town meeting would discuss amicably, but none the less trenchantly, the merits and demerits of building such-and-such a bridge or setting off another school district. Irony, a low-keyed voice, dialect spiced with folk sayings, understatement or overstatement—all would be employed as a way of making points with as little offense as possible to anyone.

James Russell Lowell: *The Biglow Papers*

Seba Smith set a pattern that found many imitators. The whole subject of Yankee humor is too large for this study and is somewhat extraneous to it. But mention—necessarily brief—should be made of another fictional Yankee villager very much akin to Jack Downing. This is James Russell Lowell's Hosea Biglow of the well-known *Biglow Papers*, which appeared in two series, the first in 1848 focusing on the Mexican War and the second in 1867 dealing for the most part with the Civil War and its aftermath. It was possibly to Lowell's disadvantage that, unlike Seba Smith, he was not a countryman, though the Cambridge he grew up in was quite rural in atmosphere. Seba Smith wrote more or less in his native idiom and the result was a highly authentic reproduction of Maine speech. Lowell, by upbringing, spoke a more formal English, that of the educated classes of the Boston area, so that in Hosea's speech he was attempting something somewhat alien to him, though he claimed to know rural New England intimately and asserted that writing in its dialect was like writing in his native tongue.[21] At any rate, he knew what he was doing; in his introductions, especially that of the second series, he discourses accurately and lengthily on the peculiarities of New England rural dialect and echoes Dwight in claiming that New Englanders speak their language "with a far higher popular average of correctness"[22] than the British country people. Yet as one listens to Hosea Biglow's speech, one senses that it falls slightly short of the real thing—and not solely because it is written in verse.

It may be asked: Why did Lowell make the effort in these *Biglow Papers* to present his criticism and discussion of national events in the dialect of a backcountry New England farmer? One answer—a simple and quite convincing one—would be that Seba Smith had led the way. But there is another important reason. By the time Lowell began writing *The Biglow Papers*, the myth of the New England town as a breeding ground for pure democracy and practical, yet somewhat moralistic, people notable for wit, common sense, and honest thinking had become a matter of widespread belief. The general public had been prepared by the Downing letters for the first series of *The Biglow Papers*, which initially appeared in the Boston *Courier* in 1846. Later a more select readership was captured by the second series, which was published in the *Atlantic Monthly* during the Civil War. The belief in the folk wisdom of the New England villager had thus spread to people of a wide range of education and sophistication. One is reminded of the high prestige that the peasants of western Ireland enjoyed among the intelligentsia of Dublin during the struggles for home rule and independence.

It should be carefully noted that Lowell went to great lengths to empha-

size the village background of Hosea Biglow, just as Seba Smith never let
the reader forget that Jack Downing was the product of the Down-East
town of Downingville. Indeed, Smith from time to time had Downing
return there, as if to reinvigorate at its source his inborn wit and good
sense, to say nothing of refreshing his dialect. Jack Downing is a product of
Downingville, and no mistake; and Hosea Biglow is a product of the rural
town of Jaalem, and no mistake about that. Homer Wilbur, the Jaalem
pastor, ludicrously pedantic though he is in his comments about Hosea,
seems to authenticate him, so to speak, as a genuine product of New England village culture. But more important, Homer Wilbur's remarks, along
with the other mock editorial apparatuses, drive home to the reader that
Hosea is not merely presenting his own opinions; he is a spokesman for his
typical New England community. The grass roots of New England, if not of
America, are speaking. The closely knit community, the church, the town
meeting all form a background that lends prestige to Hosea's utterances.
He is the voice—his readers would remember—of those New England
towns which figured so critically in the American Revolution and had been
singled out by Thomas Jefferson and John Adams as strongholds of
American democracy. One could laugh at the misspellings, the violations of
standard grammar, the quaint idioms and metaphors—and one was supposed to laugh at these. But one could not laugh at the sound ideas cloaked
in this regional speech. Indeed, the ideas gained prestige from the speech,
and the speech from the ideas. New England country dialect, for many,
seemed to be the true *vox populi* in America.

Hosea's last "Paper" in the second series is described as having been
delivered before the Jaalem March meeting of 1866. Dealing with Recon-
struction, it is critical of the policies and procedures being followed in the
South and offers Yankee common and moral sense as a corrective to a
deplorable situation. But it is the town meeting that is hearing the speech
and that approves of it. The conscience and the best political judgment in
the nation, Lowell implies in this and, other of *The Biglow Papers,* is to be
found in up-country towns of New England. The readers of the *Atlantic
Monthly* and of the daily newspapers, at least in the North, were ready to
accept this assumption. It is noteworthy that as far back as 1775 John
Trumbull in *M'Fingal* had used a fictional town meeting as a forum in
which to present the opposing views of Tories and Revolutionaries, much
to the advantage of the latter, of course. There was nothing original in
Lowell's setting for Hosea's speech.

Oddly, however, Hosea Biglow and his Cambridge-born creator were
less subtle in their approach than Jack Downing and his small-town creator,
Seba Smith. For example, Lowell makes much more use of misspellings
and supposedly phonetic spellings than does Smith, who attempts to repro-

duce Downing's dialect not only through orthography but through characteristic prose rhythms. Lowell, writing in verse, denied himself this element of rhythmic realism—or perhaps attempted and failed, for, as Frost's poems attest, it is possible to catch in verse the cadences of New England speech. Also, Lowell failed to reproduce Yankee irony and indirection as well as Smith does. Hosea blurts out, "Ez fer war, I call it murder."[23] But Downing, commenting on the Mexican War as was Hosea, launches deadpan into a calculation of the cost, which he presents as reasonable, of annexing Mexico. Mexico City has been seized, and

> Santa Anna has cleared out the night afore with what troops he had left, and is scouring about the country to get some more places ready for us to annex. When he gets another place all ready for the ceremony, and gets it well fortified, and has an army of twenty or thirty thousand men in the forts and behind the breastworks, we shall march down upon 'em with five or six thousand men, and go through the flurry [note understatement]. After they have shot down about half of us, the rest of us will climb in, over the mouths of their cannons, and annex the place; and so on, one after another [note matter-of-factness].
>
> It is pretty hard work annexin' in this way; but that is the only way it can be done. It will be necessary for the President to keep hurrying on his men this way to keep our ranks full, for we've got a great deal of ground to go over yet. What we've annexed in Mexico, so far, isn't but a mere circumstance to what we've got to do.
>
> Some think the business isn't profitable; but it's only because they haven't ciphered into it fur enough to understand it. Upon an average, we get at least ten to one for our outlay, any way you can figure it up—I mean in the matter of people. Take, for instance the City of Mexico. It cost us only two or three thousand men to annex it; and we get at least one hundred and fifty thousand in that city, and some put it as high as two hundred thousand. Some may find fault with the *quality* of the people we get in this country, jest as if that had anything to do with the merits of the case. They ought to remember that in a Government like ours, where the people is used to voting, and where every nose counts one, it is the *number* we are to stan' about in annexin', and not the quality, by no means.[24]

Jack Downing is the kind of Yankee who would cast his vote for the recently remarried minister as hogreeve and mean it as a token of good will rather than an insult—as not only the individual voter but the whole town, including the victim, would fully understand. Similarly, the countryman could recommend as national policy the slaughter of tens of thousands of men over a period of many years and show how good the bargain would be and expect the reader or listener to interpret his words as saying exactly the opposite of their surface meaning. But for this kind of irony to function, one has to assume a rather homogeneous society. The New England town was such, and in the town meetings irony would not be likely to backfire. Apparently, also, the whole Northern United States of the 1840s was sufficiently homogeneous for irony like Downing's to serve its purpose. In our mid-twentieth century it is noteworthy that no such irony was leveled against the Vietnam War, which surely was as deserving of it as the Mexican War. Will Rogers, dead these forty or more years, was the last who could approach a national audience on political issues in the manner of Seba Smith speaking through Jack Downing or James R. Lowell speaking through Hosea Biglow.

The message that the two rustic commentators, Downing and Biglow, delivered on the subject of Manifest Destiny and expansionist wars was partly in contrast and partly in harmony with the millennial utterances of the preachers like Timothy Dwight and Lyman Beecher. These two, as we have seen, considered the New England way, especially as it existed in the villages, to be predestined to save the nation and ultimately the world. Lowell and Smith obviously did not subscribe to any such grandiose concept. But they believed that New England rural folk possessed enough sense and common decency to act as a corrective to national military excesses. In the Yankee towns the moral tutelage of the church and the principle of democracy embodied in the town meeting had bred restraint, a respect for others, a sense of balance that was conspicuously lacking among large segments of the population, especially in Washington and elsewhere south of the Mason-Dixon Line. To a certain extent, then, these comic village characters provided the conscience as well as the simple reasonableness that the nation badly needed, and in this way they may be said to have exemplified the beneficial New England influence that the preachers had so enthusiastically celebrated.

But insofar as the Downings and Biglows deplored the spread of American influence and power by military means, they were thwarting the spread of the American way and the New England way beyond the already established boundaries. Settlers from the New England and other northeastern states were fanning out across the northern half of the nation, carrying with them their religion (by no means always Congregational), their commitment to education, and, in many areas, varying modifications of town-meeting government. There was no strong objection to this except from the Southern states. But New Englanders like Lowell and Smith apparently did not believe that the destiny of the nation included the spreading of American ways and ideals by means of military conquest. They were doubtless well aware that in large sections of the country the democracy of the New England towns had not been introduced or taken root—as the prophets of an earlier time believed it would—and they of course could observe that the Americanism being spread in the Southwest was characterized by such undemocratic and supposedly un-Yankee institutions as slavery. Thus the humorous New England commentators assumed the role of injecting the values and common sense of their own region into the stream of national policy. Their hope was to stem the excesses resulting from messianic notions that characterized manifest destiny—which, ironically, had much in common with the old Puritan sense of divine mission. The nation had lost its sense of balance, these commentators were saying, and Lowell saw its main hope in a reaffirmation of the older values of rural New England.

Structure and Origins of Town Government

> The history of New England is written imperishably on the face
> of a continent, and in characters as beneficent as they are endur-
> ing. In the Old World national pride feeds itself with the record
> of battles and conquests;—battles which proved nothing and
> settled nothing; conquests which shifted a boundary on the map,
> and put one ugly head instead of another on the coin which the
> people paid to the tax-gatherer. But wherever the New En-
> glander travels among the sturdy commonwealths which have
> sprung from the seed of the Mayflower, churches, schools, col-
> leges, tell him where the men of his race have been, or their
> influence has penetrated; and an intelligent freedom is the monu-
> ment of conquests whose results are not to be measured in square
> miles. Next to the fugitives whom Moses led out of Egypt, the
> little shipload of outcasts who landed at Plymouth two centuries
> and a half ago are destined to influence the future of the world.
> James Russell Lowell, "New England Two Centuries Ago"
> (1865)[1]

Next to theology and church polity as major concerns in nineteenth-
century writing about New England towns and their culture was an interest
in the origins and structure of town-meeting government. For the most
part, the authors thus far considered were writing about the towns as they
existed a hundred and fifty or more years after their founding, though in
Dwight's and Stowe's works we do get occasional glimpses into the colonial
past, along with some theorizing about it. Full focus on the origins of New
England institutions did not occur until almost the middle of the
nineteenth century, when a group of historians and social scientists began
to direct their attention to the development and roots of local governments
in the region's early settlements.

Church and Civil Government

The towns that Dwight and others described in such Edenic terms were
the result of five or six generations of New England experience, not to

mention European backgrounds and influences. The first settlements—like Plymouth, Salem, and Boston—were, of course, founded by groups directly from England, many of whom, but by no means all, shared the same dissenting religious views and perhaps had been neighbors or fellow parishioners in the old country or, in the case of the Pilgrims, as exiles in Holland. The common background and religious convictions among at least a nucleus of the first settlers made for oneness of purpose and contributed to political and social harmony, though these communities were not free from discord, as the cases of John Lyford and John Oldham in Plymouth and of Anne Hutchinson and Roger Williams in Massachusetts Bay amply testify.

In addition these first colonies were business enterprises as well as havens for worship in forms not tolerated in England. The colonists themselves, as well as their backers in London, expected a profit from their investment of effort and money. Thus, though Governor Bradford likened the Pilgrims' venture to that of Joshua entering into the promised land, and Governor Winthrop could speak of the future Boston as a city on a hill, both were concerned with the fur trade, the fisheries, agriculture, or any other source of profit. Nor did the two motives necessarily clash. According to Calvinism, which was the theology favored by the settlers, worldly success could be considered a sign of approval by God, Who would naturally see to the material comforts of His elect.

Each of the two motives or impulses—the spiritual and the materialistic—found expression in two autonomous institutions—the church and the civil government, which in theory, though hardly in fact, were entirely separate. The Congregational form of church polity, which had its beginnings in England and its full development in the New World, was adopted by almost all Connecticut and Massachusetts churches from earliest times and later prevailed in other parts of New England, including the Baptists in Rhode Island, who, though differing in theology, followed Congregational polity. Also, in all New England colonies except Rhode Island, the Congregational Church was the established religion, supported by taxes levied on all persons in a town, and it remained so in several of the states until well into the nineteenth century. However, the individual congregations were virtually autonomous everywhere except in Connecticut, where, after the adoption of the Saybrook Platform in 1708, a polity somewhat resembling that of the Presbyterian Church was followed, with the result that the self-determination of congregations was to a degree, but far from entirely, curtailed.

Once a congregation was gathered and the members covenanted after the model of the primitive church, the members would elect from their number several elders and deacons. For their pastor, if the congregation was a large one, they might have to search outside their group, for only men of thorough learning and piety were considered eligible for such positions. Sometimes, as in early Plymouth, years would pass before suitable clergymen could be found, and in these cases the elders would conduct the meetings for worship, though they were not empowered to administer communion or to baptize. When a qualified candidate was found, the congregation would vote whether or not to appoint him. If approved, he would then be ordained by a simple laying on of hands by the elders and the neighboring ministers. The new incumbent would, of course, have been carefully examined as to his theology, and he would have covenanted with his congregation to preach only in accord with the agreed-upon doctrines. If he deviated theologically or was otherwise displeasing, he could be removed from his office by vote of the church membership. Membership, however, was limited usually to those who qualified as having had "experiences" indicating they were among the elect; and they would have to present "evidence" of such experiences, though the rigidity of these requirements varied in different places and times. By no means all inhabitants of a town would have full voting privileges in church affairs, but for full members the church was democratically governed.

The voting qualifications in the civil affairs of the towns were more democratic than those of the churches. Any male inhabitant twenty-one years old or older with a small property or income was eligible to participate in town meetings and vote on town matters and in the election of local officers. Only for a brief time—and that in Massachusetts—was full church membership a prerequisite for freeman (that is, voting) status. However, in the election of colony officers or town representatives to the General Courts, or legislatures, they had to be church members even after that requirement was dropped for voting on town matters. The towns, usually isolated from one another by distance and bad roads, had to be as self-sufficient as possible and needed the cooperation of all inhabitants, rich and poor, church members or not. Thus the democracy of the town governments was based on necessity rather than on any specific ideology. A community on the edge of a wilderness—and most New England towns were so situated when first settled—could not exist long without solidarity and singleness of purpose among all its people. The most practical way to achieve this was to have everyone included in the planning and policymaking of the town.[2] It should always be remembered, however, that the towns were created by acts of colony or, later, state legislatures, which spelled out the duties and functions of the town governments and specified the numbers and types of town officers.

Early American Commentators on New England Town Government

New Englanders have from earliest times been fascinated by the past, not only of the region as a whole but of their individual towns. Governor Bradford in his *Of Plimmoth Plantation* and Governor Winthrop in his *Journal* each wrote his colony's history as it was happening. Bradford intended his work, organized in the form of annals, to be read by future generations for the lessons it contained about God's and man's doings in the trying first decades of the plantation. One of his main concerns was to preserve Plymouth as a closely knit civil and religious community, and within twenty-five years after its founding the reader finds Bradford lamenting the loosening of community bonds, the dispersal of the old settlers to other towns, and the onset of instability and wickedness. Though much can be learned from *Of Plimmoth Plantation* in regard to church and government affairs on both a colony and town level—and we can clearly discern the beginning of typical New England town government there[3]—Bradford conveys this sort of information only incidentally. A fine social historian, probably without especially intending to be, he is in no way a political scientist.

Much the same can be said of many later colonial New England historians. Authors like Cotton Mather, Thomas Hutchinson, and William Hubbard do not involve themselves in analyses of the economic and governmental structure of the towns or colonies. Some, like Bradford, are interested in holding up the past as a model for the decadent present. Others are mainly concerned with assessing God's relationship with New England over the years as evidenced in His providences. Many, of course, combined these two intentions, and from the time of John Cotton the historians, particularly if they were clergymen, were motivated by a desire to explain the "New England way" in religion. But notably lacking among these historians, diarists, and writers of annals was an interest in any but the religious, moral, and social aspects of town life; to civil government they paid very little attention. This kind of interest did not develop significantly until after the Revolution. Its emergence then was doubtless a result of an intensifying sense of national identity.

The part played by the New England town meetings in the years immediately before and during the Revolution attracted nationwide attention. The historical facts were that the Revolution began in New England, that some of the most devoted advocates of independence, like Samuel Adams, James Otis, and Joseph Warren, used the Boston town meeting as their forum and as a base for instituting the famous Committees of Correspondence to gain the concerted support of other New England towns acting through their own town meetings, thus unifying all New England behind the cause of independence.

In 1782 John Adams, when asked by the Abbé de Mably for advice concerning a history that he proposed writing of the American Revolution, replied that as far as New England's part in the conflict was concerned, the Abbé should direct his attention to the town governments, the religious congregations, the schools, and the militia, all four of which were closely interconnected. In discussing town government, Adams emphasized its influence in encouraging debate on public matters and in reaching rational decisions based on majority opinion. He pointed out how crucial to the success of the Revolution had been a citizenry so trained. In regard to the churches, Adams noted that much the same democratic processes were found in their polity. The parsons were chosen by the people and might be dismissed by them, and they lived with the people as any other citizen would, sharing with them the same privileges and duties. Each town, Adams went on to say, was compelled by state law to maintain its own schools; four colleges—Harvard, Yale, Dartmouth, and the College of New Jersey (Princeton)—were available to the New England boy with intelligence, ability, and ambition. Finally, Adams described the system of militia. All males from sixteen to sixty years were required to be enrolled in a militia company, each town having its own, which would be part of a regiment with a full staff of officers elected by the men. Each man was further required to provide himself, at his own expense, with a firelock and a supply of ammunition, and certain days were set aside for compulsory training and drill.

Adams summarized his remarks with a patriotic flourish: "Behold, sir, a little sketch of the four principal sources of that prudence in council and that military valor and ability, which have produced the American Revolution, and which I hope will be sacredly preserved as the foundations of the liberty, happiness, and prosperity of the people."[4] Since the system of schools, local government, and religious organization, as described by Adams, applied almost exclusively to New England, he would seem to be giving his native region a major share of the credit for winning American independence.

Adams, seven years earlier in a letter to his wife (October 29, 1775), had admitted an "overweening prejudice in favor of New England, which I feel very often, and which, I fear, sometimes leads me to expose myself to just ridicule."[5] He then listed the advantages that New England had over the other colonies and "every other part of the world that I know anything of."[6] Among these advantages were the fact that "the people are of purer English blood" than those of other colonies (there were fewer Scotch, Irish, Dutch, French, Danish, and Swedish) and the fact that they had left England "in purer times than the present."[7] He also found New Englanders to be more moral and better educated, owing to the legal requirements that each town have a school and a minister. The system of town government he praised for the outlet it provided for each male citizen's acquired and native abilities and for the training it provided in public affairs. Finally he noted with approval—as Dwight did later—the absence of the principle of primogeniture in the distribution of land.

John Adams's enthusiasm was echoed elsewhere in the newly founded nation. Thomas Jefferson, not motivated by local pride as Adams was, bluntly proclaimed the New England towns to be "the wisest invention ever devised by the wit of man for the perfect exercise of self-government and for its preservation,"[8] and advocated for Virginia a similar system of "ward" governments. In 1813 in a letter to John Adams he outlined his recommendations in some detail. The wards would be five or six miles square—about the size of a New England town. Elementary education would be compulsory, and promising students would be sent to college at public expense. Roads, police, elections, local militia, and the simpler forms of justice would be under the control of the people of the ward, who would be called to meeting at least once a year on a fixed date throughout the state. At these meetings, matters of statewide and national concern could be discussed and opinions reached and recorded. Each one of these "little republics,"[9] as Jefferson called them, would closely resemble a New England town in its autonomy in local affairs and in its direct influence on state and national policies and actions. The project was a favorite with Jefferson, and he frequently referred to it in his writing.

Timothy Dwight, as we have seen, was an early writer on New England town life in all its aspects. To him the New England town offered the best social order existing in the United States in his day and held the most promise as a model for the future development of the expanding nation. His approval was as enthusiastic as that of either Adams or Jefferson. This type of uncritical assessment persisted through the first half of the century and beyond. The words used in 1852 by the popular historian George Bancroft in describing New England just before the Revolution are typical:

> New York had been settled under large patents of land to individuals; New England under grants to towns; and the institution of towns was its glory and its strength. . . . New England was an aggregate of organized democracies. But the complete development of the institution was to be found in Connecticut and the Massachusetts Bay. There each township was also substantially a territorial parish; the town was the religious congregation; the independent church was established by law; the minister was elected by the people, who annually made grants for his support. There, too, the system of free schools was carried to great perfection; so

that there could not be found a person born in New England unable to write and read. He that will understand the political character of New England in the eighteenth century, must study the constitution of its towns, its congregations, its schools, and its militia."[10]

Foreign Commentators on New England Town Government

In the meanwhile foreign travelers had become intensely interested in New England towns as social and political phenomena. For example, the Englishman Edward Augustus Kendall, in his *Travels through the Northern Parts of the United States in the Years 1807 and 1808,* described at length the civil and religious polities of New England towns and, interestingly, discovered resemblances to English shire and parish governments.[11] Members of Lafayette's party, visiting the United States in 1825, are said to have been fascinated by New England towns. But most renowned among the admirers from abroad was Alexis de Tocqueville, who made an extended visit in the 1830s and in his famous book *Democracy in America* (1838) devoted many pages to what he saw in New England. The towns, he believed, were superb instances of democracy in action, successful in most ways and perfectly suited to the needs and character of the people. Pursuing the subject, he sought information from the New England historian Jared Sparks, who supplied him with a succinct and clear description of town-meeting government.[12] It was with the appearance of Tocqueville's book that public attention both in America and in Europe was seriously brought to bear on the New England town, though much of what Tocqueville had to say on the subject paralleled Dwight's account, and his enthusiasm had been anticipated not only by Dwight but by John Adams and Thomas Jefferson. But Americans are prone to let Europeans guide them in their tastes and interests. As Charles Francis Adams observed, Tocqueville made the town meeting famous.[13] Even Emerson's *Historical Discourse,* published three years before *Democracy in America* and describing Concord town government as an apex of perfection in human affairs, could not compare even as a faint whisper with the transatlantic commentator's promptings as to what we should think about town meetings.

Yet Emerson's *Discourse* was actually a very early example of a flood of New England town histories that were to be written during the remaining two-thirds of the century, especially after 1850 and down to the present day. Local history, research into the past of New England culture, reaching to its roots if possible, had become, along with genealogy, a regional and, to a lesser degree, a national preoccupation. Town, county, and state historical societies were founded, and many of these issued bulletins and other publications and held meetings at which papers were read and discussed. It was during this same period—beginning perhaps a bit ahead of it with the work of Catharine Sedgwick—that the belletrists began to concentrate on village settings and subjects for their fiction, poetry, and essays. These authors, who were later labeled local colorists, reached top production shortly after the Civil War, when, according to literary historians, readers and writers alike developed a new and sharpened interest in the various sections of the supposedly reunited nation. At the same time various universities and larger historical societies began to direct their research efforts toward the problem of the origin of New England town government. Numerous theories were put forth and much controversy ensued, but the problem has not been solved to the present day.

Early Theories of the Origin of Town-Meeting Government

The various theories as to the origin of town-meeting government are too numerous for detailed presentation here. But summaries of several of the more striking ones and an account of some of the debate that they sparked will be interesting and instructive.[14]

An early, influential, and extremely able study was a paper titled "The Origin, Organization, and Influence of the Towns of New England," read by Professor Joel Parker before the Massachusetts Historical Society in December 1865, and later published in the Society's *Proceedings*. Parker had been a judge in New Hampshire, but at the time he delivered his paper he was on the faculty of the Harvard Law School. Not surprisingly, his approach is somewhat legalistic. He points out that the charters for the settlement of Plymouth and Massachusetts Bay conferred on the planters the power to establish governments within their assigned territories, to pass and enforce laws, and generally to oversee the welfare of the colonists. Thus empowered, the plantations, which soon assumed the status of towns, proceeded to establish polities that would meet the basic needs and the aspirations of the inhabitants. Professor Parker identified these needs and aspirations as "religious liberty, self-government, and freehold titles"[15] to land. It was in the expectation of attaining these that the immigrants in large numbers crossed the Atlantic. If the colonies had been administered by royal governors enforcing laws enacted in England and if the land had been held, as in the Hudson Valley, by manorial proprietors, the New England colonies, Parker believed, would have attracted few settlers and, incidentally, liberty of religion would hardly have existed. (Of course, it did not exist in the early days.)

But the degree of self-government provided by the charters, which were designed to fit the needs of commercial corporations, was not sufficient for the colonists' purposes, and soon they were striking out on their own. The suffrage was extended, the variety and number of elective offices were increased, and, above all, the towns were organized as separate and to a large extent autonomous bodies only loosely connected with the larger corporation (or colony). "It is through the action of these town incorporations," Parker asserted, "that the Puritan principles have been sustained, the New-England character formed, the industry and economy of the people promoted, the education of the whole population provided for, and perhaps the independence of the country secured."[16]

Parker's views parallel quite closely a summarizing statement made by Tocqueville, whom Parker seems to have admired:

> The native of New England is attached to his township because it is independent and free: his cooperation in its affairs ensures his attachment to its interests; the well-being it affords him secures his affection; and its welfare is the aim of his ambition and of his future exertions. He takes a part in every occurrence in the place; he practices the art of government in the small sphere within his reach; he accustoms himself to those forms without which liberty can only advance by revolutions; he imbibes their spirit; he acquires a taste for order, comprehends the balance of powers, and collects clear and practical notions on the nature of his duties and the extent of his rights.[17]

Dwight, had he lived to read this passage, would have shared Parker's respect for Tocqueville.

Parker further believed that town-meeting government was something unique in history and that in establishing it the New Englanders had not been greatly influenced by Old World models. In support of this conclusion he cited two town historians. One of these, Francis Baylies, in his *An Historical Memoir of the Colony of New Plymouth* (1866), found that "the origin of town-governments in New England i involved in some obscurity. The system does not prevail in England. Nothing analogous to it is known in the southern states; and, although the system of internal government in the middle states bears a partial resemblance to that of New England, it is in many respects dissimilar. Those who are strangers to our customs, are surprised to find the whole of New England divided into a vast number of little democratic republics."[18] Parker omits to mention that Baylies did believe that town government owed something to the polity of the independent (Congregational) church of the colonies. The second local historian whom Parker quotes is Richard Frothingham, who in his *The History of Charlestown* (1845–49) described New England towns as "peculiar in their independence, and the organization of their government," which seemed "in the light of to-day so simple and reasonable," but "perhaps existed nowhere else."[19] Similar speculations as to the uniqueness of New England town government occur frequently in the writing on the subject.

Frothingham did, however, suggest that possible precedents for the New England town governments could be found in "those little independent nations, the free cities of the twelfth century; or the towns of the Anglo-Saxons, where every office was elective."[20] Parker rejects this suggestion, reasserting that there were no precedents.

Frothingham had, indeed, done little more than point out an analogy. But others were eager to establish a direct line of descent from the practices of the Germans two thousand years ago or from even more ancient sources. Here again Tocqueville may have provided a hint when, in introducing his discussion of American townships, he wrote: "The village or township is the only association which is so perfectly natural that, wherever a number of men are collected, it seems to constitute itself. The town or tithing . . . exists in all nations, whatever their laws or customs may be: it is man who makes monarchies and established republics, but the township seems to come directly from the hand of God. But although the existence of the township is coeval with that of man, its freedom is an infrequent and fragile thing."[21]

Germanic-Origin Theory: Herbert B. Adams

The New England town, all agreed, was characterized by a large measure of political freedom for its inhabitants and for itself in its relations with colony or state. The obvious course for those who took Tocqueville's remarks seriously and also wished to establish a credible ancestry for New England town-meeting government was to search back into English history and beyond that into the history and habits of the Saxons and the Angles before their invasion of Britain. A number of historians instituted such a search, with results satisfying to them though not universally accepted. The most famous, as well as most romantic and glamorous, of these attempts was a paper by Herbert B. Adams, "The Germanic Origin of New England Towns," which he read before the Harvard Historical Society on May 9, 1881, and published the next year in the Johns Hopkins University Studies in Historical and Political Science, of which he was editor.

Adams continued his research into the early records of New England towns and published his findings in other essays in the Johns Hopkins series, all of which tended to support his Germanic-origin theory. Indeed, beginning in 1881, the Hopkins Studies became the chief outlet for publication of material, both theoretical and factual, on towns and local communities not only in New England but elsewhere in the country. An article by Oxford professor of history Edward Augustus Freeman, in the first volume and first number of the Studies (1881), set the tone and direction of many of the ensuing essays on New England towns in later volumes. The whole approach, in fact, was an extension to America of the work and speculation of European historians seeking to establish common roots for the local institutions of all Aryan peoples. Freeman, in this essay titled *An Introduction to American Institutional History,* stated bluntly that "the institutions of Massachusetts and Maryland . . . are part of the general institutions of the English people, as those are again part of the general institutions of the Teutonic race, and those are again part of the general institutions of the whole Aryan family."[22]

Another British historian, John Richard Green, in his *History of the English People* 1877–80), which was highly esteemed in America, offered further stimulus to the search for institutional roots. Green traces English town and borough government and even Parliament back to the *tun* and *moot* of village freemen in Friesland and Schleswig. He writes: "It was in these tiny knots of farmers that the men from whom Englishmen were to spring learned the worth of public opinion, of public discussion, the worth of the agreement, the 'common sense,' the general conviction to which discussion leads, as of the laws which derive their force from being expressions of that general conviction."[23]

It was in this climate of scholarly and public interest that Herbert B. Adams's "The Germanic Origin of New England Towns" appeared. Highly readable, however sweeping and sensational in its statements, the essay attracted immediate notice. Even before its publication in 1881, part of it was read before the Stockbridge, Massachusetts, Village Improvement Society—a model and pioneer group of its kind—and printed the same day in a Pittsfield newspaper. After it was published in the Johns Hopkins Studies, demand for it in western Massachusetts was high and the Great Barrington School Board designated it for reading in their high school history curriculum.[24]

The reason for the popularity is obvious. Hitherto there had been no lack of praise of New England village culture and town-meeting government. The essayists, the fiction writers, the travel writers, the historians had all joined the chorus. But none had added the touch of romance that Adams supplied. What was needed was an ancestry, a colorful past, for town institutions—in other words, a romanticizing, but not at the expense of historical accuracy. Herbert B. Adams was equal to the task. He began modestly at first, leading the reader by easy steps to his main thesis. The first sentence of his essay is far from startling: "The reproduction of the town and parish systems of Old England under colonial conditions in America is one of the most curious and suggestive phenomena of American history."[25] It will be remembered that Edward Augustus Kendall, in his *Travels through the Northern Parts of the United States,* had in 1807 remarked on the resemblance of New England town governments to English parish organization. Others had observed the similarity, and a group of historians were saying rather reasonably that the New England towns had developed from the English parishes, in which the vestry—consisting of the male members of a local church—were charged with functions like those of the New England towns, such as care of the poor and maintenance of roads. The vestry met very much in the manner of a New England town meeting and elected officers with titles and functions similar to many of those in the New England towns. The theory was simple and plausible, and the famous English observer of American political life James Bryce subscribed to it. In his book *The American Commonwealth* (1891) he stated unhesitatingly: "The Town meeting is the English vestry, the selectmen are the churchwardens, or select vestrymen, called back by the conditions of colonial life into an activity fuller than they exerted in England even in the seventeenth century, and far fuller than they now retain."[26]

But Herbert Adams, taking his cue from Freeman, does not stop with anything so tame as the English-parish theory. After developing at some length the concept that "these little communes [the towns] were the germs of our state and national life,"[27] he launches his main thesis: "Town institutions were propagated in New England by Old English and Germanic ideas, brought over by Pilgrims and Puritans, and as ready to take root in the soil of America as would Egyptian grain which had been drying in a mummy-case for thousands of years. The town and village life of New England is as truly the reproduction of Old English types as those again are reproductions of the village community system of the ancient Germans."[28] Adams then quotes Richard Green at length and cites other authorities such as Montesquieu, who had traced the origins of the English Constitution to the inhabitants of the German forests as they were when Tacitus described the customs of the Germans of eighteen hundred years ago. We need not accompany Adams on his excursion through the Odenwald and the Black Forest of Germany, in which regions he discovered "surviving features of the ancient village community system as described by Tacitus."[29] Nor is it necessary to follow him across the North Sea as he reveals the persistence in England of the old Teutonic way, brought there by the "Saxon pirates."[30] The second transplanting of these institutions, this time across the Atlantic Ocean by the Pilgrims and Puritans, is the revelation for which Adams has been preparing his readers.

His very full and detailed presentation of the development of towns in the New World should be read in its entirety; only the general drift of it can be indicated here. Concentrating on the Pilgrims, Adams shows that in the layout of the town of Plymouth and the enclosure of it by a fence, in the early communal cultivation of the soil and the later apportioning of it among families, and above all in the self-government in town-meetings— "the Saxon *Tun Gemot*"[31]—the Pilgrims, like the other New England Colonists, were giving evidence of the fact that they were "merely one branch of the great Teutonic race, a single off-shoot from the tree of liberty which takes deep hold upon all the past."[32] Adams sarcastically asserted:

> Most writers, especially local historians, assume that New England towns are either the offspring of Puritan virtue and of the Congregational church, or else that they are the product of this rocky soil, which is supposed to produce free institutions spontaneously, as it does the arbutus and the oak, or fair women and brave men. But the science of Biology no longer favors the theory of spontaneous generation. . . . It is just as improbable that free local institutions should spring up without a germ along American shores as that English wheat should have grown here without planting.[33]

Ignoring Adams's rather elephantine humor—and the fact that in some respects his own Germanic-origin theory seems more romantic than scientific—one can detect the spirit of the times in his statement. The reference to "The science of Biology"—not just "biology" in lower case— reveals a state of mind that was becoming increasingly widespread. By 1881, when Adams was writing, Darwin's *On the Origin of Species by Means of Natural Selection* had been in print for twenty-two years. The theory of evolution had seized the imagination of the social as well as the biological scientists. A search for the origins from which the New England town evolved would thus carry one back not only to the Teutonic *tun gemot* but even farther afield or backward in time to the Russian *mir* and the Hindu *panchayat*. The territory was vast; the opportunities for hypothesizing were limitless, as were the opportunities for romanticizing.

Germanic-Origin Theory: James K. Hosmer

The culmination of the Germanic-origin theorizing was in another of the Johns Hopkins Studies, James K. Hosmer's *Samuel Adams: The Man of the Town Meeting* (1884), which has some of the qualities of historical fiction, though it was doubtless the result of sound research. To Hosmer a truly healthy democracy is almost impossible without a basis in the folkmoot, which trains the people to think for themselves and make decisions concerning their government. According to him, Anglo-Saxons carry a folkmoot tendency in their genes. Thus, though in England in the seventeenth century the folkmoot did not exist in pure form, the Pilgrims and all other English settlers in New England automatically established folkmoots.

There are several corollaries to Hosmer's views, and he faces them unflinchingly. Since the folkmoot seems to be solely an Anglo-Saxon (or Teutonic originally) institution, large admixtures of other races in New England towns would result in less effective town-meeting government. Hosmer notes that this has already occurred in many communities where there have been sizable influxes of Irish and French-Canadians. John Adams would very likely have shared Hosmer's view and concern; and other writers of the century—notably Charles Francis Adams and James Bryce—called attention to the supposedly damaging effect of foreign immigration on town meetings. Second, Hosmer points out that the growth of many towns to the size of cities renders the folkmoot unworkable and representative government has to be established in its place. He sees this deplorable change in more and more municipalities as the nation becomes industrialized and as the birthrate rises and the immigrants pour in. Yet he took comfort in the fact that thirteen million of the nation's population were descendants of the original Massachusetts Bay colonists and among these the instinct for folkmoot democracy lingers and will continue to influence the country's politics. He quotes from Bancroft's *History of the Formation of the Constitution* (1882) a statement made to Madison to the effect that New Englanders are "amazingly attached to their own custom of planting townships."[34]

The great age of the New England folkmoot, Hosmer thought, was in the years just before and during the Revolution, the inception and success of which he attributed largely to the town meetings in hundreds of towns throughout the region. And among all these town meetings, that of Boston was the leader—"the hot-bed of sedition,"[35] a Tory called it—and the guiding spirit of the Boston town meeting was Samuel Adams, whom Hosmer, straining a metaphor, nominates as a second "Father of our country."[36] In town meeting Adams could gauge and at the same time form public opinion, and from his town meeting he launched his famous program of Committees of Correspondence, involving communities all over New England. The organization of townspeople through their local meetings provided the independence movement with an impetus felt far beyond the borders of New England and brought about the eventual separation from Great Britain.[37]

During the nineteenth century, Hosmer believed, the influence and number of town meetings had declined, the change of Boston to city government in 1822 (with a population of 22,000) marking the end of an era. But in remote sections, not yet industrialized or significantly penetrated by

French-Canadians and Irish, he still found the town meeting in almost pristine purity. One of these, apparently that of his own home town of Northfield, Massachusetts, he described in action with picturesque detail and a touch of nostalgia, but above all with a profound respect reminiscent of Emerson's "Historical Discourse," which work Hosmer knew and mentions in a footnote.

Church-Origins Theory

Adams's theory and even Hosmer's more extreme version of it are fascinating and to a certain extent plausible. They at least convey a sense of institutional continuity that seems to be a human need, especially in a new country.[38] More significantly, Adams and Hosmer may have helped fill a gap left in the national, especially the New England, consciousness by the weakening of religious orthodoxy. But to many people who retained their old religious faith, the new theories were unacceptable. New Englanders, and to a greater or lesser degree all Americans, had for two hundred years regarded the founding and the prospering of the colonies as providential—God's plan for a chosen race or people. A later extension of this idea was the belief in the millennium in which the United States would lead the world—again as God's chosen nation. A people holding these convictions would at first not be happy to learn that one of their cherished institutions was pagan in origin. The good things that America and especially New England enjoyed both as colonies and as a nation were considered to be the beneficial results of reformed religion and to have been bestowed by God's grace. A debt to ancient Rome or Greece might be acceptable, and one to the Old Testament Hebrews would be joyfully acknowledged, but one to the barbaric tribes of Germany would be indignantly rejected.

There was, indeed, even in the late nineteenth century a group of theorists who still claimed to find the origins of New England town institutions in the polity of the Congregational Church, as it existed both in England and in America—a hypothesis that would have a strong appeal for the religious. The most sweeping statement of this view is found in the writing of J. S. Clark, who asserted that not only the town governments but the entire governmental structure of the United States "sprang up spontaneously from that system of church polity which our New England fathers deduced from the Bible."[39] Other historians, among them John Fiske and Noah Porter, admitted certain church influences but did not share Clark's extreme views. Porter's position is especially interesting, since as a professor of moral philosophy at Yale and later president of the college, his career closely paralleled that of Timothy Dwight in an earlier generation.

Like Dwight, Porter was a staunch Calvinist carrying on the theological tradition associated with Yale. In 1888, then seventy-seven years old, he stated in an address to the New England Society of Brooklyn, New York, that "out of the church grew the town; or rather the town was evolved or developed along with the church."[40] But the church was preeminent—the root from which grew all other phases of the political, economic, and cultural life of the community. The New Englander, he insisted, was a "*public soul*," not the inveterate "individual, separated from, or disbelieving in organized society."[41] In other words, the New Testament idea of a church as a neighborly group, of limited size, living and worshiping in close fellowship was the germ of the New England town—and the writers of the Saybrook Platform, Timothy Dwight, and many others would be in full agreement. Porter points out that the meeting house, located geographically at or near the center of a town, was formerly used as an all-purpose civic center—for town meetings and other public functions. Nor did any one find this custom irreverent; for, aside from the fact that the Puritans did not believe a church building to be sacred, religion was so basic to the town's existence that all activities were regarded as inseparably associated with it.

Racist Implications in Theories of Town Origins

But the notion that town institutions derived from remote, primitive, and secular roots was gaining strength and invalidating, at least among historians, the theories of men like Clark and Porter. In the 1880s we have seen that the Germanic-origin thesis was widely accepted. And interestingly, this theory does not wholly reject the older, religious notion that Anglo-Americans are a chosen people. Tacitly it is assumed that the Aryans, or Caucasians, especially the Germanic subgroups, are superior beings. Furthermore, this element of racism predated by many years the work of writers like Freeman and Herbert Adams. We recall, for instance, John Adams's statement, in a letter to his wife, that he had "an overweening prejudice in favor of New England,"[42] and based his prejudice on the fact that the population of New England, unlike that of other colonies, was of virtually unmixed English blood. Adams's "prejudice" was, in fact, so narrow as to include only the English; apparently he considered other Teutonic peoples, like the Dutch and the Swedes, to be inferior.

Dwight and Emerson also expressed pride in an English, or Saxon, racial as well as cultural heritage, but it remained for the Vermont lawyer George Perkins Marsh to broaden the racial base to include the Goths—as he called the Germanic branch of the Aryans—in a discussion of the roots of the

racial superiority of New Englanders. In a *Discourse* delivered before the
Philomathesian Society of Middlebury College in 1843 and printed the
same year, Marsh, like John Adams, stated his belief that the first settlers in
New England had left the old country at a time when its culture was at a
higher point—by which he meant less contaminated by strains other than
Gothic—than during previous or later centuries. To Marsh, English civilization was a product of Roman influences superimposed on an ancient
Gothic foundation, and in his opinion the Roman, or Latin, strain was
ruinously corrupting. However, the migration to New England took place
during the Reformation—a period that not only produced much of England's great literature, theology, and philosophy but also marked a high
tide of opposition to all things Roman, most prominently, of course, the
Roman Church. With the accession of the Stuarts, whom Marsh considered
despicable tyrants, the Gothic tide ebbed and has not risen again in England. Thus New England was left as the outstanding exemplar of Gothi-
cism, and hence of human civilization, in the modern world, for Marsh
seems not to consider other Gothic-derived cultures to be the equal of that
of England at the time of the migration to the New World.

Marsh is unrestrained in his enthusiasm and reckless in his claims. "The
immigration of the first settlers of New England,"he asserts, "contemplated
in its causes, its circumstances, and its results, is the noblest and most
touching incident in all history. . . . It was the spirit of the Goth, that guided
the May-Flower [*sic*] across the trackless ocean; the blood of the Goth, that
flowed at Bunker's Hill."[43] Such unscientific hyperbole is remarkable, and
indeed incredible, considering that Marsh was later the author of a closely
reasoned and documented pioneer work on ecology, *The Earth as Modified
by Human Action* (1874), for which he is justly honored today.

Exactly what, according to Marsh, were the superlative qualities of the
Goths? In the first place, they were not barbarians but "the noblest branch
of the Caucasian race."[44] Second, the Goth is characterized "by the reason
[in the Kantian and Coleridgean sense of intuition], the Roman, by the
understanding [an inferior form of cognition]; the one by imagination, the
other by fancy; the former aspires to the spiritual, the latter is prone to the
sensuous. The Gothic spirit produced a Bacon, a Shakespeare, a Milton. . . .
In literature and art, the Goth pursues the development of a principle, the
expression of a thought, the realization of an ideal."[45]

As Marsh progresses through his *Discourse*, it becomes apparent that the
terms *Gothic* and *Roman* could be replaced by *romantic* and *classic* without
altering his thesis. Thus it is not surprising that he mentions a concern for
freedom and a respect for the will of the people—so characteristic of romantic minds—as being quintessentially Gothic. "The Goth holds that government springs from the people, is instituted for their behoof, and is

limited to the particular objects for which it was originally established; that the legislature is but an organ for the solemn expression of the deliberate will of the nation, that the coercive power of the executive extends only to the enforcement of that will."[46] Marsh does not specifically mention town governments, but they fit perfectly into his larger statement of the Gothic ideal of government. Indeed, to Marsh this ideal had become most fully realized in New England, the function of which region, as the country expanded westward, he says, would be to keep these ideas alive and pass them on to newer communities. In material prosperity New England would be surpassed by other regions. "But the mighty West," he prophesies, "will look back with filial reverence to the birth-place of the fathers of her people, and the schools of New England will still be nursing mothers to the posterity of her widely scattered children."[47] Dwight's and Lyman Beecher's vision of New England as the civilizer and missionary of the nation had lost none of its luster.

Thus the notion that New Englanders were in some way a special people—whether God's elect or simply of superior racial stock—kept cropping up, and we find it in the writing of John Adams, Charles Francis Adams, Marsh, and Hosmer, as well as among the religiously orthodox. England had for centuries considered herself a redeemer nation, and New Englanders like the Mathers, Edwards, and Dwight were pretty sure that the mantle had been transferred to New England. The potential for prejudice, if not downright racism, as non-English immigrants poured into the region, was great.

Reassessment of Theories of Town Origins: P. Emory Aldrich

Marsh's ideas, though related to the theorizing regarding town origins, remained somewhat peripheral to it. Most controversy centered around the vestry (English parish) theory, the Congregational Church theory, the Germanic-origin theory, and the "without-precedent" theory (of men like Joel Parker). It was time, at last, for a review and a reassessment of all the theories; and two such attempts were made and the results published, one in 1884 and the other in 1892, each one somewhat ironically including yet another theory.

The first was the work of P. Emory Aldrich, who in a report to the American Antiquarian Society summarized and rejected most of the theories put forth up to that time. Thus he finds Tocqueville's remarks, some of which he quotes, to be "ideal, or speculative, rather than . . . historical,"[48] and he looks with skepticism on the many efforts to trace town origins back to Medieval free cities, Anglo-Saxon *tuns,* King Alfred's "Hundreds," Teutonic tribal customs, or Aryan institutions. He also rejects the notion, held by so many from John Adams onward, that all American freedoms originated in New England town institutions. He does, however, cite with approval Judge Joel Parker's and Francis Baylies's opinion that the town governments were not structured on any racial or national model but were unprecedented and unique in history.

"A careful study of the primitive institutions of all times and countries," Aldrich wrote, "can hardly fail to convince the inquirer . . . that there were no pre-existing models for New England towns. These towns were original creations, formed to meet the exact wants of the settlers of a new and uninhabited country, and the founders of a new State."[49] Furthermore, Aldrich reminds us that the towns derived their powers from colonial— later, state—governments, empowered by their charters to institute laws for their own governance and that of the towns within their boundaries. Town governments thus could in no way be regarded as having spontaneously evolved from deeply ingrained racial custom or instinct. They were dependent entirely on a central government, which carefully spelled out and limited their powers and duties. Indeed, the towns were actually smaller corporations existing by sanction of larger corporations, the colonies, which in turn existed by charters that listed in detail their powers and duties.

Reassessment of Theories of Town Origins: The Symposium of 1892

The second reevaluation of theories of the origins of town government took place in a symposium held at the January 1892 meeting of the Massachusetts Historical Society. On this occasion Charles Francis Adams read a lengthy paper, later published in the Society's *Proceedings,* on "The Genesis of the Massachusetts Town, and the Development of Town-Meeting Government," which was followed by discussion and critiques by three other scholars. Adam's research on the subject had been extensive and specific, for he was about to publish in this same year "A Study of Church and Town Government" as the third part of his *Three Episodes in Massachusetts History.* Over four hundred pages in length, this study was the result of a painstaking examination of the records of Braintree, Massachusetts, and of Quincy, which had split off from Braintree, from the time of their first settlement to 1888, when Quincy was chartered as a city and ceased to hold town meetings. Among New England town histories this work was, and remains, a model, and the fact that a man of Adams's prominence and ability undertook to write it indicates the keen interest aroused by New England local history and town government. In it he included a summary of his remarks to the Massachusetts Historical Society.

Charles Francis Adams introduced his paper with comments on changes in his own beliefs concerning the origin of Massachusetts towns. To within a few months of his preparation of this paper, he states, he had traced the New England system of government by town meeting to "common-law English vestry"[50] as modified and developed by the nonconformist churches in Great Britain and the Congregational churches in New England, and he quotes from an earlier version of his paper, which he had discarded: "The Massachusetts congregational society [*sic*], thus developed out of the vestry, under its new conditions and in process of time itself developed in the most obvious way into government by town-meeting."[51] This was an ingenious combining of the vestry theory and the Congregational-Church theory, but it no longer satisfied Adams. His dissatisfaction resulted from adverse comments made by two fellow members of the Society, Judge Mellen Chamberlain and Abner C. Goodell. These two, at a meeting of the Society two years before, had criticized theorists like Hosmer and Herbert Adams, whom they labeled "the New Historical School," for their efforts to find New England town origins in the distant past. They praised the members of this "school" for their resort to ancient records, but still held that they had misinterpreted their findings or twisted them to support their hypotheses. Chamberlain and Goodell, who prided themselves as hard headed realists, had made painstaking searches in government, church, and court records in arriving at their conclusions, which, so far as New England town origins were concerned, rejected as fanciful and romantic almost all the preceding speculation on the subject—one major exception being Judge Joel Parker's views. Finding his ideas thus challenged, Adams had extended his research beyond Braintree and Quincy, to include the records of the other Massachusetts towns of Dorchester, Hingham, Weymouth, Cambridge, and Boston.

Adams begins his paper with a reference to the English historian Richard Green and a comment on the "widespread interest and admiration" aroused by the town meeting "since Tocqueville made it famous a half a century ago."[52] He briefly mentions the propounders of the Germanic-origin theory and quotes Freeman's remarks about the direct relationship of New England institutions to those of "the whole Aryan family," but warns that the analogies and resemblances are no "evidence of descent."[53] Certainly his investigations into the histories of Braintree, Quincy, and neighboring towns provided no support, he assured his listeners, for the theory of ancient origin or of development from the Anglican vestry or Congregational Church polity. But to Adams the impulse to devise still another theory of town origins was irresistible, and he proceeded to announce one—though it had, in fact, been suggested by Joel Parker in 1866, bore some similarity to Aldrich's views, and had been developed quite succinctly by Goodell much more recently. Adams's theory, however derivative, was that town government in New England was at first modeled after the provisions for corporate organization laid down in the charter of the Massachusetts Bay Company, a conclusion that has not found much favor since Adams's day but that deserves a brief recapitulation.

According to this so-called Massachusetts charter theory,[54] the town governments of the state and colony were "of purely secular origin, and had no connection with church organization, except that certain members of the church were freemen [voters in Colony affairs] and inhabitants of the town, and the town was under legal obligations to maintain the church."[55] He compared the inhabitants of each town to the stockholders in a corporation. The town-meeting government of the towns was hence a government by stockholders, the selectmen (chosen by the inhabitants) being the equivalent of a modern board of directors. As time went on the functions of the secular government and the number of its officers increased, while the organization of the churches remained the same; and thus the secular and the religious activities of the community grew farther and farther apart.

Adams's paper was followed by comments by other members of the Society, the first being that of Abner Goodell, given *in absentia* in a letter which another member read. Goodell heartily endorsed Adams's theory, found corroboration of it in his own researches into the histories of Salem and Boston, and commended Adams's use of the records of a number of towns to establish his points. Goodell's only point of difference with Adams was on a collateral matter—Adams's failure to see the distinction between "inhabitants" and "proprietors" in the seventeenth century. The nature of this distinction need not concern us here.

The Honorable Mellen Chamberlain, the second commentator, was more verbose than Goodell. As author of a paper on "the New Historical School" he rejected, as did Goodell, the Germanic, the parish-vestry, and similar theories. Except for some minor differences, he too found Adams's paper to his liking. He highly commended the good sense of his fellow judge Joel Parker, who had regarded New England town government as "essentially indigenous"[56] and without close precedent in history. He summarized his position as follows: "[The New England Towns] were native to the soil, and planted by English emigrants with the instincts, traditions, and methods of their race, but controlled, nevertheless, by their charters, patents, or royal commissions, and the conditions of situation utterly unlike those which surrounded them in England."[57] As a sole concession to the theorists whom he is criticizing he asserts that the "aptitude of the English race for government is greater than that of the Latin or Celtic races, chiefly by reason of its experience in legislative bodies, among which may be reckoned English town-meetings and parish vestries."[58] But the expression of this talent or aptitude in New England was "something the precise like of which does not appear in recorded history."[59]

The final commentary on Charles Francis Adams's paper was made by Professor Edward Channing of Harvard, who had previously printed, as one of the Johns Hopkins University Studies, an essay on *Town and Country Government in the English Colonies of North America.* In this essay Channing had argued that the governmental institutions of the colonies were part of "the continuous history of the English people."[60] He particularly empha- sized the influence of English parish polity on that of New England towns, though he admitted the influence of new economic and political conditions. Thus it is not surprising to find him disagreeing with Charles Francis Adams and Judge Chamberlain, both of whom had in fact included him in the New Historical School that had aroused their disapproval. In his cri- tique of Adams, Channing still insisted that his own "theory of the con- tinuity of American and English history is in itself a correct theory."[61] However, he is at pains to show the weaknesses of the Germanic theory of Herbert Adams, and herein he is in agreement with Charles Francis Adams and Chamberlain. The "continuity" on which he insists is that extending from English parish organization to New England towns, always allowing for modifications resulting from differences between conditions in the New and Old Worlds.

Channing's remarks closed the symposium, as Adams called it, in which almost every theory of New England town government received some at- tention. Close to a hundred pages in the *Proceedings* were needed to pro- duce the texts of the papers delivered. Which theory, or combination of the theories, if any, deserves the greatest credence is not so significant as the fact that the subject received so much learned and earnest attention—and this is merely a fraction of the attention accorded it during the preceding forty or fifty years. The causes of this almost obsessive preoccupation is of more interest than the exact details of each theory put forward. A major, if not the sole, cause lay in a state of mind, a pervasive conviction, that can be found in a follow-up paper that Charles Francis Adams read before the Society in June of 1892. In it he attempted to answer minor objections of the commentators on his previous paper, but in addition he included a quotation from "the preface to a work privately printed but never pub- lished," expressing a degree of New England chauvinism seldom equaled.

Adams's claim is that "Massachusetts is one of the half-dozen communities" in the world's history that has had "a message to deliver to mankind" of such power as to permanently affect the course of civilization for the better.

> The Hebrews developed the idea of the one God and his command-ments,—an idea and a code which have since become the basis of all law and civilization. The Athenians next came forward, embodying the prin-ciple of popular government through discussion . . . only now struggling into general acceptance. Rome developed that idea of imperial organiza-tion which is the key-note of modern as opposed to ancient history. England originated parlimentary or representative government, and brought it into practical use. It was for Massachusetts to assert the abso-lute equality before the law."[62]

Adams further maintained that the chief avenue of the propagation of this principle of absolute equality, insofar as it existed, was the towns, the influence of which soon became felt not only in New England but eventu-ally on a national scale, in spirit if not in the actual forms of political institutions. This contention is unsurpassed in its sweeping claims even by Dwight or Emerson or Marsh, and it amounts to a secularized version of the belief held by so many New England theologians that the millennium was not only approaching but that the United States would be the first to feel its effects, and that in the process New England would lead the nation. What Jonathan Edwards had only hinted, Adams categorically stated as certainty.

Recorders of Social and Economic Decline in Rural New England

The children left [the farm], drawn by dreams of gains the city or
the sea or the far West offers; and the parents are gone, too, now.
The shingles and clapboards loosen and the roof sags and within,
damp, mossy decay has fastened itself to walls, floor and ceiling of
every room. Gaps have broken in the stone walls along the road-
way, and the brambles are thick, springing on either side. In the
front yard is a gnarled, untrimmed apple tree, with a great broken limb sagging to the ground, and about, a ragged growth of
bushes. As time goes on, the house falls, piece by piece, and at last
only the shattered frame stands, a grim memorial of the dead
past.

> Clifton Johnson, *The New England Country* (1893)[1]

The Rural Towns in Serious Trouble

While members of the historical societies were arguing about the origin of
New England town institutions, the towns themselves in the rural regions
were in very serious trouble. The realization of what was happening first
appeared among the writers of fiction and an occasional poet. If Rowland
Robinson, Seba Smith, and James Russell Lowell had, for the most part,
good things to say about life in the New England towns, others were not so
genially disposed, particularly as the century wore on. Authors like Rose
Terry Cooke, Mary E. Wilkins Freeman, Edward Bellamy, and Edwin Arlington Robinson were writing about the New England rural scene in a
mood of deep pessimism. The reasons for their gloom are complex and
manifold. The years following the Civil War—the period in which these
authors wrote—were a time of widespread disillusionment. The millennial
hopes central to Dwight's thought and, in the background at least, in the
thought of many others, could not be so confidently entertained after the
nation had temporarily disintegrated and become whole again only after
enormous expenditures of life and property and a severe erosion of spiritual values. Yet the pessimism, though pervasive, did not affect with equal

severity all authors writing about New England. Indeed, in the case of Rowland Robinson and that of James Parton, as we have seen, the effect was minimal, but few or none retained the prewar confidence that the nation as a whole would eventually see the light and adopt beneficent New England ways and thus become a world leader in an uninterrupted march toward universal justice, peace, and happiness. Many, in fact, seemed to wonder whether New England ways were actually as beneficent as had previously been thought.

Another much more tangible cause for pessimism among New England writers was the region's general sociological and economic decline. The emigration from the rural districts either to the West or to the manufacturing cities drained off large numbers of the population and left some towns virtually abandoned. The exodus westward was at first considered part of New England's mission in establishing the expanding nation as a Christian commonwealth preparatory to the reign of Christ on earth. But as time went on and the emptying of rural areas gained the momentum made possible by the Erie Canal and the railroads, cause for alarm was all too apparent. We have heard Rowland Robinson's lament over the emigration from Vermont. Edwin Arlington Robinson at the end of the century was writing dark-hued poems about deserted houses and ghost villages in his native Maine, and a few years later Robert Frost wrote of the cellar holes, abandoned farms, and lonely graveyards that made the New England hill country a haunted land. For over half a century after the Civil War—which itself, of course, tooks its toll of the region in men killed, not to mention those lured away by easier living conditions that they thought they saw elsewhere—a pall of gloom and defeatism hung over New England and cast its shadow on a generation of writers. The governments of the several states became alarmed, conducted investigations, took measures that were generally ineffective, and ended, usually, by standing back and wringing their hands as the decay continued. Newspapers and magazines, including some of the most prestigious ones, published article after article on the crisis, along with New England local-color fiction, which ranged in tone from despair to cheery affirmation of the old values.

Atlantic Monthly Articles

Some magazine articles on rural decline in New England are worth notice for the graphic, if depressing, account they give of what had happened in a region that one hundred years earlier had been found so idyllic and so full of promise by the author of *Greenfield Hill*. A good sampling of the writing on the subject in the periodicals will be four articles appearing in the *Atlantic Monthly* between 1897 and 1899. In its May 1897 issue the *Atlantic* carried as its lead contribution two essays under the general heading "Problems of Rural New England." The first, by Philip Morgan, had the title "A Remote Village." Morgan begins with a description of the pleasant aspects of the life of the town, which, unnamed, is located in extreme northern New Hampshire, ten miles from a railroad. He chuckles over general-store gossip, with its spicing of Yankee humor and tall stories; he lauds the storekeeper's generosity in donating medicine to the poor; he records his delight in the slow pace of village existence, with its pastimes of hunting, fishing, breaking colts, and community dancing. He notes that the townspeople are descendants from solid English Puritan stock and that some of the women are remarkable for their beauty. Here are the people and the sort of community that Dwight, Stowe, and Emerson saw as the hope of America and perhaps of all mankind.

Such is the surface impression conveyed by this remote town. A slightly closer look reveals a very different image. For example, drunkenness and threats of violence mar the pastoral charm of the village dances, at one of which, we learn, a suspected murderer is in attendance. Writing in the voice of one of the townspeople, Morgan confides: "The number of illegitimate births among us is large. In fact, it is so large that a definite amount has been fixed by common consent as the proper one to be paid by the putative father to the parents of the unmarried mother. Four hundred dollars, I understand, is the prevailing sum."[2] Divorce is common, as is adultery. Morgan quotes Samuel Taylor Coleridge as saying that when a rural environment "does not benefit, it depraves. Hence the violent, vindictive passions and the outrageous and dark and wild cruelties of very many country folk."[3] In the town that Morgan depicts, cruelty to animals and women is common. The mountain people sell illegal liquor and stage degrading orgies. "There are whole families sunk in a slough of vice and poverty, from which, occasionally, some enterprising son or daughter will emerge,—perhaps only to fall back again in a moment of temptation or despair."[4]

Yet theft is unknown in the town, as a result not of a sense of honesty but of a fierce sense of "equality," for to steal is to admit one's victim's superior wealth. The people's manners are, in general, good—"coarse," perhaps, yet "never vulgar."[5] But there is "a want of reverence in the village. There is no person or group of persons to set a standard of manners or of morals for the rest of the community. Nobody looks up to anybody else,—not even to the minister,"[6] nor is there respect for age. Grammar is generally bad. In winter a monthly bath is deemed sufficient for cleanliness. Still, among the townspeople there are gentlemen—in spirit if not in manners.

Religion has almost died out of the community, Morgan finds, and the ministers are second-raters and poorly paid. Church attendance is confined almost exclusively to the elderly and to women and children. "Our theology," Morgan confides, "has decayed into a vague, sentimental adherence to the doctrine of justification by faith, and a belief in instantaneous conversion."[7] Morgan sees a need for the old religion, which, though it was terrifying, dignified human beings by placing within themselves the momentous choice between salvation and damnation. (Some would question whether this choice existed in the old religion.) The former force wielded by religion—so important in forming New England character—has been lost but is sorely needed to curb the passions of the townspeople. Morgan fears for the future and wonders whether New England character, having reached a culmination of strength during the Civil War, has not been declining ever since.

The second of the pair of articles in the May 1897 *Atlantic Monthly* on "The Problems of Rural New England" was written by Alvan F. Sanborn under the title "A Farming Community," and establishes a direct contrast with Morgan's report. Here is a town that, except for its theology, would gladden the heart of Dwight had he known it. Indian Ridge, as it is called, possesses libraries, a Masonic lodge, a dramatics club, and a progressive church in which the doctrine of salvation by good works and morals is preached. The inhabitants still adhere to the old-time practice of banding together to help a neighbor in some major project like a house-moving. The village general store is like a clubhouse—a place where the men gather to play checkers and talk politics. Indian Ridge does credit to New England village culture.

But Sanborn was no Pollyanna optimist. Two months after the publication of his glowing picture of Indian Ridge, the *Atlantic Monthly* carried another article by him describing a totally decadent New England town. This piece, "The Future of Rural New England," presents conditions in the community of Dickerman, unidentified as to locality except as being in the central part of a New England state. Dickerman has a population of 1,500, living in ramshackle, unpainted dwellings. The hundred-year-old "Orthodox" Church, frigidly Calvinistic, is plastered on the outside with circus posters, as is the Baptist Church. The diet of the inhabitants is mainly pork; the women are mean-tempered; the people are blind to the surrounding beauties of nature. The schools are taught by half-educated girls. The only circulating library is that connected with the ineffective Sunday school. In the individual homes the reading matter consists of ancient religious tomes—never opened—and popular trash. Civic pride is almost nonexistent, and the town meetings are devoted to paring down appropriations and to squabbling among the various sections of town about which will receive the most out of the tax receipts. Election to office is sought for its ego-flattering value rather than from a civic-minded desire to serve. Votes are bought and sold. Prohibition does not stop the selling of liquor once the selectment have been "fixed." The churches exert some influence on their members' drinking habits, but can in no way correct their lack of civic virtue. The farmers are unintelligent, shiftless, and notable for "deaconing" (that is, cheating) their customers.

Sixty years earlier, around 1840, Dickerman had been a wholesome and prosperous town. Sanborn assigns the usual reasons for its decline: the lure of the Gold Rush; the railroads, which provided easy access to attractive jobs in the cities; the Civil War; the Western migration. But the most basic cause of decline, he believes, was the failure of the farms to yield a profit, partly because of poor soil and unfavorable climate and partly because of the laziness and demoralization of the farmers, who had taken to aping city ways and hankered after city luxuries. As for the future of Dickerman and hundreds of similar towns, Sanborn regarded farming as being no longer an important source of income. Whatever agriculture remained would be carried on by foreign immigrants who had not been spoiled for hard work. Summer vacationers, city people establishing country estates, contact with the outer world by means of trolley lines (this was in 1897) would bring about marked and beneficial changes. But the values and way of life of an old-time rural village would be extinct.

In the same gloomy vein is a two-part article by Rollin Lynde Hartt, "A New England Hill Town," published, also in the *Atlantic Monthly,* in April and May 1899. The community Hartt described is in amazing contrast to Harriet Beecher Stowe's Cloudland, the hill town that in *Oldtown Folks* she presents as a sanctuary for all the most cherished New England qualities. But she was writing about a period not long after the Revolution, and Hartt was dealing with the rural culture of close to a century later.

Hartt's approach was sociological. The plight of his hill town is held up for close scrutiny, and the chief lesson that emerges is one in genetics. The cities and the West have drained away the more intelligent, energetic townspeople and left the inferior ones to interbreed and thus to perpetuate and to accentuate their weaknesses. A family that intermarries over several generations reproduces the family oddities and abnormalities in increasingly concentrated form and in increasing numbers of persons. Mental defectives become more numerous; the moral sense vanishes along with normal mental powers. Misers and misanthropes and eccentrics of all sorts abound. Some of the people live in a state of near savagery, and a race of poor white trash is evolved.

Obviously, under such conditions the community institutions—the church, the schools, the town-meeting government—can be nothing but grotesque caricatures of what they are intended to be and very likely once were. Some of the older people and an occasional entire family who have contacts outside the town or whose children have gone away to college still maintain stricter, more traditional standards, but there are not a sufficient number to leaven significantly the degenerate average. Many of the hill towns, Hartt found, were communities without hope. They were, he thought, "an anachronism,"[8] and like Coleridge he questioned the psychic salubrity of country living in general.[9]

A complete outsider, Rudyard Kipling, who in the 1890s resided briefly in Brattleboro, Vermont, reported similar conditions. The farms, he found, were either abandoned or unproductive. Loneliness and poverty on the countryside spawned perversions of behavior and extravagant religious beliefs. Demoralization was the norm, and insanity was widespread. The silent, neglected land awaited new and more caring inhabitants—immigrants from Europe or rusticators from the cities.[10] When we remember that the New England town included not only a village, or several villages, but also the countryside for several miles around, and that originally this territory formed a compact unit held together by the church, the schools, and the town meeting, we realize that the loneliness and desolation that Kipling reported are symptoms of nothing less than the breakdown of the town system, with its sense of common purpose, tradition, and values.

In the years after the Civil War many authors—most of them New England villagers themselves—wrote quantities of stories and novels in which the social, economic, and moral decay of the countryside were reflected with varying degrees of intensity. Among them were Edward Bellamy, Sarah Orne Jewett, Rose Terry Cooke, Alice Brown, Mary E. Wilkins Freeman, and Edith Wharton—all widely read in their day. These "recorders of the New England decline,"[11] as Fred Pattee called them, were influenced by the trend toward realism in American fiction and made an effort to deal with conditions as they actually saw them. Some of these somber fictional reports from the country towns preceded those of the nonfiction writers like Hartt, Morgan, and Sanborn. Indeed, Hartt commends one of them, Mary E. Wilkins Freeman, for the accuracy of her observations. Others deserved similar commendation; and in considering this large body of fiction, the reader should not be limited to only one writer. A selection of just which individual works and authors to concentrate on is difficult, because much more of the writing than can be discussed is of real literary merit. In the remainder of this chapter, I have chosen to examine rather carefully two novels of the nineteenth century—Mary Wilkins Freeman's *Pembroke* (1894) and, as an example of a late-nineteenth-century disillusioned reading of New England history, Edward Bellamy's *The Duke of Stockbridge* (1879). A brief consideration of the fiction writers' treatment of the New England way of dealing with the poor, at this period increasingly numberous, will be included, as will a discussion of several writers' treatment of the disruptive effects of the rise of large-scale industry on town culture.

The New England of Mary E. Wilkins Freeman

Mary E. Wilkins Freeman's (1852–1930) life and career are worth examining in some detail, if for no other reason than to show how much she was a part of the rural and village environment from which she drew her material as an author. She was thoroughly a New England countrywoman; and, significantly, after her marriage at the age of forty-nine and her removal to suburban New Jersey, the quality of her writing deteriorated, and her personal existence, torn from its roots, gradually became a prolonged misery of frustration and humiliation. Both her parents were descended from early settlers in the colony of Massachusetts Bay. She was born in 1852 and passed her first fifteen years in Randolph, Massachusetts, fourteen miles south of Boston, a distance at that time sufficient to set the town outside the big-city orbit. Family circumstances were modest, her father, Warren Wilkins, being a carpenter; and Mary was nurtured on the values and goals that a middle-class New England village girl would take for granted. When Mary was fifteen the family moved to Brattleboro, Vermont, where the father became a partner in a drygoods business. Though slightly larger than Randolph and a somewhat popular health resort, Brattleboro was still a country town; and nearby, in the narrow valleys leading back from the Connecticut River, were tiny, already decadent towns, where farmers fought a losing battle with the rocky soil and harsh climate.

Mary Wilkins Freeman's first important publishing success was with a story titled "A Humble Romance," which appeared in *Harper's New Monthly Magazine* in 1884. That same year she returned to Randolph and lived there until her marriage to Dr. Charles Freeman in 1902 and her removal to New Jersey. From the time of publication of "A Humble Romance" until her death in 1930 she turned out a steady stream of tales and novels. A few of her short pieces—for example, "A New England Nun," "A Village Singer," "Sister Liddy"—rival the works of Anton Chekhov and Katherine Mansfield in their realistic artistry and power in evoking atmosphere. Nothing better in their genre has been written in America. As representations of small-town life in New England, they are supreme. In addition to many volumes of short stories, Freeman published thirteen novels, two of which are stunning accounts of village life. Of these *Jane Field* (1893) is an in-depth study of the havoc an overdeveloped conscience can wreak in a

woman's life. The second, and the greater of the two, is *Pembroke* (1894),
the most penetrating, lengthy fictional presentation of New England village
life ever written. As a country girl Freeman had been exposed in her
mother's and relatives' kitchens to female gossip, which, as she realized, is a
form of the storytelling art. Much of her fiction intentionally conveys a
gossipy flavor. The story "On the Walpole Road" is a fine example, but
Pembroke more subtly echoes the tones of village gossip—which is, of
course, the villagers' revelation of how they look upon themselves and their
community.

The basic plot situation in *Pembroke* was in fact suggested by an actual
occurrence in Randolph. The action in the novel itself, elaborated from
this incident, is summed up in the words of a townswoman who, in a late
chapter, is purveying local news to a visiting relative as the two drive in a
buggy about the town:

> "Do you see that house? . . . the one with the front windows boarded
> up, without any step to the front door? Well, Barney Thayer lives there
> all alone. He's old Caleb Thayer's son, all the son that's left; the other one
> died. There was some talk of his mother's whippin' him to death. She
> died right after, but they said afterwards that she didn't, that he run
> away one night, an' went slidin' downhill, an' that was what killed him;
> he'd always had heart trouble. I dunno; I always thought Deborah
> Thayer was a pretty good woman, but she was pretty set. I guess Barney
> takes after her. He was goin' with Charlotte Barnard years ago—I guess
> 'twas as much as nine or ten years ago, now—an' they were goin' to be
> married. She was all ready—weddin'-dress an' bonnet an' everything—
> an' this house was 'most done an' ready for them to move into; but one
> Sunday night Barney he went up to see Charlotte, an' he got into a
> dispute with her father about the 'lection, an' the old man he ordered
> Barney out of the house, an' Barney he went out, an' he never went in
> again—couldn't nobody make him. His mother she talked; it 'most killed
> her; an' I guess Charlotte said all she could, but he wouldn't stir a peg.
> "He went right to livin' in his new house, an' he lives there now; he
> ain't married, an' Charlotte ain't. She's had chances, too. Squire Payne's
> son, he wanted her bad"[12]

To complete the story as it develops in the last pages, Barnabas becomes
desperately ill from overwork cutting wood in winter in a swamp, and he
lies alone and disabled in his half-finished house. Charlotte, in defiance of
"what people might think," goes to him and nurses him day and night.
Barnabas's will veers in another direction and he forgives Charlotte's father
and marries her—a happy, love-conquers-all ending for Victorian tastes.

Such is the plot of *Pembroke*. Before considering it more closely, we might
glance at a contemporary commentary on the novel, that of Edwin Arlington Robinson in 1894, in a letter to his friend Harry de Forest Smith.

Robinson was impressed by the haunting quality of the book's simple plot and by the somber background against which the partly suppressed, but consuming, emotions of the characters are revealed. The novel, to him, was redolent with the very essence of Puritanism. Its happy ending, he thought, in no way detracted from its tragic implications. He recommended *Pembroke* to readers with open minds and some ability to sympathize with what might be unfamiliar to them.[13]

Robinson himself was in a position to understand Freeman's book. He himself had been brought up in an economically depressed town, Gardiner, Maine, which in its post-Puritan attitudes was not unlike her Randolph and her fictional Pembroke. Robinson in his Tilbury Town poems presented a gallery of portraits of village and rural persons similar to many found throughout Freeman's writing—persons whose lives have been shattered or stunted by isolation, by warped wills, by crippling flaws of character induced, we are made to feel, by something decadent, even evil in their environment. Though we need not assume a direct influence by Freeman on Robinson, his characters like Aaron Stark the miser, the pathetic, loveless Aunt Imogen, the utterly lonely and empty Tasker Norcross—all in poems named after them—would find soul-mates in her stories and novels. Nor was Robinson alone in applauding Freeman's authenticity. We have seen that R. L. Hartt in his two *Atlantic Monthly* articles under the inclusive title "A New England Hill Town" praised the sociological accuracy of Freeman's work. In the same year (1899), also in the *Atlantic*, Charles Miner Thompson, in an article "Miss Wilkins: An Idealist in Masquerade," commented, like Robinson, on the residual Puritanism in her writing and thinking—especially as regards the diseased will.

Freeman had consciously and deliberately steeped her work in the manifestations of a decadent Puritanism that Robinson and Thompson had found in it. In the "Introductory Sketch" of an 1899 edition of *Pembroke* she stated her purpose in this fictional record of life in a New England town. Her novel, she wrote, was "originally intended as a study of the human will in several New England characters, in different phases of disease and abnormal development."[14] The strength of will and sensitivity of conscience fostered by the early Puritans, she pointed out, had been necessities perhaps for survival; but these qualities became almost psychopathetic as they lingered on in a hypertrophied state two centuries or more later, with no wilderness to subdue, no Indians to fight, and no New Jerusalem to build. Thus the will and conscience became enmeshed in petty quarrels and feuds, and in obsessions with trivia. "*Pembroke*," Freeman goes on to say, "is intended to portray a typical New England village of some sixty years ago [about 1840], as many of the characters flourished at that time, but villages of a similar description have existed in New England at a much later date, and they exist to-day in a very considerable degree"[15]—hundreds of them, she later states. One might add that they exist, though in lesser numbers, at present.

Sherwood Anderson in *Winesburg, Ohio* (1919) presented his readers with a series of portraits of persons he described as village "grotesques." Freeman anticipated him by twenty years with an equally impressive exhibition of eccentricities, compulsions, and other psychoneuroses. Barnabas, for example, in *Pembroke*, not only suffers from a wrong-headed pride, in his quarrel with Charlotte's father, but contracts crippling rheumatic fever as a result of an obsessive attachment to the Puritan work ethic. Driven by a relentless will, he chops wood all winter during periods of storm and cold when other men are crouched by their kitchen fires. "He stood from morning until night hewing down trees, which had gotten their lusty growth from the graves of their own kind. Their roots were sunken deep among and twined about the very bones of their fathers which helped make up the rich frozen soil of the great swamp."[16] The forest growth feeding on the decay of former forests symbolizes, obviously, the destructively vigorous persistence of the Puritan heritage. Similarly, Barnabas's bent and twisted back, which becomes evident after his breaking his engagement with Charlotte, represents the warping of his character by his excessively developed Puritan will—"a terrible will," Charlotte realized, "that won't always let him do what he wants to himself."[17] It is interesting to remember that the farmer Seth Higgins, in Harriet Beecher Stowe's *Poganuc People*, had just such a will.

Charlotte herself possesses a formidable but more constructively directed will, which enables her, for instance, to defy custom and the church's minister and deacons when she decides to nurse the desperately sick Barnabas, and to be alone with him day and night in his house. Her refusal to consider any other suitor—notably Squire Payne's highly eligible and decent son—during Barnabas's ten years of totally ignoring her may seem less than reasonable or constructive, but at least her determination does not border on the morbid and does, at long last, result in a desirable outcome.

The same cannot be said of Deborah Thayer, Barnabas's mother. A fundamentalist Calvinist, she is aptly named after the Old Testament warrior prophetess. Completely assured that she is one of God's elect, she assumes that what she wills is God's will, for God often achieves His goals through His chosen people. "Deborah's blue eyes gleamed with warlike energy," we are told, and as she listened to the imprecatory psalms "she confused King David's enemies with those people who crossed her own will."[18] When her first child died one morning, she devoted the afternoon of the same day to washing her windows. After Barnabas broke his engagement, she banished him from the house, their wills having clashed like swords.[19] When her daughter becomes pregnant out of wedlock, Deborah turns her out into a snowstorm. Taking refuge with the village whore, the daughter is eventually found, is married in shotgun fashion to her lover, but ever afterward carries a burden of guilt and is, of course, disowned by her mother.

In her cooking Deborah spoons gravy "as if it were molten lead; . . . she might . . . have been one of her female ancestors in the times of the French and Indian Wars, casting bullets with the yells of savages in her ears."[20] She thrusts medicine at her sick son Ephraim, who has severe heart trouble, "as if it were a bayonet and there were death at the point."[21] She literally whips the Assembly's Catechism into the boy, despite the doctor's orders that such treatment might kill him. The Lord, she believes, has entrusted her with her son's soul; better that he dies than not learn the rudiments of her, and Calvin's, doctrines. Shortly after a beating, Ephraim does die, though the immediate cause is his exertion in a forbidden sledding episode of which his mother is not aware.

There are in *Pembroke* a number of other "grotesques" who need not be described here. The interesting question is, What is Freeman's assessment of her fictional community as the rather typical New England village that she says it is? As we have seen, Pembroke is in many ways an unpleasant place. Public opinion and gossip rule the townspeople's minds and actions. Yet it is a closely knit community, albeit imperfect, and partly because group opinion does matter. Moreover, certain dignitaries—the Orthodox minister, the doctor, the selectmen, Squire Payne—function as integrating influences. Their various activities are respected, and their position as leaders is recognized. Freeman makes it very clear that the inhabitants of Pembroke share a strong, almost tribal sense of identity, as is underlined by her description of a cherry-picking festivity engaged in by the young folks of the village—a sort of midsummer rite. Though utterly innocent, the occasion is characterized as being "like a little bacchanalian rout in a New England field on a summer afternoon, but they did not know it in their simple hearts."[22] Of similar significance is the traditional custom of the Pembroke children's collecting wild flowers on May Day and leaving bouquets of them at the townspeople's doors.

Thus there is in Pembroke a strong sense of community, which Freeman sees as an asset, or at least a potential one if only it could break through the outworn forms of thought and feeling imposed on it by a distant past. *Pembroke* may therefore be classed as incidentally—not by its main purpose—an anti-Calvinist novel, though Freeman was herself a converted member of the Congregational Church; and she may be grouped with such novelists, mainly associated with the Berkshires, as Sedgwick, Judd, Bellamy, Holmes, and Longfellow, most of whom advocated that the old religion of fear be supplanted by one of love, as a first step in the reformation and spiritual resuscitation of New England towns. Freeman also counts on love to break down the barriers between person and person and individual and community in Pembroke. With Barnabas and Charlotte love does eventually triumph, but in a way little different from that in which it triumphs over misunderstandings and other obstacles in conventional love stories.

More impressive is the case of Deborah Thayer in relation to the community. After her sickly son's death, it was commonly believed that she had killed him by whipping him, counter to the doctor's orders. There was talk of excommunicating her from her church; socially she was shunned. But one day after several months the truth became known: the boy's forbidden sledding had caused his ailing heart to fail. The doctor's wife and another woman call to inform her, realizing the remorse she must be suffering. This act of neighborly compassion, of Christian love, is an important episode in the book. When Deborah hears the information, Freeman writes that "her face worked like the breaking up of an icy river."[23] However, Deborah's health has been undermined, and she dies almost at once from the shock of good news.

But first she calls her estranged daughter and son to her, perhaps now having undergone a conversion quite different from the one that long ago had entitled her to church membership. That first conversion had set her apart from all but her fellow "saints"; the second reconciled her with humanity, including her own children. Freeman's point may be a suble one: the old Puritan church covenant of fellowship was too restricted. Even in early Plymouth and Massachusetts Bay it excluded large numbers of the inhabitants. It made for pride, self-righteousness, intolerance on the part of the covenanted members. A more inclusive covenant was needed—one that recognized and encouraged a sense of community, the whole community. Deborah Thayer, who represented the sternest side of Old Testament religion as practiced by the Puritans, has become softened, Christianized, one might say, by a lifting of community condemnation of her. Perhaps Freeman is saying that Old Testament oriented New England needed to shift its focus a bit toward the New Testament.

The Town Poor

The plight of the town poor became a subject of many stories by New England regional writers of the late nineteenth century, a stark indication of the economic and social distress of the area. Indeed, even the earliest fiction writers were not blind to the problem. Catharine Sedgwick provides hints that squalor and insanity were not notably absent from her beloved Berkshires. Sylvester Judd, as we have seen, in the opening chapters of *Margaret* depicts the shiftless drunkenness of shanty dwellers in western Massachusetts. But later authors dealt more graphically and more frequently with the grinding poverty and accompanying evils endemic in the remoter parts of New England.

From their founding until very recently, New England towns have had to cope with their own poor; only in the last decades have the state and federal governments taken over most of the responsibility. And the towns were not remarkable either for sympathy with, or generous provisions for, their indigent inhabitants. The two ways devised for dealing with pauperism have been mentioned in connection with Rowland Robinson. To repeat, one was the notorious New England poorhouse, which also frequently seved as an asylum for the insane. In these establishments would be gathered the down-and-outers of the town—men, women, and children, in varying conditions of health or decrepitude. Those who were able would work at household tasks or on the farm that was usually connected with the almshouse.

The other way of dealing with the poor was to place them in private homes, the assignment of each pauper going to the person who at town meeting bid the lowest figure for a year's support. Each town, moreover, elected overseers of the poor, whose function was to see that all paupers for whom the town was responsible received at least minimum relief. In a society still under the sway of Calvinist attitudes, as were the rural communities of New England, a degree of disgrace would attach to the condition of being poor. God, it was thought, tended to favor His elect with material prosperity in this world in addition to granting them salvation in the next. A pauper would be suspected of being out of God's favor and very likely headed for damnation. Thus to "go on the town" would be viewed as an ignominy to be avoided if at all possible—and of course it would be a *public* ignominy, for every one knew who the poor were and often they would be discussed by name in town meeting.

An almshouse, with its miserable inmates and mean-minded, parsimonious supervisors, was the scene of the depressing events in Rowland Robinson's story "The Fourth of July at Highfield Poorhouse." Mary Wilkins Freeman, always the realist, treats the subject more dramatically in her story "Sister Liddy," one of the finest of all New England local-color tales. Here the mentally ill, the senile, the impoverished—children as well as adults—mingle in a scene of misery in a poorhouse set among stubble fields, bleak and bare beneath a pelting November rain.[24] Meaningless, repetitive conversation, the prattle of children, the shrieks of demented women produce a jarring discord; death is the only escape from a living hell.

Freeman's volumes are thickly populated with the poor who are not quite "on the town" and who, with stubborn pride, are resisting that fate to the point of starvation. Thus in her story "An Honest Soul" an indigent seamstress faints from hunger as she desperately strives to survive in her tiny cottage,[25] and in *Pembroke* an elderly woman, also nearing starvation, submits to being taken to the poorhouse only when the selectmen force her. Yet Sarah Orne Jewett, in her story "The Flight of Betsy Lane," manages to draw a cheery picture of life in Byfleet poorhouse, where, she writes, "the inmates were by no means distressed or unhappy; many of them retired to this shelter only for the winter season, and would go out presently, some to begin such work as they could still do, others to live in their own small houses; old age had impoverished most of them by limiting their power of endurance; but far from lamenting the fact that they were town charges, they rather liked the change and excitement of a winter residence on the poor-farm."[26] As Jewett proceeds to a description of the maladies and misfortunes of the individual inmates, the rosy hue of the scene becomes somewhat darkened. But the poor farm of fictional Byfleet stands as an exception among similar institutions as they appear in the work of other New England writers of the time. Or the fact that Byfleet poorhouse afforded such desirable pleasures may be taken as a commentary on how little else the town had to offer its elderly and its destitute.

The second method of dealing with the poor—that of boarding them out with the lowest bidders—struck even Sarah Orne Jewett as inhumane. Her story "The Town Poor" examines the plight of the impoverished Bray sisters, who have been disposed of in that manner. The words of another character in the story poignantly describe the humiliation and the misery of this luckless pair:

> "They give their consent to goin' on the town because they knew they'd got to be dependent, an' so they felt 't would come easier for all than for a few to help 'em. They acted real dignified an' right-minded, contrary to what most do in such cases, but they was dreadful anxious to see who would bid 'em off, town-meeting day; they did so hope 't would be somebody right in the village. I just sat down and cried good when I found Abel Janes's folks had got hold of 'em. They always had the name of bein' slack and poor-spirited, an' they did it just for what they got out o' the town. The selectmen this last year ain't what we have had."[27]

The system was working as might be expected. The two women, of genteel background, had suffered the indignity of virtually being put up for auction. The Abel Janeses had undertaken to support both for five dollars a month and make a profit. Mrs. Janes was surly about the extra housework. One can imagine the wretchedness of the hapless boarders.

Since women did not vote in town meetings in Jewett's time, we may hope that the Bray sisters were not present as they were being "bid off." Such was not the case with the poor whose treatment is described in Rowland Robinson's "An Old-Time March Meeting." In this generally good-humored piece Robinson records a debate over the propriety of "bidding off" the paupers, and it is to the credit of human nature that before this matter could be put to a vote "a few made earnest protest against this barbarous but then not uncommon custom."[28] Yet the vote is "to let out" the support of the poor, and of course the stingiest man in town is the lowest bidder.

Doings such as these and scenes in poorhouses were not included in earlier literary descriptions of New England rural life. Can one imagine Timothy Dwight, for example, discussing in *Greenfield Hill* the condition and treatment of the local poor? Indeed, according to him, in that Utopian community there was no poverty. Even in the four volumes of his *Travels in New England and New York* Dwight avoided such matters. Nor does Harriet Beecher Stowe, one of the most prolific and realistic depicters of village life in New England, give much space to the hardships of poor people at the mercy of the town. It remained for later authors, those of the last third of the nineteenth century, to face a reality that was damaging to the carefully etched image of the New England town as a high point in the history of civilization and that hinted at more fundamental problems than earlier authors chose to recognize. Yet none of the writers of fiction who touched on the question of poverty was entirely negative about New England rural life. They were merely more honest than their predecessors.

Edward Bellamy's *The Duke of Stockbridge:* The Past Revisited

Another New England author of the postbellum period, Edward Bellamy (1850-98), took it upon himself to examine town government and social structure in New England at the end of the eighteenth century. What he found was contrary to the accounts given by historians like Charles Francis Adams and George Bancroft and by statesmen like Jefferson and John Adams. In his novel *The Duke of Stockbridge*, published in the Great Barrington, Massachusetts, newspaper the *Berkshire Courier* in 1879 and in book form in 1900, Bellamy wrote of rigid class stratification and economic oppression as it existed, according to him, in a New England town in the first years of the nation's independence. The events described in the novel are mainly drawn from accounts of Shays's Rebellion. The scene is none other than Catharine Sedgwick's beloved Stockbridge; and her father, Theodore Sedgwick, plays a prominent part in the action. Choosing to examine a New England town of considerable importance in the state and country during an agrarian revolt, Bellamy traced the causes of the upheaval to the economic conditions of the time and region, to class antagonisms and divisions, and to the aspirations and resentments of the rural populace. For Bellamy knew, as we have seen that Catharine Sedgwick knew, that deep-seated dissatisfactions and grievances had generated the rebellion of the New England farmers and that it was short-sighted and unjust to refer to Shays and his followers simply as a lawless and vicious mob without probing for the causes that made them behave as they did.

Samuel Eliot Morison has described Bellamy's carefully researched book as "one of the greatest historical novels . . . . It gives a more accurate account of the causes and events of Shays' Rebellion than any of the formal histories do."[29] But Bellamy also brought to his book a profound sense of social justice. A native of Chicopee Falls in a heavily industrialized section of western Massachusetts, he had seen the miseries and exploitation of the factory workers of his time and had witnessed the struggles of labor to better itself. Though trained as a lawyer, he never practiced law; instead, mainly in the years after writing *The Duke of Stockbridge,* he became involved in journalism. Concerned as he was with social problems, he eventually wrote his masterpiece, the immensely popular utopian novel *Looking Backward: 2000–1887* (1888), which was so influential that a political movement, that of the Nationalist party, was founded to promote its principles. Doubtless some of what Bellamy had learned in writing about Shays's Rebellion made itself felt in this later and greater book.

Bellamy was not the first New England novelist who had seriously written about Shays's Rebellion. Ralph Ingersol Lockwood (1798-1858?), a Connecticut-born lawyer, published anonymously a novel titled *The Insurgents* (1835), in which he explored in depth and with sympathy the causes of the rebellion. But Lockwood was a practicing lawyer who wrote scholarly books on the law, and he could not condone the suppression of the courts and other excesses perpetrated by the Shaysites at Northampton, Springfield, and elsewhere. The rebels, Lockwood agreed, had real grievances—a heavy burden of taxes and debts combined with a worthless currency—which should have been heard and redressed through legal and constitutional channels. James Bowdoin, who was governor of Massachusetts during the rebellion, was right, Lockwood thought, in sending troops to quell the revolt. But the novel makes its point without resort to diatribes or wholesale condemnation. It records the conditions prevalent in the decade after the Revolutionary War, presenting the political and social life of the times in realistic detail. Lockwood notes the part played by town meetings in the uprising and by county conventions—a legacy from the Revolution, but having no legal sanction—held by insurgent delegates from the various towns; and he has some vivid scenes of fighting and rioting. On the whole, his treatment is reasonably balanced and open-minded.

But Bellamy in his novel is frankly and vehemently on the side of the Shaysites, even when they are behaving in utter defiance of the laws and the courts. Chapter 1, "The March of the Minute Men," describes the moment in Stockbridge when the local militia are departing northward to take part in the Battle of Bennington. All classes—the gentry, the farmers, the shopkeepers—are on hand to see off the troops. Harmony and good will are the moods in a community sharing the efforts and anxiety of a momentous undertaking. But chapter 2, "Nine Years Later" (i.e., 1787), presents the bitter farmers and workingmen gathered in the local tavern. The angry conversation dwells on the hard times that are driving the common folk into bankruptcy. Taxes, depreciated money, sheriff's sales, imprisonment for debt, the harshness of the courts, and the unconscionable greed of the lawyers have made life unbearable. One of the drinkers arouses no opposition when he states: "I callate we wuz a dern sight better orf every way under the King, 'n we be naow. The Tories wuz right, arter all, I guess. We'd better a let well nuff 'lone, an not to a jumped aouter the fryin-pan intew the fire."[30] The angriest complaints come from the returned veterans, who nine years before had marched off as heroes to fight for the Colonies' independence.

The leader among the Stockbridge rebels, both in history and in the novel, is Perez Hamlin. Arriving home belatedly from South Carolina, where he had been soldiering, he finds his brother Reuben in the Great Barrington jail, a place of "indescribable filth,"[31] where he has languished for a year because he could not pay a debt he owed to a Stockbridge deacon. From Reuben, Perez also learns that their father is about to be evicted from his farm for failure to keep up his mortgage payments. Perez's anger grows as it finds more and more to feed on, but it scarcely exceeds that of most of his fellow townsmen. With a talent for command, and experience in war, he soon finds himself the leader of the insurgents. The events that follow are historically based, though Bellamy avails himself of a fiction writer's privilege of taking some liberties with details. The most notable deviation from history—and the most regrettable from the literary viewpoint—is the love affair that he dreams up between Perez, who in real life was married, and Desire Edwards, who never existed at all. Timothy Edwards, her father, had existed, however; he was the son of Jonathan

Edwards, at one time a missionary to the Stockbridge Indians. The younger Edwards is a local merchant, of course violently opposed to the rebels.

Edwards is also one of the three selectmen of Stockbridge, the other two being Squire Jahleel Woodbridge and Squire Theodore Sedgwick. As the most powerful and wealthiest citizens of the town, the three constitute a sort of political and social aristocracy. Their chief concern is to protect their property and position from mob action and to amass more wealth, if convenient, through foreclosures and sheriff's sales. With the backing of several other men of wealth and position, they regard themselves as absolute rulers. Meeting in a back room of Edwards's store and sipping "choice old Jamaica," they and a few of their intimates sit in council. There "the affairs of the village are debated and settled by these magnates, whose decisions the common people never dream of anticipating or questioning."[32]

Why, one may ask, have the people permitted this usurpation? At town-meeting time could not this ruling hierarchy have been voted out of office and persons more responsive to the needs of the people elected? There are a number of possible answers. In the first place, during colonial times, when Stockbridge was founded, the idea of a ruling class was more acceptable than it was later, and for a period after the Revolution the colonial attitudes lingered. For example, in the towns along the Connecticut River a group of politically and socially influential men—known as the "River Gods"—were kept more or less continuously in office as selectmen and representatives in the General Court. In the Berkshires somewhat the same situation prevailed, and notably so in Stockbridge, where confirmed enemies of democracy like Theodore Sedgwick habitually held the reins of government. As for the electorate's retiring such persons from office, historians tell us that in the late eighteenth century in western Massachusetts "only a fraction of those who could vote exercised the privilege."[33] Indeed, lethargy was so pervasive that frequently towns did not bother to send representatives to the state legislature. Until a crisis like Shays's Rebellion arose, the townspeople of all classes seem to have been content with things as they were. Also Stockbridge, like most New England villages of the time, was still under the strong influence of the government-supported Congregational Church, which traditionally taught that respect was due not only to all elected officials but also to persons of high social and economic status.

Thus when Perez, having gained control of the town, is about to have Timothy Edwards and others of the "magnates" flogged, as the "magnates" had caused others of the humble classes to be flogged, the Stockbridge minister, Parson West, expostulates: "But man . . ., you have forgotten that these are the first men in the county. They are gentlemen of distinguished birth and official station. You would not whip them like common offenders. It is impossible. You are beside yourself. . . . As a minister of the gospel I protest! I forbid such a thing."[34] Making no impression on Perez with these words, the Parson tries another approach: "Christ said that if any man smite you on the right cheek, turn to him the other also." Perez's rejoinder is: "If that is your counsel, take it to those who are likely to need it. I am doing the smiting this time, and it's their time to do the turning."[35]

Though "West is not a political parson,"[36] the temporal rulers of the town are pillars of the church; Timothy Edwards, for example, is a deacon. Furthermore, Parson West's theology is strict Calvinism of the type preached by Samuel Hopkins, under whose guidance West—once "notoriously affected with Arminian leanings"[37]—had been brought back to sound doctrine. Preaching a vengeful and punitive God, he warned that one must rejoice in the divine justice evidenced in the affliction of the damned, even if oneself were among that wretched company. In short, divine power in any form, however brutal, must be venerated and praised. By analogy the power of magistrates and selectmen, though not infallible, deserves respect. The hold of the church on most of the people of Stockbridge is amply demonstrated in their strict observance of the Sabbath, which, as in Puritan times, extends from sundown Saturday to sundown Sunday. Strife-torn though the town was, the old Sabbath ways were followed and honored. To the townspeople the parson would be the guardian of these ways and he would gain stature from his identification with the ancestral religion. Such a man would be a natural ally of the ruling clique. Perez's defiance of the minister was the act of a desperate and infuriated man.

This clique rule was, and is to some degree, quite common in New England towns, as one may discover by an examination of a number of randomly selected town reports. Year after year, in many cases, the same persons are elected to important positions. Certain families may hold monopolies on offices during several generations, so that something like hereditary rights and claims come to be tacitly accepted. The popular vote, however, has always been decisive, and if a certain functionary or family of functionaries behaves utterly outrageously they may be displaced. The lengthy tenure enjoyed by some individuals and families is frequently the result of their better education, their superior abilities and experience, which would increase with the years, and their greater wealth, which would foster in them a deep concern for the prosperity of the community and would impress the populace, whose religion formerly taught that God showers the good things of this world on those He favors. These temporary quasi aristocracies, which had existed from the earliest days of the Plymouth and Bay colonies, were not necessarily harmful to a town. Indeed, they were often beneficial, and the townspeople, with gratitude for their leaders, would address them as "Squire" (usually pronounced "Square") and refer to them as the "town fathers."

But in Stockbridge at the time of Shays's Rebellion, according to Bellamy, the self-appointed aristocracy, supported hitherto by the suffrage of a passive electorate, was beneficial to no one's interests but their own. Their attitude is revealed when the people do become aroused and show their discontent with their rulers. Squire Sedgwick speaks for his class when he says: "I like not this assembling of the people to discuss political matters. We must look to it, gentlemen, or we shall find that we have ridded ourselves of a king only to fall into the hands of a democracy, which I take it would be a bad exchange."[38] That the people did not—perhaps preferred not to—assemble in the legal forum of the town meeting indicates their loss of faith in the town's officers, who doubtless, in any event, would not cooperate in the gathering of such meetings—though, according to law, meetings had to be called if a sufficient number of voters so petitioned.

In *The Duke of Stockbridge* we see New England town government in a state of collapse, as any government might be when beset by revolt. Jefferson, John Adams, Timothy Dwight, all of whom were aware of the troubles in rural Massachusetts, would not have been pleased with the state of civic affairs in towns like Stockbridge, where all they had said in praise of New England town government seemed to be negated. But the commotions were confined mainly to Massachusetts, and even there by no means all towns were in such disarray. In some, the town meetings upheld the insurrection; others remained neutral. Jefferson, however, did not condemn the Shaysites, and thought that the system of town government would eventually gain by it. On hearing of the troubles, he wrote from Paris, where he was serving as United States minister: "I hold it that a little rebellion now and then is a good thing, and as necessary in the political world as storms in the physical. . . . It is a medicine necessary for the sound health of government."[39] Dwight, on the other hand, was not so philosophical. He regarded the uprising as the work of an unruly mob, mistakenly seeking redress by force for admitted grievances. In the four volumes of his *Travels*, however, Dwight devotes only part of one paragraph to Shays and his doings, and emphasizes the minimal loss of life in the fighting—thus providing further evidence of the inherently peaceful nature, as he saw it, of New Englanders even during an armed rebellion.[40]

Industrialization

Edward Bellamy's sympathy with the exploited farmers of Stockbridge may well have been a projection of his sympathy with the mill workers in the Connecticut River Valley village of Chicopee Falls, where he had been born and lived much of his life. Chicopee Falls, the site of textile mills and a variety of other factories employing many native and immigrant operatives, was typical of numerous medium-sized mill towns that had proliferated along rivers and smaller streams in New England during the nineteenth century. This industrialization, indeed, accounted for much of the depletion of the population of the remote rural areas as described by writers like Hartt.

The pace of industrialization was rapid. Many agricultural townships, if suitably located near a source of water power or on the route of one of the newly built railroads, were transformed into manufacturing centers, and much of the old way of life disappeared. At the beginning of the century these towns and those not so favorably situated had been largely self-supporting. Farmers grew sufficient food for their families and raised the sheep and flax from which the women made the family's clothing and bedding, and the forests supplied fuel and lumber. Each farmstead was in fact a tiny industrial complex involving a multitude of skills and occupations. Any surplus of farm or home products would find a market in the local community, where it might be disposed of in barter, or it could be transported by wagon or sledge to the larger towns and cities. In every township there would also be a number of artisans and small-scale entrepreneurs—a blacksmith, perhaps a shoemaker, a wheelwright, a miller, a storekeeper or two—whose services or commodities could be paid for in money or in produce. Thus the towns back from the sea and along the coast away from the deep-water harbors were to a great extent self-sufficient. Only the port cities depended crucially on trade with domestic or foreign markets. But as the century wore on, commerce became more and more concentrated in a few major ports on the Atlantic seaboard, though the whaling and fishing towns like New Bedford, New London, and Gloucester continued to thrive. Smaller ports like Salem (see Hawthorne's "The Custom House" in *The Scarlet Letter*) lost most of their shipping, and even Boston suffered from competition with New York. The moneyed classes of New England perforce turned to manufacturing as a substitute for commerce. As Frederick Jackson Turner phrased it, "the harbors were yielding in importance to the waterfalls."[41]

The mushrooming of textile mills along the Merrimack and the growth of the cities containing them—with Lowell in the lead—are the most dramatic illustrations of this shift, but the pattern was repeated elsewhere in the region on somewhat lesser scales. One immediate effect was to hasten the decrease in the rural population. Many young women from the hill-country farms took jobs in the mills only on a temporary basis, with the intention of returning home after a few years with a sum of money to launch them into matrimony. But many young men also went to the factory towns and stayed there in preference to the rigors and discouragements of tilling New England's hilly and rocky soil, especially as the farms now had to compete with produce from the fertile West, for which the railroads and waterways had opened up the Eastern market.

In the first half of the century, however, manufacturing was by no means confined to cities and towns along the major rivers. Throughout New England, along any stream bed with a dependable flow of water, one can find today the remnants of dams that once powered local mills. Many of these were family operations, doing little business outside the immediate neighborhood. But some, even in the remote towns, were more extensive enterprises that sold their products farther afield, perhaps even in the distant cities if transportation were available. For example, one historian records that in northeastern Vermont and northern New Hampshire, a number of the smallest towns had one or more industries, including woolen mills, tanneries, foundries, and iron works.[42] In the Berkshire Hills of Massachusetts, in the words of another historian, "the town of Sheffield . . . possessed just prior to 1830 two gristmills, five sawmills, two carding machines, two clothiers' works, three tanneries, one manufactory of hats, two cabinet makers' shops, several limekilns, several blacksmiths and wagonmakers" and a distillery.[43] In the hundred years after 1830, "Sheffield lost nearly 800 of its 2500 population, and all its industries . . . , save one lime works, a sleepy gristmill, and a small plant which ground marble dust."[44] Writing in 1871, James Parton, on visiting the Berkshires, reported that the region was still "prosperous," owing to its many diversified industries, though he deplored the ugliness of some of the factories and regretted that the employment they offered made for a shortage of farm laborers and domestic servants and attracted more foreign workers than could readily be assimilated into the Yankee culture.[45]

When these industries remained small, they caused relatively little change in the social and cultural structure of the towns. However, when they grew into large operations—as they often did, without approaching the proportions of the colossi on the Merrimack—the old way of life was severely disrupted. Frederick Jackson Turner reports: "Mill villages, made of company houses adjacent to the pond and dam with 'the proprietor's residence perched on the hillside,' began to give a different look to the landscape of southern New England and to indicate a changing society."[46]

The spread of railroads throughout New England in the 1840s and 1850s contributed to the growth in size and profits of the larger manufacturing concerns but had the opposite effect on the out-of-the-way smaller ones. One might have thought that the new accessibility to city markets would have aided the small rural industries, as, for a time, it aided the farmers. But these industries could not compete in price with the larger ones, either in the city markets or in their home territories, where low-priced, mass-produced products arrived by rail. The resultant demise of many small-town industries lessened local demands for farm products and increased unemployment. With the arrival on the Eastern seaboard of Western grain and meat the New England farmer's plight became critical. The exodus from the farms accelerated; poverty and decay settled like night over much of the countryside. Conditions described by observers like Hartt became endemic.

These phases of industrialization in New England—the rise of a highly diversified and broadly based rural industry and its gradual but disastrous decline as manufacturing, centered in larger towns, was monopolized by fewer and bigger corporations—figure importantly in the works of New England writers of fiction in the last century. The destruction of a village industry is vividly described in Mary Wilkins Freeman's *Jerome: A Poor Man* (1897), a novel weak in plot but strong in its analysis of forces responsible for the decline of morale in rural New England.

In the novel, Upham is a fictional village situated quite obviously in Vermont at a considerable distance from a larger town named Dale, through which a newly built railroad will soon pass. Most of the inhabitants of Upham are on the verge of destitution already, and the poorhouse is always full. One of the few bulwarks against utter poverty is a shoe industry run by the proprietor of the local general store. As in Freeman's native Randolph, Massachusetts, during her childhood, some of the townspeople of Upham sew shoes on consignment in tiny shops in or adjacent to their homes. The finished shoes are sold by the storekeeper to a dealer in Dale, who ships them on to the cities. The arrangement is far from satisfactory, for the persons who sew the shoes receive sweatshop pay; but it at least brings some money into a desperately depressed community. However, the coming of the railroad to Dale has soon made possible the production of machine-made shoes there for the Boston market, at a cost with which the village dealer cannot compete. The home industry of Upham collapses, just as that of Randolph had collapsed when the great factories of Brockton began the mass production of shoes. The villagers, already embittered by long years of hard times, are outraged.

"'It was an unlucky day for Upham when that railroad went through Dale,'" a man laments.

"'Curse the railroad, an' curse all the new ideas that take the bread out of poor men's mouths to give it to the rich,' said a bitter voice, and there was a hoarse amen from the crowd."[47]

So much for shoe manufacturing in the hill village of Upham. What happens in Dale, which now has become a medium-sized manufacturing town, or perhaps, eventually, a city? Sarah Orne Jewett, an optimist about most things connected with New England, describes such a town in a short story, "The Gray Mills of Farley." The town of Farley has become more and more dependent on its mills, which at first drew their laborers from the neighboring farms but later attracted Irish and French-Canadian immigrants. The mill owners are greedy; wages, when there is employment, are at a starvation level. When the mills shut down, most of the population of Farley is faced with disaster. Jewett offers no remedy, other than Christian charity.[48]

Freeman in another of her novels, *The Portion of Labor* (1901), reveals the plight of the workers in a really large manufacturing city, modeled perhaps on Brockton. In this book the social and economic chasm between the rich factory owner and the poor mill hands—Swedes, Yankees, Irish, Slavs—has become unbridgeable. Central to the plot is a workers' strike, which results in widespread distress. The suffering of the operatives and their families and the unfairness of their situation are made movingly clear. Needless to say, not a vestige of the New England village way of life can be found in this industrial city, except for the overdeveloped conscience and pride of heritage of several of the Yankee workers. Nor does Freeman—the daughter of a workingman, who had known his share of hard times—offer any solution beyond the admonitions contained in a passage from Ecclesiastes quoted by one of the native New England workers: "Live joyfully with the wife whom thou lovest all the days of the life of thy vanity, which He hath given thee under the sun, all the days of thy vanity, for that is thy portion in this life and in thy labor which thou takest under the sun."[49]

William Dean Howells (1837–1920) in his novel *Annie Kilburn* (1888), laid in a mill town named Hatboro'—which is somewhat smaller and more solidly Yankee than the city in *The Portion of Labor*—found similar class divisions, misunderstandings, and miseries, but probed more deeply for their causes and possible cures. Unlike Freeman, who had written mainly from the point of view of the poor, Howells focuses upon the merchants, the mill owners, the professional persons, and the summer folk in nearby South Hatboro'. Hatboro' is presented as once having been a typical inland New England town, primarily agricultural with a nucleus of professionals, artisans, and tradespeople to meet the population's needs. It may be assumed also that it had a few light industries, though Howells omits mention of them. A rather harmless social stratification also existed, for there were several old-line families whose education and social and intellectual refinement identified them rather vaguely as New England Brahmins. The men of this small group entered the learned professions, especially the law in the case of Hatboro'. Yet these families were not regarded as a class completely apart and they enjoyed the respect and affection of the other townspeople. Even at the time of the action of the novel, the people regarded them with a good will denied to the mill owners, the wealthy merchants, and the summer people.

The railroad on which Hatboro' is situated, the consequent coming of large textile, hat, and shoe mills, and the development of the nearby summer resort have effected a total transformation. Outside of town there are still farmers who retain their traditional conviction that they are as good as any one else, if not a little better, and deal with all people accordingly. But there has also been created a proletariat whose members, on the verge of poverty, live across the tracks from the well-to-do, for the railroad literally as well as symbolically has divided the community into two antagonistic camps.

There are no labor strikes and accompanying violence in *Annie Kilburn,* as there are in Freeman's *The Portion of Labor.* Indeed the mill hands are represented in the novel by only one or two characters of secondary importance, whereas most of the characters in Freeman's novel are of the working class. Howells's chief interest is in examining the relation of the privileged minority to the social divisions that have occurred in a town like Hatboro'. Fresh from reading Lev Tolstoy's *What Then Shall We Do?,* he was himself agonizing over the problems resulting from the widening social and economic disparities between the rich and the poor. The heroine of the novel, Annie, who is the daughter of an old family and is afflicted with a painfully sensitive conscience, attempts to improve matters by "good works," as do the summer folk, whose consciences, though less developed than Annie's, stir them to half-hearted and ineffective efforts. Many contribute their prestige, time, and money to these efforts; but the local Orthodox (Calvinist) minister knows that good works are not enough. A Tolstoyan of sorts, without realizing it, he is aware that charity or any well-intentioned aid without unfeigned brotherhood will seem patronizing to the workers and will only broaden the gulf it was designed to bridge. The minister himself, who was once a factory worker, has idealistic plans for establishing cooperative boarding houses for the workers and for educating them in night classes, but he proposes to conduct his experiment in Fall River, where the problems are much more pressing than in Hatboro'. He is run down by a railroad train before he can embark on his plan, and Annie attempts to carry out the boarding-house scheme in Hatboro'. While not a total failure, the idea is far from a resounding success. Howells, in this novel, offers no solution, though later in *A Traveler from Altruria* (1894) and other works he was to do so in strictly Tolstoyan terms. The novel *Annie Kilburn* leaves us with the saddening picture of a traditional New England town set adrift on the perilous waters of nineteenth-century industrialization. Most of the attractive and stabilizing characteristics of the old community—of which Timothy Dwight would doubtless have approved enthusiastically—have vanished, and no new stability is in sight.

The flight of New England industries from the countryside to the cities and the tendency of the cities to specialize in a single type of manufacture, such as textiles or shoes, persisted until the onset of the Great Depression. But economic collapse brought disaster to manufacturing centers like Manchester, New Hampshire and Lowell and Fall River, Massachusetts. The cessation or curtailment of production of a city's chief or sole industry threw large numbers of workers on relief and severely depressed all other segments of the community's economy. Nor in most cases was there any chance of returning to the old one-industry basis of comparative prosperity. Even before 1929 many companies had been moving their operations to the South, where labor, nonunionized, was cheap and plentiful. The Depression greatly accelerated this exodus. The only recourse was the introduction of many small industries of different types to take the place of the vanished, all-engrossing large one. This process promptly began and continued with remarkably favorable results, though some of the larger cities (e.g., Fall River and New Bedford) are still far from being out of the woods.

Along with the process of diversification in the big manufacturing centers, a variety of new, small-scale industries sprang up in smaller communities. A partial return to conditions in the previous century was taking place. But industries alone were far from being the sole answer to the economic problems of the hinterland and remote coastal regions. Recreation and tourism had assumed the status of an industry. For a century or more New England had attracted summer vacationers. The increase in automobile travel brought them in larger numbers to all areas. In the 1930s and 1940s one of the region's supposed liabilities—its long, snowy winters—turned out to be an asset, as skiing and other winter sports became a national craze. Snowbound mountain communities, accustomed during the previous two hundred years to an eight-month hibernation, suddenly found themselves the centers of lucrative year-round activity. In addition, greater mobility because of the motor car and improved highways made commuting to industrial jobs in relatively distant towns feasible for the backcountry residents. Areas of the Appalachia type of poverty still remain, but in general rural New England for the past fifty years has been staging an economic comeback.[50]

At Ease in Zion: Sarah Orne Jewett and Emily Dickinson

There is no better way of learning American history than to find
out what one can of the story of an old New England town.
Sarah Orne Jewett, "The Old Town of Berwick"[1]

Why so *far*, Jennie, wasn't there room enough for that young
ambition, among New England hills, that it must spread its wings,
and fly away, and away, till it paused at Ohio? *Sometimes* think my
dear Jennie was a *wee bit uneasy* in her own home and country, or
she never had strolled so far, but won't reproach her any, for it's
sad to be a stranger, and she *is* now. Why I can't think what would
tempt me to bid my friends Good bye. I'm afraid I'm growing
selfish in my dear home, but I do love it so.
Emily Dickinson, in a letter of Jane Humphrey.[2]

Sarah Orne Jewett and South Berwick, Maine

Two of nineteenth-century America's finest authors, Sarah Orne Jewett in
prose and Emily Dickinson in poetry, shared not at all the negative views of
New England village life conveyed in the work of authors like Mary E.
Wilkins Freeman and Edward Bellamy. Sarah Jewett (1849–1909), the
daughter of a country doctor, was descended from one of the oldest and
most prosperous families of her native South Berwick, Maine. In her girlhood she often accompanied her father on his rounds in the neighboring
countryside and thus could observe at firsthand the way of life of Maine
rural and village people; and instinctively, it seems, she focused her attention on the pleasant and admirable aspects of what she saw. But she was not
perpetually a wearer of rose-colored spectacles, as Edith Wharton once
accused her of being. She was, in fact, by no means blind to the misery and
abnormalities present among the country folk of her region, as is indicated
by stories like "The Town Poor," which has just been discussed. She herself
had the desire to become a physician like her father, but the times were not
right for a woman to enter the profession. She realized her ambition imagi-

natively, however, in writing *A Country Doctor* (1884), the story of a girl who forgoes marriage and does succeed in becoming a physician.

Jewett's all-engrossing interest in New England, especially Maine, had its roots in a fascination with the town of her birth. In an article titled "The Old Town of Berwick," printed in the *New England Magazine* in 1894, she traces from its beginning the history of Berwick, which for almost two hundred years included the town of South Berwick. A brief but detailed and carefully researched piece of local history, her essay is a model of its kind. Added merits are its clear, flowing prose and the author's patent enthusiasm for her subject. The outbursts of local chauvinism that occur here and there may be forgiven her; actually they seem appropriate to this sort of writing, as long as one may be sure, as is the case here, that the author is thoroughly acquainted with her material. One would be ungracious indeed to find fault with her when she almost fiercely asserts: "I am proud to be made of Berwick dust. . . . Her children and the flock of her old academy are scattered everywhere. . . . They have started many a Western town; they are buried in Southern graves for their country's sake; they are lost in far northern seas."[3] Jewett, indeed, thought of herself as the literary spokeswoman, or recorder, of the life and culture of her native region. She might have quoted those words of Vergil—"*Primus ego in patriam mecum. . . . deducam musas*"—which Willa Cather, who had learned much from Jewett, quotes in *My Antonia* to explain, by implication, her literary interest in the Nebraska prairies.[4] For each, the region in which she grew up was worthy of serious and sympathetic literary treatment. Perhaps no greater compliment could be given a culture.

Attachment to her native town and fascination with its past, in which her ancestors had been so deeply involved, are behind the impulse from which Jewett's writing sprang and account also, perhaps, for her relatively favorable pictures of rural and coastal Maine. In this respect she resembled Rowland Robinson, who was similarly devoted to the locale in which he was born and wrote of it with a pen that was usually highly approving and only occasionally unflattering. Mary Wilkins Freeman, on the other hand, apparently had weaker, or less happy, associations both with her native Randolph, Massachusetts, and with Brattleboro, Vermont, where she lived during her adolescence and early womanhood.

Yet Jewett was not a sentimentalist. For one thing her zeal for accuracy in her facts and her talent for close observation—learned, perhaps, from her physician father—precluded an excess of sentimentality. But also she was influenced by developments in the social sciences of her day. Her approach was sometimes that of the folklorist, sometimes that of the social historian, sometimes that of the ethnologist. In her preface to *Deephaven* (1877), which is a series of sketches of life and characters in a Maine seaport suggestive of her own South Berwick and of neighboring York, she quotes from George Sand's *Légendes Rustiques* as follows: "Le paysan est donc, si l'on peut ainsi dire, le seul historien qui nous reste des temps antehistoriques. Honneur et profit intellectuel à qui se consecrerait à la recherche de ses traditions merveilleuses de chaque hameau qui rassemblées ou groupées, comparées entres elles et minutieusement disséquées, jetteraient peut-être de grandes lueurs sur le nuit profonde des âges primitifs."[5] [The peasant then, so to speak, is the sole remaining historian of prehistoric times. Honor and intellectual profit to any one who would devote himself to the search for every hamlet's traditions, which taken altogether or in groups, compared with one another and minutely analyzed, would perhaps cast much light into the deep night of primitive epochs.] Actually, Jewett has much in common with those historians who attempted to trace the New England town meeting back to its supposed Germanic or Aryan origins. How well she was acquainted with their speculations, which did not receive widespread publication until the 1880s, is a matter of conjecture.

Sarah Orne Jewett: *The Country of the Pointed Firs*

Jewett realizes the goal suggested by George Sand more fully in another book, published nineteen years after *Deephaven*. Having spent several summers at Tenant's Harbor, a coastal hamlet almost one hundred miles east of Portland, she came to know the life of that fisherman's community as thoroughly as she did that of the Berwick area. From her knowledge was born admiration—and her greatest book, *The Country of the Pointed Firs* (1896), one of the high points in American local-color writing. In this loosely constructed novel—it is really a series of episodes involving more or less the same characters—the narrator (clearly Jewett) arrives one summer at Dunnet Landing, as the town is called in the book, in search of peace and seclusion in which to write. More sophisticated in background, education, and experience than any of the villagers, this visitor from a less remote part of New England gradually discovers that she has returned to an earlier phase of her own culture; and it is this step-by-step realization that provides the book's main interest. Woman of the world though she is, she enters into a close and genuine friendship with the local grower and dispenser of herbs, the widow Elmira Todd, with whom she boards and lodges. The medicinal use of herbs, of course, reflects the timeless folk wisdom of the sort mentioned by George Sand. Yet in rural New England in Jewett's day such use of herbs was commonplace and "experts" in their curative properties were to be found in most of the outlying towns. Some of the herbs and their uses had been learned from the Indians. Others had been known and used in the old countries. But in either case they betokened a continuity of human culture that spanned the centuries back to the beginning of recorded history and beyond.

Jewett, or the narrator, saw other tokens of the same continuity as well as of the universality of certain human traits and aspirations. The rocky, mountainous coastline of eastern Maine reminded her of Greece, and in some respects the people resembled, she thought, the ancient Greeks of history and mythology. Seeing Elmira Todd standing on a cliff above the breaking sea and gazing out on the channel where her husband had been drowned in shipwreck, the narrator discerns in her a resemblance to Antigone mourning her slain brother.[6] Elsewhere Mrs. Todd reminds the narrator of a Caryatid and, as an herbalist, of an enchantress or a "huge sibyl."[7] Mrs. Todd, who is one of the great woman characters in American fiction, "might belong to any age, like an idyl of Theocritus."[8] But such comparisons involve not only Elmira Todd. A group of persons crossing a field to a family reunion

> might have been a company of ancient Greeks going to celebrate a victory, or to worship the god of harvests in the grove above. It was strangely moving to see this and to make a part of it. The sky, the sea, have watched poor humanity at its rites so long; we were no more a New England family celebrating its own existence and simple progress; we carried the tokens and inheritance of all such households from which this had descended, and were only the latest of our line.[9]

Allusions of this sort in Jewett's book were by no means confined to persons, myths, and rites of ancient Greece. Santa Teresa is paraphrased as saying "that the true proficiency of the soul is not in much thinking, but in much loving," and the narrator adds, "Sometimes I believed that I had never found love in its simplicity as I had found it at Dunnet Landing in the various hearts of Mrs. Blacket and Mrs. Todd and William"[10]—Mrs. Blacket and William being Mrs. Todd's mother and brother. Elsewhere is a description of William's fiancée, a woman who had taken up sheep raising, as standing "far away in the hill pasture with her great flock, like a figure of Millet's high against the sky."[11] To the narrator these inhabitants of a remote Maine coastal town were perpetuators of ancient and archetypal human traditions. Jewett, or the narrator of *The Country of the Pointed Firs*, had sought the farthest reaches of the coast to renew her sense of identity with her racial past. She discovered in her Maine fishing village strands of culture that led her back to the origins of all Western civilization and beyond into the realm of myth. Thus her quest was similar to that of the explorers of town origins but more convincing in its results than theirs, since she was concerned, not with a specific political institution, but with the most basic and inclusive human relationships—those within the family, of the individual with the community, of man with nature, and of man with God.

Yet life at Dunnet Landing is not a continuous glow of love and geniality and revelations of age-old folk customs. Jewett, with her deep commitment to truth, did not dedicate her talents to deception. Dunnet Landing has its miseries as have all communities down through the ages, and it also has its share of eccentric characters. Such a person was Joanna Todd, a relative of Elmira's husband, who had been "crossed in love"[12] and, being prone to religious melancholy, exiles herself on a tiny, barren offshore island, where she lives the year round in a crude shack and subsists on her vegetable garden, clams, a few chickens, and an occasional bundle put ashore by men sailing or fishing in the vicinity. Her choice of a way of life was accepted by the townspeople once they were convinced that she could not be persuaded to live otherwise. The narrator, still seeking connections with the past, comments: "I had been reflecting upon a state of society which admitted such personal freedom and a voluntary hermitage. There was something mediaeval in the behavior of poor Joanna Todd."[13] Another eccentric is Captain Littlepage, who, in Mrs. Todd's words, "had overset his mind with too much reading" and had become prone to "spells."[14] The narrator witnesses one of these "spells," in which the captain tells of a region he has visited to the north of Hudson's Bay inhabited by persons "neither living nor dead,"[15] apparently waiting for death.

Less psychotic than Littlepage but definitely eccentric is the elderly woman in the short story "The Queen's Twin," a sequel to *The Country of the Pointed Firs* and often printed with it. This woman, who also lives alone remote from the village but, unlike Joanna, in a comfortable house, was born on the same day, at the same hour, as Queen Victoria, and like the Queen, had married a man named Albert and had had a son named Edward. Once while in London with her husband, who was supercargo on a merchant vessel, she saw Victoria passing by in the royal carriage. She imagined that the Queen noticed her among the gazing crowd and from that time on she had regarded the Queen as her closest friend. Her house is full of mementos of Her Majesty, and walking alone in the woods she tells the Queen her troubles. "You see," the Queen's Twin confides, "there is something between us, being born at just the same time; 'tis what they call a birthright. She's had great tasks put upon her, being the Queen, an' mine has been the humble lot; but she's done the best she could, nobody can say to the contrary, and there's something between us; she's been the great lesson I've had to live by. She's been everything to me. An' when she had her Jubilee, oh, how my heart was with her!"[16]

One may draw a variety of conclusions about characters like Joanna,

Captain Littlepage, and the Queen's Twin. Jewett's feeling about them is one of sympathy combined with amusement. They are what Mrs. Todd calls "curiosities of human natur',"[17] and their fellow townspeople take a certain pride in them. As psychiatrists would say, these eccentrics have made an adjustment, and Jewett admires the tolerance of a society that permits persons to adjust in odd ways without heaping contempt or scorn on them. Other observers might see something lacking in a community where self-realization is achieved so strangely and unproductively. Mary Wilkins Freeman, for example, in her famous story "A New England Nun" deals with a recluse who, unfortunate in love, may be compared to Jewett's Joanna Todd. Freeman's nun, Louisa Ellis, has reduced her life to a preoccupation with meaningless trifles. Unlike Joanna, who has managed to survive the rigors of life on a barren island, Louisa has no physical hardships to overcome; her manner of living demands no prodigies of energy, ingenuity, or endurance that merit admiration. Rather, Louisa is simply a futile, frustrated human being who arouses at best a feeling of grudging pity. The same may be said for most of the multitude of eccentrics who people Freeman's pages. To her they represented deplorable deficiencies, and she treated them as lost, unhappy persons, in many cases the victims of a materially and spiritually impoverished environment. Jewett's assessment was by no means so negative. In *The Country of the Pointed Firs* she finds the little Maine coast fishing community to be a favorable place for individual fulfillment, even if occasionally the fulfillment is a bit strange.

Like so many of her fellow New England writers, Jewett was extremely conscious of the community aspects of the life of her region, and she liked to think that individualism could flourish within the type of community she depicts. But this happy combination of individualism and a sense of community, she seemed to think, could exist best, if at all, among a homogeneous population. Jewett was immensely proud of her own Anglo-Norman ancestry. She was, indeed, an ardent anglophile, as were many Americans in her day, a hundred years after the Revolution, during which her father's family had been Tories. In South Berwick the feeling of kinship with England was stronger than any ancient bitterness against her; a memorial service was held there on the death of Queen Victoria.

In a book for children, *The Story of the Normans* (1887), Jewett sings the praises of her and New England's ancestral stock. The combining of Anglo-Saxon and Norman culture and bloodlines, she assures her young readers, produced a superior breed of men and women and accounts for the superiority of the English in literature, art, music, horticulture, shipbuilding, and war.[18] New England, to her, is simply an offshoot of Old England, and it shares fully in the latter's preeminence.[19] Nor was Jewett unique in her opinion concerning this kinship with England. At about the same time,

Lucy Larcom in her autobiographical *A New England Girlhood* (1889) wrote of her native Beverly: "Her spirit was that of most of our Massachusetts coast-towns. They were transplanted shoots of Old England."[20]

From this Nordic racial strain that she and others so admired, Jewett thinks the strength of individual New England character and the solidarity of New England village life have been derived—a view closely concurring with the ideas of George Perkins Marsh. Yet, though she attributed to English roots most of what she found admirable in New England, she wrote sympathetically in a number of stories—for example, in "Between Mass and Vespers," "A Little Captive Maid," and "Where's Nora?"—of the Irish immigrants, about whom most old-line Yankees of her time could not think of enough disparaging things to say.

Emily Dickinson and Amherst

New England villages have produced their share, and more, of notable American writers. The most remarkable of them all was Emily Dickinson, who was born and brought up and lived all but a few months of her life in the Massachusetts college town of Amherst. Emily Dickinson, like Sarah Orne Jewett, was of patrician stock. Her ancestors for generations had been respected and prosperous. Thus her deep and glowing feeling of attachment to village life, like that of Jewett, may have derived from her comfortable circumstances and sense of being deeply rooted in her region's culture.

Dickinson ranks as a world poet, among the greatest, but she was village poet as well. Visiting her in 1870, Thomas Wentworth Higginson asked her "if she never felt want of employment, never going off the place & never seeing any visitor." Her reply was "I never thought of conceiving that I could ever have the slightest approach to such a want in all future time."[21] Higginson's query bore particularly on Dickinson's choice of a life as a virtual recluse within her father's house, but her answer may be taken to reflect her feelings about Amherst. Later she assured Higginson that she didn't "care for roving,"[22] and that the grounds of her house were "ample—almost travel."[23] As a girl at Mt. Holyoke Female Seminary, only a few miles south of Amherst, she lamented to her brother that the faces that surrounded her were "not like home faces"[24]; and of a visit home from the Seminary she wrote to a friend: "Never did Amherst look more lovely [though the season was early winter] to me and gratitude rose in my heart to God, for granting me such a safe return to my *own* DEAR HOME."[25] On the few occasions when she was away for any length of time, her attachment to Amherst expressed itself in condemnation of the places she was visiting. She announced herself "rich in disdain for Bostonians and Boston,"[26] and she worried lest her brother Austin be harmed by living in that city. Of Washington, D.C., which she visited while her father was a representative in Congress, she wrote: "All is jostle here—scramble and confusion."[27] Cambridge, Massachusetts, she described as a "Wilderness."[28] Like Thoreau she might paraphrase the psalmist: If I forget thee, O Amherst, may my right hand forget her cunning.

Richard B. Sewall has written of Emily Dickinson's father's "home centeredness"[29] and his reluctance to travel; the trait seems to have been exaggerated in Emily. To the Dickinson family Amherst was as much of the world as they needed or desired. In an age when so many New Englanders were emigrating to the West, this seems to have been almost a congenital family idiosyncrasy, but more likely it was a result of extremely deep roots in the community. For almost a century Dickinsons had been prominent in town and college affairs. Emily's father, Edward, for example, not only served as a representative in Congress and in the State legislature but was treasurer for years of Amherst College, in the founding of which his own father had played a major role. All the Dickinsons, except Emily, became full (i.e., converted) church members.

Emily, of course, was not active in town political affairs; as a woman she could not have been. In her youth she led a thoroughly normal social life, but by the age of thirty she had ceased even to attend church. Later she confined herself to her house and grounds. She became a sort of living legend, a village eccentric, accepted, respected, loved, and as such was a real presence in the community. For she did not rebel against Amherst, not even against its dominant Calvinist religion, about which she remained ambivalent. Throughout her life she numbered clergymen among her closest friends—Charles Wadsworth, Thomas Wentworth Higginson, and Amherst's own Jonathan L. Jenkins. In Amherst she was completely at liberty to work out her spiritual problems, or at least attempt to. She was not in agreement with authors like Sedgwick, Judd, Holmes, or Henry Ward Beecher that the supplanting of orthodoxy with a more liberal religion would be the saving of New England towns. Though she herself did not conform to the Calvinistic doctrine of the Amherst Congregational Church, her family did, and she seems not to have respected them the less. Indeed, in her writing she made free use of traditional theological concepts and terminology—"justification," "hope" (of conversion), "grace," "sanctification"—and she quoted, or alluded to, the Bible innumerable times.

Emily Dickinson as a poet dealt with the concerns and questions that have been the subjects of great literature and art down through the centuries. She wrote about nature, love, life, death, humanity's relation with God—matters that from time to time occupy the thoughts of all thinking people. But her approach was always that of a sensitive and intelligent, not to say supremely talented, New England villager. Her subjects are the eternal ones; but the materials from which her poems are fashioned were those available in Amherst and, of course, in the books she read. She wrote that she saw "New Englandly,"[30] and she might just as accurately have expressed herself with another coinage, "Amherstly." Half ironically, she composed a poem describing the limitations of her experience:

> On the Bleakness of my Lot
> Bloom I strove to raise—
> Late—My Garden of a Rock—
> Yielded Grape—and Maise—
>
> Soil of Flint, if steady tilled
> Will refund the Hand—
> Seed of Palm, by Lybian Sun
> Fructified in Sand.
>
> (#681)

One suspects irony because Dickinson obviously did not consider her lot bleak, and she repeatedly said so. She made do gladly and brilliantly with what she had at hand.

Thus she modeled her prosody on that of the Congregational hymn-book—a form of folk verse, familiar to all churchgoers in Amherst. Her vocabulary is spiced with country words and colloquialisms like "heft," "a'nt," "whiffletree," "angleworm," and "scaffold" (in the sense of *hayloft*),[31] which were offensive to some ears in her time. For her images and symbols she drew heavily, of course, from nature, but equally heavily from the very rich store supplied by the ways of life in her village and the surrounding farmlands of a New England town. Explicitly or implicitly, Amherst is present in the great majority of her poems. Thus of a butterfly, whose transformation from its larva state has been a perennial symbol of resurrection, she wrote:

> The Butterfly's Assumption Gown
> In Chrysoprase Apartments hung
> This afternoon put on—
>
> How condescending to descend
> And be of Buttercups the friend
> In a New England Town—.
>
> (#1244)

In the second stanza Dickinson is saying that the butterfly, fully equipped for its assumption, seems to have found Amherst no less preferable than heaven. Elsewhere she is more explicit:

> I went to Heaven—
> 'Twas a small Town—
>
> (#374)

In another poem she commiserates with the departed, whatever their lot:

> I'm sorry for the Dead—Today—
> It's such congenial times
> Old Neighbors have at fences
> It's time o' year for Hay.
>
> And Broad—Sunburned Acquaintance
> Discourse between the Toil—
> And laugh, a homely species
> That makes the Fences smile—
> . . . .
> A Trouble lest they're homesick—
> Those farmers—and their Wives—
> Set separate from the Farming—
> And all the Neighbor's lives—
>
> A Wonder if the Sepulchre
> Dont feel a lonesome way—
> When men—and Boys—and Carts—and June,
> Go down the fields to "Hay"—.
>
> (#529)

As to what heaven is really like, she speculates:

> What is—"Paradise"—
> Who live there—
> Are they "Farmers"—
> Do they "hoe"—
> Do they know that this is "Amherst"—
> And that I—am coming—too—.
>
> (#215)

Doubtless Emily Dickinson would wish the last four questions answered affirmatively, reassuring her that Paradise is not very different from Amherst. But in one respect she hopes it will be different—that there she will not be isolated as "unconverted" in a family and community where all, it was hoped, would undergo conversion. In Heaven, Dickinson hopes:

> Ransomed folks—wont laugh at me—
> Maybe—"Eden" a'nt so lonesome
> As New England used to be!
>
> (#215)

But this bit of negativism was exceptional and transient. Dickinson was always slightly touchy about the fact that she had never undergone conversion, and she expressed her feelings in terms descriptive of a village woman's frustration on a shopping errand to the local dry-goods store:

> I asked no other thing—
> No other—was denied—
> I offered Being—for it—
> The Mighty Merchant sneered—
>
> Brazil? He twirled a Button—
> Without a glance my way—
> "But—Madam—is there nothing else—
> That We can show—Today?"
>
> (#621)

The meaning of "Brazil" need not sidetrack us: it is unlikely that Dickinson is referring literally to the South American nation. Rather she must mean the reddish dye of that name— a not improbable article for a shopper to be seeking. Symbolically it may stand for eternal life (attainable only through conversion), or for something more worldly. But in any event the Mighty Merchant seems to be God, and Emily is finding him difficult. He never did give her conversion—which she sought earnestly, in her early years, at least—and He may have denied her other things.

But if God and her own future, not to mention the present, seem puzzling, she will eventually learn the answers, just as in a country school a child learns the answers to simpler questions from a seemingly omniscient teacher:

> I shall know why—when Time is over—
> And I have ceased to wonder why—
> Christ will explain each separate anguish
> In the fair schoolroom of the sky—
>
> (#193)

Dickinson, as has been said, was not involved or interested in the political affairs of her town, and only to a limited extent in its economic life (e.g., her poem about the Amherst and Belchertown Railroad, "I like to see it lap the miles" [#585]). But she was acutely aware of the fundamental rhythms that were common to the life of Amherst and, for that matter, of all humanity: the cycle of the seasons, the passage of the day from sunrise to sunset. Death particularly engaged her thoughts, and she wrote repeatedly on it. In New England towns death was a public affair. The cemeteries were—and are—owned and maintained by the towns; in former days the towns owned their own hearses. More significantly, the manner in which a person died was a matter of widespread concern: the parson would be at the deathbed, as would close relatives and friends. The focus of interest would be in evidence in a person's dying moments as to whether she or he was among the saved or the damned. Dickinson wrote numerous poems on death and dying: for example, "I heard a Fly buzz—when I died" (#465), "There's been a Death, in the Opposite House" (#389), and "Because I could not stop for Death" (#712). Most poignant, perhaps, is a poem describing an abandoned graveyard:

> After a hundred years
> Nobody knows the Place
> Agony that enacted there
> Motionless as Peace
>
> Weeds triumphant ranged
> Strangers strolled and spelled
> At the lone Orthography
> Of the Elder Dead
>
> Winds of Summer Fields
> Recollect the way—
> Instinct picking up the Key
> Dropped by memory—.

(#1147)

The cemeteries are the symbols of the New Englander's connection with a past and they keep him aware of it, and this awareness is strongly felt in New England villages, both by visitors and by permanent residents. A sense of continuity, we are told, is good for the health of any community. Dickinson did not so much realize this as feel it, experience it, as the basis of her attachment to Amherst. Obliquely perhaps, but none the less unmistakably, she was a devout celebrator of the life in the New England town of her birth.

Old Home Week

Farewell to Ridgefield! Its soil is indeed stubborn, its climate
severe, its creed rigid; yet where is the landscape more smiling,
the sky more glorious, the earth more cheering? Where is society
more kindly, neighborhood more equal, life more tranquil?
Where is the sentiment of humanity higher, life more blest?
Where else can you find two thousand country people, with the
refinements of the city—their farms unmortgaged, their speech
unblemished with oaths, their breath uncontaminated with alcohol, their poorhouse without a single native pauper?

Daniel Webster once said, jocosely, that New Hampshire is a
good place to come from: it seems to me, in all sincerity, that
Ridgefield is a good place to go to. Should I ever return there to
end my days, this may be my epitaph:

> My faults forgotten, and my sins forgiven,—
> Let this, my tranquil birthplace, be my grave:
> As in my youth I deem'd it nearest heaven—
> So here I give to God the breath He gave!

Samuel Griswold Goodrich, *Recollections of a Lifetime*[1]

The conditions of decay and desertion that blighted the New England
countryside in the last decades of the nineteenth century and were described in the fiction of writers like Edith Wharton and Mary Wilkins
Freeman were causes of the greatest distress among the political, business,
and cultural leaders of the region. Individual farms were being abandoned
at an ever-accelerating rate so that many towns found that their population
had declined to only half of what they were in the first or second quarter of
the century. Some localities and villages became totally depopulated; the
forests grew back, and all that remained of the vanished settlements were
networks of stone fences that once separated meadows and pastures; miles
of unused, washed-out roads winding among and over the hills; brush-
choked graveyards with headstones toppled by tree roots and shattered by
frost; and empty cellar holes—sometimes whole villages of them—with
nearby lilac bushes and dying, unpruned apple trees planted long ago by
the departed householders. In some cases a single generation had sufficed
for the completion of the cycle of clearing the forest, establishing a farm,

and abandoning it to the encroaching armies of alder, juniper, and gray birch. Larger areas of New England, indeed of the hilly parts of the whole northeastern United States, are more forested today than at the time of the Revolution. In parts of New Hampshire, for example, farmland is a rarity, if it exists at all. The same is true in much of Vermont, western Massachusetts, and western Connecticut.

"Come Back, Come Back"

A region in which such losses of population and agriculture are taking place is a region in deep economic and social crisis. Something had to be done to revitalize the deserted and depressed countryside, and a partial remedy was initiated in the 1890s by Governor Frank Rollins of New Hampshire, whose state was among the hardest hit. Rollins's idea was to declare an annual Old Home Week, to be held by individual towns each summer and, it was hoped, to be attended by persons who had moved away or by descendants of such, who might be attracted by the idea of renewing contact with their ancestral soil and reestablishing their New England identities. The return of these people with ties to a town would bring badly needed cash, would provide excitement in the otherwise lethargic existence of the townspeople, and might result in some of the visitors' buying an abandoned farm, perhaps their ancestral one, for use as a summer residence—thus adding to the local tax base and otherwise bolstering the economy. Occasionally, moreover, some prodigal son or daughter might be so moved by the homecoming as to donate a substantial sum for some community project. The appeal was frankly sentimental. General invitations were issued by the Governor, and individual ones were sent out by the various towns to their former inhabitants.

The eloquence of Governor Rollins in support of his idea is worth sampling; the following effusion is from an article in the *New England Magazine* of July 1897:

> Sons and daughters of New Hampshire, wherever you are listen to the call of the old Granite State! Come back, come back! Do you not hear the call? What has become of the old home where you were born? Is it still in your family? If not, why not? Why do you not go and buy it this summer? Is there any spot more sacred to you than the place where you were born? No matter how far you have wandered, no matter how prosperous you have been, no matter what luxurious surroundings you now have, there is no place quite like the place of your nativity. The memories of childhood, the friendships of youth, the love of father and mother cling about it and make it sacred. Do you not remember it—the old farm back among the hills, with its rambling buildings, its well-sweep casting its long

shadows, the row of stiff poplar trees, the lilacs and the willows? I wish that in the ear of every son and daughter of New Hampshire, in the summer days, might be heard whispered the persuasive words: Come back, come back![2]

The "whispered" words—if Governor Rollins's outburst may be called a whisper—were heard. Old Home Week was a success and soon was an established custom in New England and in other states. Some time in the summer, originally at the end of August, many of the strayed sons and daughters, or their descendants, did come back. Some bought farms for summer residences; others signified "their appreciation of the friendly Old Home Week invitation by sending here and there a substantial check for a new drinking fountain, a statue or memorial window in honor of some deceased worthy, a public park, a tablet for some historic landmark, or the liquidation of a burdensome church debt."[3] Picnics, bonfires, parades, lectures, concerts, family reunions were the entertainment offered. Maudlin poems were composed and recited and printed. As one commentator has put it, the programs "were marked both by variety and verbosity."[4]

Old Home Week appealed to the nostalgia and the pride of birth of emigrants from New England towns. In many areas where such emigrants had settled, New England Societies had long since been formed and some still exist. The original purposes of these are indicated in a statement issued by the one in Cincinnati at the time of its establishment in 1845: "Its objects are, to cherish the memory and perpetuate the principles of the original settlers of New England; to collect and diffuse information respecting New England and New England emigrants to other parts of the country, especially to the West; and to extend charity to the needy of New England descent."[5] Its membership was composed of men of New England birth and ancestry, and among its activities was the assembling of a library of books about New England and the sponsoring of a course of lectures on the region.

As reported in the *New England Historical and Genealogical Register* of July 1848, "The descendants of New England ancestors do not wish to forget the land of their fathers. In whatever part of the world they are found, they are proud to have it known whence they originated. New England Societies are springing up in the south and in the west."[6] Two quotations from the bombast marking a meeting of the New England Society of Marshall, Michigan, in 1848, testify to the fervor generated in such groups. The following was spoken by the president of the society: "Massachusetts.— 'There she stands.' When the waters which bore the Mayflower to her coast, shall cease to wash her shores, then will her children forget the trials, the sufferings, and the virtues of their fathers."[7] A second outpouring from one of the members is stronger in enthusiasm than in grammar: " 'The Old

Bay state'—Whose Franklin drew lightning from the clouds, and whose Morse learned it how to talk. May she with her dialect of Electricity, Electrize the world."[8]

With sentiments like these prevailing among New England emigrants, it is easy to understand the success of Governor Rollins's plaintive appeals in behalf of Old Home Week. The sentiment was more literately, though no less feelingly, expressed by Catharine Sedgwick years earlier in her didactic novel *Home* (1835). Noting that "Americans are sometimes reproached with being deficient in that love for the home of childhood, which is so general a feature of the human race,"[9] she denies the truth of this allegation in the case of emigrated New Englanders. The Yankee boy, she avows,

> goes, but his heart lingers at the *homestead*. Many a yeoman who has felled the trees of the western forest have we heard confess, that through weary months he pined with that bitterest of all maladies, homesickness; and that even after years had passed, no day went by, that his thoughts did not return to his father's house, nor night that did not restore him to *the old place*. And when age and hardship have furrowed his cheek, and grayed and thinned his hair . . . , he may be seen travelling hundreds and hundreds of miles to revisit "*the old place*,"—to linger about the haunts of childhood, and live over for a few brief days, the sunny hours of youth.[10]

Sedgwick goes on to observe that despite "the *West* with mines of gold in its unbroken soil alluring them", many New Englanders "still linger about *the old place*,—still patiently plough our stony hills, and subdue our cold morasses."[11]

Transplantation of the "New England Way"

A more impressive gauge of emigrant New Englanders' attachment to their native and ancestral towns was their habit of transplanting New England ways and institutions in the places where they settled. Dwight would have been delighted by the multitude of towns, populated by New Englanders and modeled on New England towns, that were springing up across the northern half of the United States. To begin with, the Ordinance of 1785, sponsored by Thomas Jefferson, stipulated that the Northwest Territory be divided into townships six miles square and that Section Sixteen of each township be set aside for the support of public education. The rest of the township, divided into sections and subdivisions of sections, would provide, it was hoped, for a population of small freeholding farmers. Thus in a region including the present states of Ohio, Indiana, Illinois, Michigan, Wisconsin, and part of Minnesota, three of the characteristic features of the New England town were present—its land area, a population of small, independent landowners, and a strong commitment to education, all three either mandated; or at least encouraged, by act of the Continental Congress. The influence of Jefferson, who so greatly admired New England town democracy, is unmistakable.

Public education flourished in the territory, and the control of the district schools was largely in the hands of the inhabitants, who would meet as a body to make decisions and transact school business. These meetings were thoroughly democratic, eventually involving women, who were granted suffrage in school matters and had the right to serve on district boards. Some commentators believe, quite plausibly, that the school districts in these areas and others farther west provided training in self-government comparable to that afforded by the churches in early New England.[12]

Churches of various denominations—with Congregationalism dominant in communities settled by New Englanders—were of course established as new settlers arrived and the townships began to fill up. But the systems of town government were by no means uniform throughout the region. In areas populated predominantly by settlers from the South, the county form of local government was adopted, which left most powers centered in the state government; areas with populations predominately from the Middle States, especially New York and Pennsylvania, followed the example of those states and adopted a modified form of town government. In the northern parts of the territory, notably Michigan, Northern Illinois, and Wisconsin, and later the Dakotas and other regions, in which the homesteaders were mainly from New England or of New England stock, the towns governed themselves by town meetings somewhat in the New England manner. The role of the counties was thus less important in these areas, though not so minimal as in New England.

The case of Illinois is interesting and instructive. Early settlement of the state had been by Virginians, under whose influence the county system prevailed. Later, after the Missouri Compromise of 1820, there was an influx of New England immigrants in northern sections, to whom the county system, with centralization of power in the state government, was unfamiliar and objectionable. When Illinois was admitted to the Union in 1818 as the twenty-first state, it consisted of fifteen counties with "no power given to communities to control local affairs, or to enact by-laws,"[13] except that each township established and controlled its own schools. In 1848 the constitution was revised to permit the counties, if its inhabitants so voted, to reorganize into townships with strong local governments. The northern counties quickly made the change; the southern lagged. But most of Illinois' 102 counties eventually came over to the township system, a modified form of New England town organization, which became a model for other states.

Under the Illinois arrangement each town is a corporation. Annual town meetings are held each April for the election of town officers and the transaction of local business, such as the sale of town property, the directing of officers in the exercise of their duties, the levying of taxes for roads. "The town officers are a supervisor, who is *ex-officio* overseer of the poor, a clerk, an assessor, and a collector, all of whom are chosen annually; three commissioners of highways, elected for three years, one retiring every year; and two justices of the peace and two constables, who hold office for four years."[14] The voters choose a moderator on town-meeting day. However, the general governmental powers of such a meeting would be more restricted than in the New England town meeting.

A somewhat similar system obtains in other, but by no means all, states— Ohio and Indiana are notable exceptions—within and immediately to the west of the boundaries of the Northwest Territory. The influence of New England models is apparent, though there were important differences. For example, the center of population of a township may be incorporated as a village with a governing body (sometimes a village meeting) and by-laws of its own. In some states these municipalities "are considered parts of the township, and as such vote in town-meeting on all questions touching township roads, bridges, the poor and schools."[15]

Thus an Old Home Week visitor to New England, if he came from the West, would be impressed perhaps by how much his new home resembled his old, and this in itself would contribute to his feeling of identity, of belonging to an ongoing culture.

Old Home Week Described in Edith Wharton's Novel *Summer*

The institution of Old Home Week attracted the attention, some of it satirical, of a number of authors, notable among them Edith Wharton (1862–1937), and Robert Frost. Even in the squalid, decadent, fictional Berkshire town of North Dormer, the scene of Wharton's stark novel of New England village life, *Summer* (1917), Old Home Week was an annual event. Aside from the uses the celebration has as a backdrop for some of the action of the story, Wharton seems genuinely fascinated by the event as a sociological phenomenon. She calls it a "form of sentimental decentralization," apparently meaning that it is a force that, at least temporarily, draws people from densely to sparsely populated areas; and she observes wryly that "the incentive to the celebration had come rather from those who had left North Dormer than from those who had been obliged to stay there, and there was some difficulty in arousing the village to the proper state of enthusiasm."[16] The implication, then, is that the returning North Dormer-ites remembered things about the town that they thought made it worth revisiting and that either no longer existed, if they ever had, or were not considered attractions by the permanent residents. Simple nostalgia might have been the sole motive of returning, and Wharton reports that in speeches for the occasion "beautiful things [were said] about the old oaken bucket, patient white-haired mothers, and where the boys used to go nut-ting."[17] But Wharton indirectly suggests that something else more substan-tial may have drawn the visitors—perhaps a feeling of loyalty to the ideals, however violated, on which the town's way of life had formerly been based and a vague recognition of it as a place where human happiness and fulfillment might be achieved. One of the leading planners of the program, a rather gushing woman, does allude to the importance of setting "the example of reverting to the old ideals, the family and the homestead, and so on,"[18] but Wharton seems to be employing sarcasm here. In a speech she puts in the mouth of Lawyer Royall at one of the gatherings, her intention seems more positive. Royall admits that he, too, had once left North Dor-mer but had not succeeded in the outer world and had "come back for good" as had other young men who had failed to realize their ambitions. Indulging in a pun, he continued, "For *good*. There's the point I want to make . . . North Dormer is a poor little place, almost lost in a mighty landscape: perhaps, by this time, it might have been a bigger place, and more in scale with the landscape, if those who had to come back had come with that feeling in their minds—that they wanted to come back for *good* . . . and not for bad . . . or just for indifference."[19]

Royall goes on to address those young men who may be thinking of leaving "to follow the call of ambition" elsewhere: "Let me say this to you, that if ever you do come back to [your old homes] it's worth while to come back to them for their good. . . . And to do that, you must keep loving them while you're away from them; and even if you come back against your will—and thinking it's all a bitter mistake of Fate or Providence—you must try to make the best of it, and to make the best of your old town." He concludes with the statement: "The best way to help the places we live in is to be glad we live there."[20]

Wharton, we know, was interested in folkways, whether those of New York's Four Hundred or North Dormer's villagers. In spite of the commer-cial impulse behind it, Old Home Week, which was reaching its point of widest observance when she was writing *Summer*, could be regarded as a sort of tribal custom, somewhat like the Bowdoin family reunion in Jewett's *The Country of the Pointed Firs*. North Dormer, as a social unit roughly equivalent to a tribe, could preserve a modicum of identity through the yearly ingathering of its scattered inhabitants. In this way, too, those born there, or with ancestors from there, could maintain their identity and sense of roots in the past. Hence the need of keeping the town as decent a place as possible and of strengthening or reviving the "ideals" that had supposedly been the support of its founders and early residents. Wharton does not deny the existence of such ideals in the past, however obviously they are lacking in the present. But if we assume, as we should, that she means the reader to take Lawyer Royall's remarks seriously, then she does not consider North Dormer a hopelessly decadent community. The possibility of its renewal in mind and spirit remains. *Summer* is one of the most negative books ever written about a New England town; but its negativism is not quite total.

Robert Frost: "The Generations of Men" and "Directive"

Robert Frost (1874–1963) also, at least occasionally, entertained an interest similar to Edith Wharton's in Old Home Week, and like her he gave utterance to it with irony mingled with seriousness. Quite literally, Frost's "The Generations of Men" is a poem about Old Home Week. Less literally, "Directive" reflects the Old Home Week impulse. No one, probably, will take issue with this comment on "The Generations of Men," which seems to have been sedulously ignored by the critics (perhaps because they are unaware of its context and hence do not enjoy its many ironies). But the suggestion that "Directive"—that poem so loved by the explicators because, as Frost suggests,[21] it presents problems of interpretation comparable to those of some of T. S. Eliot's major poems—is in any way associated with so banal, so Babbitty an institution as Old Home Week will not meet with a uniformly favorable reception. Yet the two poems, though different in the level of their literary sophistication, have much in common, as to both theme and intention, and these likenesses deserve notice.

Doubtless Frost looked upon Old Home Week (many a celebration of which he must have witnessed) with a great deal of amusement. Yet there are many types of amusement; it may be derisive, it may be sympathetic, it may be warily ironic. I suggest that in "The Generations of Men" Frost's amusement was a composite of the latter two—irony and sympathy. After all, Frost did not take his own New Hampshire ancestry lightly, and he too was a returnee to New England, not for a week but for a lifetime. No one could hold greater pride in a New England background or admire its cultural traditions more. At the risk of being trite, one might say that Frost found his identity in New England. He had returned *indeed* to the source, had bucked the western migration, much as his own West-Running Brook and the eddy within it moved counter to customary directions. Symptomatic of his feelings was his addiction to buying farms, none of them very fertile, in New Hampshire and Vermont. The impulse behind at least some of these purchases is half-humorously described in "A Serious Step Lightly Taken," the persona of which asserts that on his newly acquired land he will complete another three-hundred-year cycle of his family's cultivation of New England soil.

We are told that Old Home Week generated innumerable sappy, doggerel poems on subjects connected with the event. Frost's "The Generations of Men" and other poems on related themes obviously do not belong in this large group of trash. Fortunately Frost took steps to neutralize the sentimentality inherent in the subject by including an irony, a humor, that he must have realized was directed against a tendency within himself. He was later irked that Amy Lowell failed to see and appreciate this humor.

"The Generations of Men" begins:

> A governor it was proclaimed this time,
> When all who would come seeking in New Hampshire
> Ancestral memories might come together.
> And those of the name Stark gathered in Bow,
> A rock-strewn town where farming has fallen off.[22]

As the poet tells it, the cellar hole of the original Stark homestead[23] has been discovered up a back road in the township. Each returning Stark has been provided with a card indicating his or her exact position on the many-branched tree of this famous New Hampshire family, and a day has been set for the whole relationship to meet at the cellar hole (incidentally, Frost's first title for the poem was "The Cellar Hole"). The arrangement is quintessentially in the spirit of Old Home Week and is marked by a pointless sentimentality exploited for the economic interests of town and state, harmless but surely laughable. Yet to many, including Frost, beneath the fanfare and folderol lay a significance having to do with the perpetuation of traditional values.

The Stark descendants, however, do not take the matter very seriously—and here is one of the ironies of the poem—for a light rain on the appointed day keeps all but two of them from the meeting that had been so elaborately prepared as the culmination of their return to Bow. The two who did keep the appointment are a young man and a young woman, who "idled down"[24] to the spot from opposite directions. The man has a card proving his Stark ancestry; the woman has three such cards, for she is descended from three branches of "the old stock."[25] (Note that "stock" and "Stark," as pronounced in New England, constitute a pun—another of Frost's desentimentalizing touches and a way of universalizing the poem's

subject.) The humor of the situation is not lost on these two, whose intellectual sophistication is revealed by their highly literate speech, the wit of their
repartee, and their literary and mythological allusions. Yet it is just such
persons who would discern whatever of value or substance lay beneath the
surface effusions of Old Home Week. These two might seriously

> try to fathom
> The past and get some strangeness out of it.[26]

Frost is on very thin ice in this poem and at any moment could break
through into schmaltzy depths of sentiment. As the poet makes very clear,
the couple who meet here at the ancestral cellar hole are about to embark
on a courtship that will eventuate in marriage, after which they will build a
summer home on the old foundation, including in their new house, perhaps as doorsill, a piece of charred timber from the original structure.
Thus the dearest wish of the governor—that of enticing persons of New
Hampshire origins to buy an abandoned farm as a summer residence—is to
be realized, with sentimental overtones that would delight the governor
beyond his wildest dreams. And what better subject for Old Home Week
doggerel! Yet as Frost wrote it, poking gentle fun at the whole concept of
Old Home Week, "The Generations of Men" is obviously not doggerel and
it is sentimental only to a degree. The realistic depiction of the site and the
low-keyed, restrained dialogue keep sentimentality within bounds, as does,
of course, the ironical treatment of the whole charade of the reunion. But
more than anything else the sense of proportion exhibited by the two
young Starks—their New England suppression of whatever pride they may
have covertly taken in their ancestry, their playful evocation of their pro-
genitors' comments—makes the poem a meaningful statement on the perennial human need of having roots, identity, and, above all, a code to live
by. The most serious remark in the poem—perhaps the only serious one—
is:

> What counts is the ideals,
> And those will bear some keeping still about.[27]

We are told that Frost constantly quoted or paraphrased these lines.[28]
Yet even in this statement, he has slyly left us with an ambiguity based on
two meanings of the word "still." Does he mean that one should not speak
about the "ideals" or that they should be retained? To a New Englander,
Frost's words might imply that the two interpretations are reconcilable.
New Englanders tend "to keep still"—say nothing—about really important
matters—about "ideals," for instance—that they still believe worth preserving. Of course, another possible interpretation, for which a somewhat

plausible case could be made, is that the "ideals" were rather unimpressive, if they ever existed at all, and one had better not talk about them.

"The Generations of Men" is an early poem, but in subject and theme it anticipates "Directive," published thirty-three years later. We have seen that Frost himself was somewhat sarcastic about the favorable critical reception of "Directive." The fact is, his sarcasm was not without cause. "Directive" advances an idea, or an attitude, that had its first statement in 1913 in "Ghost House" and had been restated many times in the ensuing decades in poems dealing with the desertion of New England farmlands—the idea that "what counts is the ideals." Furthermore, over the years much the same set of images kept reappearing in these poems: uninhabited houses or the cellar holes of houses already vanished; lilac or raspberry bushes, or apple trees, near the housesite; roads that no longer lead anywhere but usually ascend a hill or a mountain; a well, or spring, or brook; meadows and pastures reverting to forest; and disused graveyards. What each of these objects may symbolize, if anything, in the various poems in which they appear, cannot be definitely determined, as the myriad differing interpretations of "Directive" make evident. Each reader may, and should, assign his own meanings and values to these recurring objects.

Of one thing, however, we may be certain: a major purpose of Frost in these poems was to evoke the atmosphere of a region, of a culture, that had been abandoned and left to return to a state of nature. Obviously the spectacle is a disturbing and saddening one to the poet, who sees in it implications involving more than New England. "The land was ours before we were the land's,"[29] Frost wrote in "The Gift Outright." The hill country of New England was the settlers' for a few decades, but the ruinous evidences of their brief sojourn proclaim all too clearly that the land did not possess them. Did these fugitives from New England become possessed later by the lands they fled to in the West, or did they withhold themselves there also? The answer need not be given here, but Frost seems to say that America is still not spiritually possessed by its people. At any rate, the experience of the emigrant farmers during their New England stay had been fragmentary and incomplete, and thus they left the New England hills as fragmented, incomplete persons.

Though it is too late to begin over again, a return, in spirit at least, to the deserted villages and abandoned farms and even a sacramental drink from the ancestral wells might be needed if our culture, marked with incompleteness, is ever to "be whole again,"[30] the wholeness being derived from a realization of the continuing presence of the past—in this case, the hill-country phase of the past. The "tireless folk, but slow and sad"[31] of "Ghost House," Frost's first poem on the desertion of the New England countryside, live in the American present, and the recognition of this existence is essential to the wholeness of American society. Obviously, not only New England is involved here, but the whole of American pioneering and the transitory relations with the soil that it fostered.

The success of Old Home Week, which was by no means confined to New England, derived from the human need for a contact with the past, the need for a sense that one's life exists not in temporal isolation but in continuity with former generations. A return, after a long absence to one's childhood home or the home of one's ancestors, is an emotion-arousing experience that has been celebrated in song and poetry as long as those arts have existed. Frequently, of course, such song and verse are of a rather shallow, platitudinous quality, and this seems to have been especially true of the Old Home Week doggerel already alluded to. Thus the dilemma is great for a poet who recognizes, as did Frost, the validity of the spiritual or emotional impulse behind the desire to return home but realizes that he must repudiate both the materialism that exploits the impulse and the mawkishness that tends to degrade it. Frost, as we have seen, resorted to irony and humor as decontaminants. As far as was within his powers, which were very considerable, he appeals to the impulse, honors it, but spares it from the usual Old Home Week dishonesties. He could also present rural New England as it actually was, a deserted and abandoned region of crumbling houses and weed-choked cellar holes, and not pretend that nothing had changed since the exodus fifty or more years before. The returnees would find something very different from what they or their forebears had left. They would find ruin and decay instead of an energetic, thriving, if perhaps misdirected, society, and the spectacle, to the sensitive at least, would not so much sate their nostalgia as generate in them feelings of regret, even misgivings concerning the past of which they were a continuation.

Robert Frost: Other Poems on New England's Past

"The Generations of Men" and "Directive" are, of course only two of a sizable number of Frost's poems dealing with New England's past. "The Black Cottage" ranks high among such poems and provides a remarkable example of Frost's use of irony—in this case the minister's irony directed against himself—to keep sentiment within bounds. Another poem in this category is "The Birthplace," which has received less than its share of critical attention. In it the poet describes an abandoned homestead—with its accompanying spring and surrounding network of stone walls—where a large family of boys and girls has grown up and later scattered far and wide. Here again the danger of lapsing into pathos is severe, but Frost surmounts the danger by a clever personification of the mountain, which, he writes, "seemed to like the stir" for a while but then "pushed [the family] off her knees."[32] A similarly high potential for excessive emotion is present in the subject of Frost's "In a Disused Graveyard." But he short-circuits this potential by a simple half-humorous, half-serious remark—which, moreover, is based on fact—that now even the dead avoid this cemetery, for no one is buried there any more. He ends with a quatrain in which he again resorts to personification:

> It would be easy to be clever
> And tell the stones: Men hate to die
> And have stopped dying now forever.
> I think they would believe the lie.[33]

The mood of gentle irony reminds one of Emily Dickinson's treatment of a graveyard as an ever-growing community in the poem beginning "Who occupies this house."[34]

Frost's irony borders on the comic in "Of the Stones of the Place," in which the persona offers to send to a New Englander in the West a stone from the emigré's ancestral farm to "keep the old tradition safe."[35] The recipient can say of it that it serves as

> The portrait of the soul of my Gransir Ira.
> It came from where he came from anyway.[36]

The appropriateness of the stone as a reminder of New England and its past deserves some comment. Where New Englanders tried to farm they had first to remove innumerable stones from the soil, and to dispose of them they built them into walls. The toil, the hopes, the disappointments these walls represent go beyond the power of words to tell, and Frost, sensibly, never made the attempt—directly at least. But in one of his most famous—and most variously interpreted—poems, "Mending Wall," he calls attention to these monuments of the epical struggle of former generations of yeomen. The wall in Frost's poem does not really need rebuilding, since it serves no present purpose, and perhaps never did, aside from being a means of getting rid of unwanted rocks. But the persona himself has in-itiated the mending because he feels the wall deserves preservation for other than practical reasons—though certainly not for the fatuous reason given by his neighbor. The "something . . . that doesn't love a wall"[37] is the same something—nature—that the original builders of the wall struggled against and overcame, at least temporarily. To preserve the results of their labor is to pay respect to the tradition, perhaps the "ideals," they represent; but very wisely Frost does not lecture us to this effect. A lecture would be far less impressive than a simple description of the act.

The "something . . . that doesn't love a wall" in New England does not love a meadow either, as Frost makes clear in "The Last Mowing," which may be taken as a companion piece to "Mending Wall." The building of a wall is only a part of the process of creating a meadow from a rock-strewn forest, and the meadow is the place where the farmer's labors reach fulfillment—a place even of joyous labor, as Frost intimates in "Mowing" and "The Tuft of Flowers." Thus the decision to let a meadow revert to woodland is a momentous one that would touch the most insensitive feelings. Even nature, as she takes over, proceeds gently, filling the meadow for a few seasons with flowers, like offerings on the coffin of a dead hope, before the final obliterating onslaught of the forest.

Yet, as Frost states in "The Need of Being Versed in Country Things," the witness of these natural processes must hold his emotions in check or he will fail to understand the human significance of what is happening. The pervasive thought in the background of the aggregate of Frost's poems of desertion and abandonment is that human beings are responsible for what they do or do not do—for the desertion, for example, of a farm or a countryside—but that nature acts with signal indifference to human failures and successes. When a family or a group of families leaves land they or their forebears have prepared with great industry and hope for human uses, an act of rejection has taken place, and a sense of that rejection, with all the disappointment and disillusionment it implies, remains as a sort of aura on the land that the settlers briefly possessed but that failed to possess them. The question that haunts Frost's poems on such subjects is whether something less tangible but more important—such as the original settlers' confidence in themselves and their land or the sense of rightness and goodness that sparked their pioneering efforts—may not have been rejected along with the acres that in a sense had failed them.

Have the "ideals" of the first settlers vanished from New England's hills along with the settlers themselves? Have the "ideals" perhaps vanished from all America and not from New England alone? Was Emerson right when he wrote:

> The God who made New Hampshire
> Taunted the lofty land
> With little men?[38]

In his poem "New Hampshire" Frost skirts these questions, either not choosing or not being able to answer them. Instead, having quoted Emerson, he quotes another Massachusetts poet, Amy Lowell, who disparaged the people of New Hampshire. Frost continues:

> And when I asked to know what ailed the people,
> She said, "Go read your own books and find out."[39]

The reader is left to surmise whether Frost accepted this comment about his poems. The fact that he does not bother to reject it is perhaps his way of answering the questions posed above, though more likely it indicates that he had no definite answers, or that no final answers are possible.

Twentieth-Century Writing on New England Towns to 1960

By the latest census Arlington has—well, I forget whether four or six, or fifteen more or fewer people than it had at the time of the American Revolution. That is, it has stability. But an American kind of stability, made up not of stagnation and immobility, but of constant rediscovery of stable elements in a shifting community life—churches, books, education, civic responsibility, shared good times, neighborly feeling, a solidarity which makes everybody feel safe.

Dorothy Canfield Fisher, *Memories of Arlington, Vermont*[1]

"But anyway we all live in the same place, and when it's a place like North Domer [a New England village] it's enough to make people hate each other just to have to walk down the same street every day."

Spoken by a villager in Edith Wharton's *Summer*[2]

Writings about rural and village New England continued to appear in the twentieth century in undiminished volume, and in all the major literary forms—novels, short stories, drama, essays. Factual studies of individual towns, states, or localities have also proliferated, some of them straight histories, others cultural studies, combining historical, sociological, descriptive and other approaches. In addition, a number of periodicals, such as *Yankee, Vermont Life, Down East,* devote their pages in part to the presentation of details about country and community life either in all of New England or in one of the six states. This flood of material may be dealt with only by sampling it. Thus, in this and the next chapter, several authors and books of various types have been selected to be discussed, with necessary brevity, as to both their individual qualities and as representative of the larger output of which they are a part.

Affirmers of the Tradition: Dorothy Canfield Fisher and Thornton Wilder

The large volume of twentieth-century writing about New England's rural culture reflects attitudes varying from a stark "realism," with emphasis on degeneracy and decline of all sorts, to pollyanna optimism. Along this spectrum appear works of differing degrees of merit—from sentimental trash to competent and at times brilliant literary art. And frequently, in the work of the same author are found conflicting strains of optimism and pessimism. From writer to writer, and within the work of each, the tone may be comic or tragic, satirical or idealistic, or combinations of these.

Among the affirmers of the New England way, Dorothy Canfield Fisher (1879–1958) is undoubtedly the most romantic and idealistic. Dorothy Canfield (as a writer she usually used her unmarried name) was born in Lawrence, Kansas, where her father, a Vermonter, was librarian at the State University. She was educated in the Middle West and later at Columbia University, where she received her Ph.D. degree in 1904. In 1907 she moved to the southern Vermont town of Arlington, which her ancestors had helped to found and in which Canfields had been living for 150 years. Proud of her background, she became an ardent advocate of New England ways, especially as they existed in Vermont. Arlington was henceforth her home and the setting for much of her fiction. By oral tradition and through her reading she became steeped in local and state history and folklore. For example, as regards the early territorial quarrels between New York and Vermont, she became as ardent a partisan as Ethan Allan himself.

Canfield wrote much fiction and nonfiction on a great variety of subjects. Among her books voicing her enthusiasm for Vermont are *Hillsboro People* (1915), *Raw Material* (1923), *Seasoned Timber* (1939), and *Vermont Trdition* (1953). The first two are collections of stories and sketches drawn from her Arlington experience and background. *Seasoned Timber* is a long novel set in a similar town. *Vermont Tradition* is history, or as she phrases it in her subtitle, "The Biography of an Outlook on Life." All four celebrate New England community life and do so in the most glowing terms.

The old sense of community solidarity, Canfield finds, persists. To her, New England townspeople are still notable for their tolerance, and their sense of fair play and for their dedication to personal independence, respect for individual rights, and realization of the importance of education, for which they are ready to make major material sacrifices. Their town meetings and town government, Canfield is convinced, function effectively as bastions of democracy. And the serenity of the Vermont way of life is symbolized by the calm beauty of the mountains among which it flourishes.

In *Vermont Tradition*, her most substantial book, Canfield turned to history. But it is history told with a frank personal bias, at times quite emotionally expressed. The theme is simply stated: Vermont ways are admirable; they represent American democracy in its purist form; and they should be cherished not only by all Vermonters but by the nation, and should be imitated by all peoples of the world. She finds among the Green Mountains the millennial perfection that Dwight discerned in the Connecticut River towns, though unlike Dwight she does not use religious orthodoxy as a touchstone of progress. What she most admires Vermonters for is their concern with education. Dwight, of course, put education in second place after religion. Thus Canfield writes with admiration of a town meeting in Arlington when the people chose to build a school rather than repair some decrepit highway bridges. The fact that the most vocal pro-school participant in that debate was a second-generation Irishman in an assembly composed almost entirely of old-line Yankees was to Canfield simply a proof of the Vermonter's refusal to permit irrelevancies like race, creed, or national origin to cloud his judgment.

Much of Canfield's writing reiterates ideas long since expressed by writers about New England. In the following passage, for example, are echoes of thoughts expressed by Timothy Dwight and George Perkins Marsh, among other nineteenth-century authors:

> In the nearly two centuries of life in the Green mountains, the spirit of the community has produced several thousand—no, a million or more if you include those who emigrated when grow up—men and women who, by the act of living together in accordance with local tradition, have made for each other an unvaryingly safe and orderly social framework for widely varying individual lives. The doors of that old home-society have been left open so that those who thought they might be freer in another tradition to develop the best possibilities within them could walk out unhindered. . . . Those who have stayed at home here, and those who have taken their ideals and standards far and wide over the nation, have given proof that freedom can be orderly, can be beneficent to all who share it.[3]

There are other echoes of Dwight and earlier millennialists, even including Jonathan Edwards, in a hint that Canfield makes to the effect that the New England state of Vermont may be a leader, a model, in a future, though uncertain, attainment of a just and equitable social order for all humanity. "What chance," she asks, "have we—have we any chance at all, we men and women on the globe?—to carry forward the standard which we here call the Vermont tradition, but which is so infinitely more than Vermont's? Our nation calls it the American ideal, but it is infinitely more than American. World-wide, it is the democratic spirit, and that is another name for the guess, the mighty hope, that human beings are capable of uniting to help each other live."[4]

Canfield sees it as a "paradox that out of a tradition which strictly enjoins letting the neighbors alone should emerge the actual practice of collective action." But she finds the paradox "logical," for "the tradition makes human contacts safe."[5] The obvious manifestation of the tradition is the town meeting, which she concedes can often be tedious, petty, and spiteful but which somehow accomplishes its purpose of bringing the people together to transact business necessary to the well-being of their community. In this accomplishment she sees a hope for mankind—"a bunch of quite ordinary men and women, if they are not permanently separated into rival competing classes or groups, are really able, in spite of human rancor, to get together on how to run things—for everybody's benefit, not for any one or any few."[6]

In complete harmony with the lyricism that Canfield often brings to play in her discussion of Vermont towns is Thornton Wilder's perennially popular play *Our Town* (1938), which seems archetypal in its nostalgic evocation of some generally accepted views as to what life in a small town is like. The fictional scene of Wilder's drama, Grover's Corners, New Hampshire, could in many respects be any idealized small town, but its author has gone out of his way to localize it by the use of many New England place names and having his characters speak with New England accents and speech rhythms. The characters, like people the world over, are born, get married, raise families, and die, but Grover's Corners is presented as a peculiarly pleasant place, with an orderly and closely knit social structure in which to live through this cycle. The choice of New Hampshire for the setting is perhaps appropriate since so many communities throughout the United States were founded by New Englanders and retain many New England characteristics. Consciously or not, Wilder was capitalizing on the mystique that in many American minds surrounds New England towns.

Affirmers of the Tradition: John Sterling, Bernard De Voto, John Gould, and Clarence Webster

A note of affirmation similar to Dorothy Canfield Fisher's was sounded again and again in the decades between the World Wars. Two notable essays were John Sterling's "New England Villages," published in the *Atlantic Monthly* of April 1923, and Bernard De Voto's (1897–1955) "New England, There She Stands," published in *Harper's Magazine* of March 1932. Sterling describes a summer visit in a coastal New England village fictitiously named Fairport, which had been the home of the author's ancestors. Describing himself as one of many temporarily returned emigrés, he meditates on changes, especially in religious views and practices, but is struck most by the community's enduring qualities of "sincerity and kindheartedness, its rightmindedness, and good-will to men"; and like so many before him, he recommends this supposedly typical New England town as "a pattern for many a more pretentious but less righteous community."[7]

In contrast to Fairport, Sterling discussed in the same essay a larger town, which he names Dale. Here society is more stratified. The rich upper class attend the lovely "Orthodox" Congregational Church, where they hear extremely unorthodox "Emersonian" sermons.[8] The Unitarian Church, where Emersonian preaching would be appropriate, is less fashionable. The conclusion, then, is that the upper-class townspeople of Dale lack some of the simple sincerity characteristic of the citizens of Fairport; yet they do well by their town, for along with retaining at least the name of their ancestral religion, they preserve their old homes in top repair and fill them with antiques belonging to the region. In their way, they are also preserving the traditions of their forebears. Sterling's examination of the two New England towns results in an optimistic report.

Bernard De Voto's essay "New England, There She Stands" is more substantial and even more positive than Sterling's in its assessment of the present state of New England's culture. To begin with, he echoes many earlier observers in stating: "The New England town . . . has adjusted itself to the conditions of its life. It is a finished place."[9] Writing in the depths of the Great Depression, DeVoto believes New Englanders are better prepared than most Americans to survive national economic collapse. The Yankee is accustomed to defeat; his Puritanism has taught him not to expect too much from humanity; overcoming a hostile climate and niggardly soil, the Yankee "built his commonwealth. It was a superb equipment for his past; it may not be a futile one for our future." And echoing prophecies as old as the *Mayflower* and the *Arbella,* DeVoto asserts: "[New England] is the first permanent civilization in America. . . . It will be the elder glory of America."[10]

Two books that appeared in the 1940s—inspired perhaps by the worldwide Nazi threat to democracy—are noteworthy for their highly favorable presentation of village and rural ways in New England. The earlier of these, written by John Gould (1908–) of Maine, and illustrated with numerous photographs, was titled *New England Town Meeting: Safeguard of Democracy* (1940)—a paean to town government as it still exists in parts of Gould's state and presumably elsewhere in New England. Using an actual town as an example, Gould notes the inalienable privilege of every townsperson to put forth views on subjects under discussion, without being shut off, so long as the rules of the meeting are not violated. "Each voter brings his . . . independence into the hall, and from the congregation results a majority decision in which unity is attained without any one losing the least bit of his own separate self"[11]—a situation which Gould believes has carried over into state and national politics. Debate in town meetings—which Gould correctly describes as legislative assemblies—represents all points of view: the farmer contributing folk wisdom, the bankers supplying financial calculations, the school superintendent appealing to reason, the highway workers spicing the discussion with a bit of cussing. the women representing the interests of the children. Normally, the debate is dignified, though arguments *ad hominem* occasionally erupt. A sense of community is expressed in, and strengthened by, a resistance to ever-increasing state and federal encroachments on the prerogatives of the towns. Over the years, Gould points out, town meetings in Maine have undergone some changes, though none so drastic as to undermine the institution. The participation of women after about 1920 toned down some of the more picturesque and profane utterances during debate, and, after a slow start, more and more women were elected to offices. The presence of sizable groups of "foreigners"—for example, French-Canadians—who tend to vote in blocs (as Charles Francis Adams noted in Quincy fifty years earlier) altered the character of meetings—for the worse, Gould thinks. Also, new residents fresh from the cities injected into discussions an idealism that had no relation to the hard realities of town life. However, Gould takes satisfaction in the ease and speed with which the exurbanites assimilate to rural ways and thinking. Thus, except for the cliquish "foreigners," the future of the town meeting, Gould is assured, in the less densely populated areas of New England looks bright. The practice, common in most small New England towns, of having school children of all ages attend the meetings—and the holding of mock "March meetings" in the schools themselves—will tend to perpetuate community pride and an appreciation of a fundamental political practice.

A book similar in intent to Gould's, also written in a popular style but with serious purpose, is Clarence Webster's *Town Meeting Country* (1945), in which the author assumes the role of a countryman, seasoned in village and rural ways, as opposed to the callow newcomer from the city, whether as a summer or permanent resident. The town-meeting country of the title is northeastern Connecticut and adjacent strips of Massachusetts and Rhode Island—an area settled in Colonial times but, Webster thinks, still rural and definitely vintage New England in its values and customs. The town meeting, as in Gould's book, is presented as the backbone of democracy in New England and the purest example of democracy in the nation. The time coverage of the book is roughly the three hundred years since the region had been occupied by the white man, but the emphasis is on the present and recent past. Anecdotal and informal in style, it makes good reading and, when allowances are made for the author's enthusiasms, provides a reasonably reliable account of the social and political situation on the New England countryside.

From Affirmation to Negation: Mary Ellen Chase

It is possible to discern in the recent writing about rural New England culture two trends that stem from the nineteenth century. The authors representing one of these trends takes a critical, sometimes pessimistic view of the people and communities they are describing. They are prone to dwell upon weaknesses of character, social decay, loss of ideals and standards, poverty, and other types of social and economic distress. Traces of this outlook can be found as far back as in Catharine Sedgwick's writing and it occasionally is hinted at in Harriet Beecher Stowe's; but it came to be a major, if not dominant theme only in the late nineteenth century, especially among magazine writers like R. L. Hartt and Philip Morgan and in the fiction of Rose Terry Cooke and, most notably, of Mary E. Wilkins Freeman and Edith Wharton. The second trend, one of affirmation, at times romanticizing, was the norm in Sedgwick and Stowe and Henry Ward Beecher but attained its fullest literary expression in the stories and sketches of Sarah Orne Jewett.

Dorothy Canfield Fisher is obviously in the Jewett tradition. A slightly younger contemporary of hers, the Maine author Mary Ellen Chase (1887-1973), combines the two trends, though in most of her work she is an affirmer. Up to about the middle of her literary career her work echoes Jewett's enthusiam and optimism about all aspects of Maine life and history. In her later work the assurance and affirmation are lacking, but the Jewett manner of writing remained. *The Country of the Pointed Firs* was "my ideal," she said, "when I first began to try to write. So far as that ideal goes, it has never lost its secure place."[12] During her childhood, Chase had met Jewett and had confided to her that she wished to write books. Jewett assured the child that she would, "and good books, too, all about Maine." Jewett, Chase wrote, " is justly the master of us all." Her praise is unstinted: "Even the best among us distantly follow her footsteps, stumbling and fumbling among the words which she so perfectly set down on paper, among the people whom she so unerringly portrayed, among the marshes and islands, the coves, the hills, the villages which she saw with a vision denied to all other Maine authors."[13] But, as will be seen, Chase was somewhat less of an optimist than her "master" regarding Maine and its future.

In her early writing, however, her faith is firm. The tone of her autobiographical book, *A Goodly Heritage* (1932), an account of her childhood and girlhood in Blue Hill, Maine, is set by the Psalmists' words, which serve as a motto for the volume and from which the title is drawn: "The lines are fallen unto me in pleasant places; yea, I have a goodly heritage" (Psalms 16:6). With this book Chase joined the company of authors of an earlier generation, like Samuel Griswold and Lucy Larcom, who wrote nostalgic reminiscences of their upbringing in New England villages. Chase's Blue Hill was, and is, a village of great charm, situated on the lovely stretch of coast between Penobscot Bay and Mount Desert Island. It shared in Maine's long and distinguished maritime tradition, in which Chase's forebears had figured importantly; and the town had suffered from the decline of that tradition, as did all but the larger, deep-water ports of New England.

In the clipper-ship days mariners from Blue Hill and nearby towns sailed to every continent, but always retained their close attachment to New England and their native communities. Their voyagings around the world, as Chase and Jewett have both pointed out, made them less parochial, less impressed with the petty side of village life, but in no way diminished their ingrained sense of the superiority of their tradition over all others in the world. Their belief in the superlative qualities of New England as God's chosen land was as strong in them as in the elder Puritans. Chase in much of her writing shared this belief, so similar to Canfield's feelings about Vermont. It was in this unshakable attachment to home that Chase found the sources of the strength of will and character of the old seafarers. Had they not been so deeply rooted in New England and its past, they would not have sailed so far and with such assurance. This is the theme of much of Chase's writing.

Blue Hill, according to her account, afforded its sons and daughters exactly the foundation needed for success and fulfillment: beautiful natural surroundings, a strong commitment to family, effective but enjoyable education in the town's elementary schools and its fine academy, an active and vital religious life, and the all-inclusive sense of belonging to a firmly established community. Chase's family, to be sure, was among the most prominent in the town. Her father, a successful lawyer, was active politically in state and local affairs. But in her opinion at least, the benefits available in her town and others like it were not enjoyed only by a privileged few.

Three of Chase's novels—*Mary Peters* (1934), *Silas Crockett* (1935), and *The Edge of Darkness* (1957)— have their settings in Maine coastal towns and are accounts of communities as much as of individual characters. The first two are carefully researched repositories of social and economic history. Of the two, we shall focus on *Silas Crockett* because of the impressive breadth of its historical coverage. In this novel the life of the town, Saturday Cove, in which the action is centered, is described in its every aspect and detail during a span of one hundred years. As I have written elsewhere,

> one hears the mallets and saws, smells the tar and hemp of the shipyards, sees the sleek vessels glide down the ways in the great shipping decade of the 1830's, and walks the streets with the outlandish sailors just off ships from Rio or Cadiz. Later one scents the mackerel and herring shoveled by scale-flecked fishermen from the holds of schooners in from the Banks during the less glamorous years when Saturday Cove lived by fishing. One attends weddings, births, funerals, and bubble-blowing parties with the children, sharing the joy and sorrow of each.[14]

Most striking—and true—among the claims Chase makes for Saturday Cove and similar New England seaports is that they possess a simple, aesthetically pleasing dignity of appearance almost unique in this nation. Their achievement of an architectural synthesis of the best in other traditions—Greek, Roman, Georgian, even medieval—is totally appropriate, she believes, for a culture which, like that of America, is itself a synthesis. But in the architecture of New England, especially of Maine, this process achieves its highest expression. Chase would find appropriate to her Maine seaports the remarks made by Carl Bridenbaugh about inland New England towns: that they attained "the only successfully blended beauty of natural and man-made environment that America has even known"; and Bridenbaugh added a remark with which Chase would even more enthusiastically agree: "A solid unity among the people produced this synthesis and insured its success."[15]

Silas Crockett is the chronicle of a family as well as of a community, and it traces the decline of the Crocketts as part of the decline of the seaport. Male members of the Crockett family, originally masters of clipper ships, eventually sink to the unutterably ignominious level of ferryboat captains, and finally one of them is compelled to earn his living as a gutter of herring in a canning factory. But the town of Saturday Cove and its inhabitants retain some of their character, despite the vanishing shipping and the inroads of summer "rusticators," who regard the "natives" (scions of sea-captains in world trade) as menials on hand to serve them. At the end of the century covered by the novel, one has not, however, lost confidence in the strengths of character of the Crocketts. Somehow they will perpetuate the tradition from which they are descended. Saturday Cove is still there in the midst of the Great Depression; the spiritual forces that built it and sustained it have not expired. In Chase's view, a restrained optimism is justified.

Between the writing of *Silas Crockett* and *The Edge of Darkness*—a period of over twenty years—Chase's confidence in the durability of New England values fell sharply, though she never completely gave them up for lost. *The Edge of Darkness* was Chase's favorite among all her books—fiction or nonfiction—and it is her most pessimistic. Suggestive of Jewett's *The Country of the Pointed Firs* in that it records the life of a fishing village by providing a series of character studies, its emphasis on social and economic decline that amounts to degeneration is in the vein of the grimmest commentaries on New England's ills. The title of the book, indeed, is a Maine expression for the dusk that precedes the darkness of night. "This story is set," Chase wrote, "in no definite or discernible place, but instead in any one of many small and isolated fishing communities on a coast long familiar to me."[16] Her acquaintance with such communities, which were far different from her own Blue Hill, can be traced back to her own youthful experience working for the Maine Sea Coast Mission, an organization that strives to alleviate some of the hardships that mark the life of impoverished inhabitants of the more remote parts of the area.

The town that Chase describes is sunk deep in decadence. The one survivor from better days was Sarah Holt, the widow of one of the deepwater sea captains, whom she used to accompany on his voyages in distant oceans. She has just died, and with her death is broken the last link the town had with the era of Maine's maritime preeminence. Long since, the population has lost whatever strengths of character it might once have had, and it is now composed, with rare exceptions, of feckless, ambitionless, demoralized, and in some cases depraved descendants of once estimable families. Among them are a part-time prostitute, a hopeless drunkard, poachers, couples whose marriages have frozen in hate, and fanatics in frantically evangelistic religions. Chase, in presenting this cast of characters, rivals Edith Wharton's depiction of small-town depravity (in *Summer*) and far outdoes Mary Wilkins Freeman. Only the proprietors of the local store in Chase's novel, Lucy and Joel Norton, think about meaning and purpose in life, and their lot is economically a dreary one.

When the Widow Holt dies there is a faint stirring of spirit among the inhabitants, who, despite their demoralization, had with varying degrees of awareness felt her influence. But with her death the long moribund community also dies. There is nothing left—for the present, at least—but a group of people haphazardly thrown together within the boundaries of a township that is destitute of spiritual, moral and aesthetic standards. Yet an inveterate optimist might see one faint afterglow of hope in the words of Joel Norton at the end of the book: "I've always noticed on this coast how just at the edge of darkness, the sky often holds a long, steady glow or light."[17] The town has lost its maritime tradition and with it its contacts with the outside world. It has also lost its old religion, with its rigorous morals and stern, but intellectually challenging, theology. And with these it has lost, most disastrous of all, its sense of community. Will the "long, steady light" that Joel observes eventually return, after a period of darkness, and brighten over a coast that no longer belies its heritage? Chase supplies no answer.

Negation: Edith Wharton and James Gould Cozzens

Mary Ellen Chase's *The Edge of Darkness* is the story of a town first and of individuals second. And it is the story of a town whose spiritual bearings have either ceased to exist or have become distorted or meaningless. Strength of will has become sheer stubbornness; religion has become an empty parroting of the catechism; thrift has become miserliness. But the town had not quote reached the extreme state of decay of those towns described a generation earlier in the *Atlantic Montly* by observers like Hartt and Sanborn. The author whose picture of rural New England most closely agreed with theirs—no influence need have occurred—was Edith Wharton, who wrote two novels, *Ethan Frome* (1911) and *Summer* (1917), both reflecting the bleakness and sterility of existence in the Berkshire Hills. Wharton was not a New Englander, but she had lived for some years in Lenox, Massachusetts, and had had ample opportunity to become aware of the ways of villagers and farmers roundabout, with both of which types she deals in her two novels. Though she uses fictitious place names, there can be no doubt as to the locale she has in mind. Wharton belongs in that long line of writers of fiction dealing with the hill country of western Massachusetts, including Catharine Sedgwick, Oliver Wendell Holmes, Henry Wadsworth Longfellow, Herman Melville, Nathaniel Hawthorne, Edward Bellamy, and Rachel Field. Among these authors, Wharton's view of the region was the most somber.

Wharton explains as follows the impulse that led her to write *Ethan Frome:*

> For years I had wanted to draw life as it really was in the derelict mountain villages of New England, a life even in my time, and a thousandfold more a generation earlier, utterly unlike that seen through the rose-colored spectacles of my predecessors, Mary Wilkins and Sarah Orne Jewett. In those days the snow-bound villages of Western Massachusetts were still grim places, morally and physically: insanity, incest and slow mental and moral starvation were hidden away behind the paintless wooden house-fronts of the long village street, or in the isolated farm-houses on the neighboring hills. . . . "Ethan Frome" was written

after I had spent ten years in the hill-region where the scene is laid, during which years I had come to know well the aspect, dialect, and mental and moral attitude of the hill-people.[18]

Wharton's dig at Freeman and Jewett is unfounded and inaccurate, but *Ethan Frome,* which recounts a personal tragedy afflicting a rather decent and intelligent farmer, is indeed a dismal story. It is the better known and artistically the superior of Wharton's two Berkshire novels, but it is less significant than *Summer* as a study of rural poverty and decay. In *Ethan Frome* the town exists only in the background, providing the rigid, in-humane public opinion that forces Ethan into lifelong unhappiness. In *Summer* much of the action takes place in a village named North Dormer, which lacks all the more wholesome qualities of community life and shares in the pervading degeneracy of the region. Wharton in her autobiography, *A Backward Glance,* assures us that this novel is based on the actualities of conditions in the Berkshires; for example, the rural slum from which her heroine—or anti-heroine—originates was described to her in detail by her Lenox rector, who had, moreover, been summoned there to officiate at a funeral similar to the one described in the book. A brief summary of the novel will amply reveal its tone and mood.

Charity Royall, whose mother was a prostitute and father a thief, had been brought down from the Mountain—a locality noted for its lawless and sordid ways—by Lawyer Royall to live as a foster child with him and his wife. Assuming her benefactor's name, she entered the life of the village, a place where shotgun weddings were frequent, and poisonous gossip and hateful grudges were the norm of daily life. The lawyer, whose wife is dead at the time the novel opens, is an alcoholic, and is often in the company of disreputable women in nearby Nettleton (which answers the description of Pittsfield). But he treats his foster daughter honorably, except for one time when, apparently drunk, he propositions her in her bedroom. We are led to believe, however, that he is essentially well-intentioned, intelligent, and even somewhat idealistic—as we have seen in his Old Home Week speech discussed in chapter 11—but his good impulses have been thwarted by the deadly, petty social environment in which he lives.

Charity herself does not rise above the prevailing lax morals of North Dormer. A young man, Lucius Harney, comes to the town to make draw-ings of some of its colonial houses for an architectural journal. Charity, who keeps the local library (the books are rotting from disuse and lack of care) the few hours a week it is open, meets Lucius when he comes to the library in search of information. Shortly thereafter we find Charity driving him about the countryside in a buggy as he examines interesting buildings. The two are sexually attracted to each other and soon are meeting frequently in an abandoned farmhouse, with the result that Charity becomes pregnant. Harney, already engaged to a girl of his own class, has no intentions of marrying Charity, though after a confrontation with Lawyer Royall he protests that he has. Royall has been aware of what has been going on. Previously, in an angry scene in Nettleton, where Charity and her lover had gone for a Fourth of July celebration, Royall, drunk and accompanied by a party of revelers, had met the pair and had accused Charity of being a loose woman—with the result, perhaps, that Harney saw no harm in treating her as such. In the early stages of her pregnancy Charity, now deserted by Harney, visits an abortionist in Nettleton who does a thriving business among the girls of North Dormer and similar nearby towns. But Charity's purpose is to ascertain definitely whether or not she is pregnant, not to seek an abortion.

Assured that she is pregnant, she heads for her childhood home on the Mountain and is overtaken on the way by Parson Miles of North Dormer. It turns out that Charity's mother has just died and that the parson has been summoned to preside at her burial. Scenes of incredible sordidness take place in the mountain shanty where the dead woman lies and later at her grave. When the minister leaves, Charity insists on remaining in her "home," but the next morning revulsion overcomes her and she flees. On the road she meets Lawyer Royall, who, knowing but not saying that she is pregnant, takes her to Nettleton where the two are married.

This outline of Wharton's brief novel can leave no doubt as to how she viewed the conditions of life in rural New England, or at least in the section of it that she knew the best. The picture is one of utter decadence; a mountainous countryside peopled by shiftless, drunken, degenerate outcasts; small villages, like North Dormer, with "its mean curiosities, its furtive malice, and its sham unconsciousness of evil,"[19] and a county seat where the villagers can go to get drunk and have abortions. The region has been deserted by its best people, as Lawyer Royall says in his Old Home Week speech. None of the traditional institutions, like the church, the town meeting, or the schools, functions effectively, and Wharton has little to say about them.

Symbolic of what she believes has happened to the region is her description of a farmhouse originally built in the architectural style of an earlier era, as was evidenced by the "fan-shaped tracery of the broken light above the door, the flutings of the paintless pilasters at the corners, and the round window set in the gable."[20] But now "the paint was almost gone from the clapboards, the window panes were broken and patched with rags, and the garden was a poisonous tangle of nettles, burdocks and tall swamp-weeds over which big blue-bottles hummed."[21] The location beside a swamp, the weeds, the flies (generated by maggots and hence associated with death) harmonized with the dilapidation of the dwelling and the demoralization of its weak-minded, drunken inhabitants.

Such decaying relics of a once-prosperous past used to be common in New England and still may be found, though many have been bought and restored by summer people and retirees from the cities. But the rural slums of which they were a part have not vanished; rickety shacks and decrepit trailers have taken their place.[22] Wharton's picture was bleak, perhaps exaggeratedly so, but it was based on reality—the complete breakdown in large areas of New England of traditional rural and village society. She put in fiction what the magazine writers and others had reported in nonfiction about their findings in the backcountry and what Mary Wilkins Freeman had more than hinted at, despite the "rose-colored spectacles" that Wharton unfairly accused her of wearing.

Half a generation after publication of Wharton's *Summer,* James Gould Cozzens (1903-1978), in his novel *The Last Adam* (1933), subjected a Connecticut farming community to an almost equally devastating analysis. Granville Hicks has described *The Last Adam* as one of the outstanding fictional studies of a town in American literature. This may be extravagant praise, but the novel is strong in plot and characterization as well as in sociology. Though born in Chicago in 1903 and brought up from boyhood on Staten Island in metropolitan New York, Cozzens was well acquainted with New England. Both his parents were of New England stock or background, and *The Last Adam,* which Cozzens published at the age of thirty, may owe much to his six years in the Kent School in the same area of Connecticut in which the novel is set.

New Winton, Cozzens's fictional town, is an agricultural community in which may be found almost every form of human weakness—and a few of the human strengths that such places were traditionally reputed to foster. Politics, which in New Winton were mainly conducted behind the scenes instead of in open town meeting, were based on personal feuds and on greed in matters of taxation and public spending. The one town meeting described in the book is a farce in which the first selectman, whom Cozzens, contrary to law and custom, for some reason has acting as moderator, is utterly ignorant of parliamentary procedure and incompetent as a person. The meeting degenerates into chaos, with the first selectman's wife leading the hecklers.

Gossip of the most vicious sort is the chief pastime of the citizens of New Winton; and sexual morality, a problem in New England towns since the landing of the Pilgrims, has reached a nadir of laxity. The wealthiest family, the Bannings, of old New England stock, is composed of a husband, who ineffectively serves as a justice of the peace; a wife who controls her husband and attempts, unsuccessfully, to control the town; an empty-headed, conceited son who attends Yale; and a rather pathetic but utterly brattish daughter recently expelled from finishing school. Among other inhabitants who figure in the novel are various self-serving town officers, several local storekeepers and businessmen, an impoverished woman who eventually becomes demented after the death of her daugher, a rather likable and intelligent, but nosy, telephone operator, and a number of farmers and workingmen. The stars of the cast are Dr. Bull, who is "the last Adam," and his mistress of long standing, Janet Cardmaker, an unmarried, elderly woman who runs her ancestral dairy farm with the help of a hired man. Both Dr. Bull and Janet Cardmaker are old-line New Englanders, though the doctor had been born in Michigan and had moved back to New Winton, the home of his forebears, after getting his medical degree.

Dr. Bull and his mistress represent much that is decadent in New England, but there is also in their characters a glimmering of some of the more admirable traits of past generations. Referring to Janet, Cozzens writes:

> From talking mainly to men, her tones had taken on something male. Hearing that plain accent, that ruminative inflection given to words sober, positive, well-considered, you could see best not Janet, but out of a strangely vanished past, certain composed, farm-weathered faces; the men of an older Connecticut standing quiet, their grave eyes in direct regard, their opinions simply and unhesitatingly spoken—for they were as good as you were; a reticent, unpolished courtesy made them willing, for the moment, to assume that they were no better than you were.[23]

Most of the townspeople in New Winton, though they keep up a pretense of belief in the equality of all, have lost the calm self-assurance that Cozzens apparently sees as the foundation of rural Connecticut character. Dr. Bull and Janet have not lost it, but in them it exists, rather unattractively, as a defiant arrogance, a flaunted disregard for the opinions and feelings of others. With these two, as with many of Mary Wilkins Freeman's characters, the old New England virtues have gone sour, have become defects of character—willfulness, quarrelsomeness, contemptuousness. The result in Dr. Bull is that he shamefully neglects his duties as the sole member of the town's board of health, a job he considers little more than a sinecure providing a rather small supplement to his income. A real regard for his town and its people—and he scorns both—would have prompted him to investigate the latrines at a temporary construction camp, the waste from which polluted the local water supply with a particularly virulent strain of typhoid bacillus. As it is, an epidemic breaks out, with dozens ill and several deaths. In the emergency Dr. Bull does fall to and work to the point of exhaustion, but in his more normal daily practice we have seen him neglecting mortally ill patients while he goes off on a rather puerile expedition hunting rattle-snakes.

New Winton, nestled among the Connecticut hills, is described as a pic-ture-book New England farming town. But its inhabitants are in no way a credit to its architectural and natural beauties or to its presumably admir-able traditions. Perhaps Cozzens thought that these traditions and the in-stitutions growing out of them never were so impressively effective as many believed them to have been. At any rate, in the twentieth century in New Winton human weaknesses—the sins of Adam, to use the old phrase—are rife, spoiling the Edenic setting, no matter how many rattlesnakes Dr. Bull, the last Adam, may dispose of.

[13]
Writers on New England Towns since 1960

> Most people believe . . . that any problem in the world can be
> solved if you know enough; most Vermonters know better.
> John Gardner, *October Light* (1976)[1]

In the work of a number of authors writing during the past twenty years
about New England village and rural life, the note of pessimism that
characterized Wharton's, the later Chase's, and Cozzens's works on the
subject persisted and intensified. Four of these writers—Shirley Jackson,
John Cheever, John Updike, and John Gardner—have won for themselves
a wide readership and well-deserved acclaim as literary artists. In their
novels and short stories about New England they are more objective and
analytic than their immediate predecessors, and thus they achieve a dis-
tancing of themselves from their material that generates in the reader an
assurance as to the authenticity of what he is reading. Perhaps these
strengths result from the fact that three of the authors are not native to
New England—though they have lived there for varying periods—and the
fourth, John Cheever, though a native, has lived most of his creative life in
New York City and Westchester County. In any event the use of New
England settings by these four outstanding authors of our generation
underlines the continuing concern of American readers with the region
and its way of life.

Shirley Jackson

Shirley Jackson (1919-65) by no means specialized in New England
stories. In much of her village fiction, which is a relatively small part of her
output, she refrained from localizing her settings. Born in San Francisco,
she lived her first fourteen years in the Bay Area of California. In 1933 she
moved with her family to Rochester, New York, where she finished high
school and attended the University of Rochester, later transferring to Syra-
cuse University. Upon graduation she married Stanley Edgar Hyman, who

was to become a literary critic of some standing, and the couple moved to New York City. In 1945 they left the city for North Bennington, Vermont, where, with the exception of the years 1949 to 1951 at Westport, Connecticut, they remained for the rest of Shirley Jackson's short life. As a writer Jackson specializes in fantasy, humor, the supernatural and occult, and mental abnormality, usually combining two or more of these. Her novels and stories generally deal with individuals or small groups, often in isolated and architecturally grotesque houses; towns and other communities exist mainly in the background. But there are several short stories and at least one novel, *We Have Always Lived in the Castle* (1962), in which villages and their inhabitants figure crucially. Though much of her writing was done just before and during the 1950s, her preoccupation with racially inherited superstitions and with psychiatric problems places her work in a very different category from that of the writers considered in the previous chapters.

Jackson's best-known story, "The Lottery," is an exploration of communal village psychology. Laid on the green of a country village in the present time, the tale describes the selection by lot of a sacrificial victim who is immediately stoned to death by the assembled farmers and townspeople and their children. The traditional purpose of the sacrifice, occurring annually at approximately the summer solstice, was to ensure a good corn crop, but now this purpose seems more or less to be forgotten, except by the oldest citizens. For most of the participants it is merely a time-worn custom lacking real significance. The conductors of the rite are leading citizens of the town. Frighteningly noticeable is the solidarity of the people—their sense of being a tightly knit, even sacred social unit—in the ancient spirit of the New England social covenant. The town is all-important; the individual must be ready to give his life for its well-being. The people who are gathered on the green gossip and joke familiarly just as they would at a Fourth of July celebration or at a town meeting. The lottery is but an episode in their yearly routine, another occasion when the people meet and strengthen the bonds that hold them together.

Published in the *New Yorker* in 1948, "The Lottery" released an avalanche of puzzled, vituperative, or waggish letters upon the author and editors. Many letter writers inquired if such rites actually were practiced in remote areas of the nation. Pressed for an explanation, Jackson said that her purpose had merely been to tell a story, but that it could be taken as illustrative of the human potential for evil and cruelty—a theme embedded in much of her writing. She reports that the idea of "The Lottery" came to her as she was walking along a peaceful street in North Bennington, and that she completed the tale within a few hours on the same day.[2] Jackson has stated that she laid her story in her "own village."[3] Yet cruelties in "The Lottery" need not—and should not—be taken as uniquely applicable to a New England town except insofar as such a town resembles countless others around the world. But as an allegory of innate and universal human viciousness, stupidity, and credulity, it can be taken seriously.

There are, however, certain distinctively, though not exclusively, New England qualities in "The Lottery." Jackson's conviction of the innate human potential for evil is, of course, thoroughly Calvinistic (though theologically she was surely not a Calvinist). The scapegoat theme of the story, traceable in part to James George Frazer's *The Golden Bough*,[4] had close parallels in the treatment of witches in New England, notably those of Salem, about whom Jackson later wrote a book for adolescents. Indeed, a curious analogy exists between Jackson's transplanting primitive rites and attitudes into modern America and the efforts of nineteenth-century theorists to find Germanic and Aryan origins for the New England town meeting. But while the earlier theorists regarded the supposed connection of town meeting with the ancient gemot as an indication of the system's basic soundness, Jackson's anthropological interpretation emphasized the lingering evil and terror latent in village societies. Critics have pointed out the likenesses of some of Jackson's tales to such works by Hawthorne as "Young Goodman Brown," *The Scarlet Letter*, and "The Gentle Boy," which reveal their author's belief in what Herman Melville called "something, somehow like Original Sin."[5] In addition, Jackson shared Hawthorne's view that children, far from being little angels, have the capability of being little devils. Clearly devoted to her own children and amused by them, she wrote two autobiographical books relating episodes in their upbringing. These books she titled, humorously but suggestively, *Life among the Savages* (1953) and *Raising Demons* (1957).

In these books also she has much to say about her relationship with the Vermont townspeople, with whom she got on well and by whom she was liked, especially for her sense of humor and her participation in community affairs. Yet she was under no illusions regarding rustic living. In North Bennington she and her husband, as city people and as members of the Bennington College community, were outsiders on two counts. Among primitive tribes and in secluded rural settings like some New England towns, outsiders tend to arouse gratuitous suspicion and hate.

Among Jackson's stories dealing with the rejection of outsiders, two need special mention. One, titled "Flower Garden" (1949), tells how a city person newly arrived in a country town enters enthusiastically into her new life, makes at least one good friend among the villagers, grows a fine flower garden, but makes the mistake of hiring and being decent to a black handyman, whom she on occasion innocently permits to enter her house. This unorthodox behavior—a flaunting of a local prejudice—estranges her friend and results in her being cold-shouldered out of town. Another story, "The Summer People" (1950), develops the outsider theme with overtones of terror absent in "Flower Garden." An elderly couple have for years summered on a rather remote lake in New England. Like other "summer people," it has been their invariable custom to return to the city immediately after Labor Day. But one year they decide to stay later. Their announcement of this intention dismays their neighbors and the nearby townsfolk, who keep saying summer residents always leave on Labor Day. The elderly couple, the Allisons, are of two minds about the local people. Mrs. Allison at one point remarks to her husband that it is "horrible to think into what old New England Yankee stock had degenerated"; and Mr. Allison replies, "It's generations of inbreeding. That and the bad land."[6] But a bit later the wife, having made a purchase in a local store, describes the townspeople as "so solid . . . and so *honest*." The husband agrees, adding: "Makes you feel good, knowing that there are still towns like this."[7] These contradictory remarks are time-worn clichés voiced by city and suburban people when speaking of rural folk.

The Allisons soon learn how superficial their thinking has been. The townspeople are not only surprised by the couple's decision to stay on; they are also angered by it. As if by concerted effort—though probably, one supposes, by the spontaneous operation in a number of individuals of a communal hatred of outsiders—the Allisons are subjected to a series of rebuffs and, eventually, hostile acts that reduce them to a state of helpless terror. They discover that the solid, honest storekeeper has knowingly sold them damaged goods; the grocer will no longer deliver their orders; the man who provides their kerosene for light, heat, and cooking will no longer supply them; their mail is tampered with; their car is vandalized; their telephone wires are cut. At the end of the story the terrified pair are waiting in darkness in their remote lakeside cottage while a thunderstorm rumbles around them.

In two of Jackson's novels are echoings of the Lizzie Borden murder case, of which Jackson had made a study. In *The Sundial* (1958) the village near the mansion that is the main setting of the novel is famous as the place where a fifteen-year-old girl supposedly murdered her father and mother and two brothers with a hammer. Though the girl was acquitted, she was generally considered guilty; and she and her home, where she continued to live, became major tourist attractions, much to the economic benefit of the town. But otherwise the community does not figure importantly in *The Sundial*—a novel of combined fantasy, humor, and suspense.

In Jackson's last completed novel, *We Have Always Lived in the Castle* (1962), a village and its inhabitants play a major role. The chief character, eighteen-year-old Mary Katherine Blackwood, nicknamed Merricat, whom many critics consider the most impressive character study in all of Jackson's works, had at the age of twelve killed her parents, by placing arsenic in the sugar bowl from which they sweetened their blackberry dessert. In addition, an uncle was made desperately ill by the poison but has survived as a permanent invalid. One sister, Constance, beloved by Merricat, escaped entirely because, as Merricat knew, she did not like either blackberries or sugar. The murderess herself was undergoing punishment upstairs, where she was frequently banished without dinner. Constance had cooked the meal and after the fatal seizures had emptied and washed the sugar bowl before its contents could be analyzed. The reason that she gave for this suspicious act was that there was a spider in the bowl; the real reason was to protect Merricat, whom she suspected. Like Lizzie Borden, Constance was tried and acquitted because of inconclusive evidence. She returned to her family home just outside the village to live in total seclusion with her sister and her ailing uncle. Here we find her as the novel begins. The townspeople are convinced of Constance's guilt and treat her and Merricat cruelly.

Since Constance is emotionally incapable of going to town to shop, this duty falls upon Merricat, who, gravely psychotic, lives in a world of dreams, among them a fantasy of escaping to the moon. On her twice-weekly shopping ventures in the village Merricat is jeered at by children and shunned and derided by adults. Store clerks, sidewalk loafers, housewives are in a tacit conspiracy to torture her, though they believe that her sister, not she, is the murderess. The Blackwoods, as members of a small upper class in this New England town (that it is in New England is made clear by references to town meetings), have always been disliked. The present disgrace of the family now makes them legitimate targets for scorn, contempt, and hate. The picture is not pretty—no prettier than in "The Lottery"—but more believable.

The story reaches a wild climax when the Blackwood house catches fire through Merricat's carelessness. The volunteer brigade promptly arrives and does its duty by saving the lower half of the building in spite of cries from the gathered mob that it be allowed to burn to the ground. But once the flames are quenched, the chief fireman picks up a stone and hurls it through a window. The crowd closes in, destroying whatever the fire has left and surrounding the two women and taunting them viciously. The mob in "The Lottery" seems tame and controlled compared to this one. Quiet is restored only when the village doctor announces that the aging uncle has died—not by poison but by heart failure. At least a respect for the dead remains among the villagers. Later, a few citizens partly redeem themselves by bringing food offerings to the two women, who remain barricaded in the half-ruined house.

Jackson's writing, including other works than those discussed here, are to a greater or lesser degree fantasies, but fantasies rooted in what their author sees as truths about human nature. The human potential for evil, to her, is almost limitless, whether it surfaces in a Dachau or in a Vermont village. Most disturbing about her presentation of innate evil is that so many of the people in her fiction, as individuals or en masse, make so little effort to struggle against it.

John Gardner

John Gardner, another author who has lived in the Bennington area and written fiction laid in Vermont, also recognized in the human makeup an innate evil but along with it an inner tendency to oppose it. The resulting conflict is basic to Gardner's Vermont novel, *October Light* (1976). Like Jackson, Gardner resorts to fantasy to make his points, but his points are much more explicit than hers. He has something very definite to say on a number of subjects: a human being's responsibility for his actions, the problems of guilt, traditional values versus the values, or lack of them, of the present time. *October Light* has its setting on a hill farm in the town of Bennington. Much more than Jackson, Gardner is at pains to recreate this setting in realistic detail, and he is eminently successful in his efforts. Having been brought up on his family's dairy farm in Batavia, New York, he can describe the yearly round of farm activities from firsthand experience. To such descriptions and those of the cycle of the Vermont seasons he brings a poetic lyricism.

The hill-farmer James Page, the protagonist of *October Light,* is quoted as saying: "Most people believe . . . that any problem in the world can be solved if you know enough; most Vermonters know better."[8] So did old-time Calvinists. Though James Page is not conventionally religious, he is very much a Vermonter, and Vermont from its settlement in the late eighteenth century had a bifurcated tradition: Its greatest hero, Ethan Allen, was strongly deistic and anti-Calvinist, and was the putative author of *Reason the Only Oracle of God* (1784), a book denounced from orthodox pulpits as sheer atheism. Allen is frequently mentioned in *October Light* as a major component in Page's cultural heritage. But presented also is Allen's contemporary Vermonter, the hellfire-and-brimstone Calvinist preacher Jebediah Dewey. And finally, James Page carries some of the genes of his ancestor General John Stark, the hero of the Battle of Bennington. The past, indeed, lives on in complex and contradictory ways in the heritage by which James Page attempts to direct his life; and Gardner emphasizes this persistence of the American past by using as mottoes for the book and its sections quotations from Jefferson, Charles Biddle, John Dickinson, Franklin, John Adams, and Washington. Bennington, one of the oldest and the most historic towns in Vermont, served Gardner as an embodiment of a tradition common to the state, to New England, and to the nation. In his descriptions of Bennington he presents not only a geographical but a spiritual and intellectual landscape.

James Page, aged seventy-three, is a dairyman and a bee-keeper; he is also a hunter, a drinker, and an "ornery," stubborn, opinionated character suggestive of some of the people in Mary Wilkins Freeman's stories, but more given to thought. His problems, frustrations, and inner conflicts are numerous—and most of them stem from the clashing facets of his personality as it has been formed and twisted by two hundred years of Vermont background. For example, on a simplistic level he hates Roman Catholics exactly as the Reverend Jebediah Dewey must have hated them. Thus he opposes and thwarts the marriage of his son, whom he has bullied since childhood, to an Irish Catholic girl; for this and other reasons the young man sinks into alcoholism and eventually kills himself. Hostile to much that is modern, James Page so despises the "entertainment" offered by television that he fires his shotgun through the screen of his sister Sally's set. Like a true old-time Yankee, he speaks up at town meeting to "block progress— keep to our old covered bridges, for instance, though the richest and smartest people in town want concrete for their darn trucks and bulldozers."[9]

The action of the novel arises from conflict between James Page and his sister, an impoverished widow now forced to live with him. James disapproves not only of his sister's addiction to television but also of most of her opinions, which do violence to his ancestral values. In a rage one day, brandishing a stick of stove wood, he chases Sally upstairs and locks her in her bedroom, where she in turn bolts the door from the inside and refuses to come out. Members of the family and the local doctor and a preacher— all commonplace persons but endowed with sound rural common sense— attempt to break the deadlock but with no success. During her imprisonment, Sally reads a subliterary fantasy novel dealing with smugglers, pirates, and UFOs. Some of the events in the novel, she finds, parallel the oppressive acts of her brother; and much of the story is given verbatim as she reads it, to the artistic detriment of *October Light* as a whole. Since Sally is able to nourish herself with apples in an attic connecting with her room, she cannot be starved into submission. Enraged, James contrives a device that will discharge a shotgun at her if she opens her door. She places above her door a crate of apples that will fall on any one who enters.

Matters grind to a crisis. James gets drunk at a tavern and miraculously escapes death when he wrecks his truck on his way home. His daughter, entering her Aunt Sally's room, is crushed unconscious by the falling crate. But the daughter recovers after a stay in a hospital; and as the novel closes, a truce between Sally and James has emerged.

What are the strengths of *October Light?* The events in it are almost as fantastic as those in the works of Shirley Jackson. The major characters are eccentric or grotesquely warped. Yet in the light of Gardner's own stated convictions, one must assume that there is a purpose in the novel beyond that of entertaining the reader by shock and suspense. In his recent, controversial book, *On Moral Fiction* (1977), Gardner writes that he agrees "with Tolstoy that the highest purpose of art is to make people good by choice."[10] In the case of *October Light,* the reader's impulse to make good choices in his own life would have to stem, if at all, from the spectacle of the sorry mess that Sally and James make by choices dictated almost entirely by stubbornness. Yet, with James at least, this stubbornness has been generated by values, blindly held perhaps, that are basic in American history and life. His intransigency is actually a relentless clinging to tradition.

James was not alone in his refusal to discard the past. He had found a like thinker in Norman Rockwell, who once lived twelve miles up the valley in Arlington and whom James had met and admired. As interpreted by Gardner and understood by James, Rockwell, though seemingly secure "in this safe, sunlit village in Vermont where they were still in the nineteenth century,"[11] was actually a pessimist deploring the "decay" of the old ways and the values they represented but trying to recapture them in his paintings in the forlorn hope, perhaps, that they might again find favor among his countrymen and gently prod them to make themselves "good by choice."

James Page has a realistic grasp of the history of Vermont. He is aware, for example, that Ethan Allen was a blasphemer and a drunkard as well as a hero of the American Revolution. But James believes deeply in the constructive vitality of the Vermont tradition, and here he would agree with another resident of Arlington, Dorothy Canfield Fisher. His conflict with his sister arises entirely from her acceptance of the spurious values that he sees supplanting the older ones, which he refuses to discard. James identifies strongly with his town, his state, and his nation—very likely too strongly, for in doing so he has become an anachronism. But the sense of community, of belonging to a geographical and political area, is very much alive in him and cements his attachment to his convictions. He consciously regards himself as an embodiment of the three-hundred-year-old rural tradition of New England.

Yet in the late twentieth century the old ways and virtues may not be adequate for dealing with life's problems. In *On Moral Fiction* Gardner writes that he began *October Light* "with the opinion that traditional New England values are the values we should live by: good workmanship, independence, unswerving honesty [James Page never lies], and so on—and one tests these opinions in lifelike situations, puts them under every kind of pressure one can think of, always being fair to the other side, and what one slowly discovers, resisting all the way, is that one's original opinion was oversimple."[12] What Gardner apparently discovers is that James is too firmly locked into the New England values. Thus unlocking becomes a major theme of the novel—the unlocking of winter by spring, the unlocking of doors, and the unlocking of emotions. The ancestral values, if they are to work, must also be unlocked from the constricting confines of long-held prejudice. With James an emotional and intellectual unlocking begins after the booby trap set by his sister almost kills his daughter. But the thaw is not complete until, from information supplied by Sally and memories of remarks made by his wife before her death years ago, he pieces together the reasons for the suicide of his son Richard. During his boyhood, Richard had been made to feel worthless by the perfectionist demands made on him by his father, who later thwarted his marriage. As a young man Richard, a drunkard now, had played a Hallowe'en prank on his sickly uncle, Sally's husband, and the resulting shock had caused the uncle's death by heart failure. Richard had left the scene without attempting to help the dying man, and pangs of conscience drive him further into drink and despair. After he confesses to his mother, whom he has sworn to secrecy, she tells James that their son is sick as a result of "something he's done."[13] The father confronts the young man, ordering him to reveal what he has done. Richard retorts, "Tell you, you old bastard?"[14] James slaps him. That night Richard hangs himself.

James's new vision of his past reduces him to tears, but not maudlin tears. His stature in the reader's eyes is not diminished, nor is the worth of his inherited values negated. He has been humanized, "unlocked," by a realization of his own fallibility and the fallibility of even Vermont standards when enforced too rigidly. Outraged by the decay of the old virtues, he had lashed out too zealously and violently against the new. But he was not about to replace the old with the new.

Published in 1976, *October Light,* with its quotations from the founding fathers and its frequent references to Ethan Allen, was intended as a bicentennial novel. Like Norman Rockwell's paintings, many of which depict scenes from New England villages, Gardner's book may be taken as a warning that all is not well—that the principles on which the country was established have been abandoned too hastily, too nearly completely. But it should also be taken as an admonition against an adherence to the past so tenaciously as to shut out understanding of the present.

John Cheever

Two present-day authors, John Cheever and John Updike, have written novels with settings in Massachusetts coastal towns, where life is characterized by a sophistication and complexity not found in the Vermont villages of Gardner's and Jackson's fiction. Cheever (1912–82), a native of the Boston suburb of Quincy, has lived during most of his writing career in Westchester County, New York, and much of his fiction deals with affluent suburban settings and characters. But two of his novels, *The Wapshot Chronicle* (1957) and *The Wapshot Scandal* (1965), are laid in part in a fictional Massachusetts town, St. Botolphs, founded in early Puritan days. *The Wapshot Chronicle*, which focuses more closely than its sequel on the village setting, will be our chief concern here.

The Wapshots, whose fortunes and misfortunes in the second third of the present century are the subject of *The Wapshot Chronicle*, are descendants of passengers on Governor Winthrop's ship the *Arbella*, which arrived in Massachusetts Bay in 1630. For generations the Wapshots, a family of wealthy seafarers, had been leading citizens of St. Botolphs. In the time recorded in the novel, their prestige has badly slipped but has not entirely vanished. The present Wapshots are notable mainly for their eccentricities rather than for their accomplishments in commerce or the professions. Leander Wapshot, the ranking male representative of the family, operates a passenger ferry, the *Topaze*, down an estuary and across a bay to a seaside amusement park. Even as a ferryboat captain—about as low a position as the scion of world navigators could sink to—Leander is incompetent, for he wrecks the *Topaze* on a rock, and later the salvaged vessel is converted into "The Only Floating Gift Shoppe in New England."[15] The chronicle of Wapshot seafaring has run its downward course to the ultimate bottom, where it is mired in New England's "summer business," as tourism has rather accurately been called. Leander had protested by getting drunk on the opening day of The Floating Gift Shoppe, committing a public nuisance, and firing a pistol, with no effect, at the crowd gathered for the inaugural festivities. Later, as he swims in the river, he dies by drowning, as did his mythological namesake while swimming the Hellespont.

Leander's cousin Honora is the wealthiest, most influential, and most eccentric surviving Wapshot. Tolerated locally, in fact respected, she rules her family with her purse. It is she who owns the *Topaze* and decides to let Leander's wife convert it into a gift shop. She exerts a further control on Leander's family by promising to leave her sizable estate to his two sons, Moses and Coverly, provided each marries and has a male heir. Justifying his characterization of Honora, Cheever (or the narrator) explains: "It is not my fault that New England is full of eccentric old women and we will merely give Honora her due."[16] But Honora's eccentricity surpasses that of most of the quaint village characters so abundant in New England local-color stories. One oddity is her refusal ever to pay her federal income tax an omission that, upon its discovery, necessitates her flight to Italy. Later, tracked down and extradited, she returns home; her property is confiscated; and though not previously an alcoholic, she quickly drinks herself to death.

These disastrous events account for the title of *The Wapshot Scandal,* in which they are recorded. They also bring to an end the Wapshot preeminence in St. Botolphs. The ancestral family farmhouse on the edge of town has fallen into decay and, by local hearsay, is haunted by the ghost of its former occupant, Leander. Leander's two sons have previously gone out into the world in pursuit of careers and wives to bear the sons upon whom their inheritance depends. But their marriages, while producing the sons, have otherwise been miserable, and their lives in various cities and suburbs have been empty. Moses has become a drunkard and Coverly a woman-chaser; and, of course, their hoped-for inheritance has vanished.

"I only want to be esteemed,"[17] Leander Wapshot had once said; and to some extent the community does esteem him. Mostly this esteem is a traditional one connected with a family name closely identified through generations and centuries with the history and well-being of the town. In St. Botolphs the past still counts for something. The Wapshots had only to live up to their part in the tradition to receive the continuing respect of the citizenry. Thus Honora's eccentricities do not seriously damage her standing, because she personally retains the dignity expected of a Wapshot. Also, she is aware of her responsibility as a favored citizen and, above all, is totally loyal to the town. To her, "St. Botolphs was the fairest creation on the face of the earth."[18] Nor is she alone in this sentiment. Coverly, about to leave home to seek a living, avows that "there is no place finer in the world than St. Botolphs,"[19] and he promises that he will return once he has "made his fortune."

Leander, like Honora, conducted himself as befitted a Wapshot, taking it as his function to serve as a reassuring symbol of the town's continuity. "He went skating on Christmas Day—drunk or sober, ill or well—feeling it was his responsibility to the village to appear on Parson's Pond. 'There goes old Leander Wapshot,' people said—he could hear them—a splendid figure of continuous and innocent sport that he hoped his sons would carry on. The cold bath that he took each morning was ceremonious—it was nothing else since he almost never used soap."[20] Leander attempted to instill in his boys not only a sense of family dignity but also a joy in their surroundings, especially the natural beauties—described lyrically in this book—of the countryside, the sea, and the lakes and forests of inland New England.

But there is self-deception in the part Leander plays. He seems to have ignored the fact that St. Botolphs, for all its Currier and Ives and Christmas-card quaintness, was also "a country of spite fences and internecine quarrels," where a pair of twins could live "until their death in a house divided by a chalk line."[21] In fact, Leander most of his life has lived in a delusion of security—a "conviction of the abundance of life . . . the feeling that the world was contrived to cheer and delight him."[22] But truth is forced upon him. Honora's largesse, on which he has always relied in keeping up his image as the scion of an ancient family, proves to have strings attached: she high-handedly disposes of the *Topaze;* she interferes, moreover, in Leander's upbringing of his sons; and she urges (unsuccessfully) Leander and his wife to convert the family farmhouse into a tourist home.

The fact is, however, that the town, and not Leander, has betrayed the past, and has done so with the crotchety acquiescence of Honora, who despite her fierce and demanding pride of ancestry cannot share Leander's dismay as he sees "raised on the ruins of that coast and port, a second coast and port of gift and antique shops, restaurants, tearooms, and bars where people drank their gin by candlelight, surrounded sometimes by plows, fish nets, binnacle lights and other relics of an arduous and orderly way of life of which they knew nothing."[23] Yet one cannot hold the town totally responsible for this betrayal of history. The town has been swept by the winds of change, the hurricanic fury of which in the outer world has all but destroyed Moses and Coverly Wapshot. Cheever's Wapshot books are laments, not so much for the past as for the present's rejection of whatever of promise the past once held for the future.

John Updike

John Updike (1932-) was born and spent his boyhood in Shillington, Pennsylvania, situated between Philadelphia and Reading. He attended Harvard, from which he graduated in 1954, and for several years worked on the staff of the *New Yorker,* to which he is still a regular contributor. Since 1957 he has lived some distance north of Boston in or near Ipswich, a coastal town retaining to a unique degree its colonial atmosphere. Much of Updike's writing has no bearing on the subject of this study, nor does most of the impressive body of criticism written about the work of this popular and gifted author. But one novel, *Couples* (1968), laid in the fictional town of Tarbox, presents a memorable picture of an ancient New England town in the process of engulfment by suburbia—in a stage of transition comparable to that of Cheever's St. Botolphs.

Tarbox has much in common with Ipswich. With a population of perhaps 10,000, it is located about as far south of Boston as Ipswich is north
and thus has attracted commuters seeking "the simple life." Also like Ipswich, it has some small-scale manufacturing; is situated on the seashore
with a fine beach, dunes, and salt marshes; and has preserved many of its
colonial buildings, most notably a Congregational church with a 125-foot
steeple topped by a five-foot-long weathercock, whose eye is an English
penny.

The important characters in *Couples* are mostly recent arrivals who have
formed an intimate community within the larger one. Not native to the
place, many of them "belonged to that segment of their generation of the
upper middle class which mildly rebelled against the confinement and
discipline whereby wealth maintained its manners during upheavals of
depression and world war."[24] Thus liberated, they settled "in unthought-of
places, in pastoral mill towns like Tarbox, and tried to improvise . . . a fresh
way of life. Duty and work yielded as ideals to truth and fun."[25] The male
members of the couples represent a large variety of occupations: there are
two investment brokers, one dentist, three research scientists, and two
building contractors. All but the dentist and the contractors work in Boston
or Cambridge. The women remain at home caring for their children and
houses and, in several cases, directing community projects. Ethnically and
religiously the mix is typical of a "good" suburb of an American city. Predominantly the couples are WASP, but among them are one oriental, one
Irish-Catholic, and one Jewish couple, and one of the husbands is of Dutch
extraction. The Irish couple, the Dutch-American Piet Hanema, and one
of the wives, Foxy Whitman, are the only persons in the lot who attend
religious services. The couples' social life consists of innocent amusements
like tennis and other outdoor sports; not-so-innocent drinking parties; and
not-innocent-at-all (if traditional standards are applied) adulterous promis-
cuity among themselves, though several of the couples seem to refrain
from this pastime.

The detailed and lengthy stretches of the novel devoted to "explicit
sex"—which have prompted some to describe the book as "the thinking
man's *Peyton Place*"[26]—need not concern us. One's feeling about such intru-
sions, so *au courant* ten or twelve years ago—is a personal matter. Nor does
space allow for more than a perfunctory discussion of the Freudian elements or of the echoings of classical mythology and medieval legend in this
richly textured book. According to the dust jacket of the first edition, the
ten couples constitute a "magic circle, with ritual games, a religious sub-
stitution, a priest (Freddy Thorne) and a scapegoat," the latter being Piet
Hanema, the Dutch-American builder. Like Shirley Jackson, Updike knew

The Golden Bough and found in it parallels between primitive societies and present-day New England villages. Piet, the scapegoat in *Couples,* is not chosen by lottery, but he is as much a victim of bad luck as if he had been. The psychological need for a scapegoat among these rather sophisticated and well-educated people becomes acute as their way of life begins to take its toll—divorces, loss of jobs, resort to psychoanalysis. The continued alcoholic partying and clandestine or open adultery strain nerves and tempers, and eventually hedonism becomes a horror.

Piet, sexually the most promiscuous of the group, makes one of the wives, Foxy Whitman, pregnant. The abortion of this pregnancy is arranged by the dentist, Freddy Thorne, who as payment for his service demands and gets one night in Piet's wife's bed. Thorne's wife, Georgine, a former mistress of Piet's, turns informer and accuses Piet and Foxy of "poisoning the air."[27] Foxy's and Piet's spouses eventually get divorces. In short, Piet's fiasco demands some sort of atonement: "The couples, though they had quickly sealed themselves off from Piet's company, from contamination by his failure, were yet haunted and chastened, as if his fall had been sacrificial."[28] Indeed, even before his downfall Piet had seen himself as a "scapegoat type."[29] Perhaps he is the most logical one to fall into the role, for he retains enough traditional religious scruples to make his fate meaningful to him. Brought up in the strict Calvinism of the Dutch Reformed Church, he continues, in Tarbox, to attend the Calvinist—though less rigidly so—Congregational Church, the colonial architecture and supposedly superb carpentry of which he admires. He and Foxy Whitman attend this church in spite of the vacuity of the pastor, who preaches Christianity in the language of commerce and investment banking. Moreover, Piet suffers from an excruciating consciousness of death and is dependent for his peace of mind on his angelic, long-suffering wife—one of the few characters in the book who are not despicable, contemptible, and hateful.

Thus the concept of retributive justice can be applied to Piet's debacle, since he loses his wife, his job, and the esteem of his peers. This Calvinist churchgoer ranks as a champion in breaking the seventh and tenth commandments. Moreover, he violates most of the principles that he holds or pretends to hold. He admires good workmanship but, with his partner, constructs shoddy tract houses on the outskirts of town. He is in awe of death but stands by while a bulldozer rips up an Indian burying ground. He respects the past but supervises the construction of phony colonial effects in a local restaurant. His friends accuse him of destroying whatever charm Tarbox still retains. Piet's ostracism is well-deserved, and his eventual departure from town caused no regrets.

The "priest" of the novel, Freddy Thorne, fills the role also of the traditional Lord of Misrule—in Scotland called the Abbott of Unreason—who at Christmas time served in the King's court or in the City of London as master of merriment, much of it disrespectful of the established religious and social order. At one point Piet refers to Freddy as "the local game-master"[30]; yet at another time Piet feels toward Freddy, in his dentist's garb of "sacerdotal white,"[31] the same "fondness a woman might feel toward her priest or gynecologist or lover—some one who has accepted her worst."[32] Freddy with his obscenities sets the extremely uninhibited tone of the couples' amusements. Yet he does preach a religion of sorts. "We're a subversive cell," he pontificates. "Like in the catacombs. Only they were trying to break out of hedonism. We're trying to break back into it. It's not easy";[33] and elsewhere he announces, "People are the only thing people have left since God packed up. By people I mean sex."[34] Not highly sexed himself, in fact somewhat hermaphroditic, he empathizes with both men and women, and he eggs on both sexes in their philandering. His androgynism seems to lend him a prestige that celibacy confers on more orthodox priests. In any event, Piet's fondness for Freddy is misplaced, for Freddy decrees Piet's downfall and banishment.

Updike by no means neglects the larger town community that envelops the "magic circle" of the couples. The Plymouth County town of Tarbox has roots in the deepest Puritan past. Its common, with its surrounding seventeenth-century saltbox houses; its streets "named for the virtues"[35] (Charity, Temperance, Prudence); and above all its vintage colonial church place Tarbox at the very core of the New England tradition. But Updike finds the town, which is representative of the region and the nation, to be in decline—not merely in transition—and he shares his discovery with the reader by recording a number of disturbing symptoms. The "sexual liberation" of the couples, though it results in various miseries, is not especially important among these symptoms. After all, Governor Bradford of Plymouth, a few miles south of Tarbox, had in 1642 witnessed in his beloved community an outbreak of wickedness that included drunkenness, fornication, adultery, and sodomy. Punishment of the malefactors was always severe; but the most spectacular fell upon a youth, Thomas Granger, who practiced "buggery . . . with a mare, a cowe, tow [sic] goats, five sheep, ·2· calves, and a Turkey"[36]—a record of iniquity beside which Piet Hanema's plodding adultery with a dozen or so Tarbox housewives pales to insignificance. The Plymouth magistrates dealt with Granger, the indisputable choice for a scapegoat, as prescribed by Leviticus. After all the animals he had buggered—there was some difficulty in selecting the right sheep— were "kild before [Granger's] face,"[37] the youth was put to death. If Plymouth could extricate itself—as it did—from such foulness, surely nearby Tarbox 325 years later could survive an outbreak of adultery and rather mild drunkenness. In a sense the couples are traditional in their amusements—as traditional as human nature and its frailties.

Much more disturbing is the force embodied in the bulldozer that Piet and his partner hire to level Indian hill, graves and all, preparatory to building some tract houses. "What do you do when you see [bones]?" Piet asks the black operator of the bulldozer. "Man, I keep movin,'" is the answer.[38] Better not linger, or think about what one is doing. Disrespect for the past, for the dead, comes close to being disrespect for humanity itself, and herein may be found the most distressing symptom of Tarbox's twentieth-century illness.

And the old religion, the wraith of which still haunts the lovely Tarbox church, is powerless to cure Tarbox's illness, for the religion has been infected also, perhaps for a long, long time. The church building on one occasion struck Piet as "a stately hollow blur."[39] Its weathercock, which shifts as the winds change and has always looked upon the world with the coin of the realm—an English penny—for an eye, is a rather obvious symbol. When the church is struck by lightning and burns as if through a judgment of a wrathful and fed-up God, the ancient carpentry is revealed as basically unsound, despite Piet's admiring surmises from the look of the exterior. Only the penny-eyed weathercock is ultimately preserved. The new church is to be "a modern edifice, a parabolic poured-concrete tent-shape peaked like a breaking wave."[40]

It is at town meeting—that sacred political relic of New England—that the present-day Tarbox is most clearly revealed. Piet observed that "town meeting that spring [of his debacle] smelled of whiskey. . . . A few feet above the swamp of faces hovered a glimmering miasma of alcohol, of amber whiskey, of martinis hurriedly swallowed between train and dinner, with the baby-sitter imminent." Tarbox has become more and more a town of commuters who thronged into housing developments like those built by Piet on either side of the village and had brought with them their "VW buses and Cézanne prints. . . . Self-assured young men" have taken over the meeting and silenced the once-dominant "droning Yankee druggists, paranoid clammers, potbellied selectmen." A young associate professor of sociology, "a maestro of parliamentary procedure,"[41] has been elected moderator, and several persons from the couples group serve on important town committees.

Town meeting in Tarbox is surely different from what it was a few years earlier, but is it necessarily less effective? Updike, who throughout the book is a recorder rather than an arbiter, does not say, though he seems a bit nostalgic for the more villagy atmosphere of past meetings. At least the institution has not vanished in Tarbox, though there is ominous talk of switching to representative town meetings.

Recent Nonfiction

Nonfiction studies of New England towns continue to be published in undiminished numbers. Many are historical accounts of individual towns, based on minutes of town meetings, on land deeds, on church records, and the like—a type of book that has been appearing for 150 years and more. An exceptionally notable one is Sumner Chilton Powell's *Puritan Village: The Formation of a New England Town* (1963), a study of the settling and early years of Sudbury, Massachusetts. Winner of a Pulitzer Prize and already a classic in its genre, Powell's book attempts, with great success and plausibility, to trace back the land and governmental practices of Sudbury to the various English villages from which the first inhabitants came. The research is impressive and the style highly readable. Its method adds a new dimension to local history.

A more general study is Michael Zuckerman's *Peaceable Kingdoms: New England Towns in the Eighteenth Century* (1970), which emphasizes the need and striving for harmony in the colonial towns, and describes, with a plethora of examples from town records, the means used to achieve this end, which when achieved, Zuckerman contends, resulted in a sameness and mediocrity in community life. Another author, Page Smith, has published a much broader study, *As a City upon a Hill* (1966), taking its title from John Winthrop's address to the passengers on the *Arbella* in 1630. Smith deals with the American town in general but presents the New England towns as archetypal and nationally influential. He traces back the spirit and goals of American towns to the church covenants common in New England in Colonial and later times. His disregard of the fact that even in the earliest settlements many inhabitants were not church members and hence technically not under the covenant weakens but does not completely invalidate Smith's thesis. During the first hundred and more years in New England the church was an overwhelming force, which remained very considerable at least to the Civil War. The covenants expressed a sense of community and mission that affected all inhabitants in and outside the church.

The town as a viable institution, capable of dealing with changing conditions and problems resulting from the spread of cities in New England, is the theme of Paul Brooks's *The View from Lincoln Hill* (1976), a study of the town of Lincoln, which over the years had been transformed from a farming community to a suburb of Boston. Brooks writes primarily from the point of view of a conservationist. Correctly asserting that Lincoln, like so many New England towns, had benefited from the first settlers' careful planning of their villages and method of distributing and using land, he finds a similar purpose and spirit in 1976, and thus Lincoln, though a suburb, has remained a place of rural, residential beauty, with open spaces and public lands, rather than becoming engulfed in urban sprawl. The farms are gone, but forests and green areas have been preserved. This achievement Brooks attributes to the persistence of the traditional local government and to the fact that the original community solidarity continued to find expression in town meetings.

The demographic composition of Lincoln has changed. City people, commuters, have moved in; after long years of an almost exclusively English-descended population, large numbers of persons of other national origins, mainly Irish, have taken up residence. But the fears of John Gould and C. F. Adams that with the passing of a homogeneous population town life, especially town-meeting government, would decline in quality are not shared by Brooks. Lincoln has thrived since the arrival of non-English elements, who soon participated in local affairs. Indeed, during the period since its population became diversified, the town faced and solved some of the most difficult problems it had ever confronted—the chief one being how it could be saved as a community that retained most of the old ways and preserved much of its original rural atmosphere and beauty.

Brooks feels that Lincoln has found the answer to this problem. The Puritan settlers, he states, considered their land to be not so much something to be owned as to be protected in trust. Despite the changes the centuries have brought, this view has not entirely vanished, at least in Lincoln. "Though the farms are now few," Brooks concludes, "the principle endures: a principle that once made, and can still make, the New England town a model for a happy marriage between man and the land."[42] Brooks sees the towns of the nation—not only of New England—as major forces in the conservation of a habitable environment. Though he cannot by the wildest stretch of the imagination be described as a millennialist, the perennial notion, going back to 1620, that New England's destiny is to lead the way to salvation—in this case environmental salvation—is to be found implicit in his pages.

The Future of New England Towns

Paul Brooks, John Gould, and Clarence Webster, as we have seen, are among many who are optimistic about the continuance of New England towns in something resembling their traditional form as functioning communities. All agree that there are forces working against the continued existence of town-meeting government and a closely knit community life as known in the past three centuries. Size, for example, is a major adverse force, and one that little can be done about. Once the population of a town rises into five figures it ceases to be a compact community. Its inhabitants identify themselves more and more with various religious, political, ethnic, and occupational groups. Interests become diversified; the needs of the municipality become more complex; sheer numbers make town meetings impracticable. Such towns may petition their legislatures for charters as cities; or they may choose the rather unsatisfactory alternative of government by representative town meetings, in which elected delegates act in behalf of the voting population.[43]

Least destructive of town spirit and government is the influx of ethnic groups. Homogeneity is lost to some extent, especially as regards religion, though long before people of "foreign" origin appeared in any numbers in the towns, the dominance of orthodox Congregationalism had been shattered by inroads of Methodists, Baptists, Episcopalians, Unitarians, and others. So far as government goes, the presence of residences not of "Anglo-Saxon" background has not had the dire results that some old-line Yankees feared. Indeed, it is a rare town in New England today that does not number among its town officers one or more persons with French-Canadian, Polish, Irish, Italian, Portuguese, or other non-English names. Assimilation to New England ways has been rapid and thorough. Similarly, the large numbers of exurbanites, of whatever religious or national origin, who have recently come to live in rural towns, have, as John Gould found, only temporarily disrupted traditional routines or disturbed older attitudes. They, too, tend to fall in line with both desirable and undesirable small-town ways.

A greater threat to New England town solidarity and independence is the increasing takeover by the state and federal governments of functions and duties formerly assigned to the towns. The support of the destitute—once a local responsibility resting on an elected committee, the Overseers of the Poor—now is defrayed by welfare administered by state and national agencies. Centralized schools have done away with district schools and their individual committees, and in some instances towns have no schools at all, either elementary or secondary, all children being bused to some other location. Each town still has a school committee, but often it works in cooperation with committees from other towns. Since education has been one of the main unifying local enterprises—in late years stronger than the churches—towns that lose some or all of their schools are so much the poorer in incentives to community action.

In other ways, too, towns have become less independent. Gone forever is the old rural economy that made many a community almost totally self-sufficient in regard to food, clothing, fuel, and other commodities, and to most services, like blacksmithing, the milling of grain, and the sawing of timber. The local police, or constables, are no longer the most important agency of law enforcement but share that function with state police and enlarged sheriff's departments. Town roads are still important and their upkeep constitutes one of the chief remaining functions of the towns, but state highways are built through the towns independently of local control.

The shrinkage of town powers continues. In some instances—for example, in the care of the poor—the shift of responsibility to centralized agencies has been desirable and advantageous to all concerned. In other instances, as with the schools, the gains may not have offset the losses. One thing is certain, however. The towns are no longer the little independent democracies that the historian Bancroft described in the 1840s. Yet what independence they retain—and it is considerable, especially in the matter of taxation, town planning, and local ordinances—they guard zealously and utilize quite fully.

Here and there in remote parts of New England one finds towns that the influx of newcomers, whether from the cities or from foreign lands, has passed by and in which state and federal encroachments have been at a minimum. Such a town is Swans Island, Maine, situated five or six miles south of Mount Desert Island. The population of this town has decreased from 765 in 1880 to perhaps 400 today. The number of summer visitors and residents is increasing, but they have never been, and are far from becoming, the chief source of income for the island as they are, for example, on Martha's Vineyard. The year-round inhabitants are for the most part descended from the original settlers, who around 1800 came from the coastal towns of Massachusetts. Thus they are direct descendants from the original Puritans and Pilgrims. By occupation most of the males were originally fisherman-farmer-sailor—that versatile combination so common until quite recently in coastal New England, especially Maine. There were some granite quarrying and lumbering on the island years ago, but primarily the townspeople won their livelihood from land and sea—particularly the latter. They were not the world-girdling seafarers that Mary Ellen Chase wrote about, but they were active in coastwise, even West Indian schooner trade, and their fishing voyages carried them northeastward to Cape Breton and the Banks and southwest to Virginia. They were skillful sailors in their home waters, as treacherous as exist anywhere, but their graveyards contain numerous memorials to men and whole families lost at sea.

The farming has long since been abandoned on Swans Island's rocky land, and the island's vessels no longer ply the coastwise trade or sail to distant fishing grounds. But the sea is still the major source of income—lobstering, scalloping, herring seining, some offshore trawling. The men are as skillful as ever on the water, guiding their boats among the fog-shrouded reefs and racing tides with uncanny precision. The town is still a compact unit, still somewhat isolated, though the state underwrites a ferry service to the mainland. The elementary school is still the island's own, a source and center of common interest and activity; there has never been a high school, and now, as always, those seeking secondary education must "go away," though at present they can commute daily on the ferry. The roads are still one of the town's most important responsibilities, though considerable state money is available for their maintenance. Also, until recently, the town operated its own cooperative electric power plant, which not long ago brought the island into the electronic age. Another town project from time to time has been the support of a physician, with help from the Maine Sea Coast Mission. In other words, though the island, like all other New England towns, has lost some of its functions and responsibilities, it has taken on others and so remained more self-sustaining than many mainland towns.

Thus change has taken place, but much remains the same, particularly in the character of the people and in their joint enterprise in running public affairs. Some years ago the author attended town meeting on Swans Island. Following tradition, the meeting took place in early March, when winter still prevailed. The morning of the meeting the water of the harbor was skimmed with new ice and snowdrifts lay deep along the edge of the woods. But the roads were clear; the weather was favorable; and the people early began to converge on the place of assembly, the Oddfellows Hall, a structure that would sicken the heart of Mary Ellen Chase, so counter is its monstrous ugliness to her cherished theories about Maine architecture.

By no means all the voters attend. Some are simply not interested. Others are contrary, vowing that they will give the "town fathers" enough rope to hang themselves rather than coming to their aid by being present. Eventually, some thirty-five persons have arrived, mostly in ancient automobiles sufficiently serviceable only for the island's few miles of road. The hall is far from full, but the meeting is brought to order by the first select-man and proceeds to the nomination and election from the floor of a moderator—a way of choosing that officer once quite usual and still legal, but no longer commonly practiced. Old ways persist on Swans Island.

I have described this same meeting elsewhere[44] in detail unnecessary for present purposes, but some impressions of it may be of interest. The moderator, a man of soft voice and easy manner, gives every evidence of having served many times in that capacity. The meeting continues with dignity; the townspeople, armed with their printed Town Reports, participate with intelligence and restraint. Their town, their daily lives, their money are involved; and there are potential causes for heated debate. Yet these people must live together on an island and rancor must be avoided as much as possible. No disparaging words are spoken; no insults exchanged. One by one the fifty-four articles on the warrant are acted upon. Officers are elected and later sworn in; tax rates are voted; allocation of money is made. Miscellaneous matters are discussed: the repair of the town wharf; the improvement of the town dump, found to be a breeder of rats.

At noon there has been a break in the proceedings, during which the attenders partake of an excellent lunch served by the island women for the price of one dollar. This is truly a social interlude, in which the island's sense of being a community, a partially self-governing, self-contained entity is in full evidence. As a result, the afternoon's work goes even more serenely than before, with occasional touches of humor. By twilight all business has been finished and the townspeople rattle homeward in their well-worn vehicles. An important job has been done, though there is no talk about the glories of democracy or smug allusion to the large numbers who stayed at home out of inertia or spite. Those who have wished to have a say in public affairs have had the opportunity and have conducted themselves creditably.

On Swans Island the town system works adequately, if not perfectly. It works with a similar degree of efficiency in numerous other small communities equally remote or nearly so. In larger towns it works in a perhaps less traditional manner, but the machinery, the system, is there and is often used effectively. Towns like Swans Island exemplify the old ways as practiced, to the best of their ability, by direct descendants of the people who first followed them three centuries ago in the colonies of Plymouth and Massachusetts Bay. Some New Englanders regard communities like Swans Island as perpetuators of past strengths and virtues, much as Irish nationalists regard the Aran Islands as guardians of an age-old Irish tradition. In both cases there is idealization, myth-making; but ideals and myths are essential to any culture.

Notes and References

Chapter 1 "God Has Never Forsaken That Country"

1. John Winthrop, "A Modell of Christian Charity," in *The Puritans: A Sourcebook of Their Writings*, ed. Perry Miller and Thomas H. Johnson, 2 vols. (New York: American Book Co., 1938), 1: 198–99.

2. Timothy Dwight, *Travels in New England and New York*, ed. Barbara Miller Solomon, 4 vols. (Cambridge, Mass.: Belknap Press of Harvard University Press, 1969), 1: 122.

3. Charles E. Cunningham, *Timothy Dwight, 1752–1817* (New York: Macmillan, 1942), p. 105.

4. Ibid., p. 107; Stephen Berk, *Calvinism vs. Democracy: Timothy Dwight and the Origins of American Evangelical Orthodoxy* (Hamden, Conn.: Archon Books, 1974), chap. 6.

5. Philip Freneau in 1772 published a poem titled "The American Village"—his first verse to be printed—that was a favorable treatment of a New York village. Freneau omitted the poem, which is undistinguished, from later editions of his work. It may be found in *The Poems of Philip Freneau*, ed. Fred Lewis Pattee, 3 vols. (1907: reprint ed., New York: Russell & Russell, 1963), 3: 381–94. John Trumbull published in 1775–82 a mock epic, *M'Fingal*, in which he employed a New England town meeting as a setting for a satirical presentation of Tory and British points of view, but this poem is hardly a celebration of village life and values. See *The Poetical Works of John Trumbull* (Hartford, Conn.: Samuel G. Goodrich, 1832).

6. *The Major Poems of Timothy Dwight, with a Dissertation on the History, Eloquence, and Poetry of the Bible* (Gainesville, Fla.: Scholarly Facsimiles and Reprints, 1969), p. 371. Dwight's own happy experience in Greenfield Hill must have strengthened his belief that New England towns were smiled upon and showered with blessings by an approving Deity. During his years there he was a leader in education as well as a venerable clergyman. His academy, which was ahead of its times in admitting girls as well as boys, drew students from other states and countries. The church records reveal no serious dissension between him and his congregation, and the town records indicate that this was a peaceful period in Fairfield as a whole. When he was called to the presidency of Yale College, he was hesitant about leaving, and his parishioners strongly opposed the move. When a convocation of neighboring clergymen advised that he accept the call, he acted accordingly. The disappointed townspeople then thought of suing for breach of contract; but eventually they decided against this measure and let him go with their good wishes. At Greenfield Hill, Dwight had fulfilled completely his ideal of a Christian minister's place and influence in a community. (See the Minutes of the Town of Fairfield and Records of Greenfield Hill or Northwest Society and Church Records, Fairfield, Connecticut.)

7. Dwight, *Major Poems*, p. 378.

8. Ibid., p. 381.

9. Ibid.

10. Joel Parker, "The Origin, Organization, and Influence of the Towns of New England," *Proceedings of the Massachusetts Historical Society* 9 (1866): 15–16.

11. Moses Coit Tyler, *A History of American Literature During the Colonial Period, 1607–1765*, 2 vols. (New York: G. P. Putnam's Sons, 1909), 2: 312. Also Jared Eliot, *Essays upon Field*

Husbandry in New England and Other Papers, 1748–1762, ed. Harry J. Carman and Rexford G. Tugwell, Columbia University Studies in the History of American Agriculture, no. 1 (New York: Columbia University Press, 1934), p. xv.

12. Eliot, *Essays,* p. 137.

13. Ibid., p. 137.

14. Ibid., p. 138.

15. Ibid.

16. Another Connecticut poet, David Humphreys, who was a friend and contemporary of Dwight's, wrote a poem about the British attack on Fairfield titled "An Elegy on the Burning of Fairfield in Connecticut." The author, who claims he was writing "on the spot," describes "the scorched elms" and the "faded green"—the desecration of two characteristic and symbolic features of New England villages. Humphreys, indeed, writes as if he were describing the destruction of a holy city. (The poem may be found in *The Columbian Muse: A Selection of American Poetry from Various Authors of Established Reputation* [New York: J. Carey, 1794], pp. 112–14.)

17. Dwight, *Major Poems,* p. 466.

18. Ibid., p. 502.

19. Ibid., p. 506.

20. Cunningham, *Timothy Dwight,* p. 335; Berk, *Calvinism,* p. 21.

21. Ernest Lee Tuveson, *Redeemer Nation* (Chicago: University of Chicago Press, 1966), p. 110.

22. Dwight, *Major Poems,* p. 516.

23. Berk, *Calvinism,* p. 21.

24. Printed in Hartford in 1817 by Peter B. Gleason and Company; in 1793 a similar committee of the General [Congregational] Association of Connecticut published *An Address to the Inhabitants of the New Settlements in the Northern and Western Parts of the United States* (New Haven, Conn.: T. and S. Green, [1793]). Dwight was not a member of that committee.

25. *An Address* (1817), p. 3.

26. Dwight, *Travels,* 3: 186.

27. Ibid., 2: 321.

28. Ibid.

29. Ibid.

30. Ibid., p. 317.

31. Ibid., p. 318.

32. Ibid., p. 333.

33. Quoted in William Bradford, *History of Plymouth Plantation, 1620–1647,* ed. Worthington C. Ford, 2 vols. (Boston: The Massachusetts Historical Society, 1912), 2: 115.

34. Charles Francis Adams, *Three Episodes in Massachusetts History,* 4th ed., 2 vols. (Boston: Houghton, Mifflin & Co., 1894), 610ff.

Chapter 2 Reports on the Promised Land: Dwight's *Travels in New England and New York,* and Other Commentators

1. Dwight, *Travels,* 1: 7.

2. Most early-nineteenth-century writing about New England villages was in prose, but the poetic impulse that prompted *Greenfield Hill* was not dead, as is attested by Enoch Lincoln's *The Village: A Poem with an Appendix* (Portland, Me.: Edward Little and Co., 1816). Lincoln, later governor of Maine, claimed to be describing a typical New England community, identified as the Saco River Valley town of Fryeburg, Maine. Employing a variety of verse forms, as did

Dwight, he devotes considerable space to scenery and to Indian lore, but never gets down to the specifics of village life. Generalizations like "Our blest New England's fruitful soil/Requires no culture by servile toil" (p. 23) are typical. The Appendix deals almost exclusively with slavery, which Lincoln deplores. Still another poem, unsigned, *The Populous Village, A Poem Recited before the Philermenian Society of Brown University, September, 1826* (Providence, R.I.: published by the Society, 1826) echoes Dwight and Goldsmith in its praise of a New England type of village (its precise location is unnamed), describing the churches, the schools, and the inn, and celebrating the prosperity and happiness of the inhabitants.

3. Dwight, *Travels*, 1: 5.

4. Ibid., p. 9.

5. Ibid., p. 8.

6. Ibid., p. 6.

7. Jonathan Edwards, *An Humble Attempt to Promote Explicit Agreement and Visible Union in Prayer . . .* , in *Apocalyptic Writings of Jonathan Edwards*, ed. Stephen J. Stein, *The Works of Jonathan Edwards*, 5 vols. (New Haven, Conn.: Yale University Press, 1977), 5: 363. For discussion of Edwards's millennial views see Stein's introduction; also see C. G. Goen, "Jonathan Edwards: a New Departure in Eschatology," *Church History* 28 (1955): 33–39; Perry Miller, *Jonathan Edwards* (1949; reprint ed. Cleveland: World Publishing Co., 1959), pp. 316–20; James Carse, *Jonathan Edwards and the Visibility of God* (New York: Charles Scribner's Sons, 1967), pp. 21–22 and 175–78; and Tuveson, *Redeemer Nation*, pp. 99–100. Tuveson, *Redeemer Nation*, passim is useful in giving an overview of American millennial thought.

8. Edwards, *An Humble Attempt*, p. 170.

9. Goen, "Jonathan Edwards," pp. 39–40, n. 31.

10. Miller, *Jonathan Edwards*, p. 198, quoted from a sermon delivered by Edwards in 1745.

11. Dwight, *Travels*, 1: 238–54.

12. Walt Whitman, *Leaves of Grass*, ed. Harold W. Blodgett and Sculley Bradley (New York: W. W. Norton & Co., 1968), p. 90.

13. Tuveson, *Redeemer Nation*, passim.

14. From the old missionary hymn composed in 1819 by Reginald Heber, later Bishop of Calcutta. The hymn is included in many Protestant hymnals, e.g., that of the Protestant Episcopal Church of America, edition of 1913, p. 592. The last stanza is especially millennial in sentiment:

> Waft, waft, ye winds, His story,
>   And you, ye waters, roll,
> Till, like a sea of glory,
>   It spreads from pole to pole:
> Till o'er our ransomed nature,
>   The Lamb for sinners slain,
> Redeemer, King, Creator,
>   In bliss returns to reign.

15. Carse, *Jonathan Edwards*, pp. 175f.; Goen, "Jonathan Edwards," p. 38.

16. Dwight, *Travels*, 4: 228–29.

17. Berk, *Calvinism*, pp. 87, 172, and 198; Cunningham, *Timothy Dwight*, pp. 319–28.

18. Quoted in Tuveson, *Redeemer Nation*, pp. 60 ff.

19. Quoted in ibid., pp. 57 ff.

20. Dwight, *Travels*, 4: 285.

21. Ibid., p. 284.

22. Ibid., p. 281.

23. See *An Address to the Inhabitants of the New Settlements*, pp. 4–5.

24. Ibid., p. 4.

25. Ibid., p. 5.

26. Dwight, *Travels*, 4: 226.

27. Ibid., p. 295.

28. Ibid., p. 207.

29. Ibid., 1: 128.

30. Ibid., 4: 206–7.

31. Ibid., 3: 373–74.

32. Ibid., 1: 375.

33. Ibid., 4: 244.

34. See Carl Bridenbaugh, "The New England Town: A Way of Life," *Proceedings of the American Antiquarian Society* 56 (April 17–October 16, 1946): 24. Bridenbaugh's article in its entirety may be read as a perceptive treatment of the New England town. See also Charles Grant, *Democracy in the Connecticut Frontier Town of Kent* (New York: Columbia University Press, 1961), pp. 151–52.

35. For Dwight's description of town government and its demands and effects on the citizenry see *Travels*, 1: 174–82.

36. For an extensive discussion of the emphasis on achieving harmony in New England towns in the eighteenth century see Michael Zuckerman, *Peaceable Kingdoms: New England Towns in the Eighteenth Century* (New York: Alfred A. Knopf, 1970). See also Bridenbaugh, "The New England Town: A Way of Life."

37. Dwight, *Travels*, 1: 155.

38. Ibid., p. 123. Harriet Beecher Stowe in *Oldtown Folks* (Boston: Fields, Osgood & Co., 1869) also records that in New England villages few people locked their doors at night. Indeed, this remained true until very recently.

39. Dwight, *Travels*, 4: 236. Dwight would have been delighted by the following excerpt from Bridenbaugh's "The New England Town: A Way of Life" (p. 44): "An orderly place was the average New England town. When Bryan Sheehen of Marblehead was found guilty of rape in Essex County Court in 1771 the press announced him to be 'the first Person, as far as we can learn, that has been convicted of Felony in this large county, since the memorable year [of the witchcraft], 1692.'" (Bridenbaugh was quoting from the *Massachusetts Gazette and Post-Boy*, November 18, 1771.)

40. Dwight, *Travels*, 4: 188.

41. Ibid., 2: 232–33.

42. Ibid., p. 233.

43. Ibid., p. 230.

44. Ibid., p. 231. See also Richard L. Bushman, *From Puritan to Yankee: Character and the Social Order in Connecticut, 1690–1765* (Cambridge, Mass.: Harvard University Press, 1967), especially pp. 58 ff., for a description of the distribution of landholdings in and around a town.

45. Dwight, *Travels*, 1: 122–23 and 4: 235 ff., reveals further idealization of the New England town. For somewhat more objective but favorable comment see Bridenbaugh, "The New England Town," passim.

46. James Fenimore Cooper, *The Pioneers* (New York: W. A. Townsend & Co., 1861), p. 106. It is interesting to note that in 1802 Cooper entered Yale College and three years later was dismissed for boyish misbehavior. Dwight was president of Yale at that time and the mischievous boy from New York must have come to his attention.

47. James Fenimore Cooper, *Notions of the Americans*, 2 vols. (Philadelphia: Carey, Lea & Carey, 1828), 1: 60.

48. Ibid., pp. 91–94.

49. Ibid., p. 96.

50. Ibid., pp. 98–99.

51. Ibid., p. 100.

52. Frances Wright D'Arusmont, *Views of Society and Manners in America* (Cambridge, Mass: Belknap Press of Harvard University Press, 1963), p. 195.

53. Harriet Martineau, *Retrospect of Western Travel* (London: Saunders and Otley, 1838), p. 78.

54. Ibid., p. 91. The biblical passage (Psalms 16.6) echoed in the last clause of this quotation served as the motto of Mary Ellen Chase's *A Goodly Heritage* (New York: Henry Holt & Co., 1932).

Chapter 3   Emerson and Thoreau and the Town of Concord

1. Ralph Waldo Emerson, *The Complete Works of Ralph Waldo Emerson,* 12 vols. (1903–4; reprint ed., New York, william H. Wise, 1929), 11: 49.

2. Ralph Waldo Emerson, *The Journals and Miscellaneous Notebooks of Ralph Waldo Emerson,* vol. 4. ed. Alfred R. Ferguson (Cambridge, Mass.: Belknap Press of Harvard University Press, 1964), p. 335.

3. Edward W. Emerson, *Emerson in Concord* (Boston: Houghton Mifflin & Co., 1916), p. 146.

4. R. W. Emerson, *Complete Works,* 3: 60.

5. R. W. Emerson, *Journals and Miscellaneous Notebooks,* vol. 7, ed. A. W. Plumstead and Harrison Hayford (Cambridge, Mass.: Belknap Press of Harvard University Press, 1969), p. 444. This passage also appears in Emerson's "The Method of Nature" (*Complete Works,* 1: 220).

6. R. W. Emerson, *Complete Works,* 11: 38.

7. Ibid., p. 42.

8. Ibid., p. 45.

9. Ibid., p. 46.

10. Ibid., 3: 43.

11. Ibid., 11: 46–47.

12. Ibid., p. 86.

13. Ralph Waldo Emerson, *Journals and Miscellaneous Notebooks of Ralph Waldo Emerson,* vol. 6, ed. Ralph H. Orth (Cambridge, Mass.: Belknap Press of Harvard University Press, 1966), p. 130.

14. R. W. Emerson, *Complete Works,* 11: 49.

15. Ibid., pp. 49–50.

16. In Perry Miller and Thomas H. Johnson, eds., *The Puritans: A Sourcebook of Their Writings,* 2 vols. (New York: American Book Co. 1938), 1: 199.

17. Octavius Brooks Frothingham, *George Ripley* (1883; reprint ed., New York: AMS Press, 1970), p. 310.

18. Nathaniel Hawthorne, *The Blithedale Romance,* ed. William Charvat et al. (Columbus: Ohio State University Press, 1964), p. 13.

19. Ibid., p. 24.

20. Ibid., p. 25.

21. *The Letters of Ralph Waldo Emerson,* ed. Ralph Rusk, 6 vols. (New York: Columbia University Press, 1939), 2: 369.

22. Henry David Thoreau, *The Journal of Henry David Thoreau,* 14 vols. (1906; reprint ed., New York: Dover Publications, 1962), 1: 227.

23. Quoted in Walter Harding, *A Thoreau Handbook* (New York: New York University Press, 1959), p. 117.

24. Ibid., p. 117; also in Thoreau, *Journal*, 9: 160.

25. Walter Harding, "Thoreau and Timothy Dwight," *Boston Public Library Quarterly* 10 (April 1958): 109–15.

26. H. H. Hoeltje, "Thoreau in Concord Church and Town Records," *New England Quarterly* 12 (June 1939): 349–59.

27. Thoreau, *Journal*, 3: 3.

28. Henry David Thoreau, *The Writings of Henry David Thoreau*, 10 vols. (Boston: Houghton Mifflin Co., 1906), 4: 397.

29. Walter Harding, *The Days of Henry Thoreau* (New York: Alfred A. Knopf, 1966), p. 206.

30. Thoreau, *Journal*, 9: 151.

31. Hoeltje, "Thoreau," p. 349.

32. Bridenbaugh, "The New England Town," p. 42.

Chapter 4   Village Fiction before 1850

1. Samuel Griswold Goodrich, *Recollections of a Lifetime, or Men and Things I Have Seen*, 2 vols. (New York: Miller, Orton & Mulligan, 1857), 1: 318.

2. Quoted in Robert J. Taylor, *Western Massachusetts in the Revolution* (Providence, R. I.: Brown University Press, 1954), p. 73, from Mary E. Dewey, ed., *Life and Letters of Catharine M. Sedgwick* (New York: Harper & Bros., 1872), pp. 49–50.

3. See Richard D. Birdsall, *Berkshire County: A Cultural History* (New Haven, Conn.: Yale University Press, 1959), pp. 33–74, for an excellent account of the Calvinist divines in Berkshire County.

4. For an account of the growth of Methodism in a typical New England town, Ridgefield, Connecticut, see S. G. Goodrich, *Recollections of a Lifetime*, 1: 210 ff.

5. Dwight, *Travels*, 1: 375.

6. Ibid., 3: 101–16.

7. In "A Shaker Bridal" in *Twice-Told Tales* and in "The Canterbury Pilgrims" in *The Snow Image and Other Twice-Told Tales*, Hawthorne clearly expresses his views on Shakerism.

8. Edward Halsey Foster, *Catharine Maria Sedgwick* (New York: Twayne Publishers, 1974), p. 120.

9. Catharine Maria Sedgwick, *Home* (Boston: J. Munroe, 1835), p. 76.

10. Ibid., p. 120.

11. Ibid., p. 115.

12. Margaret Fuller, "American Literature, Its Position in the Present Time, and Prospects for the Future," in Perry Miller, ed., *Margaret Fuller: American Romantic* (Ithaca, N. Y.: Cornell University Press, 1970), p. 244.

13. Van Wyck Brooks, *The Flowering of New England* (New York: E. P. Dutton & Co., 1936), p. 385.

14. Alexander Wilson and Prince Charles Bonaparte, *American Ornithology; or, The Natural History of Birds of the United States*, 3 vols., vols. 1 and 2 (New York: J. W. Banton, 1877), vol. 3 (London: Chatto & Windus, 1876) 1: lvii. Editions containing this letter appeared as early as 1832. The first publication of Wilson's monumental work was in 1804–14 in nine volumes. The letter was dated 1808. Travelers in the area did not seem to agree on what they saw. Sir William Strickland in his *Journal of a Tour in the United States of American, 1794–1795* (New York: New-York Historical Society, 1971) describes the country along the Connecticut River as prosperous and the villages as neat and attractive—reminiscent, indeed, of Old England.

15. Wilson and Bonaparte, *American Ornithology*, p. liv. I have supplied the word *whoring* in a space left blank either by Wilson or by his editors. What follows the sentence quoted suggests strongly that this is what Wilson had in mind.

16. Arethusa Hall, *Life and Character of the Rev. Sylvester Judd* (1851; reprint ed., Port Washington, N. Y.: Kennikat Press, [n.d.]), p. 336.

17. Sylvester Judd, *Margaret: A Tale of the Real and the Ideal, Blight and Bloom* (1851; reprint ed., Upper Saddle River, N. J.: Gregg Press, 1968), p. 232.

18. Ibid., p. 369.

19. Ibid., p. 394.

20. Ibid., p. 373.

21. Ibid., p. 379.

22. Ibid., p. 366.

23. Ibid., p. 395.

24. Birdsall, *Berkshire County*, p. 337. Much earlier in a story titled "The Wondrous Tale of a Little Man in Gosling Green" (published as a prizewinning story in *The New Yorker*, November 1, 1834) Longfellow had described a typical Down East town with its meeting house and town elections and the perennial feuding, pettiness, and curiosity of the townspeople. For a reprint of the story see T. Hatfield, "An Unknown Prose Tale by Longfellow," *American Literature* 3 (March, 1931): 136–48.

25. Henry Wadsworth Longfellow, *Hyperion and Kavanagh* (Boston: Houghton, Mifflin & Co., 1886), p. 324.

26. Samuel Longfellow, *Life of Henry Wadsworth Longfellow*, 2 vols. (Boston: Ticknor & Co., 1886), 2: 135–36.

27. Ibid., p. 54.

28. H. W. Longfellow, *Kavanagh*, p. 380.

29. Ibid., p. 380. The founder of the Millerites, William Miller (1782–1849), was a native of Pittsfield, though he had grown up in northern Vermont.

30. See Robert Lowell's long poem *The Mills of the Kavanaughs* (New York: Harcourt, Brace & World, 1951).

31. H. W. Longfellow, *Kavanagh*, pp. 354–55.

32. Ibid., p. 357.

33. Ibid., pp. 357–58.

34. Ibid., p. 358.

35. Ibid., p. 359.

36. Ibid., p. 405.

37. Birdsall, *Berkshire County*, p. 344.

Chapter 5   "A Delightful Village on a Fruitful Hill": Lyman and Henry Ward Beecher and the New England Town

1. L. Beecher, *Autobiography*, 2 vols. (New York: Harper & Bros., 1865), 1: 213.

2. Ibid., pp. 43–44.

3. Ibid., p. 45.

4. William G. McLoughlin, *The Meaning of Henry Ward Beecher: An Essay on the Shifting Values of Mid-Victorian America* (New York: Alfred A. Knopf, 1970), p. 12.

5. L. Beecher, *Autobiography*, p. 70.

6. Ibid., p. 68.

7. Lyman Beecher, *A Plea for the West* (Cincinnati: Truman & Smith, 1835), p. 11.

8. Ibid., pp. 37–38.

9. L. Beecher, *Autobiography,* pp. 205–6.

10. Henry Ward Beecher, *Eyes and Ears* (Boston: Ticknor & Fields, 1864), p. 14.

11. See foreword to Paxton Hibben, *Henry Ward Beecher: An American Portrait* (New York: The Press of the Readers' Club, 1942).

12. Robert Shaplen, "That Was New York, The Beecher-Tilton Case," *New Yorker* 30, nos. 16 & 17 (June 5 and 12, 1954), pp. 37–61 and 34–68. See also Robert Shaplen, *Free Love and Heavenly Sinners* (New York: Alfred A. Knopf, 1954) for a fuller treatment of the subject.

13. H. W. Beecher, *Eyes and Ears,* p. 35.

14. Marvin Felheim, "Two Views of the State, or the Theory and Practice of Henry Ward Beecher," *New England Quarterly* 25 (September 1952): 316–17.

15. Quoted by McLoughlin (p. 63) from the preface to the 1887 edition of *Norwood* (New York: Fords, Howard & Hulbert, 1887). A parody—always a sign of a book's popularity—of *Norwood* appeared in 1868 titled *Gnaw-wood, or New England Life in a Village,* by H. W. B. Cher, pseudonym (New York: The National News Co.)

16. See back pages of advertising in the 1868 (first) edition of *Norwood* (New York: Charles Scribner & Co., 1868).

17. Felheim, "Two Views," p. 317. Felheim (p. 316) states that the circulation of the *Ledger* was 400,000.

18. Rebecca W. Smith, in *The Civil War and Its Aftermath in American Literature* (Chicago: Private Edition, 1937), pp. 7–8, credits *Norwood* with initiating the Lincoln legend in the United States.

19. H. W. Beecher, *Norwood,* (1868 edition), p. 3.

20. Ibid., p. 177.

21. Ibid., p. 1.

22. Ibid., p. 2.

23. Ibid., pp. 4–5.

24. Ibid., p. 5.

25. Ibid., pp. 137–38.

26. Ibid., p. 138.

27. R. W. Emerson, *Journals and Miscellaneous Notebooks,* 7: 444.

28. H. W. Beecher, *Norwood,* pp. 102–3.

29. Ibid., p. 131.

30. Ibid., p. 181.

31. Ibid., p. 143.

32. Ibid.

33. Ibid., p. 144.

34. Ibid., p. 142.

35. Ibid., p. 181.

36. Ibid.

37. Ibid., p. 375.

38. Ibid., p. 374.

39. R. W. Emerson, *Works,* 1: 9.

40. Paraphrase by Neal R. Peirce, *The New England States: People, Politics, and Power in the Six New England States* (New York: W. W. Norton & Co., 1976), p. 20.

41. H. W. Beecher, *Norwood,* p. 309.

42. Ibid., pp. 277–88.

43. Ibid., p. 459. For the tendency among American clergymen at the time of the Civil War to look upon the struggle as apocalyptic, see James H. Moorhead, *American Apocalypse: Yankee Protestants and the Civil War, 1860–1869* (New Haven, Conn.: Yale University Press, 1978).

44. H. W. Beecher, *Norwood,* p. 158.

45. Ibid., pp. 286–87.

46. Ibid., p. 305.

47. Ibid.

48. Ibid., p. 306.

Chapter 6   Harriet Beecher Stowe: Interpreter of New England Life

1. Harriet Beecher Stowe, *Oldtown Folks*, p. iii. Note the almost obsessive impulse of New England writers to "interpret" their region. Cf. Catharine Sedgwick, Sarah Orne Jewett, and Mary Wilkins Freeman.

2. For a brief discussion of Stowe as a regionalist, see "Introduction" and "Bibliographical Notes" in Harriet Beecher Stowe, *Regional Sketches*, ed. John R. Adams (New Haven, Conn.: College & University Press, 1972), pp. 7–28.

3. Harriet Beecher Stowe, *The Minister's Wooing* (New York: Derby & Jackson, 1859), p. 332.

4. Ibid., pp. 23–24.

5. Ibid., pp. 24–25.

6. Stowe, *Oldtown Folks*, p. 436. See Alice C. Crozier, *The Novels of Harriet Beecher Stowe* (New York: Oxford University Press, 1969), p. 132, for comments on Calvinism and Greek tragedy. Crozier points out that Emerson also saw beauty in the orthodoxy he had rejected.

7. Stowe, *The Minister's Wooing*, p. 341.

8. Emily Dickinson, *The Poems of Emily Dickinson*, ed. Thomas H. Johnson, 3 vols. (Cambridge, Mass.: The Belknap Press of Harvard University Press, 1958), 2: 622.

9. "New England Ministers," *The Writings of Harriet Beecher Stowe*, 16 vols. (Boston: Houghton Mifflin Company, 1896), 14: 223.

10. Harriet Beecher Stowe, *The Pearl of Orr's Island* (Boston: Houghton Mifflin Company, 1896), pp. 240–41.

11. Ibid., p. 120.

12. Harriet Beecher Stowe, *The Mayflower and Miscellaneous Writings* (Boston: Philips, Sampson, and Company, 1855), pp. 321–29.

13. Stowe, *Pearl of Orr's Island*, p. 120.

14. Annie Fields, *Authors and Friends* (Boston: Houghton Mifflin and Company, 1897), pp. 199–200.

15. Stowe, *Oldtown Folks*, p. iii. Henry Ward Beecher, it will be recalled, also used the metaphor of the beehive in discussing the influence of New England. Indeed, Cotton Mather used the analogy to a swarming hive when writing of new settlements in New England.

16. Stowe, *Oldtown Folks*, p. iv.

17. Ibid.

18. Ibid., p. 368.

19. Ibid., p. 421. Compare the thought here with that in Robert Frost's "Directive," in which he locates the source of spiritual strength—not solely in New England, one assumes—in a mountain spring or well.

20. Stowe, *Oldtown Folks*, p. 421.

21. Ibid.

22. Ibid.

23. Ibid.

24. Ibid., pp. 223–27.

25. Ibid., p. 441.

26. Ibid.

27. Ibid., p. 446.

28. Dwight, *Travels*, 2: 256.

29. Ibid., p. 257.

30. Ibid.

31. Harriet Beecher Stowe, *Poganuc People* (Boston: Houghton Mifflin Co., 1906), p. 46.

32. See William A. Robinson, *Jeffersonian Democracy in New England* (New Haven, Conn.: Yale University Press, 1916), for light on the political situation in Poganuc as described in this and following paragraphs.

33. Stowe, *Poganuc People*, p. 73.

34. Ibid., p. 68.

35. Ibid., p. 226. Repeatedly in New England regional writing the touchstones of civic virtue and health are the absence of poverty and of the need to lock one's doors at night.

36. Stowe, *Poganuc People*, p. 42.

37. Ibid., p. 48.

38. L. Beecher, *Autobiography*, p. 32.

39. Stowe, *Poganuc People,* p. 67.

40. Ibid., pp. 216–17.

41. Ibid., p. 57.

42. Ibid., p. 139.

43. Ibid.

44. Lyman Beecher, "A Reformation of Morals Practicable and Indispensable," in *Lyman Beecher and the Reform of Society* (New York: Arno Press, 1972), pp. 30–32.

45. Octavius Brooks Frothingham, *Transcendentalism in New England: A History* (1876; reprint ed., Gloucester, Mass.: Peter Smith, 1965), p. 108. A sort of residual millennialism was pervasive in Transcendentalism. For example, in 1839 William Henry Channing, the nephew of the great Unitarian, wrote in the Transcendentalist *Western Messenger*, edited by him and published in Cincinnati: "We feel that a mighty power of good is stirring now in society; we believe in the coming of the kingdom of God" (in Perry Miller, ed., *The Transcendentalists: An Anthology* [Cambridge, Mass.: Harvard University Press, 1950], p. 430).

46. Thoreau, *Writings*, 4:412–13.

Chapter 7   Essays, Sketches, Humor

1. Van Wyck Brooks, *The Flowering of New England, 1815–1865* (New York: E. P. Dutton & Co., 1940), p. 407.

2. [Nathaniel Shatswell Dodge], *Sketches of New England, or Memories of the Country* (New York: E. French, 1842), p. v. The book is attributed to John Carver, Dodge's pseudonym.

3. Ibid., p. 179.

4. Ibid., p. 181.

5. Ibid., p. 186.

6. James Parton, *Topics of the Times* (Boston: James R. Osgood & Co., 1871), pp. 37–38.

7. Ibid., p. 54.

8. Rowland Robinson, *Danvis Folks* (Boston: Houghton, Mifflin & Co., 1901), p. iii.

9. Rowland Robinson, *Vermont: A Study of Independence* (Boston: Houghton, Mifflin & Co., 1892), p. 365.

10. In *Out of Bondage and Other Stories* (Rutland, Vt.: Charles E. Tuttle Company, 1936), pp. 137–47.

11. Ibid., pp. 16–78.

12. Rowland Robinson, "An Old-Time March Meeting," *Atlantic Monthly* 89 (March 1902): 312–13.

13. Ibid., p. 317.

14. In *The Best Short Stories of Sarah Orne Jewett,* ed. Willa Cather, 2 vols. (Boston: Houghton, Mifflin & Co., 1925), 2: 224–47.

15. In *Out of Bondage and Other Stories.*

16. [Seba Smith], *My Thirty Years Out of the Senate* by Major Jack Downing (New York: Derby & Jackson, 1860), p. 33.

17. Ibid., p. 43.

18. Constance Rourke, *American Humor: A Study of the National Character* (New York: Harcourt, Brace & Co., 1931), p. 28; James Russell Lowell, *The Biglow Papers, Second Series,* 6th ed. (Boston: Houghton, Mifflin & Co., 1892), introduction, esp. pp. 264–70.

19. *My Thirty Years Out of the Senate,* p. 281.

20. Ibid., p. 404.

21. Lowell, *The Biglow Papers, Second Series,* p. 280. In his "Cambridge Thirty Years Ago" (*The Works of James Russell Lowell,* 10 vols. [Boston: Houghton, Mifflin & Co., 1890], 1: 43–99). Lowell emphasizes the village and rural characteristics of his native town in the early decades of the nineteenth century.

22. *The Biglow Papers, First Series,* 6th ed. (Boston: Houghton, Mifflin & Co., 1892), p. 37.

23. Ibid., p. 65.

24. *My Thirty Years Out of the Senate,* pp. 275–76.

Chapter 8   Structure and Origins of Town Government

1. James Russell Lowell, "New England Two Centuries Ago," *The Works of James Russell Lowell,* 10 vols. (Boston: Houghton, Mifflin & Co., 1890), 2:1. The essay was first printed in 1865.

2. See Michael Zuckerman, *Peaceable Kingdoms: New England Towns in the Eighteenth Century* (New York: Alfred A. Knopf, 1970), for a discussion of the need and the desire for harmony in town government.

3. Joel Parker, "The Origin, Organization, and Influence of the Towns of New England," pp. 19–23.

4. John Adams, *The Works of John Adams,* 10 vols. (Boston: Charles C. Little & James Brown, 1850–1856), 5: 496.

5. John and Abigail Adams, *Familiar Letters of John Adams and His Wife Abigail Adams, During the Revolution* (New York: Hurd & Houghton, 1876), p. 120.

6. Ibid.

7. Ibid.

8. Thomas Jefferson, *The Writings of Thomas Jefferson,* 20 vols. (Washington, D.C.: The Thomas Jefferson Memorial Association, 1904–05), 15 (1904): 38.

9. Thomas Jefferson, *The Adams-Jefferson Letters,* ed. Lester J. Cappon, 2 vols. (Chapel Hill, N.C.: University of North Carolina Press, 1959), 2: 390.

10. George Bancroft, *History of the United States from the Discovery of the American Continent,* 10 vols. (Boston: Little, Brown & Co., 1834–76), 4 (1852): 148–49.

11. Edward Augustus Kendall, *Travels in the Northern Parts of the United States in the Years 1807 and 1808,* 3 vols. (New York: I. Riley, 1809), 1: 112 ff.

12. The information that Jared Sparks supplied Tocqueville is contained in "Observations

by Jared Sparks on the Government of Towns in Massachusetts," *Johns Hopkins University Studies in Historical and Political Science* 16 (1898): 579–600.

13. Charles Francis Adams, *Three Episodes of Massachusetts History*, 4th ed., 2 vols. (Boston: Houghton, Mifflin & Co., 1892), 2: 813–14.

14. For an effective similar attempt to summarize these theories, but with different emphases, see John Fairfield Sly, *Town Government in Massachusetts (1620–1930)* (Cambridge, Mass.: Harvard University Press, 1930), chap. 3.

15. Parker, "Origin," p. 16.

16. Ibid., pp. 16–17.

17. Alexis de Tocqueville, *Democracy in America*, ed. Phillips Bradley (New York: Vintage Books, 1954), 1: 71.

18. Quoted by Parker, "Origin," p. 19, from Francis Baylies, *Historical Memoir of the Colony of New Plymouth*, 2 vols. (Boston: Hilliard, Gray, Little & Wilkins, 1830), 1: 240. Same volume and page in 1866 ed. (Boston: Wiggin & Lunt).

19. Quoted by Parker, "Origin," p. 19, from Richard Frothingham, *History of Charlestown, Massachusetts* (Boston: C. C. Little & J. Brown, 1845–1849), p. 49.

20. Quoted by Parker, p. 19, from Richard Frothingham, p. 50.

21. Tocqueville, *Democracy*, 1: 62.

22. Quoted by Sly, "Town Government," p. 56, n. 1, from Edward Augustus Freeman, *An Introduction to American Institutional History*, Johns Hopkins University Studies in Historical and Political Science, ser. 1, no. 1, p. 13.

23. John Richard Green, *History of the English People*, 4 vols. (New York: The Bradley Co., n.d.), 1: 21.

24. Herbert B. Adams, *The Germanic Origin of New England Towns*, Johns Hopkins University Studies in Historical and Political Science, no. 2 (Baltimore, Md.: Johns Hopkins University, 1882): 49–50.

25. Ibid., p. 5.

26. James Bryce, *The American Commonwealth*, 2d ed. (New York: Macmillan Co., 1891), 1: 583.

27. Herbert Adams, *Germanic Origin*, p. 5.

28. Ibid., p. 8.

29. Ibid., p. 11.

30. Ibid., p. 23.

31. Ibid., p. 27.

32. Ibid., p. 23.

33. Ibid., p. 8. Adams might have had uppermost in mind Baylies's *Historical Memoir of the Colony of New Plymouth.*

34. Quoted by James K. Hosmer, *Samuel Adams: The Man of the Town-Meeting*, the Johns Hopkins University Studies in Historical and Political Science, ed. Herbert B. Adams, 2d ser., no. 4 (Baltimore, Md.: N. Murray, Publishing agent for Johns Hopkins University, April, 1884): 15. Hosmer was quoting from George Bancroft, *History of the Formation of the Constitution of the United States of America*, 2 vols. (New York: D. Appleton & Co., 1882), 1: 181. A native of Northfield, Massachusetts, Hosmer served as Unitarian pastor in Deerfield, Massachusetts, from 1860–66. Later he was a professor of literature at Washington University in Saint Louis. He was the author of biographies of Samuel Adams and Sir Henry Vane.

35. Hosmer, *Samuel Adams*, p. 25.

36. Ibid., pp. 36–37.

37. It is worth noting that during Shays's Rebellion Samuel Adams, opposing the county conventions held by the rebels after the model of those approved by Adams during the

Revolution, advocated reliance on "those simple Democracies in all our Towns, which are the Basis of our State Constitutions," the Constitution in turn being a sure protection against enslavement or other harm. ("Letter to Noah Webster. April 30, 1784," *The Writings of Samuel Adams*, ed. H. A. Cushing, 4 vols. (New York: G. P. Putnam's Sons, 1904–8), 4: 306.

38. The idea of extremely ancient origins of New England town meetings attracted popular attention in the late nineteenth century. For example, in 1892 appeared an article titled "The Aryan Mark: A New England Town Meeting," *Harper's New Monthly Magazine* 85 (September 1892): 577–85, in which the author, Anna C. Bracket, described a town meeting in a remote section of Vermont, where Anglo-Saxon racial roots are most in evidence. "There is nothing perhaps more distinctly Aryan than the New England Town Meeting," Bracket assured her readers; and she advises foreigners wishing to see the real United States to attend such a meeting. Oddly, the meeting that she described was not typical, since it took up no business other than electing a representative to the state legislature. Physiognomies of the supposedly Aryan stock appear in a number of black and white drawings of "town characters."

39. J. S. Clark, *A Historical Sketch of the Congregational Churches in Massachusetts* (Boston: Congregational Board of Publication, 1858), p. 13.

40. Noah Porter, "The New England Meeting House," *The New Englander* 42 (Complete Series), no. 74 (May 1888): 305.

41. Ibid., p. 309.

42. John Adams, "Letter to His Wife October 29, 1775," *Familiar Letters of John Adams and His Wife*, p. 120.

43. George P. Marsh, *The Goths in New-England: A Discourse Delivered at the Anniversary of the Philmathesian Society of Middlebury College, August 15, 1843* (Middlebury, Vt.: J. Cobb, Jr., 1843), pp. 10–14.

44. Ibid., p. 14.

45. Ibid., pp. 14–16. The vocabulary reflects that of the Kantians and American Transcendentalists; imagination, for example, was considered a higher faculty than fancy.

46. Marsh, *Goths*, pp. 16–17.

47. Ibid., p. 39.

48. P. Emory Aldrich, "Report of the Council," *Proceedings of the American Antiquarian Society*, n.s.3 (October–April 1884): 112.

49. Ibid., p. 118.

50. Charles Francis Adams, "The Genesis of the Massachusetts Town, and the Development of Town-Meeting Government," *Proceedings of the Massachusetts Historical Society*, 2d ser. 7 (1892): 173.

51. Ibid.

52. Ibid., p. 175.

53. Ibid., p. 176.

54. Sly, *Town Government*, p. 62.

55. C. F. Adams, "Genesis of the Massachusetts Town," p. 196.

56. Mellen Chamberlain, "Remarks by Mellen Chamberlain on C. F. Adams' 'The Genesis of the Massachusetts Town . . .,'" *Proceedings of the Massachusetts Historical Society*, 2d ser. 7 (1892): 216.

57. Ibid.

58. Ibid., p. 218.

59. Ibid., p. 220.

60. Sly, *Town Government*, p. 58, quoted from Edward Channing, *Town and County Government in the English Colonies of North America.*, Johns Hopkins University Studies in Historical and Political Science, 2, no. 10, p. 53.

61. *Proceedings of the Massachusetts Historical Society,* 2d ser. 7: 244.

62. Ibid., p. 447–48.

Chapter 9   Recorders of Social and Economic Decline in Rural New England

1. Clifton Johnson, *The New England Country* (Boston: Lee & Shepard, 1893), pp. 36–37.

2. Phillip Morgan, "The Problems of Rural New England: A Remote Village," *Atlantic Monthly* 79 (May 1897): 582–83.

3. Ibid., p. 583. The Coleridge quotation is from S. T. Coleridge, *Anima Poetae,* ed. E. H. Coleridge (Boston: Houghton, Mifflin & Co., 1895), p. 23.

4. Morgan, "Problems," 583.

5. Ibid.

6. Ibid.

7. Ibid., p. 587.

8. Rollin L. Hartt, "A New England Hill Town: I. Its Condition," *Atlantic Monthly* 83 (April 1899): 572.

9. Ibid., p. 564.

10. Rudyard Kipling, *Something of Myself* (Garden City, N. Y.: Doubleday, Doran & Co., 1937), p. 127.

11. Fred Pattee, *Sidelights on American Literature* (New York: The Century Company, 1922). The phrase is one of Pattee's chapter headings.

12. Mary E. Wilkins [Freeman], *Pembroke* (New York: Harper & Bros., 1894), pp. 305–6.

13. Edwin Arlington Robinson, *Untriangulated Stars: Letters of Edwin Arlington Robinson to Harry de Forest Smith 1890–1905,* ed. Denham Sutcliffe (Cambridge, Mass.: Harvard University Press, 1947), pp. 174–75.

14. Quoted from P. D. Westbrook, *Mary Wilkins Freeman* (New York: Twayne Publishers, 1967), p. 93.

15. Ibid., p. 94.

16. Freeman, *Pembroke,* p. 312.

17. Ibid., p. 68. Compare with the description of Zeph Higgins's will in Stowe's *Poganuc People,* p. 67.

18. Freeman, *Pembroke,* p. 3.

19. Ibid., p. 103.

20. Ibid., p. 146.

21. Ibid., pp. 221–22.

22. Ibid., p. 138.

23. Ibid., p. 247.

24. Mary E. Wilkins [Freeman], *A New England Nun and Other Stories* (New York: Harper & Bros., 1891), pp. 81–98.

25. Mary E. Wilkins[Freeman], *A Humble Romance and Other Stories* (New York: Harper & Bros., 1887), pp. 78–91.

26. *The Best Stories of Sarah Orne Jewett,* 2: 23.

27. Ibid., pp. 228–29.

28. Rowland Robinson, "An Old-Time March Meeting," p. 318.

29. Edward Bellamy, *The Duke of Stockbridge,* ed. Joseph Schiffman (Cambridge, Mass.: The Belknap Press of Harvard University Press, 1962), p. xiii.

30. Ibid., p. 24.

31. Ibid., p. 33.

32. Ibid., p. 6.

33. Robert Taylor, *Western Massachusetts in the Revolution* (Providence R. I.: Brown University Press, 1954), p. 33. Taylor finds that only occasionally did the voters oppose the "River Gods," who in general were able men who in most matters, at least in prosperous times, served their communities well. Theodore Sedgwick, according to Taylor, was highly typical of these town leaders.

34. Bellamy, *The Duke of Stockbridge*, pp. 197–98.

35. Ibid., p. 198.

36. Ibid., p. 150.

37. Ibid., p. 151.

38. Ibid., p. 47.

39. Quoted by Marion L. Starkey, *A Little Rebellion* (New York: Alfred A. Knopf, 1955), p. 111, from a letter from Jefferson to James Madison, dated Paris, January 30, 1787. See *The Life and Selected Writings of Thomas Jefferson,* ed. Adrienne Koch and William Peden (New York: The Modern Library, 1944), p. 413.

40. Dwight, *Travels,* 4: 237–38.

41. Frederick Jackson Turner, "New England, 1830–1850," *Huntington Library Bulletin,* no. 1 (May 1931), p. 155.

42. Cited in Harold F. Wilson, *The Hill Country of Northern New England: Its Social and Economic History, 1790–1930* (New York: Columbia University Press, 1936), p. 45.

43. Ibid., pp. 145–46.

44. Ibid., p. 146.

45. Parton, *Topics of the Times,* pp. 43–45.

46. Turner, "New England," p. 173.

47. Mary E. Wilkins [Freeman], *Jerome: A Poor Man* (New York: Harper & Bros., 1897), p. 463.

48. See Sarah Orne Jewett, "The Gray Mills of Farley," in *American Local Stories,* ed. H. R. Warfel and G. H. Orians (New York: American Book Co., 1941).

49. Mary E. Wilkins [Freeman], *The Portion of Labor* (New York: Harper & Bros., 1901), pp. 562–63.

50. For information on economic conditions in New England since 1930 see Lawrence Dame, *New England Comes Back* (New York: Random House, 1940); R. C. Estall, *New England: A Study in Industrial Adjustment* (New York: Frederick A. Praeger, 1966); and Neal R. Peirce, *The New England States: People, Politics, and Power in the Six New England States* (New York: W. W. Norton & Co., 1976).

Chapter 10   At Ease in Zion: Sarah Orne Jewett and Emily Dickinson

1. Sarah Orne Jewett, "The Old Town of Berwick," *New England Magazine* 10 (July 1894): 604.

2. Emily Dickinson, *The Letters of Emily Dickinson,* ed. Thomas H. Johnson and Theodora Ward, 3 vols. (Cambridge, Mass.: Belknap Press of Harvard University Press, 1958), 1: 197.

3. Jewett, "The Old Town of Berwick," p. 609.

4. Willa Cather, *My Antonia* (Boston: Houghton Mifflin Co., 1954), pp. 263–71. See also Jewett's preface to the 1893 edition of *Deephaven* (Boston: Houghton, Mifflin & Co.) for evidence of her conscious assumption of the role of literary spokeswoman for her region of New England.

5. Jewett, *Deephaven* (1893 ed.), p. 5.

6. *The Best Stories of Sarah Orne Jewett,* 1: 78. In editing this volume Willa Cather included all of *The Country of the Pointed Firs* as first published in 1896, plus three other tales—"A Dunnet Shepherdess," "The Queen's Twin," and "William's Wedding"—which deal with the same characters and have the same setting as *The Country of the Pointed Firs.*

7. Ibid., p. 10.

8. Ibid., p. 93.

9. Ibid., p. 163.

10. Ibid., pp. 286–87.

11. Ibid., p. 226.

12. Ibid., p. 103.

13. Ibid., p. 110.

14. Ibid., p. 21.

15. Ibid., p. 37.

16. Ibid., pp. 272–73.

17. Ibid., p. 102.

18. Sarah Orne Jewett, *The Story of the Normans* (New York: G. P. Putnam's Sons, 1887), pp. 365–66.

19. Sarah Orne Jewett, "From a Mournful Villager," in *Country By-Ways* (Boston: Houghton, Mifflin & Co., 1881), p. 117.

20. Lucy Larcom, *A New England Girlhood* (Boston: Houghton, Mifflin & Co., 1889), p. 117.

21. *The Letters of Emily Dickinson,* 2: 474. See Richard B. Sewall, *The Life of Emily Dickinson,* 2 vols. (New York: Farrar, Straus & Giroud, 1974), 1: 38–40, for a discussion of the Dickinson family's attachment to Amherst.

22. *Letters of Emily Dickinson,* 2:551.

23. Ibid., 3: 716.

24. Ibid., 1: 62.

25. Ibid., p. 58.

26. Ibid., p. 141.

27. Ibid., 2: 317.

28. Ibid., p. 433.

29. Sewall, *Life,* 1: 38.

30. *The Poems of Emily Dickinson,* 1: 204 (poem #285). Henceforth reference to Emily Dickinson's poems will be made in the text and notes by the number assigned them by Thomas Johnson.

31. Examples of each may be found respectively in poems #258, #215, #1636, #328, and #178. See Brita Lindberg-Seyersted, *The Voice of the Poet: Aspects of Style in the Poetry of Emily Dickinson* (Uppsala: Almquist & Wiksells, 1968), pp. 62 ff., for a treatment of Dickinson's regional and colloquial usages.

Chapter 11   Old Home Week

1. S. G. Goodrich, *Recollections of a Lifetime,* 1: 319.

2. Frank W. Rollins, "New Hampshire's Opportunity," *New England Magazine* 16 (July 1897): 542. The idea was not entirely new with Governor Rollins. As far back as 1845 in Berkshire County, Massachusetts, a "Jubilee" was held with the purpose of welcoming "home distinguished sons and daughters which [sic] the county had sent forth." Sermons were preached, hymns sung, sentimental doggerel recited. A prominent citizen proposed the toast: "The stock of New England . . . the stock of old England, their virtue, their intelligence with

equality added." And another proclaimed: "The Children of Berkshire. They have only to be steadfast to the principles into which they were born" (Sarah Cabot Sedgwick and Christina Sedgwick Marquand, *Stockbridge, 1739–1974* [Stockbridge, Mass.: The Berkshire Traveller Press, 1974], p. 229–31).

3. Thomas F. Anderson, "'Old-Home Week' in New England," *New England Magazine* 34 (August 1906): 676.

4. Harold F. Wilson, *The Hill Country of Northern New England*, p. 273.

5. "Anniversary of the New England Society of Cincinnati, O[hio]," *New England Historical and Genealogical Register* 1 (January 1847): 100.

6. "New England Societies," *New England Historical and Genealogical Register* 2 (April 1848): 198.

7. Ibid.

8. Ibid.

9. Catharine M. Sedgwick, *Home*, p. 115.

10. Ibid., pp. 115–16.

11. Ibid., p. 116.

12. See Edward W. Bemis, *Local Government in Michigan and the Northwest*, Johns Hopkins University Studies in Historical and Political Science, vol. 1, no. 5 (March 1883), pp. 19–20; and Albert Shaw, *Local Government in Illinois*, Johns Hopkins University Studies in Historical and Political Science, vol. 1, no. 3 (January 1883), p. 10.

13. Shaw, *Local Government in Illinois*, p. 10.

14. Ibid.

15. Bemis, *Local Government in Michigan*, p. 15. James Bryce, *The American Commonwealth*, 2d ed., 1: 560–81, contains a resumé of local government in the United States, especially regarding the town meeting. Stewart Holbrook, *The Yankee Exodus: An Account of Migration from New England* (1950; reprint ed., Seattle: University of Washington Press, 1968) provides information on the adoption of New England town government in the western United States, as does Lois Kimball Mathews in *The Expansion of New England* (1909; reprint ed., New York: Russell & Russell, 1962).

16. Edith Wharton, *Summer: A Novel* (New York: D. Appleton & Co., 1917), p. 170.

17. Ibid., p. 196.

18. Ibid., p. 173.

19. Ibid., pp. 193–94.

20. Ibid., pp. 194–95.

21. See Elizabeth Shepley Sergeant, *Robert Frost: The Trial by Existence* (New York: Holt, Rinehart & Winston, 1960), p. 394.

22. Robert Frost, *The Poetry of Robert Frost*, ed. Edward Connery Lathem (New York: Holt, Rinehart & Winston, 1969), p. 73.

23. Perhaps Frost had in mind the very first Stark home in America, which was at Derry near his chicken farm. This house burned (note charred wood in the poem) in 1736. Starks later settled in Dunbarton, a few miles from Bow, but the seven-generation removal of the couple in the poem from their common ancestors suggests that Frost was thinking of the Derry site.

24. Frost, *Poetry*, p. 74.

25. Ibid., p. 80.

26. Ibid., p. 73.

27. Ibid., p. 80.

28. Lawrence Thompson, *Robert Frost: The Years of Triumph, 1915–1938* (New York: Holt, Rinehart & Winston, 1970), p. 561.

29. Frost, *Poetry,* p. 348.

30. Ibid., p. 379.

31. Ibid., p. 6.

32. Ibid., p. 265.

33. Ibid., p. 221.

34. *The Poems of Emily Dickinson,* 2: 657, poem #892.

35. Frost, *Poetry,* p. 365.

36. Ibid., p. 366.

37. Ibid., p. 33.

38. Ralph Waldo Emerson, *Poems* (Boston: Houghton, Mifflin & Co., 1884), p. 72, quoted in Frost's "New Hampshire," *Poetry,* p. 166.

39. Frost, *Poetry,* p. 166.

Chapter 12   Twentieth-Century Writing on New England Towns to 1960

1. Dorothy Canfield Fisher, *Memories of Arlington, Vermont* (New York: Duell, Sloan & Pearce, 1957), pp. 11–12.

2. Edith Wharton, *Summer,* p. 47.

3. Dorothy Canfield Fisher, *Vermont Tradition: The Biography of an Outlook on Life* (Boston: Little, Brown & Co., 1953), pp. 390–91.

4. Ibid., p. 414.

5. Ibid., p. 410.

6. Ibid., pp. 409–10.

7. John Sterling, "New England Villages," *Atlantic Monthly* 131 (April 1923): 526.

8. Ibid., pp. 527–28.

9. Bernard De Voto, "New England, There She Stands," *Harper's Magazine* 164 (March 1932): 414.

10. Ibid., p. 415.

11. John Gould, *New England Town Meeting: Safeguard of Democracy* (Brattleboro, Vt.: Stephen Daye Press, 1940), p. 35.

12. [Richard Cary], "Editor's Epilogue," *Colby Library Quarterly,* ser. 6 (March 1962), p. 46. This issue of the *Colby Library Quarterly* is devoted entirely to material on and by Mary Ellen Chase.

13. Mary Ellen Chase, "My Novels About Maine," *Colby Library Quarterly,* ser. 6 (March 1962), p. 15.

14. Perry D. Westbrook, *Mary Ellen Chase* (New York: Twayne Publishers, 1965), pp. 80–81.

15. Carl Bridenbaugh, "The New England Town: A Way of Life," p. 21.

16. Mary Ellen Chase, *The Edge of Darkness* (New York: W. W. Norton & Co., 1957), preface.

17 .Ibid., p. 235.

18. Edith Wharton, *A Backward Glance* (New York: Appleton-Century Co., 1936), pp. 293–96.

19. Wharton, *Summer,* p. 157.

20. Ibid., p. 81.

21. Ibid., p. 82.

22. See Stan Bicknell, "The End-of-the-Road People," *Yankee* 41, no. 1 (January 1977), for an account of poverty in the northeastern counties of Vermont, which are by no means the only impoverished areas of New England.

23. John Gould Cozzens, *The Last Adam* (New York: Harcourt, Brace & Co., 1933), p. 42.

Chapter 13   Writers on New England Towns since 1960

1. John Gardner, *October Light* (New York: Afred A. Knopf, 1976), p. 10.
2. Shirley Jackson, "Biography of a Story," in *Come Along with Me*, ed. Stanley Edgar Hyman (New York: Viking Press, 1968), pp. 211–24.
3. Lenemaja Friedman, *Shirley Jackson* (Boston Twayne Publishers, 1975), p. 64.
4. Seymour Lainoff, "Jackson's 'The Lottery,'" *The Explicator* 12 (March 1954), item 34.
5. Herman Melville, "Hawthorne and His Mosses, By a Virginian Spending July in Vermont," in *Billy Budd and Other Prose Pieces*, ed. Raymond Weaver (London: Constable & Co., 1924), p. 129.
6. Shirley Jackson, "The Summer People," in *Come Along with Me*, p. 68.
7. Ibid., p. 69.
8. Gardner, *October Light*, p. 10.
9. Ibid., p. 417.
10. John Gardner, *On Moral Fiction* (New York: Basic Books, 1977), p. 106.
11. Gardner, *October Light*, p. 424.
12. Gardner, *On Moral Fiction*, p. 114.
13. Gardner, *October Light*, p. 428.
14. Ibid., p. 429.
15. John Cheever, *The Wapshot Chronicle* (1957; reprint ed., New York: Harper & Row, 1973), p. 198.
16. Ibid., p. 36.
17. Ibid., p. 205.
18. John Cheever, *The Wapshot Scandal* (1963; reprint ed., New York; Harper & Row, 1973), p. 111.
19. Cheever, *The Wapshot Chronicle*, p. 93.
20. Ibid., p. 54.
21. Ibid., pp. 81–82.
22. Ibid., p. 82.
23. Ibid., p. 139.
24. John Updike, *Couples* (New York: Alfred A. Knopf, 1968), p. 105.
25. Ibid., p. 106.
26. *Contemporary Literary Criticism*, vol. 5, (Detroit, Mich.: Gale Research, 1976), p. 449.
27. Updike, *Couples*, p. 384.
28. Ibid., p. 456.
29. Ibid., p. 318.
30. Ibid., p. 384.
31. Ibid., p. 356.
32. Ibid., p. 408.
33. Ibid., p. 148.
34. Ibid., p. 145.
35. Ibid., p. 17.
36. William Bradford, *History of Plymouth Plantation, 1620–1647*, 2 vols. (Boston: The Massachusetts Historical Society, 1912), 2: 328.
37. Ibid., p. 329.
38. Updike, *Couples*, p. 86.
39. Ibid., p. 244.
40. Ibid., p. 457.
41. Ibid., p. 386.

42. Paul Brooks, *The View from Lincoln Hill* (Boston: Houghton Mifflin Co., 1976), p. 244.

43. See Joseph F. Zimmerman, *The Massachusetts Town Meeting: A Tenacious Institution* (Albany, N. Y.: The Graduate School of Public Affairs, State University of New York at Albany, 1967) for an expression of restrained optimism regarding the future of the town meeting.

44. Perry D. Westbrook, *Biography of an Island* (New York: Thomas Yoseloff, 1958), pp. 214–244. See Eleanor A. Ott, "Vermont Country Calendar," *Natural History* 90, no. 3 (March 1981): 73–83, for a record of the persistence of the traditional ways and values in a Vermont town.

Bibliographic Note

General Commentaries

The literary scene in New England is described in Robert Spiller et al., eds., *The Literary History of the United States*, 3d ed., 3 vols. (New York: Macmillan Co., 1963), passim, and in Van Wyck Brooks, *The Flowering of New England* (1936) and *New England: Indian Summer* (1940), both published in New York by E. P. Dutton & Co. For a more specialized treatment of rural New England authors see Perry D. Westbrook, *Acres of Flint: Writers of Rural New England, 1870–1900* (1951; reprint revised ed., subtitled *Sarah Orne Jewett and Her Contemporaries*, Metuchen, N. J.: The Scarecrow Press, 1981). Two cultural studies of typical New England regions are Richard D. Birdsall, *Berkshire County: A Cultural History* (New Haven, Conn.: Yale University Press, 1959), and Dorothy Canfield Fisher, *Vermont Tradition: The Biography of an Idea* (Boston: Little, Brown & Co., 1953). A useful companion piece to Birdsall's book is Robert Taylor, *Western Massachusetts in the Revolution* (Providence, R. I.: Brown University Press, 1954), which provides a graphic account of rural New England in times of crisis, particularly during Shays's Rebellion.

Accounts of industry, agriculture, and economic conditions in general are Frederick Jackson Turner, "New England, 1830–1850," *Huntington Library Bulletin*, no. 1 (May 1931): 153–97; and Harold F. Wilson's landmark study, *The Hill Country of Northern New England: Its Social and Economic History* (New York: Columbia University Press, 1930). Two other revealing social and economic studies with narrower focuses than Wilson's are Percy W. Bidwell, "Rural Economy in New England at the Beginning of the Nineteenth Century," *Transactions of the Connecticut Academy of Arts and Sciences*, 20: 241–399, and George Frederick Wells, *The Status of Rural Vermont, 1903* (St. Albans, Vt.: Printed by the Cummings Printing Company for the Vermont State Agricultural Commission, 1903). For recent assessments of economic and social conditions in New England see Lawrence Dame, *New England Comes Back* (New York: Random House, 1940); R. C. Estall, *New England: A Study in Industrial Adjustment* (New York: Frederick A. Praeger, 1966); and Neal R. Peirce, *The New England States: People, Politics and Power in the Six New England States* (New York: W. W. Norton & Co., 1976). Not to be overlooked is Betty Flanders Thomson, *The Changing Face of New England* (New York: Macmillan Co., 1958), a description of the climate, geology, and geography of the region but relating these to its history, culture, and economy.

The centrality of religion in the early development of New England towns is well known. The doctrines and the secular influences of Puritanism have been explored by many scholars. An early discussion is J. S. Clark, *A Historical Sketch of the Congregational Church in Massachusetts* (Boston: The Congregational Board of Publication, 1858). Later and more ambitious works on New England theology are Joseph Haroutanian, *Piety vs. Moralism: The Passing of New England Theology* (New York: Henry Holt & Co., 1932); Perry Miller's monumental volumes, *The New England*

Mind: The Seventeenth Century (New York: Macmillan Co., 1939) and *The New England Mind: From Colony to Province* (Cambridge, Mass.: Harvard University Press, 1953); Chard Powers Smith, *Yankees and God* (New York: Hermitage House, 1954), the main premise of which is that New England influences, especially religious ones, were of nationwide scope; Sidney E. Ahlstrom, *A Religious History of the American People* (New Haven, Conn.: Yale University Press, 1972), which includes discussions of all phases of New England church history from 1620 to the present; Sacvan Bercovitch, *The Puritan Origins of the American Self* (New Haven, Conn.: Yale University Press, 1975), which is particularly helpful in its tracing of millennial doctrines and attitudes that have permeated New England and American history since the landing of the first Puritans. Since Jonathan Edwards's theology exerted a major influence in New England from 1750 to 1850 and since his millennial views were widely accepted, the interested reader should consult *The Apocalyptic Writings of Jonathan Edwards*, ed. Stephen J. Stein, *The Works of Jonathan Edwards*, 5 vols., vol. 5 (New Haven, Conn.: Yale University Press, 1977). Useful commentaries on Edwards are James Carse, *Jonathan Edwards and the Visibility of God* (New York: Charles Scribner's Sons, 1967) and C. G. Goen, "Jonathan Edwards: A New Departure in Eschatology," *Church History* 28 (1959): 25–40. Ernest Lee Tuveson, *Redeemer Nation* (Chicago: University of Chicago Press, 1966), provides a general discussion of American millennialism, especially that of Timothy Dwight and Jonathan Edwards.

Two studies of emigration from New England and the consequent spreading of New England town institutions are Lois Kimball Mathews, *The Expansion of New England: The Spread of New England Settlements and Institutions to the Mississippi River, 1620–1865* (1909; reprint ed., New York: Russell & Russell, 1962), and Stewart H. Holbrook, *Yankee Exodus: An Account of Migration from New England* (1950; reprint ed., Seattle: University of Washington Press, 1968).

Writings Closely Bearing on New England Towns

A valuable study of American towns in general but with sharp focus on those of New England is Page Smith, *As a City upon a Hill* (New York: Alfred A. Knopf, 1966). Irma Honaker Herron, *The Small Town in American Literature* (1939; reprint ed., New York: Pageant Books, 1959) devotes much space to the New England aspect of her subject. For a detailed and well-documented report on New England towns before the American Revolution, the reader should consult Michael Zuckerman, *Peaceable Kingdoms: New England Towns in the Eighteenth Century* (New York: Alfred A. Knopf, 1970).

The emergence of a keen national interest in the distinctive aspects of the New England town and its institutions coincided with the onset of the struggle for independence. Eloquent expressions of this interest may be found in the letters of John Adams, especially in *Works*, 10 vols. (Boston: Charles C. Little & James Brown, 1850–56), 5 (1851): 492–96; in *Familiar Letters of John Adams and His Wife Abigail Adams during the Revolution* (New York: Hurd & Houghton, 1876), pp. 120–21; in *The Writings of Thomas Jefferson*, ed. Andrew A. Lipscomb and Albert L. Bergh, 20 vols. (Washington, D. C.: The Thomas Jefferson Memorial Association, 1904–5), 15 (1904): 32–44; and in *The Adams-Jefferson Letters*, 2 vols. (Chapel Hill: University of North Carolina Press, 1959), 2: 387–92. Timothy Dwight's lengthy poem "Greenfield Hill" (1794), available in *The Major Poems of Timothy Dwight* (Gainesville, Fla., Scholarly Facsimiles and Reprints, 1969), is a seminal early idealization of a

New England village; and Dwight, *Travels in New England and New York,* 4 vols. (Cambridge, Mass.: Belknap Press of Harvard University Press, 1969), first published in 1821–22, is an exhaustive and indispensable early commentary on all phases of the subject. Useful books on the life and thought of Dwight, a pivotal author in any study of New England towns, are Stephen Berk, *Calvinism vs. Democracy: Timothy Dwight and the Origin of American Evangelical Orthodoxy* (Hamden, Conn.: Archon Books, 1974); Charles E. Cunningham, *Timothy Dwight, 1752–1817* (New York: Macmillan Co., 1942); and Kenneth Silverman, *Timothy Dwight* (New York: Twayne Publishers, 1969).

During the early years of the Republic many travelers from abroad included comments on New England towns in their accounts of their experiences. Among these were Frances Wright D'Arusmont, *Views of Society and Manners in America* (Cambridge, Mass.: Belknap Press of Harvard University Press, 1963), first printed in 1821; the Marquis de Chastellux, *Travels in North America in the Years 1780, 1781, 1782,* 2 vols. (Williamsburg, Va.: University of North Carolina Press, for the Institute of Early American History and Culture, 1963), first published in French in 1786 and in English in 1787; Edward Augustus Kendall, *Travels through the Northern Parts of the United States in the Years 1807 and 1808* (New York: I. Riley, 1809), vol. 1; Harriet Martineau, *Retrospect of Western Travel,* 2 vols. (London: Saunders & Otley, 1897), first published in 1838; and, most important of all, Alexis de Tocqueville, *Democracy in America,* ed. Philips Bradley, 2 vols. (New York: Vintage Books, 1954), vol. 1, first published in America in 1838. A later observer from abroad, Englishman James Bryce, *The American Commonwealth,* 2d ed., 2 vols. (New York: Macmillan Co., 1891), vol. 1, describes in detail and with admiration the government of New England towns.

Among numerous laudatory nineteenth-century commentators on general aspects of New England towns are James Fenimore Cooper, *Notions of the Americans,* 2 vols. (Philadelphia: Carey, Lea & Carey, 1828), vol. 1; George Bancroft, *History of the United States from the Discovery of the North American Continent,* 10 vols. (Boston: Little, Brown & Co., 1834–75), vol. 4 (1852); Jared Sparks, "Observations by Jared Sparks on the Government of Towns in Massachusetts," written in response to Tocqueville's request for information on the subject but first published in 1898 (*The Johns Hopkins Studies in Historical and Political Science,* 16: 579–600); James Parton, *Topics of the Times* (Boston: James R. Osgood & Co., [c. 1871]); George Lunt, *Old New England Traits* (New York: Hurd & Houghton, 1873).

The commentators listed in the preceding three paragraphs were for the most part admirers of New England town culture, but by the end of the century, as the rural New England economy declined, less favorable reports began to appear. Among these were Philip Morgan, "The Problems of Rural New England: A Remote Village," *Atlantic Monthly* 79: 577–88; Rollin L. Hartt, in a two-part essay, "A New England Hill Town: I. Its Condition," and "A New England Hill Town: II. Its Revival," *Atlantic Monthly* 83: 561–74 and 712–20 respectively.

The twentieth century saw no let-up in the flow of nonfiction writing about New England towns. Noteworthy are John Sterling, New England Villages," *Atlantic Monthly* 131: 520–29; Carl Bridenbaugh, "The New England Town: A Way of Life," *Proceedings of the American Antiquarian Society* 56: 19–48; and Clarence Webster's study of rural northeastern Connecticut, *Town Meeting Country* (New York: Duell, Sloan & Pearce, 1945).

Histories and studies of individual towns have proliferated during the past two centuries, and many of them supply valuable information and insights concerning social, religious, and economic conditions in the towns. The prototype of such histories is William Bradford's *Of Plimmoth Plantation,* written between 1620 and 1647 but not printed in full until 1856, now available in what is thus far its most scholarly edition, as *The History of Plymouth Plantation,* ed. Worthington Ford et al., 2 vols. (Boston: The Massachusetts Historical Society, 1912). Another among the many histories of Plymouth is Francis Baylies, *Historical Memoir of the Colony of New Plymouth,* 2 vols. (Boston: Hilliard, Gray, Little & Wilkins, 1830). Of major significance is Ralph Waldo Emerson's encomium of Concord, "Historical Address at Concord," *Complete Works of Ralph Waldo Emerson,* 12 vols. (1903–04; reprint ed., New York: William H. Wise, 1929), 11: 27–86; and for a study of Concord in the mid-nineteenth century there is no better source than Walter Harding, *The Days of Henry Thoreau* (New York: Alfred A. Knopf, 1966). Among other writings about individual towns, the following are recommended as representative of various trends: Thomas W. Higginson's anecdotal volume on Newport, Rhode Island, *Oldport Days* (Boston: James R. Osgood & Co., 1873); Charles Francis Adams's meticulously researched "A Study of Church and Town Government," in *Three Episodes in Massachusetts History,* 4th ed., 2 vols. (Boston: Houghton, Mifflin & Co., 1894), 2: 581–1009, which focuses almost entirely on Braintree and Quincy; Sarah Orne Jewett's somewhat nostalgic historical sketch of her native town, "The Old Town of Berwick," *New England Magazine* 10: 585–609; E. L. Bogart's objective study, *Peacham: The Story of a Vermont Hill Town* (Montpelier: Vermont Historical Society, 1948); Dorothy Canfield Fisher's somewhat sentimental but charming *Memories of Arlington, Vermont* (New York: Duell, Sloan, Pearce, 1957); Perry D. Westbrook's historical and sociological study of a Maine island fishing community, *Biography of an Island* (New York: Thomas Yoseloff, 1958); Christopher Rand's contrast of Past and present, *The Changing Landscape: Salisbury, Connecticut* (New York: Oxford University Press, 1968); Sarah C. Sedgwick's and Christina S. Marquand's historical and cultural study, *Stockbridge, 1739–1974* (Stockbridge, Mass.: Berkshire Traveller Press, 1974); and Paul Brook's account of a Massachusetts town's approach to present-day problems, *The View from Lincoln Hill* (Boston: Houghton, Mifflin & Co., 1976). Two important books dealing exclusively with the founding and early years of New England towns are Charles Grant, *Democracy in the Connecticut Frontier Town of Kent* (New York: Columbia University Press, 1961) and Sumner Chilton Powell, *Puritan Village: The Formation of a New England Town* (Middletown, Conn.: Wesleyan University Press, 1963).

One of the distinctive features of the New England towns was their town-meeting government. Some of the authors already mentioned—e.g., Dwight, Emerson, Baylies, and Tocqueville—described the political institutions and practices of the towns, but devoted little or no attention to the historical background of this mode of government. Not until after the middle of the century did the question of the origins of town government arouse a keen interest among historians and political scientists. An early writer on the subject was Joel Parker, "The Origin, Organization, and Influence of the Towns of New England," *Proceedings of the Massachusetts Historical Society* 9 (1866–67): 14–65. In 1882 Herbert B. Adams published *The Germanic Origin of New England Towns* as vol. 2 of *The Johns Hopkins University Studies in Historical and Political Science,* a work that cast a new and romantic, if not historically accurate, light on the subject. Adam's Germanic theory was adopted by James K. Hosmer, *Samuel Adams: The Man of the Town Meeting, The Johns Hopkins University Studies in Historical and Political Science,* 2d ser., vol. 4 (April 1884). In the same year P. E. Aldrich presented in the *Proceedings of the American Antiquarian Society,* n.s., 3

(October 1883–April 1884): 111–24, as part of "The Report of the Council," a useful review of the various theories of town origins. Among the clergy a popular theory was that town government in New England developed from Congregational Church polity. An eloquent exponent of this idea was Noah Walker, President of Yale University, "The New England Meeting House," *The New Englander* 52, no. 174 (May 1888): 305–38. The Massachusetts Historical Society Published in its *Proceedings* for 1889–90, ser. 2, 5: 320–31, a paper entitled "The Origin of Towns in Massachusetts," by Abner C. Goodell, and in 1892, ser. 2, 7: 172–211 and 441–49, a lengthy paper, "The Genesis of the Massachusetts Town and the Development of Town-Meeting Government," by Charles Francis Adams.

Two authoritative volumes on the general topic of the town meeting are John Fairfield Sly, *Town Government in Massachusetts* (1620–1930), (Cambridge, Mass.: Harvard University Press, 1930) and Joseph F. Zimmerman, *The Massachusetts Town Meeting: A Tenacious Institution* (Albany, New York: Graduate School of Public Affairs, State University of New York at Albany, 1967). A popularized account of a Maine town meeting in action may be found in John Gould, *New England Town Meeting: Safeguard of Democracy* (Brattleboro, Vt.: Stephen Daye Press, 1940). Concerning the spread and influence of town-meeting government outside of New England, James Bryce, *The American Commonwealth* (already cited) provides valuable information, as do two publications in *The Johns Hopkins University Studies in Historical and Political Science*—Albert Shaw, *Local Government in Illinois*, 1st ser., vol. 3 (1883), and Edward W. Bemis, *Local Government in Michigan and the Northwest*. Vol. 1, no. 5 (March 1883).

Fiction, Poetry, and Essays

During almost two hundred years of steady and prolific productivity, writers of fiction, poets, and essayists have supplied the most detailed and, for the judicious reader, the most nearly authentic record of life in the towns of New England. A complete biography of such writings would fill a volume. Here a representative selection will have to suffice. Timothy Dwight's "Greenfield Hill," has already been mentioned. The first author of consequence to write fiction depicting New England village life was Catharine M. Sedgwick, *A New-England Tale, or Sketches of New England* (1822) and *Redwood, A Tale*, 2 vols. (1824), both published in New York by S. Bliss & E. White. Sedgwick in general extolled the virtues of life in her native Berkshire County, Massachusetts, but she frowned upon the rigidities and hypocrisies of the lingering Puritanism of the area. Other novelists who looked favorably upon life in western Massachusetts but also deplored its persistent Calvinism were Henry Wadsworth Longfellow, *Kavanagh* (1849), available in vol. 8 of *The Works of Henry Wadsworth Longfellow*, 14 vols. (Boston: Houghton, Mifflin & Co., 1886–1891); Sylvester Judd, *Margaret: A Tale of the Real and the Ideal, Blight and Bloom* (1851; reprint ed., Upper Saddle River, N. J.; Gregg Press, 1968); and Oliver Wendell Holmes, *Elsie Venner: A Romance of Destiny* (1861), available in vol. 5 of *The Works of Oliver Wendell Holmes*, 13 vols. (Boston: Houghton, Mifflin & Co., 1892). An early volume of nonfictional sketches praising life on the New England countryside is Nathaniel Shatswell Dodge, *Sketches of New England, or Memories of the Country* (New York: E. French, 1842). Two relatively unknown novelists—Julia C. R. Dorr and D. G. Mitchell (Ik Marvel) deserve notice. Dorr's *Farmingdale* (New York: D. Appleton and Company, 1854) and *Lanmere* (New York: Mason Bros., 1856) carry on the campaign against Calvinism, as in a more genial manner does Mitchell, *Dr. Johns: Being a Narrative of Certain Events in the Life of an Orthodox Minister in Connecticut,* 2 vols. (New York: Charles Scribner & Co., 1866). Edward Bellamy harshly criticizes local government in the late eighteenth century in a novel dealing with Shays's Rebellion, *The Duke of Stockbridge,* first published as a newspaper serial in 1879 and now reissued in an edition prepared by Joseph Schiffman (Cambridge, Mass.: Belknap Press of Harvard University Press, 1962). Ralph Ingersol Lockwood, *The Insurgents* (Philadelphia: Carey, Lea & Blanchard, 1835), also wrote fictionally about Shays' Rebellion but was less critical than Bellamy concerning town government.

After 1850 regional or local color writing became increasingly popular. Seba Smith's volume of short tales, *'Way Down East; or, Portraitures of Yankee Life* (New York: J. C. Derby, 1854), brings a pleasant touch of humor to his subject. Henry Ward Beecher, *Norwood; or, Village Life in New England* (New York: Charles Scribner & Co., 1868), writes more seriously and with mild disapproval of the high Calvinism entrenched in rural New England. His sister, Harriet Beecher Stowe, shares his outlook in a series of distinguished novels: *The Minister's Wooing* (New York: Derby & Jackson, 1859), laid in Newport, Rhode Island; *Oldtown Folks* (Boston: Fields, Osgood & Co., 1869), with an up-country setting; *The Pearl of Orr's Island* (Boston: Houghton, Mifflin Co., 1896, first published in 1862); and *Poganuc People,* vol. 11 in *The Writings of Harriet Beecher Stowe,* 16 vols. (Boston: Houghton Mifflin Co., 1896–99). which, first published in 1878, draws from its author's memories of her childhood in Litchfield, Connecticut. A collection of Stowe's shorter local-color pieces, many on New England, is *Regional Sketches,* ed. John R. Adams (New Haven, Conn.: College & University Press, 1972).

As the nineteenth century drew to a close, the regional writers paid less attention to religious matters and directed their efforts to a realistic, sometimes grim, depiction of conditions in New England as they saw them. Mary E. Wilkins Freeman in a series of novels and volumes of short stories ranks high among the authors of this period. Almost all of her output is relevant; the following books are especially so: *A Humble Romance and Other Stories* (1887), *A New England Nun and Other Stories* (1891), *Pembroke* (1894), *Jerome: A Poor Man* (1897), *The Portion of Labor* (1901), all published in New York by Harper & Bros. The last two of these books deal poignantly with problems resulting from industrialization—a subject treated more forcibly by William Dean Howells in his fictional study of a small New England manufacturing town, *Annie Kilburn* (New York: Harper & Bros., 1889). Another author focusing on backcountry settings similar to those in many of Freeman's stories and achieving occasionally as stark a realism as Freeman's was Rose Terry Cooke, *Somebody's Neighbors* (Boston: J. R. Osgood & Co., 1881) and *Huckleberries Gathered from New England Hills* (Boston: Houghton, Mifflin, & Co., 1891). Somewhat lighter in tone but rich in close observation of village ways are the sketches and tales of the Vermonter Rowland Robinson, published in the following: *Danvis Folks* (Boston: Houghton, Mifflin & Co., 1901); *Out of Bondage and Other Stories* (1936); and *Uncle Lisha's Shop and a Danvis Pioneer* (1937), the two latter published as reissues of earlier writings in Rutland, Vermont, by the Charles E. Tuttle Co. Attention is also directed to Robinson, "An Old-Time March Meeting," *Atlantic Monthly* 89: 312–20.

Sarah Orne Jewett ranks with Stowe and Freeman in eminence as a New England regionalist, but her focus, unlike theirs, was primarily on the seacoast. Most of her work is germane to this study, and a convenient introduction to it may be found in *The Best Short Stories of Sarah Orne Jewett,* ed. Willa Cather, 2 vols. (Boston: Houghton, Mifflin & Co., 1925), which includes all of her famous *The Country of the Pointed Firs* (1896). In addition, *Deephaven* (first published in 1877) in the edition of 1893 (Boston: Houghton, Mifflin & Co.) is recommended for its preface and for its depiction of scenes and people in a Maine seaport.

Thus far in the twentieth century there has been no slackening in the output of fiction with New England settings and motifs. Following Jewett's example, Mary Ellen Chase, drawing from her own and her family experiences, wrote a series of distinguished novels about Maine coastal life: *Mary Peters* (1934) and *Silas Crockett* (1935), both published in New York by The Macmillan Co., deal with the clipper ship era and its aftermath. Her *The Edge of Darkness* (New York: W. W. Norton & Co., 1957) describes the deplorable social decay that set in upon the coast as shipping and seafaring ceased to be a way of life. Another book catching the atmosphere of one of the lesser New England ports is William John Hopkins, *Old Harbor* (Boston: Houghton Mifflin Co., 1909). Contrasting sharply with the calm and serenity of Jewett, Hopkins, and the early Chase, are three recent novels that deal with coastal communities in the process of conversion into summer resorts or Boston suburbs—John Cheever, *The Wapshot Chronicle* (1957) and *The Wapshot Scandal* (1963), both published in New York by Harper & Row, and John Updike, *Couples* (New York: Alfred A. Knopf, 1968).

Glowing representations of inland New England life occur in the fiction of Dorothy Canfield Fisher, notably in *Hillsboro People* (New York: Henry Holt & Co., 1915), *Raw Material* (1923), and *Seasoned Timber* (1939), the latter two published by Harcourt, Brace & Co., in New York. Edith Wharton wrote more somber treatments of the hinterland in two novels of the Berkshire Hills, *Ethan Frome* (New York: Charles Scribner's Sons, 1911) and *Summer: A Novel* (New York: D. Appleton & Co., 1917), the latter recording a rural decadence bordering on depravity. Somewhat less darkly than Wharton, but without Fisher's complacency, James Gould Cozzens, *The Last Adam* (New York: Harcourt, Brace & Co., 1933), describes a northwestern Connecticut town that has lost most of its more admirable Yankee qualities and has found no substitutes for them. Shirley Jackson, a fantasist rather than a realist, employs New England towns as the scenes of the ultimate in mob stupidity and cruelty in "The Lottery," readily available in *The Magic of Shirley Jackson*, ed., Stanley E. Hyman (New York: Farrar, Strauss & Giroux, 1966); "The Summer People," included in *Come Along with Me*, ed. Stanley E. Hyman (New York: Viking Press, 1968); and *We Have Always Lived in the Castle* (New York: Viking Press, 1968). John Gardner, *October Light* (New York: Alfred A. Knopf, 1976), has presented, also with a good deal of fantasy, the stresses in the Vermont town of Bennington as the nation enters its third century of existence.

The major poets of New England also provide insights into village life and character. Particularly recommended are Edwin Arlington Robinson, *Tilbury Town: Selected Poems of Edwin Arlington Robinson* (New York: Macmillan Co., 1953); *The Poems of Emily Dickinson*, ed. Thomas Johnson, 3 vols. (Cambridge, Mass.: Belknap Press of Harvard University Press, 1955); and *The Poetry of Robert Frost*, ed. Edward Connery Lathem (New York: Holt, Rinehart & Winston, 1975).

Personal Memoirs

Many personal memoirs and journals dating from earliest Puritan days cast much light on life in New England towns. From these records Barrows Mussey has compiled a collection of excerpts in *Yankee Life by Those Who Lived It* (New York: Alfred A. Knopf, 1947). Among individual memoirs Lyman Beecher, *Autobiography* (New York: Harper & Bros., 1865) and Samuel Griswold Goodrich, *Recollections of a Lifetime; or, Men and Things I Have Seen*, 2 vols. (New York: Miller, Orton & Mulligan, 1857) provide accounts of existence in Connecticut towns in the early nineteenth century. James Russell Lowell, "Cambridge Thirty Years Ago," *The Works of James Russell Lowell*, 10 vols. (Boston: Houghton, Mifflin & Co., 1890), 1: 43–99, describes his native town when still a rural community. Lucy Larcom, *A New England Girlhood* (Boston: Houghton, Mifflin & Co., 1889) and Mary Ellen Chase, *A Goodly Heritage* (New York: Henry Holt & Co., 1932), describe the process of growing up in Beverly, Massachusetts, and Blue Hill, Maine, respectively. Last, for the many glimpses they give of Concord, that most famous of New England small towns, the reader may consult *The Journal of Henry D. Thoreau*, ed. Bradford Torey and Francis H. Allen, 2 vols. (1906; reprint ed., New York: Dover Publications, 1962) and *The Journals and Miscellaneous Notebooks of Ralph Waldo Emerson*, ed. William H. Gilman et al. (16 vols. to date) (Cambridge, Mass.: Belknap Press of Harvard University Press, 1960–).

Index